Litwak's Multimedia Producer's Handbook

LITWAK'S
MULTIMEDIA
PRODUCER'S
HANDBOOK

A Legal and Distribution Guide

Mark Litwak

SILMAN-JAMES PRESS Los Angeles

First Edition
10 9 8 7 6 5 4 3 2 1

Library of Congress Cataloging-in-Publication Data

Litwak, Mark.
Litwak's multimedia producer's handbook : a legal and
distribution guide / by Mark Litwak.
p.   cm.
1. Multimedia systems—Law and legislation—United States.
2. Copyright—United States.
3. Multimedia systems industry—Law and legislation—United
States. I. Title.
KF390.5.C6L58   1997   343.7309'944—dc21   97-29963

ISBN: 1-879505-35-5

Cover design by Heidi Frieder/Art Head

Printed and bound in the United States of America

SILMAN-JAMES PRESS
1181 Angelo Drive
Beverly Hills, CA 90210

To Tiiu, David and Michael

DISCLAIMER

This book is designed to assist non-lawyers understand legal issues and business practices frequently encountered in the multimedia industry. It will provide readers with an understanding of basic legal principles, enabling them to communicate better with their attorneys.

Nothing in this book should be construed as legal advice. The information provided is not a substitute for consulting with an experienced multimedia attorney and receiving counsel based on the facts and circumstances of a particular transaction. Many of the legal principles mentioned are subject to exceptions and qualifications that may not be noted. Furthermore, case law and statutes are subject to revision and may not apply in every state. Because of the quick pace of technological change, some of the information in this book may be outdated by the time the book is published. Readers should be aware that business practices, distribution methods, and legislation will continue to evolve in this rapidly changing industry.

ACKNOWLEDGMENTS

I am grateful for the assistance of numerous individuals who assisted me in writing this book. I appreciate the efforts of my teaching assistants—Colleen Barberis, Justin Linam, and Howard Osias—and my secretary, Amy Lee, for their help. My law clerk, Ryan S. Gawel, did fact-checking and legal research. A number of attorneys generously agreed to review some or all of my manuscript and offer comments. These attorneys include Michael E. Morales, David Greenspan, Sam Simon, and Richard Thompson. Steve Arbuss contributed a list of relevant web sites for the Appendix.

Marketing guru Joanna Tamer reviewed my chapter on publishing and offered her insights.

Jess Foster, David Rosen, Karol Martesko, and Gary Rosenfeld reviewed the portions of my work that deal with technological issues.

I would also like to thank Michael Prohaska of SAG, Susan Gerakaris of the WGA, Bryan Unger of the DGA, and Robert Brown of AFTRA for reviewing the accuracy of those portions of the book that deal with union and guild regulations.

Finally, thanks to my publishers, Gwen Feldman and Jim Fox, for their patience and suggestions.

CONTENTS

All of the contracts in this book are available on computer disc. Write: Hampstead Enterprises, Inc., P.O. Box 3226, Santa Monica, CA 90408, Phone: (310) 859-9595, Fax: (310) 859-0806, or visit web site http://www.laig.com/law/entlaw See order form on page 336.

PREFACE

The news media has proclaimed that the multimedia revolution is upon us. Multimedia technology is expected to radically change the way we work, entertain, communicate, and educate ourselves. Telephone, cable, and entertainment companies are frantically jockeying for position as they prepare to invest the billions of dollars necessary to connect homes, businesses and schools to the information superhighway. The $15-billion worldwide electronic-games industry already dwarfs the $5.9-billion generated from the American movie industry.

The Internet, especially the World Wide Web, is growing by leaps and bounds. An estimated 60 million people worldwide have access to the Internet, and growth continues at a torrid pace. Businesses are quickly setting up web sites to advertise products, respond to customer inquiries, and make sales. Web sites have advantages over opening a store: they cost less to build and maintain, the "salespeople" are always knowledgeable, and an electronic "store" can conduct business worldwide, twenty-four hours a day. As secure methods for transmitting electronic money become accepted, Internet commerce is expected to boom.

While the promise of new technology is exciting, one should keep in mind that the public's appetite for some applications is far from certain. E-mail is a hit. Internet video conferencing is likely to become popular, even though the videophone was a flop when it was tried decades ago. Telecommuting is increasing, and people are forming virtual communities. There are more than 65,000 mom-and-pop computer bulletin-board services (BBSs).

The interactive market will become a $10-billion-a-year market by the year 2000, according to San Francisco investment house Volpe, Welty & Co. Interactive television can provide much more than entertainment. It can be used for banking, home security systems, and video teleconferencing. America Online executive Robert Pittman predicts that interactive television may capture a portion of the $75-billion-a-year catalog sales business, the $12-billion-a-year classified advertisement business, the $10-billion-a-year couponing business and the $100-billion-a-year telecommunications business.

On the other hand, the public has shown minimal interest in acquiring many of the CD-ROM programs offered for sale. A test of video-on-demand in Cerritos, California was a big disappointment. The cost of wiring a single home with fiber optics has been estimated as high as $1,000. How much are consumers willing pay to avoid standing in line at Blockbuster Video? No one really knows.

It is unlikely that interactive multimedia will supplant traditional methods of human interaction. People will always want to converse in person. Virtual stores are nice, but sometimes you want to touch the fabric and try on the pants. Just as radio did not replace theatre, and television did not destroy movies, multimedia communication will not eliminate earlier forms of communication—different media will coexist.

This book explains how multimedia programming is produced and distributed, and it explores some common legal issues that arise. Readers should note that the structure of the industry is rapidly evolving. Thus, it is often difficult to say what is customary practice. Moreover, in some instances the law has not kept pace with technology, leaving important issues unresolved. As this book goes to press, Congress is debating what changes should be made to our copyright laws to protect works transmitted in cyberspace while encouraging the free exchange of information.

I have written this book based on my experience advising multimedia developers and entrepreneurs. Many of my clients are computer savvy, but have only a vague understanding of the legal principles that affect their work, and they often know little about how multimedia products and services are marketed and distributed. This book is meant for them. I have attempted to explain the law and business of multimedia in as simple terms as possible.

This work follows several books I have written about the motion-picture industry. In *Reel Power: The Struggle for Influence and Success in the New Hollywood* (Morrow, 1986; NAL, 1987; Silman-James Press, 1994), I explained the inner-workings of the movie business. *Dealmaking in the Film and Television Industry* (Silman-James Press, 1994) and *Contracts for the Film and Television Industry* (Silman-James Press, 1994) are entertainment-law guides for non-lawyers.

I spent more than three years working on this book. Many times as I neared completion, significant technological or legislative change required me to go back and revise the manuscript. As the industry continues to evolve, some of the information may become outdated. Readers are invited to visit my web site for information on recent developments in entertainment and multimedia law: Entertainment Legal Resources at http://www.laig.com/law/entlaw/

I welcome comments and suggestions from readers. You can contact me as follows:

Mark Litwak
P.O. Box 3226
Santa Monica, CA 90408
Phone: (310) 859-9595
Fax: (310) 859-0806
E-mail: Litwak@aol.com

I hope this guide will prove useful to you.

Mark Litwak
August 1997

CHAPTER 1

INTRODUCTION TO MULTIMEDIA

WHAT IS MULTIMEDIA?

Multimedia works are based on multiple media sources such as video, text, audio, graphics, and animation. These works are typically stored in digital form on magnetic or optical media. Programs may be interactive, meaning that the user can interact and control the direction, pace, and content of the program. Current programming is primarily based on CD-ROM technology. CD-ROMs have large storage capacity (650 megabytes), are inexpensive to manufacture (less than a dollar), are compact, durable, and transfer information quickly. Digital Versatile Discs, also known as Digital Video Discs (DVD), are the next big improvement in storage devices. As more American homes go online, however, multimedia programming will increasingly be distributed over the information superhighway.

OPPORTUNITIES FOR INDEPENDENT PRODUCERS

Many independent producers are excited about the prospect of producing multimedia programs. Rapid technological developments have dramatically reduced production costs. For a producer who distributes via the Internet, a $2,000 high-end home video camera can shoot perfectly acceptable images. A home computer with inexpensive software can be used to edit the footage. Special effects, that a decade ago required hundreds of thousands of dollars' worth of equipment can be easily added. Thus, owners of personal computers can become desktop moguls, producing slick and sophisticated programming at minimal cost. Distribution may become as simple as sending E-mail.

Today's media gatekeepers, the television networks and entertainment/publishing conglomerates, will lose much of their hold over access to consumers in a world of 500-plus channels. Indeed, the entire concept of a channel becomes obsolete when viewers can order any program they want on demand. Every viewer will become his or her own programmer.

While technology holds the promise of turning a nation of couch potatoes into producers, there may not be much of a market for these new programs. Dad's homage to junior's birthday party may only interest the grandparents. Talented entrepreneurs, however, can be expected to generate innovative programs for new market niches. Such programs as *Trout Fishing in Idaho*, might not be profitable to distribute in a system that requires duplication of film prints, advertising, and shipping. But distributed over the Internet, these works could be profitable, generating a small, steady stream of income for many years.

How far into the future is such a scenario? Consider that an estimated 30 million-plus individuals already use the Internet, and their numbers are rapidly growing. Recent breakthroughs in compression technology allow full-motion video to be compressed and transmitted over channels with limited bandwidth. Digital television will permit four or more high-quality transmissions in the bandwidth that previously carried one noisy analog television signal.[1] With fiber optics, capacity is almost unlimited. It appears that engineers are close to being able to deliver 1,000 billion bits per second over a single fiber. At that rate, a hairlike fiber could deliver a million channels of television concurrently.[2] The cost of fiber optics has declined so that today it costs less than copper wire for new installations. As telephone companies replace their aging infrastructure, they can be expected to use fiber optics. Since they replace about 5% of their equipment every year, in twenty years the transition to an all-fiber-optic system could be achieved.[3]

Before that time, many consumers should have access to video on demand. They may be able to order any program ever made to view any time they desire. If you like *60 Minutes*, but are unable to view it Sunday night, you could order it on Tuesday for a small charge.[4] If your local video store does not have shelf space for the arty foreign films you like, you may be able to order them directly over the Internet from an electronic library.

Eventually there should be as much diversity in electronic programming as there is in printed matter. Electronic libraries will have several advantages over traditional libraries. Electronic libraries will not have to stock numerous hard copies of works, incur substantial storage and replacement costs, and "borrowers" need never return anything.

Of course, while technology can greatly reduce production and distribution costs, it does nothing to create demand for an independent producer's work. The cost of marketing and promoting a program may pose a substantial barrier to widespread distribution. The entertainment conglomerates will maintain an advantage here. Tomorrow's *TV Guide* may be as thick as the Yellow Pages. Viewers will have so many programs to choose from that a single program can easily get lost in the clutter. Warner Bros. can promote its programs with full-page newspaper ads and 30-second television commercials. Viewers may look to brand names, like the Sundance Channel or HBO, to help them find programs. How will the independents compete?

HOW THE INTERNET CAN HELP INDEPENDENT PRODUCERS

There are several technological developments on the horizon that may help independents level the playing field. The development of software "smart agents" could assist viewers in navigating the Internet. These agents could learn the preferences of viewers and make suggestions.

WEB SITES FOR INDEPENDENTS

INDEXES

CINEMEDIA: LINKS TO OVER 10,000 FILM AND MEDIA SITES.
http://www.afionline.org/CINEMEDIA/cinemedia.home.html

INDEX TO MULTIMEDIA INFORMATION SOURCES:
http://viswiz.gmd.de/MultimediaInfo

HYPERSTAND-NEWMEDIA MAGAZINE: http://www.newmedia.com

MEGA-MEDIA LINKS: THE NORTHWESTERN UNIVERSITY DEPARTMENT OF RADIO/TV/FILM. http://omnibus-eye.rtvf.nwu.edu/

MULTIMEDIA NEWS:
http://ourworld.compuserve.com/homepages/media4/

SCREENSITE: "A SITE FOR THE STUDY OF FILM."
http://www.sa.ua.edu/TCF/welcome.htm

YAHOO (FILM SECTION): A FILM SEARCH ENGINE.
http://www.yahoo.com/entertainment/movies_and_films/

INTERNET MOVIE DATABASE: A FLEXIBLE SEARCH ENGINE FOR A DATABASE OF MOVIES. http://us.imdb.com/

FESTIVALS

ENTERTAINMENT LAW RESOURCES: MARK LITWAK'S WEB PAGE, INCLUDING A FESTIVAL CALENDAR. http://www.laig.com/law/entlaw

MEDIA CUBE: SEARCHABLE FILM FESTIVAL DATABASE.
http://www.mediacube.de/festivals/index.html

VIRTUAL FILM FESTIVAL: "GLOBAL COMMUNITY FOR INDEPENDENT FILM."
http://www.virtualfilm.com/

[CONTINUED]

The providers of video-on-demand could collect information on viewer preferences. These lists might be used to target advertising to viewers interested in the works of independent producers. Suppose an independent filmmaker thinks his program would appeal to the same viewers who enjoyed *Fried Green Tomatoes*. If he could obtain a list of viewers who ordered that movie, the filmmaker could directly solicit them by regular mail or E-mail. This would be much more cost-

PRODUCTION RESOURCES [CONTINUED]

eMOON: PRODUCTION RESOURCE GUIDE INCLUDING CREW, EQUIPMENT, AND SERVICES. http://www.hollyvision.com/emoon/

FOOTAGE.NET: SOURCE OF INFORMATION ON STOCK FOOTAGE http://www.footage.net

LICIUM'S-MULTIMEDIA NEWSLETTER AND RESOUCE DIRECTORY: http://www.licium.com

PROMOTION

IUMA: HI-FI MUSIC ARCHIVE. http://www.iuma.com/

KALEIDOSPACE: INDEPENDENT INTERNET ARTIST. http://kspace.com/

FILM SCHOOLS

CYBERSPACE FILM SCHOOL: HOLLYWOOD FILM INSTITUTE FILM SCHOOL. http://HollywoodU.com/

CYBER FILM SCHOOL: A FILMMAKING WEB SITE. http://www.cyberfilmschool.com/

LEGAL RESOURCES

ENTERTAINMENT LAW RESOURCES: MARK LITWAK'S WEB PAGE http://www.laig.com/law/entlaw

ADVERTISING LAW: ARENT FOX ADVERTISING LAW INTERNET SITE http://www.webcom.com/~lewrose/home.html

EFF MULTIMEDIA LAW PRIMER: INTELLECTUAL PROPERTY ISSUES FOR MULTIMEDIA DEVELOPERS. http://www.eff.org/pub/CAF/law/ip-primer

ENTERTAINMENT LAW: ENTERTAINMENT, MULTIMEDIA & INTELLECTUAL PROPERTY LAW WEB SITE. http://www.laig.com/law/intnet/

HOLLYWOOD LAW CYBERCENTER: ENTERTAINMENT LAW WEB SITE http://www.hollywoodnetwork.com/Law/

effective than advertising on network television or in a general-interest magazine. Of course, allowing providers to compile this type of information raises a host of privacy issues.[5]

The Internet can be used to help promote the work of independents through such sites as Kaleidospace (http://kspace.com/). Here, artists pay a commission or monthly fee to have excerpts of their work (graphic art, text, animation, motion pictures, or music) available for sampling. Users can download excerpts for free, and then place orders to buy the work. IUMA (http://www.iuma.com/) provides a similar service for musicians and bands. Both of these sites allow unknown artists to market themselves directly, bypassing traditional distributors.

A number of companies have become Internet video distributors. California Newsreel (http://www.newsreel.org) distributes cultural and social-change motion pictures, while the Noodlehead Network (http://homepages.together.net/~noodlhed/) markets children's educational videos. Bullfrog Films distributes programs about the environment and public-policy issues. In the future, everyone may have the ability to be their own distributor.

An example of an independent who has successfully used the Internet to market his work is Brock N. Meeks. A Washington-based journalist, Meeks began writing and publishing his Cyberwire Dispatch, a hard-hitting, profane, and often amusing report distributed by E-mail and posted on the web (http://cyberwerks.com/cyberwire). Meeks' distinctive voice generated a substantial following among Net aficionados, making him a minor celebrity as a cyberspace watchdog. Distributing his work over the Internet allowed him to speak his mind without any editorial interference. His outspoken opinions, however, have gotten him into trouble. He was sued for libel after he characterized an Internet-distributed sales pitch as a scam. The case was ultimately settled without payment of damages, but Meeks did incur substantial legal fees defending himself. Today, Meeks is Chief Washington Correspondent for *Wired/Hot Wired*.

LEGAL HURDLES

Technological changes have out-paced legal developments. Our current legal system was not designed with current technology and a global marketplace in mind. Old law has to be applied to new circumstances. When information can be sent from Los Angeles to Nigeria as easily as from Los Angeles to New York, the hodgepodge of conflicting national laws can become a serious obstacle to free communication and open commerce.

While state-of-the-art technology permits the development of diverse and innovative programs, there are many legal hurdles to overcome in making even a simple multimedia program. Since interactive programming requires more content than linear programs, many more releases and/or permissions may be needed. Determining and securing all the necessary releases and rights for a multimedia project can be a tiresome and complicated endeavor.

Multimedia legal issues cross disciplines and can become exceedingly knotty. Multimedia attorneys need to be knowledgeable in the fields of publishing, telecommunications, computer and entertainment law, intellectual-property rights (copyright, patent, trademarks), torts (right of privacy, right of publicity, defamation, and unfair competition), and contract law.

If you distribute programs over the Internet, additional issues arise. The downloading of your material in another country may expose you to liability under foreign law. The global reach of the Internet means that hundreds of different systems of jurisprudence could affect you. Many countries have censorship laws; few have anything analogous to our First Amendment guarantee of free speech.

Even drafting a simple employment contract can raise a bewildering array of issues. The multimedia creator may wear several hats, blurring the traditional roles of writer, director, composer, editor, costume designer, and software developer. If you use a computer to manipulate a character's image, changing appearance, dress, and background scenery, you have performed functions traditionally handled by a writer, director, editor, costume designer, and set designer.

INDUSTRY GIANTS WRESTLE FOR CONTROL

Companies in entertainment and publishing (Time Warner, Viacom), telecommunications (Bell Atlantic), computer software (Microsoft), consumer electronics (Sony), and cable (TCI) are rushing to get on the information superhighway and stake out their turf. These industries are converging because the new medium is a hybrid of current methods of distribution. Many different types of information can be transmitted in digital form. Companies want to become players in this new arena to increase profits and to protect their existing core businesses.

This convergence has encouraged fierce competition. 20th Century Fox is no longer only competing against film distributors. It is now competing with computer software providers to create entertaining content and with telephone, cable, and wireless companies to distribute it. Likewise, cable companies are losing their exclusive access to their subscribers' homes as telephone companies have been given authority to distribute content over their wires, and as Direct Broadcast Satellite (DBS) companies begin to beam programming directly to consumers. Newspaper publishers, meanwhile, are worried that video classified ads will reduce the profitability of their newspapers. Long-distance and international carriers are concerned about new technology that allows computer users to make inexpensive international calls over the Internet.

None of the players from existing industries can control this new medium. They each bring certain strengths and weaknesses to the battle, but no one entity has all the know-how and capital necessary to dominate the field. Many companies are in discussions with one another, exploring ways in which they can combine or work together advantageously. As their industries converge, it may make sense for them to form alliances or merge with partners.

The telecommunication companies (Telcos) know a lot about operating extensive telecommunications systems. They have an installed telephone base worth $60 billion.[6] Since the phone system is fully switched and interconnected, any phone caller can connect with anyone else who has a phone—a feat beyond today's cable systems. The Telcos have little experience, however, in developing programming. As regulated common carriers, they never had to be concerned with generating the content they carried. They made money from all phone calls, even boring ones.

Telephone conversations require little bandwidth. While telephone trunk lines are largely fiber optic, the line from the local node to the home is usually copper wire, which has limited capacity to transmit multiple channels of video, data, and voice information.[7] This line was designed with one-way service in mind, although recent technological developments may permit these lines to become more interactive and carry full-motion video. Installing fiber optic lines into every home in the nation will cost an estimated $100 billion or more.

Local Telcos have operated as regulated monopolies without competition in their markets. If they hope to succeed, they will have to change the way they operate and become more entrepreneurial. While Telcos have vast financial resources, it is not clear whether they are willing to spend the billions of dollars needed to upgrade their networks to carry full-motion video. They may be reluctant to raise their debt or cut shareholder dividends, and they may not be able to obtain regulatory approval to increase phone rates to offset such investments. Even if they do raise rates, this may be counterproductive because they will face competition from new providers of phone service, such as Competitive Local Exchange Carriers (CLECS), MCI, and AT&T.

The movie studios know how to entertain audiences by producing and distributing high-quality content. But they have little experience with computer software or with the development of non-linear programming.[8] The most popular multimedia programming has not been generated by the studios, but by smaller independent companies.

Unlike the cable and telephone companies, the movie studios do not own transmission lines into viewers' homes, nor do they possess the technology and software needed to transmit programming and invoice millions of consumers. If independent filmmakers can distribute content over the Internet, or send it electronically to theaters, they could bypass the studio distribution system.

Cable companies have broadband coaxial cables reaching into nearly 60 million of the 94.2 million television households in the United States. The cable operators know how to package, market, and deliver entertainment to home viewers and collect revenue. All 11,217 cable systems do not interconnect, however, and they reach few schools or businesses. In order to build a nationwide system, the cable operators will have to agree on common standards, and they will need to lease trunk lines from the long-distance carriers or build their own. Moreover, cable systems are arranged with one-way communication in mind: from the cable head-end to the customer. Most cable systems do not currently have the capacity for upstream, or return, communication.[9]

The cable companies could possibly compete against the Baby Bells in providing local telephone service. With their access to homes, they could circumvent the Baby Bells and provide direct access to long distance carriers. They might be able to offer phone service at a lower cost, although this has not be proven. At one time, John Malone, head of cable giant TCI, bragged that his strategy was to link up with a long-distance carrier and offer homeowners a package of long-distance phone calls, brand-name entertainment like HBO and CNN, as well as home-energy management. "I can save the homeowner probably enough money on his electric bill to pay for his cable service," he said.[10] More recently, Malone delayed plans to move into telephony, refocusing his company on its core cable business and the adaptation of digital set-top boxes.[11] This technology will enable cable companies to better compete against digital satellite services, to whom they are losing customers. The digital satellite services can currently provide more channels and better-quality signals than cable systems, and the cost of owning the satellite dish has come down dramatically. While this competitor to cable may delay the cable industry's move into telephone and Internet services, cable companies could provide high-speed Internet access if they can come up with a workable cable modem.

Wireless services are expected to expand rapidly, offering another communication avenue. The auction of PCS (Personal Communications Services) licenses creates a new competitor to cellular phone service. Record sums were paid at auction for licenses to use these airwaves. Cellular phone prices have been dropping, perhaps in anticipation of forthcoming competition.

Television broadcasters and networks are expected to expand into new arenas. Digital compression technology can create several digital channels in the space occupied by one broadcast channel today. The Federal government recently announced that it will grant broadcasters digital channels. The additional spectrum space could be used by broadcasters to provide advanced digital services, thereby enabling them to compete with online services and telephone companies. Moreover, when broadcasters give back their existing channels in the next decade, the FCC will be able to reallocate this space for additional wireless services.

The electric utility companies may also become players on the information superhighway. In 1993, Arkansas Power and Light (AP&L) used bandwidth on the fiber optic network it uses for internal communication to offer an information test service to fifty homes in Little Rock. Electric power companies may be well positioned to become carriers of information because they have a large, already-installed base of fiber optic cable. Moreover, power companies have extensive rights of way that allow them access to homes nationwide.[12] The 1996 Telecom Act encourages utility companies to enter telecommunications.

The convergence of these separate industries has created difficult regulatory issues. Some industries, like telecommunications, have been regulated closely, while others, like publishing, have been able to operate without any government regulation at all.[13] Cable companies occupied middle ground. They had a local monopoly with rates regulated, but unlike the phone companies, cable companies could control the content distributed over their wires. Thus, they could choose to offer the most profitable channels, even if those channels catered to an affluent minority of viewers.

If telephone and cable companies provide similar service, should they not operate under similar rules? Since the phone companies are losing their monopoly as cellular companies and cable companies begin to offer phone service, should the phone companies be allowed to compete with cable companies on an equal basis in the arena of providing programming? The recently enacted Telecommunications Act of 1996 has changed the rules governing telecommunications in an attempt to treat all entities in a more equitable manner. It remains to be seen whether the regulations that will be adopted to implement these laws will have that effect.

HISTORY OF THE INFORMATION SUPERHIGHWAY

In the early 1970s the Department of Defense funded the Advanced Research Project Agency Network (ARPANet). This network was intended to help scientists exchange information by computer. It was designed to be a decentralized system of communication. Any number of different paths could be used to communicate from one computer to another. In the event of a nuclear war, there would be no central hub that, if destroyed, would prevent the remainder of the network from working.

Twenty years later, the National Science Foundation took responsibility for the network. The network was renamed the NSF Net, and its primary focus was to serve universities and research centers. This network would later become the Internet, an international network of computer networks used by an estimated 40 to 50 million people. Today, the Internet is growing by more than 300,000 users per month.

Groundwork is now being laid to build Internet II, the next-generation computer network that promises to be 100 times faster than the current Internet. The new network will link universities, research laboratories, and government agencies, permitting large-scale video and multimedia conferencing, telephony, distance learning, and telemedicine. Backers claim they need this new network because the commercialization and popularity of the Internet has made it too congested to handle the large data transmissions needed by researchers. Eventually, the technology developed for Internet II should find its way into popular use.

WHAT WILL THE INFORMATION SUPERHIGHWAY LOOK LIKE?

At the present time, no one knows how the information superhighway of the future will function and perform. To some extent, there is already an information superhighway: the Internet, a worldwide computer cooperative. Existing networks, such as telephone and cable companies' transmission lines and satellites, will likely be incorporated into the information superhighway. So, the backbone of the system already exists. What is needed is better on- and off-ramps that will link schools, businesses, and homes with the network.[14]

There has been considerable debate in Congress as to the shape of the National Information Infrastructure, the formal name of the information superhighway. Will there be universal access, even if it means that some consumers have to be subsidized? What protocols will be used? Will bandwidth be large enough to permit full two-way video communication (upstream/downstream bandwidth symmetry) or will we have a one-way pipeline designed with consumption in mind that permits consumers to transmit limited information such as E-mail?

We do know that the highway will transmit information digitally and it will be built and operated by private enterprise. The government will shape its development with research grants and by setting standards and regulations. Users will pay a fee for access to the network and for content, although much information may be available for free.

Data will be transmitted by a variety of computer servers. Information will be transmitted to personal computers, personal digital assistants (PDAs), smart phones, and television set-top boxes. An addressable digital set-top box has been estimated to cost $500 per home. Amortized over five years, that amounts to $8.30 a month. Keeping in mind that cable viewers today pay three or four dollars a month for their box, the increase in fees is not dramatic. Consumers may well be willing to pay a higher fee in order to have movies on demand, many more channels, videophone conferencing, digital music, high-definition television, and video games.[15] Already in existence is WebTV, which delivers Internet content directly to television sets. The company received a big boost in April 1997 when it was purchased by Microsoft.

The network will need software operating systems, user interfaces, and databanks. It is not clear at this time whose software will dominate, but it is likely that the architecture will be interactive and open so that outside companies can readily develop applications, just as they do now for the "DOS," "Windows," and "Macintosh" computer operating systems.

Software will enable viewers to easily navigate the system. A smart agent could learn the preferences of its owner and automatically retrieve those programs. It could compile customized reports of news of interest to the consumer, and shop for the best deals for products. Every viewer will be able to organize his television programming to suit his taste and schedule.

The companies that own the transmission lines may be required to operate as common carriers, like the phone companies, in which case they could not discriminate against users or content providers, nor could they censor or control what is transmitted over the network. Under such a scenario, there would be no media gatekeepers to restrict entrepreneurs who wanted to sell information services over the network.

The entertainment and cable companies, however, see the highway primarily as a way to sell their movies, entertainment, and other services to consumers. They want viewers to be able to interact with the information provider to the extent of being able to order movies on demand and shop at home. They may be less interested in enabling content consumers to become content providers who compete against them.[16] The media conglomerates might be satisfied with a network where the flow is mostly one way: from the studio to the couch potato. They may also prefer to limit access, avoiding neighborhoods that are expensive to wire or have less profit-making potential.

Aficionados of the Internet and public-interest advocates envision a switched, broadband network that could transmit a wide array of data, voice, and video signals. If there were universal access, common carriage, an open platform, and reasonable rates, such a system would allow everyone on the network to interact easily and privately with everyone else.

Dad could send his latest home movies to relatives abroad. Employees could telecommute, reducing traffic congestion and increasing efficiency. Videophone conferences could allow executives to reduce travel time, saving time, money, and lessening pollution. Democracy and civic participation would flourish if the system were truly two-way and open to everyone. Citizens would have access to a wealth of information, they could more easily organize, and they could readily communicate with their elected representatives.

New businesses would be able to market services over the system, and make sales via electronic money. With the cost of computers, video cameras, and desktop editing equipment falling, independent producers could create sophisticated, specialized programming in their garage's and then transmit it over the information superhighway to viewers. No one knows what types of new businesses might arise. After photocopying was invented, people found a host of new ways to benefit from the ability to make inexpensive copies. Businesses duplicated reports; consumers copied recipes. These new uses did not ruin the publishing industry; photocopying expanded the market for printed material by allowing individuals to self-publish specialized material. Likewise, there may be a vast untapped market for specialized multimedia programming in schools, community organizations, and businesses. Up to now, only well-financed companies could afford to create television programming, and they could only profitably make programming that appealed to a mass market.

I believe there is a vast, unrealized market for specialized programming. Students may someday create their school reports in the new medium. If they become ill they could monitor their classes by modem. Business proposals and presentations will increasingly become multimedia presentations. Companies are creating electronic catalogs and stores, complete with electronic salespeople who are always knowledgeable and available. Government could become much more efficient. Imagine using your home computer to register your car with the Department of Motor Vehicles or vote. Doctors could examine and diagnose patients over the Internet, making specialists available in rural areas at minimal cost.

The more universal the service, the more valuable it will be for both information providers and information consumers. A phone system that could only connect to a limited pool of individuals would be far less valuable than the almost universal service we have today. There is a danger that a small group of large companies could come to monopolize the market, stifling competition, innovation, and the ability of independent producers to sell their work. The large media companies have been consolidating: placing publishing, television, cable, film, and music companies under one roof. Viacom acquired Paramount and Blockbuster. Disney acquired ABC. Warner Bros. and Time merged into Time Warner, which later acquired Turner. The small entrepreneur must be guaranteed access to the information superhighway on the same terms as the large media conglomerates.

The information superhighway will have a worldwide reach. Customers in remote areas will be able to order products easily, quickly, and relatively inexpensively. Developers should keep in mind, however, that unlike many Americans, citizens in most countries are not as likely to have a computer at home. In many developed countries, computers are used primarily as a business tool, and not utilized much for in-home entertainment. In France, only 8% of home PC owners have modems.[17] Moreover, most countries do not have residential calling plans that offer local calls for no charge above the basic monthly service fee. The average cost of a three-minute local peak-rate call in Europe is about fourteen cents. These charges discourage citizens from surfing the Internet.

PRIVACY CONCERNS

Establishing a secure information superhighway is essential in order for individuals and businesses to rely on it. Security measures can include passwords, restricting physical access to the network and data encryption. Data encryption is particularly important as more information is transmitted by wireless devices, and as more financial transactions are conducted in cyberspace.

The United States government has opposed the use of encryption methods that it cannot crack. The government wants to ensure that it can monitor information vital to national security and deter criminal activities. The Clinton administration proposed a clipper chip that provides a technological back door that is accessible to government agencies. Although government agencies would be required to obtain a court order to authorize a wiretap, the proposal has met with considerable opposition. Civil liberties groups object on privacy grounds; high-tech businesses object because such a chip might hinder the sale of U.S. technology abroad.

Export laws prevent the sale of advanced U.S. encryption technology abroad. This policy does not prevent terrorists and the drug cartels from acquiring similar technology from other countries. It has, however, deterred the development of electronic money. A bipartisan group of Senators has introduced legislation (The Encrypted Communications Privacy Act, S 1587) to liberalize the export and use of digital-encryption technology.

KEY TECHNOLOGICAL DEVELOPMENTS

Fiber Optics

Optical fibers are made of transparent glass, a thin and flexible medium that transmits information with pulses of light. While each fiber is thinner than a strand of hair, it can transmit thousands of times more data than traditional copper wires. While copper wires can transmit 64,000 bits of information per second, fiber optic cable can transmit at the rate of a trillion bits per second.[18] Fiber optic cable can transmit the entire text of the *Encyclopedia Britannica* around the world in less than two seconds.[19] A single fiber can transmit 129,000 simultaneous telephone conversations. Fiber optics thus increase capacity, thereby enabling the transmission of hundreds of channels of data and interactive communication.

Fiber optics are more cost-efficient than older copper cables for trunk lines between cities and between major switching centers. Their small size and light weight allow the manufacture of cables up to ten miles long without splicing. Consequently, installation time is shortened, and fewer repeaters are needed. Fiber optics are also immune to electromagnetic interference, assuring cleaner reception.

Rewiring the nation with fiber optics into every home, however, is expensive. Therefore, telephone and cable companies have experimented with methods of transmitting more information over twisted copper pairs, the telephone wiring found in most homes, and coaxial cable, the wire used by cable operators. Different media can be used together. Fiber optic cable could transmit information into the neighborhood, with the last leg to the home relying on copper wire or coaxial cable.

Telcos have installed much more fiber optic cable than cable operators. However, cable companies are increasing their installation of fiber optics at a more rapid pace.

Digital Compression

Digital compression squeezes data into reduced channel space. Recent developments have dramatically increased compression ratios and improved video signal quality at a lower cost. Using this technology, ten to twenty video signals can be compressed and travel over the space that used to carry one channel.

To carry compressed signals, cable and television networks will need to be upgraded. In addition, households will need a cable converter box to display the compressed signal.

High-Definition Television

The development of High-Definition Television (HDTV) allows viewers to purchase a new television receiver and view programs with much better resolution, color, and sound. The image is sharper because the new sets scan almost double the lines of existing television receivers. Home viewers can thus expect a sharper viewing experience, more like a movie theater.

The new receivers, however, remain expensive, although the price will drop when they are manufactured in volume. HDTV sets are expected to cost an additional $1,000 or more above the cost of current large-screen receivers.

Although there were several competing technologies, the groups developing these technologies have merged their efforts and have agreed upon a single standard. The new system will be a digital one.

The FCC allows current broadcasters to apply for a second channel to broadcast in HDTV. This will allow viewers with ordinary television sets and those with HDTV sets to receive the same channel.

Direct Broadcast Satellite

Direct Broadcast Satellite (DBS) technology allows consumers to receive programming by using a home satellite dish to receive signals from high-powered satellites. These signals are powerful enough that homeowners only need to purchase an eighteen-inch dish. While there are significant costs to build and launch the satellites, and homeowners need to purchase a receiving dish, DBS technology alleviates the need for laying wire from the program source to the home.

DirecTV, the industry leader, had 2.4 million subscribers as of 1997.[20] In a joint venture with Microsoft, DirectTV plans on offering its subscribers access to the Internet. Hughes Network Systems has an odd-shaped satellite dish that receives both television signals and provides access to the Internet. Internet delivery via satellite is much faster than access through ordinary telephone lines.[21]

Digital Video Disc

The Digital Versatile Disc (DVD), also known as Digital Video Disc, is a new format for storage of data that has generated a lot of excitement. DVDs are five-inch optical discs that look like audio Compact Discs (CDs). But DVDs are far more versatile because they can be used for recording motion pictures and computer software as well as music, and these different types of data can be combined on a single disc.

A DVD can hold 4.7 gigabytes of data on a side, which is the capacity of seven CD-ROMs. According to Toshiba, a double-sided, double-layered disc can hold 17 gigabytes of data.[22] A DVD can hold a feature-length film with high-quality picture and sound.[23] The capacity is so great that a movie on DVD would have room for soundtracks in several languages, different sets of subtitles, and such options as allowing the viewer to choose a G- or PG-rated version of the movie.

While movies on laserdiscs never caught on big—about two million laserdisc players have been sold compared to 170 million VHS decks[24]—there are several reasons to believe that DVDs will fare better. First, the format has backward compatibility with existing CDs. Users can play CD and CD-ROM software on DVD drives. Second, DVD drives are likely to be included in the next generation of computers. Third, the storage capacity is so large that a single disc could include a motion picture, an audio soundtrack of the film's music, and a computer program incorporating the film's characters. The system has the capability of allowing parents to block violent or other objectionable scenes deemed inappropriate for children. Brought to market in 1997, several manufacturers are currently producing DVDs. In addition to the read-only DVDs now being sold, manufacturers are planning to produce write-once and rewritable discs.

The World Wide Web

The World Wide Web (WWW or the Web) is the multimedia, interactive portion of the Internet. Here, Web pages and sites contain files embedded with hyperlinks or hotlinks. These links allow users to quickly jump from one Web site to another by simply clicking on highlighted text. Graphics, sound, and digitized information of all types can be accessed quickly and easily using various icon-based Web browsers. Web sites are being used by many businesses to advertise products and, in some cases, consumers can order products online.

The creation of a variety of Web access tools has speeded the development of the Web. Hypertext Markup Language (HTML) is the formatting code used to turn an ordinary text document into a Web document with hypertext links.

Real-time audio allows sound to be heard in real time, like a radio broadcast. Thus, sound files do not have to be downloaded and played later. RealAudio (Progressive Networks, http://www.realaudio.com/) and Streamworks (Xing Technology, http://www.xingtech.com/) make live broadcasting on the Web possible.

RealAudio is a group of tools for producing, distributing, and listening to on-demand audio clips over the Internet. RealAudio permits anyone with a 14.4kbps or faster modem to listen to music on the net without first downloading the clip. It integrates into existing web browsers, and it has the ability to embed network and multimedia scripting commands into the sound stream. Thus, as narration or music plays, pages displayed on the web site can automatically turn.

The development of real-time video could enable independent producers to provide full-motion video over the Internet. This should become possible as compression technologies improve, bandwidth increases, and faster modems are adopted. A number of companies are developing video streaming (VDOnet at http://www.vdolive.com/ and Iterated Systems at http://www.interated.com/).

Sun's programming language, Java, makes the Web interactive (http://java.sun.com/). Sun's Web browser, Hotjava, uses a programming language that automatically downloads tiny applications (applets) to users' computers. Thus, if a user's computer does not have the necessary software to play a clip, Hotjava will automatically download it.

Virtual Reality Modeling Language (VRML) is a programming language that allows users to explore three-dimensional environments, or "worlds." This will allow users to move about virtual stores, select and examine objects, and allow graphical, rather than text-based, navigation of web sites.

GOVERNMENT POLICY

In 1984, Judge Harold Greene issued a decision that broke up the AT&T Bell System (Ma Bell), creating local Telcos (Baby Bells). While the Baby Bells were prohibited from manufacturing equipment, providing long-distance service, and owning content, the breakup created an industry with new companies competing for portions of the long-distance market. Long-distance rates dropped significantly. MCI and Sprint reduced AT&T's market share from 98% to about 55%.

In 1991, the prohibition preventing the Baby Bells from providing information services was partially lifted, allowing them to own news, sports, weather, and other data services distributed over their phone lines.[25] In 1993, Bell Atlantic was successful in challenging the portion of the Cable Act that prevented the Baby Bells from providing television programming.[26] A subsequent FCC ruling allowed telephone companies to provide "video dial-tone" services.

The Telecommunications Act of 1996 radically changed the law by removing barriers that prevent different industries from competing against each other. Under the new law, consumers can buy a variety of services from local and long-distance phone carriers, cable companies, and wireless providers. The Baby Bells, for instance, once they

---

BOOKS OF INTEREST

BEING DIGITAL, NICHOLAS NEGROPONTE, VINTAGE BOOKS, 1996.

CYBERSPACE AND THE LAW: YOUR RIGHTS AND DUTIES IN THE ON-LINE WORLD, EDWARD A. CAVAZOS AND GAVINO MORIN, MIT PRESS, 1994.

THE CUCKOO'S EGG, CLIFF STOLL, SIMON AND SCHUSTER, 1990. A TRUE MYSTERY STORY OF HOW A BERKELEY ASTRONOMER TRACKED DOWN A 75-CENT DISCREPANCY ON HIS BILL AND BROKE UP AN INTERNATIONAL ESPIONAGE RING.

ED KROL'S THE WHOLE INTERNET USER'S GUIDE AND CATALOG, O'REILLY & ASSOCIATES, 1993.

ZEN AND THE ART OF THE INTERNET, BRENDAN KEHOE, PRENTICE HALL, 1993.

pass a test on opening their local networks to competition, will be allowed to enter the long-distance business, and they can now enter the cable business.[27] They will also be able to connect calls across state lines within their regions without relying on long-distance carriers.

The long-distance carriers will no longer have to rely upon local telephone companies. They have been paying the local companies about 45% of their long-distance revenue for access to consumers. The long-distance companies are investing large sums to build their own local networks. AT&T purchased McCaw Cellular Communications for $11.5 billion to gain a local wireless connection that bypasses the Baby Bells.

The new law does not always promote competition. The prohibition on owning cable and telephone properties in towns with less than 50,000 residents has been dropped. Television broadcast groups can expand from 25% to 35 % of the national audience, allowing television networks to own more stations.

MAGAZINES OF INTEREST

BOARDWATCH MAGAZINE, 8500 W. BOWLES AVE, STE. 210, LITTLETON, CO 80123 (303) 973-6038. A GUIDE TO THE INTERNET WORLD WIDE WEB AND BBSS. A PLAIN-ENGLISH GUIDE TO TECHNOLOGY, PUBLISHED BY THE ASSOCIATION OF AMERICA'S PUBLIC TELEVISION STATIONS, SEPTEMBER 1993.

EDUPAGE, EDUCOM, 1112 16TH ST. NW, STE. 600, WASHINGTON, DC 20036 (202) 872-4200.

ELECTRONIC FRONTIER FOUNDATION (EFF), 1550 BRYANT ST., STE. 725, SAN FRANCISCO, CA 94103 (415) 436-9333 HTTP://WWW.EFF.ORG/

ELECTRONIC PRIVACY INFORMATION CENTER, 666 PENNSYLVANIA AVE. SE, STE. 301, WASHINGTON, DC 20003 (202) 544-9240 HTTP://WWW.EPIC.ORG/

INTERNET WORLD. MECKLERMEDIA, 20 KETCHUM ST., WESTPORT, CT 06880 (203) 226-6967.

MORPH'S OUTPOST ON THE DIGITAL FRONTIER. MORPH'S OUTPOST, INC., P.O. BOX 578, ORINDA, CA 94563 (510) 253-9816.

RED HERRING. FLIPSIDE COMMUNICATIONS INC., 2055 WOODSIDE RD., STE. 240, REDWOOD CITY, CA 94061.

WIRED, 520 THIRD ST., FOURTH FLOOR, SAN FRANCISCO, CA 94107 (415) 276-5000.

The legislation includes a ban on "indecent" material over the Internet, a prohibition that has been struck down as unconstitutional by the U.S. Supreme Court. The law also provides that future television sets include a V-Chip, which will allow parents to block selected programs.

A Clinton Administration's working group on intellectual property has been examining intellectual-property laws to consider whether they need to be modified in order to facilitate the growth of the National Information Infrastructure (NII), the government's name for the information superhighway. In September 1995, this task force issued a White Paper titled "Intellectual Property and the National Information Infrastructure" with their recommendations. The report is available from the Information Infrastructure Task Force Bulletin Board, which can be accessed through the Internet by pointing the gopher client to iitf.doc.gov or by telnet to iitf.doc.gov (log in as gopher).

Since existing intellectual-property laws were not drafted with the Internet in mind, there has been some uncertainty whether the electronic transmission of copyrighted works would be considered a violation of a copyright owner's rights. The report recommends that the transmission of copies or phonorecords by electronic transmission be considered a use that falls within the copyright holder's right to control distribution of his work. The report suggests that the term "publication" be expanded to include publication through distribution to the public by transmission. Another recommendation is that electronic transmissions of sound and musical compositions should be considered a public performance under copyright law.

Congress enacted, effective February 1, 1996, the Digital Performance Right in Sound Recordings Act. The Act is meant to provide additional protection to owners of sound recordings that are transmitted digitally. The recording industry may be moving from a distribution system in which CDs and cassettes are physically distributed to a system in which music is transmitted digitally. The Act sets forth licensing and royalty provisions and extends the mechanical-license right to digital transmissions of sound recordings.

In December 1996 a two-week conference of the World Intellectual Property Organization (WIPO) was convened in Geneva. Delegates from the United States and 160 other countries attended to discuss three draft treaties dealing with the protection of films, software, recorded music, and databases. Although an agreement was not reached on a proposed database treaty, treaties were proposed that addressed issues of how copyrighted materials delivered over computer networks would be treated. Critics charged that the Clinton Administration attempted an end-run around Congress by taking positions before Congress had held hearings and debated the issues.

The Clinton Administration's position was similar to that advocated by record companies, movie studios, and book publishers—entities that want maximum protection for copyright holders. The companies are concerned about the potential for widespread copyright piracy in a digital era, and they want stronger laws to stop unauthorized copying and distribution. Aligned against these interests are a group of information carriers such as telecommunications companies and Internet service providers, as well as computer companies, universities, libraries, and civil liberties groups. They are concerned about the rights of users to have access to copyrighted works.

After much discussion and wrangling, the WIPO conference rejected most of the Clinton's Administration's agenda. The proposal to treat transitory copies of works in computer memory as a significant act under copyright law was defeated. The Clinton Administration backed away from a proposed database treaty after the American scientific community expressed their concern that it would seriously hamper scientific research. The proposed treaties and other related documents can be found at: http://www.wipo.org/eng/diplconf/distrib/index.htm. The treaties need to be ratified by the U.S. Senate to bind the United States.

CHAPTER 2

LICENSING CONTENT

Producers often want to incorporate pre-existing works in their multimedia programs. This may involve placing text, such as a dictionary, on a CD-ROM, or producing a program about Mozart with accompanying music and photographs. There are several problems one encounters when trying to license pre-existing works.

AN UNCERTAIN MARKET

Content owners may not know what to charge to license material for multimedia use. CBS, Inc. is reportedly charging $15 per second for material in its library. Many companies have adopted a wait-and-see attitude because they are afraid to sell rights at below-market rates. If companies stand on the sidelines, the market will develop slowly.

The amount of money that a producer can afford to pay, and still recoup his investment, is relatively small at this time because of the limited market for the end product. While many new computers have CD-ROM players, many older computers do not. Retail sales of CD-ROM programs are much less than music CDs and movie videotapes, although the market for CD-ROMs and DVDs is expected to continue to grow.

Usually, owners want to know the context in which their content will be used. They may be reluctant to license a film clip, for instance, if its intended use will disparage the movie the clip came from. They may want to know the territory in which the program will be distributed, how many sales are projected, and whether the clip will be used in advertising the program.

CLEARANCE PROBLEMS

Owners of existing works may not hold all of the necessary rights needed to exploit their properties as multimedia programs. Multimedia and electronic publishing did not exist when many contracts were negotiated, therefore the question of who owns such rights may be unclear. As a practical matter, old contracts may have been lost or may be difficult to locate.

A multimedia producer cannot buy rights to put content on a CD-ROM if the seller does not own those rights. Contract language that granted rights to the seller may have been ambiguous. A contract might provide that a novelist is granting a studio the right to turn his or her novel into a motion picture. The grant could include "all allied rights." Under this language, who owns the electronic publishing rights to the novel? The studio may claim electronic publishing is an "allied right." The writer may disagree, contending that the parties never intended to transfer electronic publishing rights since electronic publishing did not exist when the contract was made.

When a studio gives a multimedia producer a license to use its footage in a new interactive program, the grant may be no more than a quitclaim release. Here, the studio sells only those rights that it may own, without promising (warranting) that it owns any rights. The multimedia producer will need to examine the contracts that purportedly gave the studio these rights in order to determine the extent of the rights the studio actually owns. The studio, however, may not want to disclose the terms of its contracts.

Whether a studio owns the right to exploit a film as a multimedia project will often turn on the language used in contracts to acquire rights to underlying content. The case law in this area is confusing and somewhat contradictory. In one line of cases, the courts state that a licensee may use a property in any manner that appears to fall within the scope of the contract granting those rights.[1] In these decisions, the courts assume that a grant of rights covers new uses or new media if the words conveying the grant are susceptible to that interpretation, even if such new uses are not specified.[2] Thus, an assignment of motion-picture rights to a play has been held to include the right to broadcast the film on television, even though television did not exist at the time the contract was made.[3]

In another line of cases, the courts assume that a grant of rights only extends to those uses that are clearly within the scope of the rights conveyed. In *Cohen v. Paramount Pictures Corp.*,[4] a composer granted to a production company the right to use his music in the film *Medium Cool*. The grant included the right to use the composition by means of television, including exhibition by pay television and subscription television. The contract reserved all other rights to the composer. When Paramount began to distribute the film in the form of videocassettes, the composer sued on the grounds that his prior grant of rights did not include exhibition by home video. The Ninth Circuit Court of Appeals agreed.[5]

FEAR OF DIGITALIZATION

Owners are concerned that if they let their work be digitalized, the work will be easily pirated by others. In digitalization, the image is converted into a series of pixels or dots. Once a work is digitized, subsequent generations can be copied without any loss in quality. Furthermore, the image can be manipulated and changed so that it does not look like the original. Multiple images can be metamorphosed into new hybrids, a practice called "morphing." Ready access to computer networks, the Internet, and bulletin boards can compound the damage by making it easy to distribute pirated works to many people at little cost.

Refusing to allow one's work to be digitized, however, does not necessarily stop thievery. A determined pirate can steal an image by simply scanning it into a computer.

Assuming that the owner of a work is willing to license it for multimedia use, a multitude of legal issues may arise.

LICENSING CONTENT

Text

Whether the multimedia producer is licensing a fiction or non-fiction work, the principal legal issues are as follows:

Copyright

Copyright law protects works of authorship, such as literary works, musical works, paintings, and photographs.[6] These creations are "things" created by people. They are called intellectual property since they are products of the mind. Copyright should not be confused with personality rights (e.g., the right of publicity and right of privacy) that people may possess to protect the use of their name, voice and personae.

Federal copyright law applies in all states. Today, state copyright law is largely preempted by federal law,[7] although state law may provide a remedy in those areas that the federal law does not preempt. For instance, state law could protect works that are ineligible for federal protection because the works are not recorded in a fixed medium of expression, a requirement for a federal copyright.

Copyright laws are territorial in their application. This means that United States copyright law applies only within the United States. The United States has joined several international copyright conventions that protect U.S. works from infringement abroad. These treaties also protect the work of foreign authors in the United States.

To be eligible for copyright protection, a work must meet four criteria:

(1) It must be original;

(2) It must be an "expression of an author";

(3) It must be of a non-utilitarian nature; and

(4) It must be in a fixed, tangible medium of expression.

If a work meets all four criteria, the creator automatically has a copyright in his work. The copyright comes into existence upon creation. The creator does not need to send any forms to the Copyright Office, say any magic words, or perform any rituals in order to be protected under copyright law. A copyright notice is not required to obtain a copyright.[8]

COPYRIGHT REQUIREMENTS

(1) ORIGINALITY

INDEPENDENT EFFORT: THE WORK MUST BE CREATED THROUGH THE INDEPENDENT EFFORT OF THE AUTHOR. THE CREATOR CANNOT COPY IT FROM ANOTHER. THE WORK NEED NOT HAVE ANY ARTISTIC MERIT. A SILLY NOVEL OR AN UGLY PAINTING CAN BE COPYRIGHTED. THE WORK HAS TO BE ORIGINAL, NOT GOOD.

(2) EXPRESSION OF AN AUTHOR

NOT CONSIDERED AN EXPRESSION OF AN AUTHOR: IDEAS, PHRASES, CONCEPTS, THEMES, AND TITLES. WHAT IS PRO-TECTED: THE CRAFTSMANSHIP AND APPROACH OF THE WRITER, THE WRITER'S SKILL IN FASHIONING AND ORGANIZING HIS WORK. IN OTHER WORDS, THE EMBELLISHMENT UPON THE IDEA.

(3) NON-UTILITARIAN NATURE

LIGHTING FIXTURES, INDUSTRIAL DESIGN OF APPLIANCES, AND ACCOUNTING FORMS ARE WORKS OF A UTILITARIAN NATURE THAT ARE NOT ELIGIBLE FOR COPYRIGHT PROTECTION.

(4) FIXATION IN TANGIBLE MEDIUM OF EXPRESSION

ACCEPTABLE MEDIUMS: ALMOST ANYTHING THAT IS STABLE AND RELATIVELY PERMANENT, INCLUDING PAPER, VIDEOTAPE, AUDIOTAPE, PAINT, CLAY, FILM, AND METAL. WHAT IS NOT ACCEPTABLE: SAND CASTLES, ICE SCULPTURES, IMPROVISED LIVE PERFORMANCES, AND ORDINARY CONVERSATIONS THAT ARE NOT RECORDED IN A TANGIBLE MEDIUM. WHO MUST FIX: THE AUTHOR OR SOMEONE UNDER HIS AUTHORIZATION MUST REDUCE THE WORK TO A TANGIBLE FORM.

Perhaps the simplest way of understanding copyright law is to think of it as a three-tiered scheme. First, the author gets a copyright in his work when he creates it, assuming that the work meets the four criteria. Second, an author was obliged, before 1989, to place a copyright notice (the word "copyright," or the abbreviation, or the copyright symbol "©"; the name of copyright holder; and the year of publication) in order to retain their copyright if they chose to publish their work. And third, if the author registers the work with the Copyright Office in a timely manner, he will be eligible for some extra, super-duper benefits, like reimbursement of attorneys' fees and recovery of statutory damages in a copyright infringement suit. But if the author does not choose to publish or register a work, he may nevertheless be protected under copyright law.

Since the United States joined the Berne International Copyright Convention in 1989,[9] a copyright notice is no longer required to protect a copyright. In other words, an author who publishes his work and fails to attach a copyright notice is protected anyway.

A producer who desires to incorporate a literary work in a multimedia program should take the following steps. First, the producer should determine whether the work is copyrighted or in the public domain. This can be difficult since a search of copyright records is rarely conclusive. Many works protected under copyright law may be unpublished and/or unregistered.

Of course, if a work fails to meet one of the above-mentioned four criteria, it is not copyrightable and must be in the public domain. It is not always readily apparent, however, whether a work has met the criteria. For example, a basic tenet of copyright law is that ideas are not protectable, only the expression of ideas.[10] In other words, the embellishment upon an idea can be protected, but not the underlying bare idea itself. Copyright law protects the craftsmanship of the author, and the particular manner in which an author expresses himself, not underlying facts and ideas.

It may be difficult to determine when an idea is sufficiently embellished upon in order for a work to be entitled to protection. While a single word is not an expression of an author,

and an entire book is an expression of an author, what about a
synopsis? Is this an "idea," or more? In *Takeall v. Pepsico,
Inc.*,[11] the court declined to find that the short phrase "You Got
the Right One, Uh-Huh," as used in a Pepsi commercial, was
copyrightable.[12]

In some instances an author is unable to protect an expression of an idea, such as when an idea can only be expressed in
one or in a limited number of ways.[13] Even when an expression can be protected under copyright law, underlying elements of the work may be borrowed. For example, historical
facts and stock scenes ("scenes a faire") are unprotected, and
can be taken from copyrighted work without violating the
author's copyright.[14]

Copyright law protects both the literal text of a work and its
structure and organization.[15] Thus, a borrower of material who
closely paraphrases the original may be liable for copyright
infringement, although the precise text of the two works differ.
The key test is whether the works are "substantially similar."[16]

In determining whether two works are substantially similar,
some courts use a two-part test. First, the works are compared
objectively, using external criteria and analysis and sometimes
expert testimony. The second part of the test subjectively
determines how the ordinary observer would view the works.

When evaluating whether a work is in the public domain,
multimedia producers should keep in mind that a work of a
U.S. author that is in the public domain in the United States
might nevertheless be protected under foreign law. Since the
market for CD-ROMs and computer programming is global,
compliance with foreign laws is of concern to U.S. producers
who want to market their products internationally. Determining whether a work is in the public domain worldwide can be
exceedingly complex.

Consider, for example, Charlie Chaplin's copyright claim to
the 1925 silent film *The Gold Rush*,[17] which is in the public
domain in the United States. The film was first published in the
United States. Chaplin, a British citizen, brought suit in Switzerland, where he was then a resident. Swiss copyright law did
not apply directly since it only protects works by Swiss nationals and works first published in Switzerland.

Switzerland protects other works, however, by virtue of various international treaties. The United States and Switzerland have a 1924 bilateral agreement, but it only applies to works of United States and Swiss nationals. Both countries are signatories to the Berne Treaty, but the United States did not join until 1989, long after the film was published. Great Britain was also a member of Berne and Chaplin was a citizen of Great Britain, but the 1908 version of Berne applied only to works first published in a Berne country, which the United States was not. Thus, it appeared that Chaplin did not have a valid copyright claim.

The 1908 version of Berne, however, extended copyright protection to works simultaneously published in a Berne signatory country. The film was published in Canada, a Berne country, in 1925. The Swiss court found this to be a simultaneous publication. Since Berne applied, the law of Switzerland applied. Under Swiss law, copyright lasts for the lifetime of the author plus fifty years, and Chaplin's copyright remained in force. At that time, the United States only protected this work for twenty-eight years. Therefore, the film was protected in Switzerland, although it was in the public domain in the United States.[18]

Now imagine that you are a multimedia developer creating a CD-ROM encyclopedia. For the entry on Charlie Chaplin you want to include a clip from *The Gold Rush*. Your research indicates that the film was first published in the United States, and under U.S. law the film has fallen into the public domain. You therefore believe that you can use the clip without obtaining any permission from the Chaplin estate. Your publisher manufactures, packages, and arranges for international distribution of your encyclopedia. When it enters Switzerland, the Chaplin estate obtains an injunction, halting distribution and causing substantial losses to your publisher and the foreign distributor. Since you have warranted (promised) in your contract with the publisher that your program has not infringed the rights of any third parties, you have breached your contract. The indemnity clause requires you to reimburse the publisher and distributor for any losses they have incurred as a result of your breach, including their attorneys' fees.

The Chaplin case illustrates the complex nature of copyright issues, the difficulty of determining the status of a work, and how treacherous it can be to rely on materials that appear to be in the public domain.

Another complication was added in 1994, when President Clinton signed the Uruguay Round Agreements Act (URAA),[19] modifying U.S. copyright, patent, and trademark law to comply with a new World Trade Organization (WTO) agreement. The U.S. Copyright Act now provides for the restoration of copyright protection for foreign works that were in the public domain in the United States while protected under foreign law.[20] Works subject to restoration are those that are: (1) in the public domain in the United States for reasons other than expiration of a full copyright term; and (2) are not in the public domain in their "source country"; and (3) are works of foreign origin. Qualifying works are automatically restored for the remainder of the copyright the work would otherwise have been granted. Remedies are limited, however, in regard to parties who have exploited such a work before the copyright was restored.

Another trap for the unwary can arise from works first published abroad. A work may be protected abroad yet be in the public domain in the United States. For example, the copyright for the classic Italian film *The Bicycle Thief* was determined to have expired under United States law since its copyright was not properly renewed in the United States. The movie was first published in Italy in 1948[22] and it remains protected there because in Italy, copyright lasts for fifty years from the first public showing.

Content borrowers need to be concerned with other foreign laws as well. Some countries, such as France, expressly recognize the moral rights ("droit moral") authors have in their work. These moral rights prevent others from changing the author's work (the right of integrity), or taking the author's name off of it (the right of paternity), even if the author has sold the physical work and the copyright to it.[23]

In other words, there are different types of rights an author may have in his work. There is ownership of the actual physical work, such as a painting. The owner of a painting can display it in one's home and can sell it. The owner cannot duplicate the painting, however, unless the owner has also secured the copyright to the painting. The copyright allows the owner the right to duplicate, distribute, and prepare derivative works, such as a T-shirt with the image of the painting on it. Then there are the moral rights an author may have in his work. These rights are separate and distinct from the owner- ship of the painting and the copyright to the painting. If a

COPYRIGHT BASICS

LIMITS ON COPYRIGHT

SOMETIMES ONE MAY USE COPYRIGHTABLE WORKS WITHOUT THE COPYRIGHT OWNER'S PERMISSION. THESE USES INCLUDE "COMPULSORY LICENSES," "BLANKET LICENSES," AND USES WITHIN THE FAIR USE DOCTRINE. UNDER A BLANKET LICENSE, FOR INSTANCE, A RADIO STATION CAN PUBLICLY PERFORM MUSIC WITHOUT SECURING COPYRIGHT PERMISSION BEFOREHAND. THE STATION MUST PAY A FEE TO THE OWNER'S AGENT (E.G., ASCAP OR BMI) FOR THE PRIVILEGE.

OWNERSHIP OF COPYRIGHT

WORKS CREATED PURSUANT TO ONE'S EMPLOYMENT ARE WORKS MADE FOR HIRE, AND, THEREFORE, THE COPYRIGHT IS USUALLY HELD BY THE EMPLOYER. WORKS CREATED BY THE COLLABORATIVE EFFORT OF SEVERAL AUTHORS ARE JOINT WORKS AND THE COPYRIGHT IS USUALLY HELD JOINTLY BY THE COLLABORATORS. LIKE OTHER PROPERTY, A COPYRIGHT CAN BE SOLD AND TRANSFERRED.[21]

DERIVATIVE WORKS

A DERIVATIVE WORK IS ANY WORK BASED ON ONE OR MORE PRE-EXISTING WORKS. DERIVATIVE WORKS INCLUDE TRANSLATIONS, MUSICAL ARRANGEMENTS, DRAMATIZA- TIONS, FICTIONALIZATIONS, MOTION PICTURE VERSIONS, SOUND RECORDINGS, ABRIDGEMENTS, AND CONDENSATIONS. ALSO, WORKS CONSISTING OF EDITORIAL REVISIONS, ANNOTATIONS, ELABORATIONS, OR OTHER MODIFICATIONS THAT, AS A WHOLE, REPRESENT AN ORIGINAL WORK OF AUTHORSHIP, ARE DERIVATIVE WORKS.

A DERIVATIVE WORK INFRINGES ON THE COPYRIGHT OF THE ORIGINAL. TO AVOID INFRINGEMENT, A DERIVATIVE WORK MUST BE BASED ON PUBLIC-DOMAIN MATERIAL OR MADE WITH THE PERMISSION OF THE COPYRIGHT OWNER OF THE ORIGINAL.

[CONTINUED]

painter has moral rights in his work, for instance, then he can sell the work, transfer the copyright, and still assert his moral right to prevent others from taking his name off the work or changing it.

Under French law, the rights of integrity and paternity are perpetual, inheritable, inalienable, and imprescriptible.[24] Thus, the heirs of an artist could object to the use of their ancestor's work, even if that work's copyright has expired. In *Huston v.*

COPYRIGHT BASICS
[CONTINUED]

JOINT WORKS

A JOINT WORK IS PREPARED BY TWO OR MORE AUTHORS WITH THE INTENTION THAT THEIR CONTRIBUTIONS BE MERGED INTO INSEPARABLE OR INTERDEPENDENT PARTS OF A UNITARY WHOLE. IT IS IMPORTANT THAT THE AUTHORS INTEND AT THE TIME OF CREATION THAT THEIR RESPECTIVE LABORS BE INTEGRATED INTO ONE WORK.

A JOINT WORK CAN BE CREATED EVEN IF THE CONTRIBUTIONS OF THE AUTHORS ARE UNEQUAL, SO LONG AS EACH AUTHOR MAKES MORE THAN A TRIFLING CONTRIBUTION AND THEY INTEND THEIR WORK TO BE PART OF A JOINT WORK. JOINT WORKS CAN ALSO BE CREATED WHEN A COPYRIGHT OWNER TRANSFERS COPYRIGHT TO MORE THAN ONE PERSON, OR WHEN COPYRIGHT PASSES BY WILL OR INTESTACY TO TWO OR MORE PERSONS, OR WHEN A WORK IS SUBJECT TO STATE COMMUNITY-PROPERTY LAWS. THUS, A JOINT WORK CAN BE BROADLY DEFINED AS ONE IN WHICH COPYRIGHT IS OWNED IN UNDIVIDED SHARES BY TWO OR MORE PERSONS, WHETHER CREATED BY JOINT AUTHORSHIP OR SOME OTHER WAY.

AS CO-OWNERS, THE AUTHORS ARE DEEMED TO BE TENANTS IN COMMON, WHICH MEANS THAT EACH CO-OWNER HAS AN UNDIVIDED OWNERSHIP INTEREST IN THE ENTIRE WORK. A CO-OWNER CAN USE OR LICENSE THE WHOLE WORK IF HE WISHES, BUT HAS AN OBLIGATION TO ACCOUNT FOR PROFITS TO THE OTHER JOINT OWNERS. A JOINT OWNER, HOWEVER, CANNOT TRANSFER ALL INTEREST IN THE WORK WITHOUT WRITTEN CONSENT OF HIS CO-OWNERS. THE COPYRIGHT TERM FOR JOINT WORKS IS LIFE PLUS FIFTY YEARS, MEASURED FROM THE LIFE OF THE LAST LIVING JOINT AUTHOR.

TRANSFERS OF COPYRIGHT INTERESTS

COPYRIGHT IS COMPRISED OF A BUNDLE OF RIGHTS, AND THE 1976 COPYRIGHT ACT EXPRESSLY RECOGNIZES THE DIVISIBILITY OF COPYRIGHT: ANY SUBDIVISION OF THE RIGHTS MAY BE TRANSFERRED AND OWNED SEPARATELY. TO BE EFFECTIVE, TRANSFERS OF COPYRIGHT MUST BE IN WRITING AND SIGNED BY THE COPYRIGHT OWNER. THIS REQUIREMENT DOES NOT APPLY TO A NON-EXCLUSIVE LICENSE.

Turner Entertainment,[25] the late American director John Huston was determined by a French court to be the author of the American film *The Asphalt Jungle*, although under American law his employer was deemed the author.

France's approach to author's rights is shared by such countries as Spain, Portugal, Italy, Greece, Belgium, and the Netherlands. Under the laws of these countries, it can be difficult for a multimedia producer to obtain all rights to component parts of a multimedia work. If a country does not have a work-for-hire doctrine, the copyright of a multimedia work would vest in the individuals who created the music, artwork, writing, photographs, and other elements that are incorporated in the final product. Ownership can turn on whether a multimedia work is classified as an audiovisual work, a composite work, or a computer program[26] because the applicable law might vest rights differently depending on the nature of the work.

If a work is in the public domain, one can use it without permission from the author. Works in the public domain include those created by the United States government, works created by authors who have abandoned their copyright, and those works in which the copyright has expired.

To determine whether a copyright has expired, one must refer to the law in effect when the material was published or created. Under the copyright law in effect before 1978, copyright lasted for twenty-eight years and could be renewed for an additional twenty-eight-year period.[27] Some copyright owners renewed their copyrights while others did not. Under prior law, failure to put a copyright notice on a work could place the work in the public domain.

Once a work goes into the public domain (with the relatively rare exception of restoration of copyrights to foreign works under the Uruguay Round Agreements),[28] a copyright cannot be revived.[29] As explained previously, some works may be in the public domain in the United States but protected by copyright law in other countries. Determining copyright protection in foreign countries can be difficult, since most countries do not require registration or deposit of copyrighted works.

If a work is copyrighted, one needs permission to use it unless the use is considered a fair use or the use is protected under the First Amendment or what is taken is not copyrightable matter (e.g., ideas). A greater amount of material may be borrowed from non-fiction works than from fictional works. Clearly, a writer can borrow historical facts from a previous work without infringing upon the first author's copyright. Moreover, since factual works, unlike works of fiction, may be capable of being expressed in relatively few ways, only verbatim reproduction or close paraphrasing will be an infringement.[30]

The multimedia producer should be cautious when borrowing from fictional works. In one recent case, the author of the book *Welcome to Twin Peaks: A Complete Guide to Who's Who and What's What* was found to have infringed the television series *Twin Peaks*. The book contained detailed plot summaries and extensive direct quotations of at least eighty-nine lines of dialogue.[31]

A producer who decides to license rights should make sure that the licensor has the necessary rights to grant. This can be difficult to determine—since a copyright may be jointly held, interests may have been transferred to third parties, and ownership may be unclear when the work was created by one person for another (i.e., a work for hire). A book author, for example, may have granted movie rights to a studio. A screenwriter, if working as an employee, probably does not own the copyrighted script he wrote; the studio will own it.

A copyright search is advisable. A copyright report may reveal a transfer of the copyright, or the licensing of some rights. If the copyright report shows that the purported owner of the literary property is not the copyright holder, or if the copyright has been sold to another, the multimedia producer will not want to buy a license.

Private research companies can check additional sources of information for potential copyright, title, and trademark conflicts. These companies may review catalogs and reference works that list publications, movies, sound recordings, and products. Keep in mind that the reports supplied by the Copyright Office, and from private research companies, do not offer a conclusion as to ownership of a copyright. These reports merely supply the information needed to determine the status of a copyright. The opinion of an experienced attorney is often needed to interpret the data.

Obtaining rights to literary works can become even more complex if the literary works have incorporated other copyrightable elements. For instance, a book may include photographs duplicated with permission of the photographer. The book author may not have acquired the copyright, or any electronic rights, to those photographs, and therefore cannot grant such rights to a multimedia producer. One would have to track down the photographer, or copyright owner, and request permission.

When text is taken from a script created by a Writers Guild of America (WGA) member for an employer, other issues may arise. While WGA members usually do not own the copyright to works for hire, they may have certain reserved rights in the material, such as dramatic, publication, sequel, and merchandising rights. These rights are defined in the Writers Guild Minimum Basic Agreement (MBA). This division of rights is called "Separation of Rights."

Titles

Titles are not copyrightable but can be protected under state and federal unfair-competition laws. The gist of an unfair-competition action is mislabeling or misdesignating a product (or service) in such a way as to cause confusion to consumers as to the origin of its manufacture.[32] Once the title of a work comes to be associated in the public mind with the work of a particular producer, it acquires what is known as a "secondary meaning." Others who attempt to trade on this secondary meaning by adopting the same or similar title may be liable for unfair competition and trademark infringement.[33]

One should conduct a title search to determine if there are any conflicts with a proposed title. One can order a title report, which will list other products or services that have used the same or similar title. If someone has used the desired title on a similar product or service in the same geographical area, that title may not be used unless it has been abandoned or a release has been obtained.

In creating a title, the use of a highly fanciful or original one is preferable because it is not likely to infringe upon other titles. Such a title will also help the creator protect the title from subsequent infringement.

Trademarks

One kind of unfair competition is trademark infringement. A trademark or service mark is a brand name—which can be a word, a symbol, or a device—used by a business to distinguish its goods or services from those of others. "Coca-Cola" and "Xerox" are trademarks. They are used to identify the origin of goods. Trade names, slogans, and package designs can also be used to distinguish one company's products from another's. These symbols are typically infringed upon when a competitor uses the same or similar symbol in a manner that causes people to confuse the source of competing goods or services.

Merely mentioning a trade or service mark in a multimedia work is not an infringement. If the mark is used to mislead the public as to the origin of manufacture of some product or service, however, there is an infringement.[34] Thus, a producer could use the word "Sony" or "IBM" in a story without infringing those marks. If those marks were used in such a way as to imply that a multimedia work was published by Sony or IBM, the use would be actionable.

Characters

Characters, especially those represented in a visual form, such as cartoon characters, can be protected under copyright law.[35] Individual personality traits of a character, however, are not copyrightable.[36]

The use of a character in a fictional work can be problematical if the character:

(1) infringes on someone else's copyrighted character, or

(2) resembles actual persons and their portrayal is defamatory or invades an actual person's privacy.[37]

These pitfalls can be avoided by licensing the use of fictional characters and obtaining depiction releases from living individuals. Another solution is to change the name and description of characters so that they are not identified with other fictional characters or living individuals.

Characters can also be protected under trademark and unfair-competition laws. A character's name, image, and dress can be a trademark.[38] One can conduct a character search to determine if any living or fictional characters with the same or similar names exist.

Tort Liability

If the material borrowed invades rights of others because it is defamatory, or it invades their rights of privacy or publicity, the borrower, as well as the original author, may be liable. When licensing rights, one should have the owner of the original material warrant that the work does not infringe upon any of these rights. The licensee should also request an indemnification clause so that if the warranty is breached, the licensee can obtain reimbursement for damages and attorneys' fees. Additional protection can be obtained by purchasing Errors and Omissions (E & O) Insurance.

Defamation

A defamatory statement is one that harms the reputation of another so as to lower him in the opinion of the community, or to deter third persons from associating or dealing with him. For example, those communications that expose another to hatred, ridicule, or contempt or reflect unfavorably upon their personal morality or integrity are defamatory.[39]

The law of defamation can be confusing because the common-law[40] tort rules are subject to constitutional limitations. To determine applicable law, one must read a state's defamation laws in light of various constitutional principles, such as those expressed in *New York Times Co. v. Sullivan*,[41] *Gertz v. Robert Welch, Inc.*,[42] and *Philadelphia Newspapers, Inc. v. Hepps.*[43]

There are several important defenses and privileges to defamation, including truth. If a program hurts someone's reputation, but what was said is true, the communication is absolutely privileged. An absolute privilege cannot be lost through bad faith or abuse.[44] So, even if one maliciously defames another, if the statement is true, the communicator will be protected.

While truth is an absolute defense,[45] the burden of proving truth sometimes falls on the defendant.[46] Multimedia producers should be prepared to prove the truth of any defamatory statements in their work.

There is a conditional common-law privilege of fair comment and criticism.[47] This privilege applies to communications about a newsworthy person or event. Conditional privileges may be lost through bad faith or abuse. This privilege has been largely superseded by a constitutional privilege for statements about public figures or public officials.

Public figures, such as celebrities, and public officials, such as senators, have a much higher burden to bear to prevail in a defamation action.[48] There are two types of public figures. One is a person who has achieved such pervasive fame or notoriety that he is a public figure for all purposes. Another type of public figure is one that has only been drawn into a particular public controversy and will be considered a public figure for a limited range of issues.[49]

For a public figure or public official to win a defamation case, they must prove that the defendant acted with "actual malice."[50] Actual malice is a term of art that means that the defendant intentionally defamed another, or acted with reckless disregard of the truth. Plaintiffs find it difficult to prove actual malice. That is why so few celebrities bother suing *The National Enquirer.* To successfully defend itself, the *Enquirer* need only show that it did not act with actual malice. The newspaper can come into court and concede that its report was false, defamatory, and the result of sloppy and careless research. Unless the celebrity can prove that the *Enquirer* acted intentionally or recklessly, the court is obliged to dismiss the case. Mere negligence is not enough for liability.

The multimedia producer should take the following steps to protect against a defamation suit:

   (1) take special care when portraying living individuals who are not public figures or public officials;

(2) make sure the communicator can prove that any derogatory statements are true and that due care was exercised
in this publication. This can be achieved by annotating
scripts with the sources of information, and documenting the truth of any derogatory statements;

(3) obtain releases whenever possible (it never hurts to
have a release, even if it is not legally required); and

(4) have an attorney closely review all scripts for potential
liability before production.

If a multimedia producer can fictionalize the subjects and the
setting without detracting from the dramatic value of the story,
the producer should do so. If a person depicted is identifiable
from the context, however, liability may result.[51] Similarly, a
disclaimer in the credits such as "Any resemblance to people,
living or dead, is purely coincidental . . ." may not protect a
producer if viewers nevertheless believe that the movie is
depicting a particular person.

Right of Privacy

The right of privacy has been defined as the right to live
one's life in seclusion, without being subjected to unwarranted
and undesired publicity. In other words, it is the right to be left
alone.[52]

Like defamation, the right of privacy is subject to constitutional restrictions. The news media is not liable for statements
that portray another in a false light if the statements are
newsworthy, unless they are made with knowing or reckless
disregard of the truth (i.e., with actual malice).[53]

Other defamation defenses apply to invasion of privacy, but
not truth. Express and implied consent are valid defenses. One
who voluntarily reveals private facts to others cannot recover
for invasion of privacy. Likewise, revealing matters of public
record cannot be the basis for an invasion-of-privacy action.[54]

Privacy actions typically fall into four factual patterns:[55]

(1) Intrusion Into One's Private Affairs: This category includes
such activities as wiretapping and unreasonable surveil-
lance. The intrusion must be highly offensive. Whether an

intrusion is highly offensive depends on the circumstances. Most people would find it offensive to discover a voyeur peering through their bedroom window. On the other hand, a salesman knocking on one's front door at dinnertime may be obnoxious, but is not sufficiently offensive to state a cause of action. Query whether the practice of a software company uploading information about a user's computer, unbeknown to the user when he registers software online, might be considered an invasion of privacy.

(2) Public Disclosure of Embarrassing Private Facts: One who gives publicity to a matter concerning the private life of another is subject to liability for invasion of privacy if the matter publicized is of a kind that would be highly offensive to a reasonable person, and is not of legitimate concern to the public. In other words, if the matter publicized is not newsworthy.[56]

An example of this type of invasion of privacy would occur if someone digs up dirt on another person, publicizes it, and the information is not of legitimate interest to the public. The First Amendment will protect producers, however, if they reveal newsworthy facts about others, even if the subjects are private individuals and they prefer to keep the facts secret.[57]

(3) Appropriation: An action for appropriation of another's name or likeness is similar to an action for invasion of one's right of publicity. The former action seeks to compensate the plaintiff for the emotional distress, embarrassment, and hurt feelings that may arise from the use of one's name and/or likeness on a product.[58] The latter action seeks to compensate the plaintiff for the commercial value arising from the exploitation of one's name and likeness.[59]

As with the right of publicity, a person cannot always control the use of his name and likeness by another. While a subject can prevent a company from putting his face on its pancake mix, the subject cannot stop *Time* magazine from putting his face on its cover.

That is because the use of someone's name or likeness as part of a newsworthy incident is not actionable.

(4) False Light: Publicity that places a plaintiff in a false light will be actionable if the portrayal is highly offensive.[60] This type of invasion of privacy is similar to a defamation action but no harm to reputation is required. An example of false-light invasion of privacy could entail a political dirty trick such as placing the name of a prominent Republican on a list of Democratic contributors. Although this person's reputation may not be harmed, he has been portrayed in a false light.

Right of Publicity

The right of publicity is the right to control the use of one's image, name and likeness[61] in a commercial context. To avoid liability, in most circumstances multimedia producers should secure a signed release giving the producer the right to use the name, voice, likeness, and identity of every person who appears in a program in all media worldwide in perpetuity. The producer may also want the right to use the image in advertising and on ancillary spin-off products.

A person's identity may be infringed when their nickname or something closely associated with them is portrayed. Johnny Carson once sued a company marketing a portable toilet under the name "Here's Johnny!" The court held that the company had misappropriated Carson's identity by use of that phrase.[62] Vanna White won a suit against an advertiser who broadcast a commercial with a robot that resembled her.[63] An actor may have the right to control the use of his or her screen personae, and the characters they portray, even if they do not own the copyright to those characters.[64]

Union/Guild Permissions

If the writer is a member of the WGA, the multimedia producer may have to sign a guild contract to employ that writer. The WGA, however, allows a production company to become a guild signatory for one production only, with minimal requirements, as discussed later.

Motion Pictures

When a multimedia producer wants to incorporate existing film or television footage in a new work, many of the same copyright, character, trademark, title, and defamation issues mentioned in the text discussion apply. Licensing issues can be more difficult, however, because a film and its underlying component parts may be owned by different parties.

For example, a film may be based on a copyrighted book. It could incorporate music, the copyright to which is jointly held by a composer, musician, and record company. Permissions may be needed from actors to use their images and voices, and from owners of rights to special effects, animation, and works of art incorporated in the film. And, what if the motion picture included clips of stock footage? This footage was probably licensed for use in the original film only.

If a film is based on a book, the studio probably bought the "movie rights" from the book's author, but the studio will not necessarily own any derivative rights, such as electronic publishing rights.

Movie studios will often insist on licensing film clips on a quitclaim basis (i.e., without any warranties as to ownership of the various rights needed). It can be an arduous task for the producer to identify all rights owners and to license the appropriate rights. This may prove impossible if the film-clip owner will not reveal the contents of its contracts, or if the contracts have been lost or destroyed.

If the film is based on another work, such as a book, the right to use the book may have expired unbeknownst to the film owner. Under federal copyright law, in effect before 1978, a copyright lasted twenty-eight years and could be renewed for an additional twenty-eight years.[65] If the author of a book licensed movie rights to a studio, and if he died before the second copyright term began, his estate would own the copyright to the second term.[66] The studio would not own such rights, even if its contract with the author purported to transfer such rights. This is the issue discussed in the *Rear Window* case.[67]

The *Rear Window* case is of concern to multimedia producers because it may limit use of copyrighted material they license. If a producer incorporates work created before 1978, which is still in its first twenty-eight-year copyright term, the producer may find that rights to the work can end abruptly if the author dies and his estate refuses to relicense it. The estate may refuse permission to use the work, even if the author agreed to assign the second term to the producer.[68]

Another potential problem arises when distribution rights to a film clip are shared by several parties, as when a studio owns domestic rights and the foreign rights have been sold to another distributor. Can the owner of such foreign distribution rights prevent a multimedia producer from distributing a program with the film clip in foreign territories? The answer is unclear.

If a film has been designated as culturally, historically, or aesthetically significant under the National Film Preservation Act of 1988,[69] and added to the national registry, additional restrictions may apply. This Act was passed in response to the movement to colorize old black-and-white movies. Under the Act, twenty-three films per year can be added to the registry. While modification of these films is not prohibited, a disclaimer must be added.

Another issue arises when a multimedia producer wants to incorporate footage of a crowd scene in her work. While filming a person in a public place is usually not an invasion of privacy,[70] incorporation of a recognizable person's identity in a film may be an infringement of one's right of publicity.

Whether a use is infringing depends upon whether the image is used in a commercial context, such as on a product, or in a newsworthy context, such as in a magazine or documentary program.[71] The latter use is protected under the First Amendment. Thus, producers should avoid incorporating a person's image in a purely commercial program, or in advertising for such a program, unless a release has been obtained.[72]

The right of publicity is not limited to a person's image. Performances and objects closely associated with one's identity may also be protected. The appropriation of a photograph of a race car with distinctive markings that was used in a cigarette ad was held to be an infringement of the driver's identity, even though his image was not shown.[73]

The unauthorized use of a celebrity's persona or voice can also violate state and federal laws against unfair competition and trademark infringement. In *Waits v. Frito-Lay Inc.*,[74] the voice of singer Tom Waits was imitated in a Frito-Lay commercial. Although Waits' actual voice was not used, the court held that this use amounted to a false endorsement of a product. The court stated that a distinctive attribute of a celebrity could amount to an unregistered commercial trademark.

Of course, a person's right to restrict the use of their name, likeness, and voice has to be balanced against the rights of others (e.g., journalists and filmmakers) under the First Amendment. Suppose a newspaper publisher wants to place a picture of a sports figure in its paper. Is permission required? What if *60 Minutes* wants to broadcast an expose of a corrupt politician? What if Kitty Kelley wants to write a critical biography of Frank Sinatra?

In each of these instances, a person's name and likeness is being used on a "product" sold to consumers. Products such as books, movies, and plays, however, are also forms of expression protected by the First Amendment. The First Amendment allows journalists and writers to write freely about others without their consent. Otherwise, subjects could prevent any critical reporting of their activities. When one person's right of publicity conflicts with another person's rights under the First Amendment, the First Amendment is often, but not always, considered the dominant right.

When a use is newsworthy, or the use is in the context of a documentary, a biography, or a parody, the First Amendment will usually protect the producer. In *Hicks v. Casablanca Records*,[75] Casablanca Records made a movie called *Agatha* about the mystery writer Agatha Christie. The film portrayed her as an emotionally unstable person who committed a crime. An heir brought suit, alleging infringement of Christie's right of publicity.

The court held that Casablanca's rights under the First Amendment were paramount to the estate's rights. The court reasoned that the First Amendment outweighed the right of publicity because the subject was a public figure, and the events portrayed were obviously fictitious.

When a multimedia producer wants to license a motion-picture clip portraying an actor, the producer should contact the Screen Actors Guild (SAG) or the American Federation for Radio and Television Artists (AFTRA) to seek permission to use the actor's image. If the performance was first recorded on film, contact SAG; if the performance was first recorded on videotape, contact AFTRA.

The unions will supply the name of the actor's agent who can then be contacted to obtain permission to use the clip. When an actor's name is unknown, it may be difficult to match his or her image with the names listed in the credits. Moreover, if an actor is not a Guild member, or is deceased, it may be difficult to locate the holder of the rights.

In working with unions and guilds, the multimedia producer should recognize that a system of fees and royalty payments for electronic publishing is just developing. Some guilds have been willing to sign One Production Only (OPO) deals with multimedia producers that do not require them to become guild signatories for all productions. The Writers Guild, for instance, allows a production company to become a Guild signatory for one production by signing a Letter of Adherence. This letter agreement does not mandate minimum scale payments nor compliance with most Guild rules. The producer need only agree to make pension and health-fund payments.

Photographs and Still Images

Still images are copyrightable, and the same copyright, trademark, character, and tort issues that arise with the use of motion pictures apply here as well. Likewise, copyright defenses predicated on fair use or the First Amendment can be invoked.

It can be especially difficult to determine whether a photograph is copyrighted, and to determine the identity of its owner. Many photographs are not registered with the Copyright Office. Even if registered, a search can be tiresome since a photograph may be untitled, or the title may not describe the image.

Some photographs are clearly in the public domain, such as those in the National Archives in Washington, D.C. For other photographs, the owner should be asked to warrant that he has all rights to a particular photograph, including releases from any identifiable persons in the photographs. The multimedia producer should request that the photograph owner indemnify the producer, should a claim arise from a third party. Photographers may own the copyright to their photographs, but do not necessarily have releases from their subjects giving the photographer the right to use the subject's image in other media or for other purposes.[76]

The license to use a photograph should include a waiver of moral rights. Permissions may be obtained for some photographs through the Graphic Artists Guild (http://www.gag.org/) or the American Society of Media Photographers (http://www.zdepth.com/asmp/).

Music

The same copyright, trademark, and tort issues that apply to use of a motion picture apply to the use of music. Determining copyright ownership can be particularly complex, as there may be several simultaneous copyright holders in a piece of music. For example, the composer may own the copyright to the composition, the lyricist may own the copyright to the lyrics, and the record company may own the copyright to a recording.[77] Moreover, ownership of each component can be jointly held by several parties, and rights can be transferred to or inherited by others.

Right of publicity issues can also arise. The recent Bette Midler case[78] considered the issue of whether the use of a sound-alike voice of a celebrity was an invasion of the celebrity's right of publicity. An advertising agency had asked Midler to sing the song "Do You Want To Dance" for a car advertisement. After she declined to participate, the ad agency hired one of Midler's former backup singers to record the song, imitating Midler's voice and style. When the advertisements were run, many listeners thought that the song was being sung by Midler. The ad agency obtained permission to use the song from its copyright owner but did not have Midler's consent to imitate her voice.

The court held that this imitation of Midler's voice infringed upon her rights. The court reasoned that when a distinctive voice of a professional singer is widely known and is deliberately imitated in order to sell a product, a tort, which is a civil wrong, has been committed in California. The court limited the holding to the facts, and cautioned that not every imitation of a voice to advertise merchandise was necessarily actionable.

Multimedia producers will need to obtain a mechanical license to reproduce a musical composition on a CD-ROM disc when the music is going to be used without an accompanying image. If the music is used with a video image, then a synchronization (sync) license is needed. If the program will be distributed on videograms (discs or tape) or CD-ROMs, the producer will need a license for those uses as well.

When music is modified, an adaptation license may be needed. A dramatic-adaptation license, for example, would permit the multimedia producer to dramatize a song's lyrics. Thus, the lyrics could be used as the basis for a screenplay or motion picture.

If copies of sheet music or lyrics accompany the CD-ROM, a print license will be needed. When a title of a song is used, a license may be needed to avoid a claim of unfair competition.[79] If a portion of a musical play or opera is included on a CD-ROM, a license of "Grand Rights" should be obtained in order to use the creative elements in the work, including dialogue, scenery, choreography, and costumes.

Public performance rights are generally not needed. That is because music on CD-ROMs, unlike music performed in nightclubs or broadcast by television or radio, is used privately. Query whether sending a song over the Internet is a public performance.[80]

There is no such thing as a standard fee to license music for multimedia productions. The more desirable the song and the more rights requested, the greater the fee. Background or incidental use of a song should cost less than a featured performance. Music publishers generally charge a fixed royalty per unit sold, or a percentage of the wholesale price per unit, or some combination. There may be one-time fixing fees and/or advances. Flat fees or buy-outs may be used for works that are unlikely to sell many units, and if the producer wants to avoid a continuing obligation to account for royalties.

Before committing oneself to use a particular piece of music, the multimedia producer should determine what rights are needed, who owns those rights, and whether the rights are available at a reasonable cost. Music that is not available or too expensive may need to be eliminated from the program. The owner of music rights is not required to issue a license for a musical work to be reproduced or adapted in a CD-ROM. The compulsory license provisions of the Copyright Act do not apply to the production of multimedia programs.[81]

A producer who incorporates music without first securing permission risks the expense of re-editing the work to delete the music. If the CD-ROM has been distributed, the owner of the unlicensed music can obtain substantial damages, reimbursement of attorneys' fees, and an injunction, pulling the offending product off of store shelves.

Digital sampling has become a hot issue in the music industry. An increasing number of artists have borrowed portions of pre-existing musical works to incorporate in their own works. Rapper Vanilla Ice, for instance, sampled the bassline from the Queen-David Bowie work "Under Pressure" for "Ice, Ice Baby." After the song became a hit, litigation was initiated. The suit was settled for an undisclosed amount.[82]

A sample is a digital recording that can be manipulated. Tone, pitch, and rhythm can be changed, and the work can be combined with other recordings. The resulting work may not sound much like the original work from which it was sampled.

Samplers reason that borrowing a single note or short excerpt from another work is not an infringement because:

(1) what has been taken is not an expression of an author (i.e., no more than an idea); or

(2) the taking is protected under the fair use doctrine; or

(3) the use is protected under the First Amendment.

The case of *Acuff-Rose Music, Inc. v. Campbell*[83] discussed these issues. The case arose after the group 2 Live Crew parodied the Roy Orbison song "Pretty Woman." The Court of

Appeals, Sixth Circuit, found that 2 Live Crew's use of the prior work was copyright infringement and not a fair use as a matter of law.[84] The United States Supreme Court disagreed, and reversed the lower court, stating that the use of the prior work could be a fair use, and whether it was needed to be determined on a case-by-case basis.[85]

While it is doubtful that taking a few notes from another work would be deemed an infringement,[86] there are no definitive rules that set forth precisely how much can be taken. Only a few cases have grappled with the issue of how much a digital sampler can remove under the fair use doctrine.[87] If the borrowed excerpt is recognizable to others, it is arguably an infringement. Thus, artists who borrow small amounts of other people's music may be liable for copyright infringement. There is no truth to the widespread belief that six or eight bars of music can be borrowed with impunity.

The identities of copyright owners can be obtained through the performing-arts guilds (SAG/AFTRA), the Songwriter's Guild of America (a trade association), or the American Federation of Musicians (AFM). AFTRA covers singers and AFM covers instrumentalists. Publishers can be contacted directly or through the Harry Fox Agency, which acts as a licensing agent for many publishers.[88]

Rights may need to be secured from a variety of parties, including composers, lyricists, publishers, agents, record companies, unions, and in some cases the heirs or assigns of the aforementioned. Songwriters often sell or assign their copyright to a publisher, who takes control of the rights. The publisher will then share royalties derived from the song with the songwriter. In some cases, the publisher may need to obtain the songwriter's approval before licensing the work. Record companies usually retain rights to their recordings, but they may need to obtain artists' approvals for some uses. Because of the complexity of licensing music, producers may want to retain a rights-and-permissions agency (i.e., a clip-clearance company) to negotiate and secure the necessary rights.

Public domain music can be used without payment.[89] Generally, compositions published more than seventy-five years ago are in the public domain, and some compositions published less than seventy-five years ago may have fallen into the public domain. Some musical works, while in the public domain in the United States, may be protected in other countries. Keep in mind that while a composition may be in the public domain, a recording of that composition may not be. In such a case, the multimedia producer will have to either locate a recording in the public domain, which may be quite old and have poor sound quality, or hire musicians and create a new recording of the composition.

The expense and burden of licensing can be avoided by commissioning original music. Here, the producer must be careful to make sure all rights are obtained. If the composer is an employee for hire, the copyright to the work product will be owned by the employer (producer). A written employment contract is needed. If the employee incorporates any existing material in the work, rights to that material must be secured.

Inexpensive music and sound effects can also be licensed from music libraries on a one-time, fixed-fee basis.

Architecture

When images of buildings are reproduced in a multimedia program, is there an infringement of copyright? Congress recently accorded copyright protection to architecture, placing it in a separate category from pictorial, graphic, and sculptural works.[90] The copyright in an architectural work, however, is limited. The copyright owner cannot prevent others from publicly displaying pictures and photographs of buildings that are visible from a public place.[91]

Of course, even if a producer does not need permission to include a building's image in a program, that does not mean that the producer can trespass on another's property to capture that image. Moreover, showing a recognizable image of a building in a derogatory light could give rise to a defamation action if the reputation of a company or individual is harmed.

Fine Art

If art work is incorporated in a multimedia production, a license may be needed. Pictorial, graphic, and sculptural works of art are copyrightable,[92] and displaying them in a program without permission could be an infringement. Remember, ownership of an art work does not necessarily include ownership of its copyright. Thus, the owner of the physical item may have the right to sell that item, but not necessarily have the right to reproduce it. The latter right is part of the copyright. California law provides that when a work of art is sold, the right to reproduce it is reserved to the artist, unless that right is transferred in writing and the writing specifically refers to the right of reproduction.[93]

Suppose a piece of sculpture appears momentarily in the background of a scene. Is permission of the copyright owner necessary? Probably not. The maker of school room charts and wall decorations that appeared in the background as scenery in a *Barney and Sons* videotape recently sued for copyright infringement.[94] The charts and decorations appeared only fleetingly and were often obscured by the actors. The court refused to issue an injunction against the producers of the videotape on the grounds that the use was so minimal that it was not infringing. The fact that the video was educational in nature was an important factor in finding a fair use. If a producer features art work in the foreground, however, a release should be obtained.[95]

When Congress passed the Visual Artists Rights Act of 1990,[96] the United States expressly recognized certain moral rights that artists have in works of visual art such as paintings, drawings, sculptures, and still photographs. As previously mentioned, moral rights include the Right of Paternity, which is the right of an author to claim authorship to his work and prevent the use of his name on works he did not create, and the Right of Integrity, which prevents others from distorting or mutilating his work. A multimedia producer who incorporates artwork in a program could be liable if the work is distorted, which may occur if the work is digitized and metamorphosed into a new form.

Recall that moral rights differ from copyright. Even when an artist sells the copyright to his work, his moral rights may prevent others from removing the artist's name or modifying his work. While the United States does not explicitly recognize moral rights, except in regard to fine art, these rights may be protected in the United States as violation of our unfair competition and defamation laws. These laws have been applied to motion pictures and other works of authorship.

Computer Software

A multimedia work will contain computer software to operate the program. This software can be developed by the multimedia creator or licensed from another. Since software is copyrightable matter,[97] it cannot be freely borrowed from another unless it is in the public domain or considered a fair use.

The fair use doctrine has been successfully invoked to protect programmers who reverse-engineer another's program, even though the process entails making a reproduction of the entire work.[98] In *Sega Enterprises Ltd. v. Accolade, Inc.*,[99] a video-game developer disassembled a copyrighted program in order to make a compatible game. The court held that this disassembly was a fair use of the copyrighted work because it was necessary to analyze those portions of the program not protected by copyright, and because Accolade had a legitimate interest in making compatible cartridges.

On the other hand, disassembly was not considered to be a fair use in *Atari Games Corp. v. Nintendo of America, Inc.*,[100] on the grounds that the defendant did not own an authorized copy of the program disassembled. The court opined that reverse engineering to discern unprotectable ideas can be a fair use when the reproduction is limited in scope and there is no commercial exploitation of protected elements of the work.

In *Apple Computer, Inc. v. Microsoft Corp.*,[101] the court held that the Apple's use of icons to represent familiar office objects, and the manipulation of icons to instruct a computer, was not protectable expression.[102] In another case, *Lotus v. Borland*,[103] a U.S. District Court held that the menu commands and menu command structure of the Lotus 1-2-3 spreadsheet program are protected expressions.[104] Here, the two spreadsheet menu trees were virtually identical. The case was overturned, however, when the Court of Appeals determined that the user interface was a "method of operation" and thus not copyrightable. The U.S. Supreme Court deadlocked 4-4 in January 1996, leaving the Court of Appeals ruling as the final word—for the time being. In reviewing the cases, it is clear that computer developers can borrow such ideas as that of using a graphical user interface (GUI) and offer functions similar to other programs. The identical copying of another program's icons, however, could be an infringement.

The processing and transmission of computer programs raise interesting copyright issues. One court has held that merely loading a computer program from a disc into the random access memory (RAM) of a computer, whereby the program would be removed when the computer was turned off, is a "copying" of the program, and therefore a violation of copyright unless otherwise privileged.[105]

In Florida, an operator of a computer bulletin board was sued by Playboy Enterprises after subscribers downloaded some Playboy photographs. The photographs had been uploaded by subscribers, not the operator, who had no knowledge of the photographs until he was served with a complaint. The court found that the transmission of the photographs was a public "display" and thus a violation of Playboy's copyright.[106] The fact that the operator was unaware of the infringement was no defense, since intent or knowledge is not required for one to infringe upon another's copyright. Producers who desire to borrow or emulate computer programs should proceed with caution and seek legal advice early.

Software names, logos, and symbols may be protected under state and federal trademark law. Recently, a federal appeals court held that the title of a newspaper column may be a trademark although the column was not marketed as a separate feature. Thus, a subsidiary component of the newspaper was deemed eligible for trademark protection. By analogy, computer program icons could be protectable trademarks.[107]

Software can also be protected under patent law, which protects the "useful arts," which means any new and useful process or machinery.[108] Thus, multimedia software (the process) and the hardware (the machine) are potentially patentable.

A patent must be applied for and granted by the federal government, after a determination has been made that the applicant is eligible for it. If the patent is granted, the inventor receives a seventeen-year monopoly on using, making, or selling the invention.[109] The United States grants patents to the first inventor, not the first person to file a patent application. Therefore, if two parties contest ownership to an invention, the first inventor is entitled to the patent.[110]

A patent cannot be granted when the subject matter sought to be patented and the prior art are such that the subject matter was obvious to people with ordinary skill in that art.[111] It can be difficult to determine non-obviousness in computer program inventions because the Patent Office lacks extensive records for this type of useful art. A "prior art search" is used to determine the state of the prior art in the field of the invention. If software is developed by an outside contractor, the agreement between the parties needs to specify who will own the copyright and any patent to the work, and which rights are being licensed. The producer should have a written employment agreement with a covenant that the employee or independent contractor assigns all copyrights, inventions (whether patentable or not), and trade secrets developed in the course of employment to the employer.

If software is licensed for use in a multimedia program, the license agreement needs to spell out which uses can be made of the acquired software. Can the software be used to develop a new product? Can it be incorporated into the final work? If a license fee is to be paid, is it a one-time fee for unlimited use or a per-unit royalty? Does the owner of the borrowed software share in the copyright of the new work?

DEFENSIVE TACTICS

Multimedia producers should consult an attorney who has expertise in multimedia production to determine what licenses may be needed. This review should be undertaken early, before a lot of time and effort are invested developing a project. A competent attorney can suggest ways the producer can reduce costs and potential liability. For instance, certain rights may not need to be purchased if the producer is willing to fictionalize a story, rely on the fair use doctrine, change an individual's identity, or add a disclaimer. An attorney can also check the chain of title of all content that has been purchased for inclusion in the program. Recall that if the seller of video footage does not own the rights needed to use the footage in a multimedia program, the buyer cannot receive those rights, irrespective of what the contract states.

Some licensors may allow the licensee to review the contracts, releases, and other documents that prove that the licensor has obtained all necessary rights. If the licensor will not permit third parties to review their contracts, the most the licensee may be able to obtain is a warranty from the licensor that he owns the rights he is selling. If possible, the licensor should indemnify the licensee for any loss sustained from breach of his warranties.

The licensee will also want the licensor to warrant that the property does not infringe upon anyone else's rights (including rights of defamation, invasion of privacy, right of publicity, trademark, and copyright) and that there are no claims or litigation outstanding in regard to the property. If the licensor is a corporation or partnership, the licensee may want the licensor to warrant that it has authority to enter into the license.

Besides express warranties found in a contract, there may be some warranties implied by law. The implied warranty of merchantability, for example, may exist even if the contract does not mention it.[112] Products can be sold without a warranty when the seller adds a prominent disclaimer notifying the buyer that the product is sold "as is" without any implied warranties.[113]

INSURANCE

To protect oneself from potential liability, the multimedia producer should consider purchasing Errors and Omissions (E & O) insurance.[114] Errors and Omissions insurance will protect the insured from negligence that gives rise to claims of defamation, invasion of privacy or publicity, copyright and trademark infringement, and breach of contract arising from submission of materials to the producer. Care should be exercised in shopping for E & O coverage since this is a relatively new product for multimedia programs. Brokers may not be knowledgable about such policies, or may not know how to obtain it. Premiums can vary considerably.

Recently, American International Group (AIG), a large insurer, announced that it would offer Patent Infringement Liability Insurance. The insurance includes coverage of expenses and damages, including attorneys' fees, incurred to defend any lawsuit alleging infringement of a United States patent. The minimum premium, however, is $50,000, with a minimum deductible of $50,000. The insured also has to pay 10% of all damages and defense costs and any punitive damages that may be awarded.

Insurance will not protect the insured from acts of intentional wrongdoing such as deliberate infringement or fraud. Therefore, the producer should be prepared to show that he was acting in good faith and followed customary clearance procedures. He should maintain records of releases and correspondence to secure rights and copies of letters from counsel in regard to what licenses are necessary.

Insurers will typically require an applicant for insurance to secure all necessary licenses and permissions. Also, a copyright report and title report will be needed, and all employment agreements must be in writing. If music is going to be used, synchronization and performance licenses will be necessary.

If the multimedia script is original, its origins must be determined to ensure that everything in it is original and nothing has been copied from another work without permission. The insurer will carefully review the project before issuing a policy.

Errors and Omissions insurance will pay for any liability incurred, as well as the cost to defend. The deductible is often $10,000 or more. When shopping for a policy, producers should inquire whether the time period covered by the insurance is based on when the claim is made or when the original infringement occurred. These types of policies are often referred to as "claims made" or "occurrence" policies.

CONCLUSION

New technology permits producers to make innovative multi-media programs. Unfortunately, legal obstacles may deter rapid development of programs. Complex rights issues are likely to arise when a producer incorporates existing works.

Multimedia producers can minimize liability by creating programs entirely from scratch or by only borrowing works that are clearly in the public domain or available under the fair use doctrine or First Amendment. If the multimedia producer is planning to incorporate outside works, or is producing material that may infringe on another's rights, a knowledgeable attorney in multimedia legal issues should be consulted early, and insurance should be purchased.

FILM-CLIP LICENSE WITH WARRANTIES

This Agreement is made and entered into on _____, 19__, by and between _____, a _____ corporation located at _____ ("Multimedia Producer"), and _____, a _____ corporation located at _____ ("Licensor").

RECITALS

A.   Licensor is the owner of the copyright to the motion picture identified on Exhibit A of this Agreement. "Film Clip" means the excerpt of the motion picture (including the soundtrack) identified on Exhibit A.

B.   Multimedia Producer is developing a digital, machine-readable, interactive multimedia work tentatively titled "_____" (the "Multimedia Program").

C.   Multimedia Producer desires to reproduce, incorporate, and distribute the Film Clip as part of such Multimedia Program.

D.   Licensor is willing to grant such rights to Multimedia Producer subject to the terms and conditions of this Agreement.

NOW THEREFORE, the parties agree as follows:

1. LICENSE

(a) Rights Granted to Multimedia Producer. Licensor grants Multimedia Producer a non-exclusive, non-transferable license and right for the Term, Territory, and Fee described in Exhibit A to:

(1) incorporate all or any part of the Film Clip within the Multimedia Program;

(2) reproduce all or any part of the Film Clip, as incorporated in the Multimedia Program, in any media now known or hereafter developed, including, but not limited to, CD-ROM, CD-I, and videodisc;

(3) manufacture, package, market, promote, sell, license, and distribute copies of all or any part of the Film Clip, as part of the Multimedia Program, both directly to end users and indirectly through distributors, dealers, resellers, agents, and other third parties.

(b) Restrictions on Use.

(1) The Film Clip is restricted to the uses described in paragraph (a). The Film Clip may not be used for any other purpose or purposes whatsoever.

(2) Multimedia Producer will not reproduce the Film Clip except for use in and as part of the Multimedia Program.

(3) While Multimedia Producer may use the Film Clip in advertising the Multimedia Program, Multimedia Producer shall not use the name of Licensor for any purposes in connection with the advertising, publicizing, or distribution of the Multimedia Work without the prior written consent of Licensor.

(4) Multimedia Producer shall not use the Film Clip in a manner or context that will be in any way derogatory to the Motion Picture from which the Film Clip was taken, any person connected with the Program thereof or depicted therein, or the Licensor and/or the literary material upon which the Film Clip is based. Furthermore, the Film Clip will not be used in any way so as to constitute an express or implied endorsement of any product or service by anyone associated with the Motion Picture from which the Film Clip was derived.

(c) Rights Reserved to Licensor. Multimedia Producer acknowledges that it has no rights in the Film Clip except those expressly granted by this Agreement. Licensor shall at all times have the right to use, or authorize others to use on a non-exclusive basis, the Film Clip in any way Licensor may desire.

(d) No Obligation to Use Film Clip. Licensor acknowledges that Multimedia Producer is not obligated or required to use or incorporate the Film Clip in the Multimedia Program.

2. CREDITS

Multimedia Producer agrees to give Licensor appropriate credit on copies of the Multimedia Program that include the Film Clip in the form specified on Exhibit A, which credit shall be displayed in the same manner as credits given to other artists and copyright owners whose works are included in the Multimedia Program.

3. THIRD-PARTY RELEASES

(a) Multimedia Producer shall not have the right to use the Film Clip until it obtains all required individual authorizations, consents, licenses, and releases that may be necessary for the use of the Film Clip under this Agreement including, without limitation:

(1) consents from those who appear recognizably in the Film Clip and from all stunt persons appearing in any stunt identifiable in the Film Clip;

(2) consents from unions and guilds to the extent required under applicable collective bargaining agreements; and

(3) if any pre-existing copyrighted works (such as music) are included in the Film Clip, licenses from the copyright owners of such works.

(b) Copies. At Licensor's request, Multimedia Producer shall deliver to Licensor copies of all authorizations, consents, releases, and licenses required to be obtained under the foregoing paragraph.

(c) Payments to Third Parties. Multimedia Producer shall pay, or cause to be paid, to the extent that the Multimedia Producer may be additionally liable therefore as a result of sales of copies of such Multimedia Programs embodying the Film Clip, all payments to applicable union pension and welfare funds, as applicable.

4. LICENSOR'S DELIVERY OBLIGATIONS

Immediately following execution of this Agreement, Licensor will provide Multimedia Producer with a copy of the Film Clip on a mutually agreeable medium that can be reproduced by Multimedia Producer.

5. LICENSOR'S WARRANTIES

(a) Authority. Licensor represents and warrants that it has the right and authority to enter into this Agreement and to grant to Multimedia Producer the rights to the Film Clip that are granted in this Agreement.

(b) Non-infringement. Licensor warrants to Multimedia Producer that the inclusion of the Film Clip in the Multimedia Work, and reproduction and distribution of the Film Clip as part of the Multimedia Work, if done pursuant to the terms of this Agreement, will not infringe upon or misappropriate the proprietary rights of any third party.

6. INDEMNIFICATIONS

Each party will indemnify, save, and hold the other (and its respective parent, affiliates, subsidiaries, agents, directors, officers, employees successors, licensees, and assignees) harmless from and against any and all damages, costs, liabilities, losses, and expenses (including reasonable attorneys' fees) arising out of or connected with any third-party claim, demand, or action inconsistent with any of the warranties, representations, undertakings, or covenants made by the indemnitor in this Agreement that results in a final adverse judgment, arbitration award or settlement with the consent of the indemnitor (not to be unreasonably withheld). The indemnified party agrees to give indemnitor notice of any action to which the foregoing indemnity applies, and the indemnitor may participate in the defense of same, at its expense, through counsel of its own choosing.

7. PAYMENT TO LICENSOR

(a) License Fee. In full and final consideration of the rights granted to Multimedia Producer in this Agreement, Multimedia

Producer will pay Licensor the Fee specified in Exhibit A within _____ days of delivery of a copy of the Film Clip.

(b) Materials Fee. In addition, Multimedia Producer agrees to pay Licensor a fee of $_____ for reproducing and delivering the master copy of the Film Clip to be used by Multimedia Producer.

8. TERMINATION OF LICENSE

(a) Termination for Breach. Licensor may terminate this Agreement only in the event of a material breach of the terms or conditions of this Agreement by Multimedia Producer which breach is not cured within thirty (30) days of written notice from Licensor. In addition to these rights of termination, each party will have the right, in the event of an uncured breach by the other party, to avail itself of all remedies or causes of action, in law or equity, for damages as a result of such breach.

(b) Effect of Termination. Upon termination of this Agreement for any reason, Multimedia Producer will immediately cease duplication of the Film Clip and production of the Multimedia Program containing the Film Clip, and will return to Licensor, at Multimedia Producer's expense, the master version of the Film Clip. However, Multimedia Producer shall have the right to distribute all copies of the Multimedia Program in Multimedia Producer's inventory as of the date of termination.

IN WITNESS WHEREOF, the parties have executed this Agreement as of the date set forth above.

[MULTIMEDIA PRODUCER]   [LICENSOR]

By: _____   By: _____

Its: _____   Its: _____

EXHIBIT A

1. **Motion Picture:**

2. **Description of Film Clip:**

3. **Term:**

4. **Fee:**

5. **Territory: Worldwide.**

6. **Credit:**

MODEL RELEASE

For $ _____ and other valuable consideration received, I hereby grant to Producer the absolute and irrevocable right and permission, in respect of the photographs that it has taken or has had taken of me or in which I may be included with others, to copyright the same, in its own name or otherwise (and assign my rights throughout the world in such photograph), to use, re-use, publish, and re-publish, and otherwise reproduce, modify, and display the same, in whole or in part, individually or in conjunction with other photographs, and in conjunction with any copyrighted matter, in any and all media now or hereafter known, for illustration, promotion, art, advertising, and trade, or any other purpose whatsoever; and to use my name in connection therewith if it so chooses. I hereby release and discharge Producer from any and all claims and demands arising out of or in connection with the use of the photographs, including without limitation any and all claims for libel or invasion of privacy.

Producer may sell, assign, license, or otherwise transfer all rights granted to it hereunder. This authorization and release shall also inure to the benefit of the heirs, legal representatives, licensees, and assigns of Producer as well as the person(s) (if any) for whom Producer took the photographs.

I am of full age and have the right to contract in my own name. I have read the foregoing and fully understand the contents thereof. This release shall be binding upon me and my heirs, legal representatives, and assigns. I further release Producer from any responsibility for injury incurred during the photography session.

Name

_____

Signature

_____

Address

_____

City, State, Zip

_____

Phone

_____

Soc. Sec. #

MUSIC AND SOUND RECORDING LICENSE

THIS AGREEMENT ("Agreement") entered into as of _____, by and between a corporation with its principal place of business at _____ ("Multimedia Producer"), and _____ ("Composer") with his principal place of business at _____.

RECITALS

WHEREAS, Composer owns the right to a certain musical composition and the master recording thereof,

WHEREAS, Multimedia Producer wishes to license rights to that musical composition and the master recording thereof as provided under the terms of this Agreement.

NOW, THEREFORE, the parties agree as follows:

1. Definitions: The terms used in this Agreement shall have the following definitions:

Audiovisual Work means the Multimedia title _____ to be developed by Multimedia Producer.

Master means the master recording of the Musical Composition embodying the performance of Composer.

Multimedia means the medium in which the Musical Composition and Master will be utilized, which includes, but is not limited to, a software program involving film, photographs, music or text.

Multimedia Discs means those Multimedia discs containing the Musical Composition and/or the Master, including but not limited to, CD-ROMs, DVDs, laserdiscs, and floppy discs for any computing platforms.

Musical Composition means the musical composition entitled _____ written by _____.

2. License Grant: Composer hereby grants to Multimedia Producer and Multimedia Producer accepts, a worldwide, non-exclusive license, with the right to sublicense, during the term of this Agreement, to do the following:

(a) reproduce and have reproduced, in digital, computer-readable, or other form consistent with the integral requirements of Multimedia, the Musical Composition for use in whole or in part in connection with the Multimedia Disc;

(b) to synchronize the Master, or a portion thereof, in time-relation with the Audiovisual Work and in any promotions and advertisements of the Audiovisual Work;

(c) to reproduce and have reproduced, distribute copies of, and publicly perform the Multimedia Discs;

(d) to create derivative works of the Musical Composition and Master in order to arrange and orchestrate for reproducing the Musical Composition or to promote or advertise the Audiovisual Work; provided, however, Multimedia Producer does not have the right to alter the fundamental character of the Musical Composition or Master, to print sheet music of the Musical Composition, or to make any other use of the Musical Composition or Master except as expressly authorized under this Agreement;

(e) to publicly perform the Musical Composition and the Master in connection with the Audiovisual Work;

(f) to use or refer to Composer in the credits, and in any promotions, advertisements, and publicity in connection with the Audiovisual Work.

3. Payment: As full and complete consideration of the license and the rights granted herein, Multimedia Producer shall pay to Composer the sum of _____ ($_____).

4. Term:

(a) This license and grant of rights made herein shall subsist, at a minimum, for the remainder of the term of all copyrights in and to the Musical Composition and the Master, and any and all renewals or extensions thereof that Composer or its successors or assigns may now own or control or hereafter own or control without additional consideration therefor.

(b) Upon the expiration of this license, all rights herein granted shall cease and terminate, and the right to make or authorize any further use or distribution of any recordings made hereunder shall also cease and terminate subject to Multimedia Producer's right to sell off its inventory of Multimedia Discs for an additional period of three (3) years.

5. No Obligation to Include Musical Composition or Master: Nothing herein shall obligate or require Multimedia Producer to include the Musical Composition or Master in the Audiovisual Work.

6. Representation and Warranty; Indemnity: Composer represents and warrants that it has the right to grant this license. Composer shall indemnify and hold harmless Multimedia Producer, its officers, directors, employees, sublicensees, customers and agents against all claims, actions or demands, alleging that the reproduction, distribution, modification, or public performance of the Musical Composition or the Master libels, defames, infringes the copyright or trademarks, infringes the publicity or privacy rights of any individual, or violates other similar proprietary rights of third parties in any jurisdiction. Composer represents and warrants that Composer has paid any American Federation of Musicians or other union re-use fees to permit Multimedia Producer to use the Musical Composition in Multimedia Producer's Audiovisual Works.

7. License Limitations: This license does not include the right to:

(a) Rent separately the Musical Composition or Master included in the Multimedia Discs or to permit purchasers or others to do so;

(b) Use the story of the Musical Composition or dramatically depict the Musical Composition;

(c) Parody the lyrics and/or music of the Musical Composition in any way;

(d) Make, sell, or distribute audio phono records of the Musical Composition or Master.

8. Arbitration: Any controversy or claim arising out of or relating to this agreement or any breach thereof shall be settled by arbitration in accordance with the Rules of the American Arbitration Association; the parties select expedited arbitration using one arbitrator, to be a disinterested attorney specializing in entertainment or multimedia law, as the sole forum for the resolution of any dispute between them. The venue for arbitration shall be Los Angeles, California. The arbitrator may make any interim order, decision, determinations, or award he deems necessary to preserve the status quo until he is able to render a final order, decision, determination, or award. The determination of the arbitrator in such proceeding shall be final, binding and non-appealable. Judgment upon the award rendered by the arbitrator may be entered in any court having jurisdiction thereof. The prevailing party shall be entitled to reimbursement for costs and reasonable attorneys' fees.

9. Miscellaneous: This Agreement sets forth the entire understanding of the parties hereto with respect to the subject matter hereof and supersedes all prior understandings, if any, whether oral or written, pertaining thereto and may only be changed by mutual agreement of authorized representatives of the parties in writing. This Agreement shall bind and inure to the benefit of the parties and their successors and permitted assigns. This Agreement shall be governed in all respects by the laws of the State of _____ as applied to agreements entered into and performed entirely within _____ by _____residents.

IN WITNESS WHEREOF, the parties have executed this Agreement as of the date indicated above.

MULTIMEDIA PRODUCER:

By: _____

COMPOSER:

By: _____

PHOTOGRAPH LICENSE AGREEMENT

This Agreement is made and entered into on _____, 199_, by and between _____, a _____ corporation located at _____ ("Multimedia Producer"), and _____ ("Photographer").

RECITALS

A. Photographer is owner of all rights to the following photograph(s):

1. _____
2. _____
3. _____
4. _____

(hereafter referred to as "Photograph" or "Photographs").

B. Multimedia Producer intends to develop, manufacture, and distribute to the general public a digital, computer-readable, interactive multimedia Program tentatively titled "_____" on the subject of "_____" ("Multimedia Program").

C. In connection therewith, Multimedia Producer desires to use and incorporate a copy of all or a portion of the Photograph in the Multimedia Program.

D. Photographer is willing to grant Multimedia Producer the right to incorporate the Photograph, in whole or in part, within the Multimedia Program, and distribute the Photograph as so incorporated, worldwide.

NOW THEREFORE, the parties hereby agree as follows:

1. GRANT OF LICENSE:

(a) Rights Granted to Multimedia Producer. Photographer grants to Multimedia Producer a perpetual, non-exclusive, worldwide, paid-up license and right to:

(1) incorporate the Photograph, in whole or in part, within the Multimedia Program and in doing so, to crop and otherwise alter and edit the Photograph, as the Multimedia Producer deems appropriate, to fit space or to enhance the function or effectiveness of use of the Photograph;

(2) reproduce the Photograph, as incorporated in the Multimedia Program, in any manner, medium, or form, whether now known or hereafter devised;

(3) sell, license, and distribute copies of the Photograph, as incorporated in the Multimedia Program, worldwide;

(4) display the Photograph publicly, as incorporated in the Multimedia Program, subject to the terms set forth below.

(5) use the Photograph, together with photographer's name and pertinent biographical data, in advertising and promotion of the Multimedia Program.

(b) Conditions of Use. The foregoing license is subject to the requirement that Multimedia Producer first obtain the consent of the identifiable persons (if any) appearing in the Photograph.

(c) Rights Reserved to Photographer. Multimedia Producer acknowledges that it has no rights in the Photograph except those expressly granted by this Agreement. Nothing herein shall be construed as restricting Photographer's right to sell, lease on a non-exclusive basis, license, modify, publish, or otherwise distribute the Photograph in whole or in part, to any other person.

2. DELIVERY: Upon execution of this Agreement, Photographer will deliver a copy of the Photograph to Producer in the form of a color slide suitable for reproduction. Such material shall remain the property of Photographer, and shall be returned to Photographer after it has been reproduced by Multimedia Producer.

3. PHOTOGRAPHER'S WARRANTIES:

(a) Authority. Photographer represents and warrants that the Photograph is original and created by Photographer, and that Photographer has the right and authority to enter into this Agreement and to grant to Multimedia Producer the rights to the Photograph that are granted in this Agreement.

(b) Non-infringement. Photographer represents and warrants to Multimedia Producer that adaption and incorporation of the Photograph in the Multimedia Program, and the reproduction and distribution of the Photograph as so incorporated, will not infringe upon or misappropriate the proprietary rights of any third party.

4. PAYMENT: In full and final consideration of the rights granted to Multimedia Producer in this Agreement, Multimedia Producer will pay Photographer the sum of $_____ upon execution of this Agreement.

5. CREDIT AND COPYRIGHT NOTICE: Multimedia Producer will give the Photographer credit in the following form: "Courtesy of _____ ." In addition, the following copyright notice must appear in connection with Multimedia Producer's use of the photograph: "Copyright © _____, All Rights Reserved."

6. INDEMNIFICATION: Photographer will defend, indemnify, and hold Multimedia Producer harmless from and against any and all liabilities, losses, damages, costs, and expenses (including legal fees) associated with any claim or action brought against Multimedia Producer for infringement of any U.S. copy-

73

right, trademark, or other property right based upon the duplication, sale, license, or use of the Photograph in accordance with this Agreement, provided that Multimedia Producer promptly notifies Photographer in writing of the claim and allows Photographer to control, and fully cooperates with Photographer in, the defense and all related settlement negotiations. Photographer shall have no liability for any settlement or compromise made without his consent.

7. LIMITATION OF LIABILITY: Photographer's liability to Multimedia Producer shall be limited to direct damages and, except as provided in the section titled "Indemnification," shall not exceed the amount of the fees paid by Multimedia Producer to photographer hereunder. In no event will photographer be liable for incidental, special, or consequential damages (including lost profits) suffered by Multimedia Producer, even if it has previously been advised of the possibility of such damages.

8. TERM AND TERMINATION:

(a) Term. This license shall remain in full force and effect for the duration of all copyrights in the Photograph, including any renewals and extensions thereof.

(b) Termination for Breach. Photographer may terminate this Agreement only in the event of a material breach of the terms or conditions of this Agreement by Multimedia Producer which breach is not cured within thirty (30) days of written notice from Photographer.

(c) Effect of Termination. Upon termination of this Agreement for any reason, Multimedia Producer will immediately cease duplication of the Photograph and production of copies of the Multimedia Program containing the Photograph. However, Multimedia Producer shall have the right to distribute all copies of Multimedia Program in Multimedia Producer's inventory as of the date of termination, unless termination is due to a material breach by Multimedia Producer.

IN WITNESS WHEREOF, the parties have executed this Agreement as of the date set forth above.

[MULTIMEDIA PRODUCER]   [PHOTOGRAPHER]

By: _____   _____

Its: _____

TEXT LICENSE AGREEMENT

This Agreement is made and entered into on _____,
199_, by and between _____,
a corporation located at _____,
("Developer"), and _____ a
corporation located at _____ ("Publisher").

BACKGROUND

A. Publisher is the owner of the copyright to the excerpt from
the book identified on Exhibit A of this Agreement ("Text").

B. Developer is developing a digital, machine-readable, interactive, multimedia work tentatively titled "_____"
(the "Multimedia Program").

C. Developer desires to incorporate the Text as part of the
Multimedia Program, and to reproduce and distribute the Text as
so incorporated, on a worldwide basis.

D. Publisher is willing to grant such rights to Developer, subject
to the terms and conditions of this Agreement.

NOW THEREFORE, the parties agree as follows:

1. GRANT OF LICENSE:

(a) Rights Granted to Developer. Publisher grants Developer a non-exclusive license and right to (1) convert the Text
into digital, machine-readable form and incorporate all or any
part of the Text within the Multimedia Program; (2) reproduce
the Text, as incorporated in the Multimedia Program, in the
Media described in Exhibit A; and (3) manufacture, package,
market, promote, sell, license, and otherwise distribute copies of
all or any part of the Text, as incorporated in the Multimedia
Program, both directly to end users and indirectly through
distributors, dealers, resellers, agents, and other third parties
within the Territory specified in Exhibit A.

(b) Restricted Use. Use of the Text is restricted to the uses
described in paragraph (a) above. Developer shall have no right
to alter, modify, or distort the Text, nor to create derivative
works thereof except to the extent specifically authorized in this
Agreement.

(c) Ancillary Uses. Notwithstanding the foregoing, Developer may use the Text or any portion thereof in printed materials that accompany the Multimedia Program for delivery to end
users, and in connection with advertising, publicizing, or distributing the Multimedia Program.

(d) Derogatory Uses. Developers shall not use the Text in

any manner or context that will be in any way derogatory to the book from which it came, the author, or any person connected with the creation thereof or depicted therein. Furthermore, the Text will not be used in any way so as to constitute an express or implied endorsement of any Program or service by anyone associated with the Publisher or the author.

(e) Rights Reserved to Publisher. Developer acknowledges that it has no rights to use the Text except those expressly granted by this Agreement. Publisher retains all rights not expressly granted herein.

(f) No Obligation to Use Content. Publisher acknowledges that Developer is not obligated or required to use or incorporate the Text in the Multimedia Program.

2. COPYRIGHT NOTICE AND CREDITS: In every copy of the Multimedia Program that includes the Text, Developer agrees to include Publisher's copyright notice, and to give credit to Publisher and the author of the book, in the form specified on Exhibit A, in the same manner as it accords credit to all other artists and copyright owners whose works are included in the Multimedia Program.

3. PUBLISHER'S WARRANTIES:

(a) Authority. Publisher represents and warrants that it has the right and authority to enter into this Agreement and to grant to Developer the rights to the Text that are granted in this Agreement.

(b) Non-Infringement. Publisher warrants to Developer that incorporation of the Text in the Multimedia Program, and the reproduction and distribution of the Text as so incorporated, will not infringe upon or misappropriate the proprietary rights of any third party, and in addition, that the Text does not contain any matter that is defamatory or that otherwise violates the privacy rights of any person.

(c) DISCLAIMER. THE FOREGOING ARE THE ONLY WARRANTIES MADE BY PUBLISHER. PUBLISHER SPECIFICALLY DISCLAIMS ALL OTHER WARRANTIES, EXPRESS OR IMPLIED, INCLUDING, BUT NOT LIMITED TO, THE IMPLIED WARRANTIES OF MERCHANTABILITY AND FITNESS FOR A PARTICULAR PURPOSE.

4. INDEMNIFICATION: Each party will defend, at its expense, any claim, suit, or proceeding brought against the other insofar it is based on a claim that arises out of its breach of any warranty, representation, undertaking, or obligation in this agreement, and will pay all damages, costs, and expenses finally awarded against the other party in connection with such claim. To qualify for such defense and payment, the party sued must (1) give the indemnifying party prompt written notice of such claim, and (2) allow the indemnifying party to control the defense and/or settlement of such claim.

5. PAYMENT TO PUBLISHER: In full and final consideration of the rights granted to Developer in this Agreement, Developer will pay Publisher the License Fee specified in Exhibit A within fourteen (14) days of the date of this Agreement.

6. TERMINATION OF LICENSE:

(a) Termination. This Agreement may be terminated by written notice if: (1) Developer does not publish the Multimedia Program containing the Text within three years after the date of this Agreement; (2) the Multimedia Program goes "out of print" in that it is not commercially available for a period of two years after its initial publication; or (3) Developer commits a material breach of this Agreement and fails to remedy such breach within thirty (30) days of written notice from Publisher.

(b) Effect of Termination. Upon termination of this Agreement for any reason, Developer will immediately cease duplication of the Text and production of copies of the Multimedia Program containing the Text. However, Developer shall have the right to distribute all copies of the Multimedia Program in Developer's inventory as of the date of termination.

7. MISCELLANEOUS:

(a) Governing Law. This Agreement shall be construed in accordance with the law of the State of _____.

(b) Arbitration: Any controversy or claim arising out of or relating to this agreement or any breach thereof shall be settled by arbitration in accordance with the Rules of the American Arbitration Association; the parties select expedited arbitration using one arbitrator, to be a disinterested attorney specializing in multimedia or intellectual-property law, as the sole forum for the resolution of any dispute between them. The venue for arbitration shall be _____, California. The arbitrator may make any interim order, decision, determinations, or award he deems necessary to preserve the status quo until he is able to render a final order, decision, determination, or award. The determination of the arbitrator in such proceeding shall be final, binding and non-appealable. Judgment upon the award rendered by the arbitrator may be entered in any court having jurisdiction thereof. The prevailing party shall be entitled to reimbursement for costs and reasonable attorneys' fees.

(c) Entire Agreement. This Agreement constitutes the entire agreement between the parties pertaining to the subject matter contained herein, and supersedes all prior agreements related thereto.

IN WITNESS WHEREOF, the parties have executed this Agreement as of the date set forth above.

[Developer]   [Publisher]

By: _____   By: _____

Its: _____   Its: _____

EXHIBIT A

1. **Text:** Pages _____ through _____ of the book titled "_____," written by _____. Copyright Registration number: _____

2. **Term:**

3. **License Fee:**

4. **Territory: Worldwide:**

5. **Credit:**

6. **Media:** All electronic or computer-readable media now known or hereafter developed, including but not limited to magnetic disc and optical disc (such as CD-ROM and DVD).

VIDEO LICENSE AGREEMENT

THIS AGREEMENT, made and entered into on _____ , 199_, by and between _____ ("Multimedia Producer"), a _____ corporation, and _____ ("Owner"), a _____ corporation.

WHEREAS, Multimedia Producer is in the business of publishing and distributing multimedia titles; and

WHEREAS, Owner has the right to grant to Multimedia Producer a license to use the Video, as defined herein, in Multimedia Producer's multimedia product.

NOW THEREFORE, the parties hereto agree as follows:

1. Definitions

1.1. Licensed Media: "Licensed Media" shall mean computer-readable media now known or hereafter to become known including, without limitation, magnetic media-storage devices, DVD, CD-ROM, laserdisc, optical discs, integrated circuit card or chip, and any other human- or machine-readable medium.

1.2. Video: The "Video" shall mean those video segments identified in Exhibit A, and all portions or adaptations thereof.

1.3. Product: The "Product" shall mean the multimedia product described in Exhibit B, which Multimedia Producer shall develop and publish in any and all of the Licensed Media.

2. Delivery: Upon the execution of this Agreement, Owner shall provide Multimedia Producer with videotape copies of the Video conforming to the specifications set forth in Exhibit B.

3. Grant: Subject to the limitations set forth herein, Owner hereby grants to Multimedia Producer a non-exclusive license in perpetuity to: (1) reproduce the Video; (2) digitize such reproductions to create "Digitizations"; (3) incorporate such portions of the Digitizations in the Products so that the aggregate length of the use of the Video in the Product does not exceed twenty (20) minutes; and (4) manufacture, reproduce, distribute, broadcast, or transmit the Product, incorporating part or all of the Digitizations through normal channels of commerce.

4. Reservation of Rights: The license granted by Owner herein shall extend only to the use of the Video in connection with the design, development and distribution of the Product in the Licensed Media. Multimedia Producer shall have no right to make any use of the Video, or any part thereof, other than in connection therewith. The license granted herein is non-exclusive, and Owner reserves the right to make any use of the Video, or to license any rights with respect to the Video to any third party.

5. Right of Consultation: Prior to the commencement of the manufacture of any Product, Owner shall be consulted over the use of the Video as part of the Product. Multimedia Producer shall provide Owner with one (1) copy of the design layout of the Product. Owner shall respond in writing within five (5) days of receipt thereof with any suggestions or comments Owner may have. Owner shall have no right to prohibit Multimedia Producer's use of the Video, except in the event of an unauthorized alteration of the Video.

6. Fee: Upon the execution of this Agreement, Multimedia Producer shall pay to Owner the fee of _____ dollars ($_____).

7. Title: The Video shall remain the sole and exclusive property of Owner and Owner shall retain all right, title, and interest, including without limitation any rights under United States or foreign copyright laws, in the Video.

Multimedia Producer, or its assigns shall have sole and exclusive title to all components of the Product other than the Video, including all patents, copyrights, trademarks, trade secrets, and other proprietary rights therein, and to whatever rights vest in the Video as part of a collective work or compilation, including without limitation the right to reproduce the Product in any or all Licensed Media. Owner will, upon request by Multimedia Producer, promptly execute, acknowledge, or deliver any papers deemed reasonably necessary by Multimedia Producer to document, enforce, protect, and otherwise perfect Multimedia Producer's rights, title, and interest in and to the Products.

8. Copyright Notice: All copies of the Product which include the Video shall bear an appropriate copyright notice.

9. Advertising: Owner shall have the right to approve all advertising, packaging, promotional, or display materials bearing Owner's name, which approval shall not be unreasonably withheld.

10. Indemnification: Owner warrants and represents that Owner has all rights in the Video necessary to grant the licenses granted herein, and has secured all necessary waivers of rights of privacy and publicity from persons depicted in the Video for use of the Video as contemplated in this Agreement. Owner, at its own expense, shall defend, indemnify, and hold harmless Multimedia Producer, its licensees, employees, and agents, from any claim, demand, cause of action, debt, or liability (including attorneys' fees) to the extent it is based on a claim that Multimedia Producer's use of the Video infringes or violates the copyright, license, or other proprietary right of a third party, or violates a third party's right of publicity and/or privacy, provided Owner is notified promptly of such claim. Multimedia Producer may, at its expense, assist in such defense if it chooses. Owner shall have the right to control the defense in any such action. This obligation shall survive the termination of this Agreement for any reason.

Notwithstanding the foregoing, no obligation of indemnification shall arise in the event of a third-party claim based solely on alterations or modifications to the Video performed by Multimedia Producer or at Multimedia Producer's direction.

Multimedia Producer warrants that the Video shall not be used in conjunction with or made a part of any Product which is libelous, slanderous, or obscene. Multimedia Producer, at its own expense, shall defend, indemnify, and hold harmless Owner, its licensees, employees, and agents, from any claim, demand, cause of action, debt, or liability (including attorneys' fees) and may assert a claim based solely on Multimedia Producer's production and distribution of the Product.

11. Limitation of Liability: Neither party shall have any liability to the other with respect to its obligations under this agreement or otherwise for special, incidental, consequential, punitive, or exemplary damages, even if that party has been advised of the possibility of such damages.

12. Termination: Either party shall have the right to terminate this Agreement upon written notice to the other party upon: (i) a material breach by the other party of any provision of this Agreement, which material breach remains uncured thirty (30) days after written notice thereof has been provided to the breaching party; (ii) an unauthorized assignment of this Agreement; (iii) termination of the business of the other party; (iv) insolvency of the other party; or (v) an assignment for the benefit of creditors or the filing of a petition in bankruptcy against the other party, which petition is not dismissed within sixty (60) days from the date of filing.

13. Arbitration: Any controversy or claim arising out of or in relation to this Agreement or the validity, construction, or performance of this Agreement, or the breach thereof, shall be resolved by arbitration in accordance with the rules and procedures of the AFMA, as said rules may be amended from time to time with rights of discovery if requested by the arbitrator. Such rules and procedures are incorporated and made a part of this Agreement by reference. If the AFAM shall refuse to accept jurisdiction of such dispute, then the parties agree to arbitrate such matter before and in accordance with the rules of the American Arbitration Association under its jurisdiction in Los Angeles before a single arbitrator familiar with entertainment or multimedia law. The parties shall have the right to engage in pre-hearing discovery in connection with such arbitration proceedings. The parties agree hereto that they will abide by and perform any award rendered in any arbitration conducted pursuant hereto, that any court having jurisdiction thereof may issue a judgment based upon such award and that the prevailing party in such arbitration and/or confirmation proceeding shall be entitled to recover its reasonable attorneys' fees and expenses. The arbitration will be held in Los Angeles and any award shall be final, binding, and non-appealable. The Parties agree to accept service of process in accordance with the AFMA Rules.

14. General

14.1. Entire Agreement: This Agreement, including Exhibit A, sets forth the entire agreement between the parties in connection with the subject matter hereof and it incorporates, replaces, and supersedes all prior agreements, promises, proposals, representations, understandings, and negotiations, written or not, between the parties in connection therewith. The making, execution, and delivery of this Agreement have been induced by no representations, statements, warranties, or agreements other than those expressed herein.

14.2. Notice: All notices will be in writing and will be delivered personally or sent by confirmed facsimile transmission, overnight letter or United States certified mail, proper postage prepaid at the addresses specified below:

To Owner at: _____

To Multimedia Producer at: _____

Either party may change the person or the address to which notices are directed by giving written notice to the other party. Personally delivered or confirmed facsimile notices will be deemed given when delivered. Notices sent by United States certified mail, return receipt requested, will be deemed given four (4) business days after dispatch. Notices sent by overnight letter will be deemed given on the next business day after dispatch. Notwithstanding the foregoing, notices of change of address will be deemed given only upon receipt by the party to whom it is directed.

14.3. Choice of Law: This Agreement has been entered into in the State of California and will be governed by those laws of the State of California which are applicable to contracts entered into and performed entirely within the State of California without regard to conflict-of-laws principles.

14.4. Modification: No modification, amendment, supplement to or waiver of any provision of this Agreement shall be binding upon the parties hereto unless made in writing and duly signed by both parties.

14.5. Waiver: A failure of either party to exercise any right provided for herein shall not be deemed to be a waiver of any right hereunder.

14.6. Severability: Whenever possible, each provision of this Agreement shall be interpreted in such manner as to be effective and valid under applicable law, but if any provision of this Agreement shall be prohibited or invalid under applicable law, such provision shall be ineffective to the extent of such prohibition or invalidity without invalidating the remainder of such provision or the remaining provisions of this Agreement. Any unenforceable provision will be replaced by a mutually acceptable provision which comes closest to the intention of the parties at the time the original provision was agreed upon.

14.7. Headings: The headings in this Agreement are for purposes of reference only.

14.8. Survival: All provisions hereof relating to assignment of rights to Multimedia Producer shall survive termination of this Agreement.

IN WITNESS THEREOF, the parties have executed this Agreement by their duly authorized representatives as of _____ , 199_.

By: _____   By: _____
     Owner   Multimedia Producer

ART WORK LICENSE AGREEMENT

AGREEMENT dated _____, and made by and between _____, a corporation organized and existing under the laws of the State of_____, with a principal place of business a _____(the "Producer") and _____, a corporation organized (the "Owner").

WHEREAS, Producer is in the business of publishing and distributing various multimedia titles;

WHEREAS, Owner has exclusive possession of, and controls all access to certain paintings, sculpture and other art work described fully in Schedule A attached hereto (the "Art Work"); and

WHEREAS, Producer wishes to incorporate digitized images of the Art Work (the "Images"), in whole or in part in combination with or as a composite of other matter, including, but not limited to, text, data, images, photographs, illustrations, animation and graphics, video or audio segments of any nature, and embody such combination or composites in computer readable media and embodiments, now known or hereafter to become known, including, but not limited to, all formats of computer readable electronic, magnetic, digital, laser or optical-based media (the "Product").

NOW, THEREFORE, in consideration of the promises and covenants recited below, it is hereby agreed by and between Producer and Owner as follows:

1. Grant: Subject to the terms and conditions set forth herein, Owner hereby grants to Producer a nonexclusive license for the term of this Agreement to:

    (i)   photograph the Art Work;

    (ii) create Images of such photographs;

    (iii) incorporate the Images only as described in Schedule A hereto; and

    (iv) distribute the Product embodying the Images.

1.1. Right to Photograph: Producer shall have the right to photograph the Art Work, provided, however that Producer complies with Owner's standard terms and conditions for the access to Owner's Art Work, which are attached hereto as Exhibit A. Within one (1) week of the execution of this Agreement, Owner shall make the Art Work available to be photographed for five (5) hours at a time mutually convenient to the parties. All photographs, including any negatives, film imprints, prints, or any reproductions thereof (the "Photographs") shall be the sole property of Owner, and Owner shall own all right, title and interest thereto, including any and all copyrights, trade secrets and other intellectual property rights.

1.2. Right to Digitize and Incorporate: Producer shall have the right to create the Images and incorporate such Images in the Product.

Upon completion of the design of the Product, including without limitation the incorporation of the Images in the Product, and prior to the commercial distribution of the Product, Producer shall submit two (2) copies of the Product, a videotape of the Product in its operational mode, as well as all accompanying packaging and documentation for the Product to Owner for review. Producer shall include a list of all Images included in the Product, and instruction on all methods by which such Images can be accessed by the user of the Product.

2. Use of Name: Nothing herein shall be construed as granting any permission for Producer to use Owner's name, logos, trademarks or other identification in connection with any Product.

3. Owner's Warmnties: Owner hereby represents and warrants to Producer that it is the lawful possessor of the Art Work. Owner MAKES NO OTHER WARRANTY REGARDING THE ART WORK, EXPRESS OR IMPLIED, AND EXPRESSLY DISCLAIMS ANY WARRANTY OF NON INFRINGEMENT, OR ANY REPRESENTATION THAT THE ART WORK DOES NOT VIOLATE A THIRD PARTY'S PRIVACY OR PUBLICITY RIGHTS, OR THAT THE USE OF THE ART WORK AS CONTEMPLATED HEREIN, WITHOUT ANY CREDIT OR ATTRIBUTION, DOES NOT VIOLATE A THIRD PARTY'S RIGHTS OF ATTRIBUTION OR INTEGRITY.

4. Proprietary Rights: The parties hereby acknowledge and agree that the Owner shall retain all right, tile and interest to the Art Work, Photographs and Images, including without limitation any copyright or other proprietary rights in and to the same. Producer shall make no use of the Art Work, Photographs or Images, other than as expressly provided herein, and acknowledges that to do so would constitute an infringement of Owner's proprietary rights therein.

Notwithstanding the foregoing, the parties hereby acknowledge and agree that, with the exception of the Images, the Producer shall retain all proprietary rights in the Product including all applicable rights to patents, copyrights, trademarks, and trade secrets inherent therein, and appurtenant thereto.

5. Indemnification: Producer shall indemnify, defend and hold Owner harmless from any claims, demands, liabilities, losses, damages, judgments or settlements, including all reasonable costs and expenses related thereto including attorneys' fees, directly or indirectly resulting from any claim asserted by a third party with respect to the Products, or the Photographs or the Images as incorporated into the Products, including without limitation a claimed infringement or violation of any intellectual property right or right of publicity or privacy or a claim of libel or defamation.

6. Term: The term of this Agreement shall be ten (10) years from the date that this Agreement is executed by both parties. This Agreement may be terminated by either party in the event that the other party commits a material breach of this Agreement and fails to cure such breach within ten (10) days of notification thereof by the non-breaching party. Producer shall have no right of sell-off upon the termination or expiration of this Agreement, unless otherwise agreed to by the parties in writing. Producer agrees that within five (5) business days of the termination or expiration of this Agreement, Producer shall: (1) return to Owner all Photographs in its possession or control, and shall destroy any and all Images, including those embodied in unsold Products, within its possession and control; and (2) certify to Owner in writing of such return or destruction.

Upon the termination or expiration of this Agreement, all rights licensed hereunder shall terminate but all provisions except for those of Section 1 shall survive such termination or expiration.

7. Compensation: Upon the execution of this Agreement, Producer shall pay to Owner a one-time, non-refundable license fee of _____dollars ($___). This fee is not an advance against royalties, and is non-refundable under any circumstance, including but not limited to a termination of this Agreement due to Owner's material breach.

Producer agrees to pay Owner a royalty (a "Royalty") which shall be equal to the greater of (1) $ ____ for each copy of each Product commercially distributed (excluding up to ___ copies of Products distributed at no charge for promotional purposes); (2) _____ percent (___%) of Sales Income (as defined herein) multiplied by the percent of data of the Product comprised by the Images; or (3) _____ percent (___%) of Sales Income. As used herein, "Sales Income" shall mean gross revenues to be received by Producer in connection with any sale, license, lease or other exploitation of the Product; provided, however, Sales Income shall exclude import/export or other taxes imposed on foreign sales; duties, sales or use taxes actually invoiced; transportation and insurance charges billed separately to customers; and actual credits, discounts, allowances and returns granted to customers. Except as herein provided, Sales Income shall be determined by using generally accepted accounting principles consistently applied.

8. Royalty Accounting: Producer will compute Owner's Royalties, if any, four (4) times per year, at the end of each calendar quarter. Within thirty (30) days after the last day of a calendar quarter, Producer will send Owner a statement (a "Royalty

Statement") covering such Royalties indicating the Royalties due Owner, if any.

9. Inspection: Owner, at its sole cost and expense, shall have the right, upon reasonable written notice to Producer, to inspect those of Producer's books and records which pertain to revenues received from sales of Products, at Producer's premises and during Producer's normal business hours. Owner may exercise this right two (2) times each calendar year and only during the term of this Agreement. All information to which Owner is provided access during such examination is confidential information of Producer, and Owner shall not use or disclose such information, except for the purposes of verifying its royalty payments. In connection with any claim by Owner that additional monies are payable by Producer under this Agreement based upon an examination of Producer's books and records as set forth in this Section, Producer will not be deemed in breach of this Agreement unless within thirty (30) days of Producer's receipt of such claim in writing, together with sufficient documentation to support such claim, Producer does not pay such additional monies so claimed by Owner.

10. Binding Agreement: This Agreement executed by the Parties sets forth the entire agreement between the Parties in connection with the subject matter hereof and it incorporates, replaces, and supersedes all prior agreements, promises, proposals, representations, understandings and negotiations, written or not, between the Parties. The making, execution, and delivery of this Agreement have been induced by no representations, statements, warranties or agreements other than those expressed herein. This Agreement shall be binding upon the heirs, legal representatives, successors and assigns of Owner.

11. Notice: All notices will be in writing and will be delivered personally or sent by confirmed facsimile transmission, overnight letter or United States certified mail, proper postage prepaid at the addresses specified above.

12. Choice of Law: This Agreement has been entered into in the State of _____, and will be governed by those laws of the State of _____, which are applicable to contracts entered into and performed entirely within the State of _____, without regard to conflict of laws principles.

13. Arbitration: Any controversy or claim arising out of or relating to this agreement or any breach thereof shall be settled by arbitration in accordance with the Rules of the American Arbitration Association; The parties select expedited arbitration using one arbitrator, to be a disinterested attorney specializing in multimedia law, as the sole forum for the resolution of any dispute between hem. The venue for arbitration shall be Los Angeles, California. The arbitrator may make any interim order, decision, determinations, or award he deems necessary to pre-serve the status quo until he is able to render a final order, decision, determination or award. The determination of the arbitrator in such proceeding shall be final, binding and non-appealable. Judgment upon the award rendered by the arbitrator may be entered in any court having jurisdiction thereof. The prevailing party shall be entitled to reimbursement for costs and reasonable attorney's fees.

IN WITNESS WHEREOF, the parties have executed this Agreement as of the date hereof.

By: _____   By: _____
Owner   Multimedia Producer

CHAPTER 3

HIRING OTHERS

THE NATURE OF INTELLECTUAL PROPERTY

Multimedia programs are a form of intellectual property—property that is a product of the mind. Since it is intangible, it cannot be physically handled like tangible personal property, such as a flashlight. Intellectual property embodied in a physical form, such as a videocassette of a copyrighted movie, can be held. It is important to understand that ownership of the physical form does not necessarily give one ownership in the underlying intellectual property. For instance, if you buy a videocassette of a popular movie, you own the individual cassette but do not gain any rights to the underlying copyright in the movie. If you purchase a painting, you may own that painting but that does not necessarily give you the right to duplicate its image on T-shirts. It is helpful to think of intellectual property as a system of rights to control the use and disposition of certain creations. The most common forms of intellectual property are copyrights, trademarks, and patents.

Because of the unusual nature of intellectual property, entrepreneurs are often confused as to the rules that govern its creation and ownership. When a real-estate developer hires workmen to construct a house, there is no question that the real-estate developer owns the house. This is not necessarily the case, however, in regard to the creation of intellectual property. The "author" of a work under copyright law could be the person hired to create the work: the painter, the writer, the photographer, the musician—not the person who hired them. Even if an artist is specifically hired to create a work for another, the copyright may not vest in the hiring party. Of course, the parties have the power to decide who owns the copyright to the work product. If they do not make such a decision before the work is created, various legal presumptions will determine ownership.

Multimedia developers and producers who hire others to assist them in the creation and promotion of programming need to proceed carefully to ensure that they own the rights to the work product created by others. A written contract is strongly recommended as it will protect the hiring party by documenting the terms of the engagement and the respective rights and obligations of the parties. The relationship of the parties can be structured any number of ways, including that of employer/employee, commissioning party/independent contractor, or collaborators who co-own a work. As will be explained, the decision as to how to structure the relationship is important because different legal presumptions will come into play.

Employers typically want all of an employee's work product to be owned exclusively by the employer. Intellectual property, such as a copyright, can be jointly held. In some circumstances, parties who jointly author a work will be presumed to share the copyright. Moreover, an employee could claim that a creation is solely owned by the employee because it was developed outside the scope of employment. To avoid ambiguity, an employment agreement should clearly state that the employer is the owner of the rights to any work product, and the agreement should define the scope of employment.

WORKS MADE FOR HIRE

The United States Copyright Act provides that an employer is deemed the author of any work made for hire unless the parties have agreed otherwise. A work made for hire is defined as either (1) a work that is prepared by an employee within the scope of employment or (2) a work that is specially ordered or commissioned, such as when a commissioning party hires a freelance artist or independent contractor, but only if the work falls within one of nine categories and the parties have signed an agreement that it is a work for hire.[1] This contract must be signed BEFORE the work is created.[2] Otherwise, the copyright will vest in the individual creator when he or she fixes the work in a tangible medium. If a multimedia producer, for instance, should fail to have a developer sign a contract before work commences, then the producer will only be able to acquire the copyright with a written assignment of these rights.

EMPLOYEE OR INDEPENDENT CONTRACTOR?

Whether the author of a work should be characterized as an employee or an independent contractor is determined on the basis of a control test and several other factors. If the hiring party has the right to control the manner and means by which the product is made, or the service is rendered, then the relationship is likely to be construed as employer/employee. If, on the other hand, the person hired has considerable discretion as to how he accomplishes the work, such as choosing his own hours and providing his own tools, then he is likely to be characterized as an independent contractor. Other factors to consider include the skill level of the hired party, and whether the hiring party provides employee benefits and withholds taxes.[3] Note that a person could be considered an "employee" under an employee-benefit law, yet be found to be an independent contractor for purposes of the work-made-for-hire statute.

The seminal decision in this area of the law is the U.S. Supreme Court case of *Community for Creative Non-Violence v. Reid.*[4] In that case, Community for Creative Non-Violence (CCNV), a non-profit organization, hired a sculptor, defendant Reid, to create a sculpture dramatizing the plight of the homeless. Reid orally agreed to create the work for a fixed sum, and did so in his studio. As he worked on the project, he was visited occasionally by CCNV representatives. They observed the progress of his work and made suggestions, most of which where adopted by Reid. After Reid delivered the sculpture, each party attempted to register the work with the copyright office, claiming the copyright as their own.

The key question for the court to resolve was whether Reid was an employee or an independent contractor. If he was an employee, the copyright would vest in CCNV, his employer, as a work made for hire. The court found that Reid's work was highly skilled and he created the sculpture with his own tools in his own studio. Moreover, he was hired for only two months, was paid a fixed sum, and had complete authority and discretion over hiring assistants. For these and other reasons, the court concluded that Reid was an independent contractor. The court then remanded the case to the district court for it to review the facts and consider the possibil-

---

WORKS MADE FOR HIRE

A WORK MADE FOR HIRE IS EITHER:

(A) A WORK PREPARED BY ANY EMPLOYEE WITHIN THE SCOPE OF THEIR EMPLOYMENT; OR

(B) A WORK SPECIALLY ORDERED OR COMMISSIONED, PROVIDED THERE IS A WRITING SIGNED BY BOTH PARTIES INDICATING THAT THE WORK IS MADE FOR HIRE AND THE WORK IS:

(1) A CONTRIBUTION TO A COLLECTIVE WORK;

(2) A PART OF A MOTION PICTURE OR OTHER AUDIOVISUAL WORK;

(3) A TRANSLATION;

(4) A SUPPLEMENTARY WORK;

(5) A COMPILATION;

(6) AN INSTRUCTIONAL TEXT;

(7) A TEST;

(8) ANSWER MATERIAL FOR A TEST; OR

(9) AN ATLAS.

ity that the parties had prepared the work with the intention that their contributions be merged into inseparable or interdependent parts of a unitary whole. If this was the case, the parties would be co-owners of the copyright.[5]

The case is illustrative for multimedia employers because Reid was hired in a manner similar to how creators of content are hired by developers. Often, free-lance graphic artists, photographers, and programmers are asked to create content, without a written contract, and on the developer's erroneous assumption that the copyright to the work product will vest with the developer.

ASSIGNMENT OF RIGHTS

To resolve any doubts as to ownership of work product, a hiring party is wise to have an assignment clause in the hiring agreement that transfers to the hiring party any rights the creator may have. Such a clause might state:

> Employee agrees that all copyrightable works created by Employee or under Employer's direction in connection with Employer's business are "works made for hire" and shall be the sole and complete property of Employer and that any and all copyrights to such works shall belong to Employer. To the extent such works are not deemed to be "works made for hire," Employee hereby assigns all proprietary rights, including copyright, in these works to Employer without further compensation.

If the hired party is not an employee but an independent contractor, the above clause should be modified by substituting "Independent Contractor" for the word "Employee." If the hiring party wants to obtain patent, trade secret, or other rights, the clause should be expanded to encompass those forms of work. A more comprehensive clause transfering the results and proceeds of an employee's work can be found at the end of this chapter.

One reason why multimedia producers want to own the initial copyright to works created for them is that they want to avoid the termination and renewal provisions of the Copyright Act. When a work is made for hire, the hiring party is considered the author and holds the renewal rights, and no termination rights are vested in another. On the other hand, if the work is acquired by assignment (i.e., the initial copyright vested in the creator of the work, who later transfers his rights to a developer), the creator is the author and the holder of renewal and termination rights.[6] Consequently, it is advantageous for the hiring party to have work done on the basis of a work-for-hire agreement rather than pay authors to transfer rights to work they created on their own. That is because a transfer of rights does not necessarily include renewal rights, and a transfer cannot restrict the author's termination rights.

Renewal rights exist in works created before January 1, 1978. The holder of the right can extend the term up to a total of seventy-five years. Termination rights allow authors and their heirs to terminate a transfer of copyright. As mentioned, termination rights cannot be assigned away by authors. Any agreement purporting to restrict the author's termination right, or an agreement by the author to make a future grant, is invalid.[7] For works created after January 1, 1978, a transfer can be terminated either thirty-five years from the date of publication of the work, or forty years from the date of execution of the grant of rights, whichever is earlier.[8] Thus, developers that obtain rights to content by assignment can only be certain that the rights will last for thirty-five years. On the other hand, developers that create product as a result of work-for-hire agreements will own the product for the full term of the copyright.

PATENTS

Under U.S. patent law, rights to an invention generally reside in the inventor or discoverer rather than his employer. Consequently, when software is developed by an employee or an independent contractor, it is extremely important for the parties to have a written agreement specifying who owns the patent. Nevertheless, even if patent rights belong to the employee, the employer may have the right to use the invention in perpetuity without paying royalties. This is known as the "shop rights" doctrine,[9] and it applies when an invention is created by an employee within the scope of employment.

Courts have justified the shop rights doctrine on the grounds that it is only fair to give an employer these rights when an invention is created on company time using company resources. At least one case has extended the shop rights doctrine to work created by independent contractors.[10] Shop rights can be expanded or restricted by express agreement of the parties, such as when an employment contract sets forth the extent of shop rights granted the employer.

Employers may use invention assignment agreements to obtain rights to inventions created by employees or independent contractors. Since it may be difficult to determine precisely when an invention was conceived, these agreements typically transfer rights to inventions conceived or reduced to practice during the term of employment. Overly broad assignment clauses may be invalid because they are contrary to public policy. California Labor Code 2870, for instance, provides that employment agreements that assign rights to an invention do not apply to inventions developed by employees on their own time without use of an employer's equipment, supplies, facilities or trade secrets. Exceptions are made for inventions that are related to an employer's business, or anticipated research and development, and for inventions that result from work performed by an employee for the employer.

PROTECTING TRADE SECRETS

An employer will want to prevent unauthorized disclosure of important proprietary information such as customer lists, business plans, trade secrets, and other confidential information. Employee turnover is high in the multimedia and computer industries. An employee who departs with valuable information can cause irreparable harm.

A trade secret can be a formula, pattern, device, or compilation of information that is used in one's business and which gives one a competitive advantage over those who do not know or use it.[11] To maintain a trade secret, it must be kept secret. Unlike patents and copyrights, there is no time limit on how long a trade secret can be protected, provided it remains secret. The laws protecting trade secrets prevent wrongful discovery or use by others, such as when someone obtains a trade secret by industrial espionage or by breaching a contract.

Employers protect trade secrets by restricting access to them. Trade secrets embodied in documents should be kept in locked file cabinets or safes. Databases that contain trade secrets must be secured so that only authorized persons have

GUIDELINES FOR DRAFTING EMPLOYMENT CONTRACTS

THE FOLLOWING GUIDELINES WILL HELP EMPLOYERS DRAFT ENFORCEABLE CONTRACTS:

1. SPEAK TRUTHFULLY: EMPLOYERS SOMETIMES "HYPE" THEIR COMPANIES, EXAGGERATING BENEFITS AND MAKING PROMISES THEY MAY NOT BE ABLE TO KEEP. IN SOME CIRCUMSTANCES, THESE ORAL STATEMENTS MAY COME BACK TO HAUNT THE EMPLOYER. EVEN IF THERE IS NO HYPE IN THE EMPLOYMENT AGREEMENT, SUCH A STATEMENT COULD BE INTRODUCED INTO EVIDENCE TO INTERPRET AN AMBIGUOUS CLAUSE.

2. DON'T STEAL EMPLOYEES OR DATA FROM OTHERS: IF A PROSPECT IS UNDER CONTRACT WITH ANOTHER COMPANY, YOU COULD BE LIABLE IF YOU INDUCE THE EMPLOYEE TO BREACH HIS EMPLOYMENT CONTRACT. YOU SHOULD CAREFULLY DETERMINE WHETHER A PROSPECTIVE EMPLOYEE IS UNDER ANY ENFORCEABLE RESTRICTIONS THAT MIGHT PREVENT HIM FROM TERMINATING EMPLOYMENT. NEVER ASK A PROSPECTIVE EMPLOYEE TO BRING TO HIS NEW JOB ANY PROPRIETARY INFORMATION FROM A PRIOR EMPLOYER. INDEED, YOU MAY WANT THE EMPLOYMENT AGREEMENT TO EXPLICITLY PROHIBIT AN EMPLOYEE FROM BRINGING ANY PROPRIETARY INFORMATION TO HIS NEW JOB.

3. GIVE THE EMPLOYEE TIME TO REVIEW THE CONTRACT: DO NOT PRESSURE THE EMPLOYEE TO IMMEDIATELY SIGN A CONTRACT OR PRESENT THE CONTRACT TO THE EMPLOYEE AFTER EMPLOYMENT HAS BEGUN. EMPLOYEES SHOULD BE GIVEN AMPLE OPPORTUNITY TO STUDY THE TERMS OF A PROPOSED CONTRACT AND CONSULT WITH AN ATTORNEY OF THEIR OWN CHOOSING. STANDARD CONTRACTS THAT ARE NOT SUBJECT TO NEGOTIATION, AND THOSE WITH TERMS THAT A COURT MIGHT CONSIDER UNCONSCIONABLE, MAY NOT BE ENFORCEABLE.

[CONTINUED]

access. Those employees allowed access to trade secrets must understand the importance of keeping the material confidential. Employers typically require employees to sign non-disclosure or confidentiality agreements, restricting dissemination of confidential company information.

Information that may not be protectable under copyright or patent law can be protected as a trade secret. A developer's software, for instance, may contain elements not generally

GUIDELINES FOR DRAFTING EMPLOYMENT CONTRACTS
[CONTINUED]

4. INCLUDE A NON-DISCLOSURE PROVISION: WHILE MANY STATES HAVE LAWS THAT PROTECT TRADE SECRETS, SOME PROPRIETARY INFORMATION MAY NOT BE CONSIDERED SUFFICIENTLY SECRET TO QUALIFY FOR PROTECTION. THEREFORE, A NON-DISCLOSURE CLAUSE SHOULD BE INCLUDED IN THE EMPLOYMENT CONTRACT, OR A SEPARATE NON-DISCLOSURE AGREEMENT SHOULD BE SIGNED UPON EMPLOYMENT. MOREOVER, A NON-DISCLOSURE PROVISION PUTS AN EMPLOYEE ON NOTICE, REMINDING HIM THAT HE SHOULD BE CAREFUL NOT TO DISCLOSE CONFIDENTIAL INFORMATION TO OTHERS.

5. COVENANT NOT TO COMPETE: A COVENANT NOT TO COMPETE RESTRICTS AN EMPLOYEE'S ABILITY TO LEAVE AND SUBSEQUENTLY COMPETE AGAINST THE EMPLOYER. USUALLY THE PROVISION IS LIMITED IN TIME AND GEOGRAPHIC AREA. IF THE RESTRICTION IS DEEMED UNREASONABLE, COURTS MAY REFUSE TO ENFORCE IT. SOME STATES, SUCH AS CALIFORNIA, PROHIBIT COVENANTS NOT TO COMPETE, WITH A FEW EXCEPTIONS.[14]

6. SIGN EMPLOYMENT AGREEMENTS FIRST: A COMPLETE WRITTEN EMPLOYMENT CONTRACT SHOULD BE SIGNED BEFORE EMPLOYMENT BEGINS. IF EMPLOYMENT COMMENCES ON THE BASIS OF A DEAL MEMO, AND ONLY LATER IS THE EMPLOYEE PRESENTED WITH A NON-COMPETITION OR NON-DISCLOSURE AGREEMENT TO SIGN, THESE LATTER AGREEMENTS MAY BE UNENFORCEABLE BECAUSE THEY ARE NOT SUPPORTED BY ADDITIONAL CONSIDERATION.

7. OWNERSHIP CLAUSE: THE AGREEMENT SHOULD CLEARLY STATE THAT, ABSENT A WRITTEN AGREEMENT TO THE CONTRARY, OWNERSHIP OF ALL WORK CREATED BY AN EMPLOYEE WILL VEST IN THE EMPLOYER, INCLUDING COPYRIGHTS, TRADEMARKS, PATENTS, AND TRADE SECRETS. THE EMPLOYER BECOMES THE AUTHOR FOR COPYRIGHT PURPOSES. TO ENSURE THAT THE COPYRIGHT IS OWNED BY THE EMPLOYER, THE SCOPE

[CONTINUED]

known by one's competitors, which may be protected as a trade secret. Even negative information, such as negative results of research, can qualify as a trade secret.[12] The fact that a certain procedure doesn't work could be of great economic value to a competitor.

Typically, trade secrets developed by employees within the scope of their employment will belong to the employer. Of course, it may not always be clear whether a trade secret was

---

GUIDELINES FOR DRAFTING EMPLOYMENT CONTRACTS
[CONTINUED]

OF THE EMPLOYEE'S WORK SHOULD BE CAREFULLY AND BROADLY DEFINED SO THAT IT IS CLEAR THAT ANY AND ALL WORK PRODUCT WAS CREATED IN THE COURSE OF EMPLOYMENT, INCLUDING WORK CREATED AFTER HOURS. TO PROTECT AGAINST AN ADVERSE FINDING THAT AN "EMPLOYEE" IS IN FACT AN INDEPENDENT CONTRACTOR (IN WHICH CASE THE COPYRIGHT MIGHT NOT VEST IN THE EMPLOYER), THE CONTRACT SHOULD PROVIDE THAT ALL WORK BY THE HIRED PARTY IS A "WORK MADE FOR HIRE" TO WHICH COPYRIGHT VESTS IN THE HIRING PARTY, AND TO THE EXTENT THAT ANY WORK IS NOT A WORK FOR HIRE, THE HIRED PARTY TRANSFERS HIS RIGHTS TO THE HIRING PARTY.

8. **ARBITRATION**: CONSIDER ADDING AN ARBITRATION CLAUSE TO RESOLVE ANY CONTRACTUAL DISPUTES. THROUGH ARBITRATION, THE PARTIES CAN AVOID PROTRACTED AND COSTLY COURT PROCEEDINGS. THE ARBITRATION CLAUSE SHOULD SPECIFY WHO WILL ARBITRATE THE DISPUTE AND THAT THE PREVAILING PARTY IS ENTITLED TO REIMBURSEMENT OF ATTORNEYS' FEES AND COSTS. A SAMPLE CLAUSE MIGHT STATE:

ANY CONTROVERSY OR CLAIM ARISING OUT OF OR RELATING TO THIS AGREEMENT OR ANY BREACH THEREOF SHALL BE SETTLED BY ARBITRATION IN ACCORDANCE WITH THE RULES OF THE AMERICAN ARBITRATION ASSOCIATION; THE PARTIES SELECT EXPEDITED ARBITRATION USING ONE ARBITRATOR TO BE A DISINTERESTED ATTORNEY, AS THE SOLE FORUM FOR THE RESOLUTION OF ANY DISPUTE BETWEEN THEM. THE VENUE FOR ARBITRATION SHALL BE LOS ANGELES, CALIFORNIA. THE DETERMINATION OF THE ARBITRATOR IN SUCH PROCEEDING SHALL BE FINAL, BINDING, AND NON-APPEALABLE. JUDGMENT UPON THE AWARD RENDERED BY THE ARBITRATOR MAY BE ENTERED IN ANY COURT HAVING JURISDICTION THEREOF. THE PREVAILING PARTY SHALL BE ENTITLED TO REIMBURSEMENT FOR COSTS AND REASONABLE ATTORNEYS' FEES.

developed within the scope of employment. To ensure owner-ship, employers should have a written employment agreement that defines the scope of employment and assigns trade secrets to the employer.

Information and know-how that may not be secret enough to qualify as a trade secret could be restricted with a non-disclosure agreement. Such an agreement should define for the employee which information is confidential. Another device used by employers to protect their proprietary information is a covenant not to compete. This provision attempts to restrict an employee from competing against a former employer. Many courts will only enforce such restrictions within a limited geographical area and for a limited time. Other states, such as California,[13] simply refuse to enforce these restrictive cov-enants on the grounds that they violate public policies that favor competition, employee mobility, and the right of an individual to earn a living.

Multimedia companies should also exercise care when dis-closing trade secrets to outside contractors, such as beta testers. A written non-disclosure agreement should be used to prevent unauthorized disclosure.

GENERAL EMPLOYMENT CONCERNS

This book is focused on issues of particular concern to persons working in the multimedia arena. Brief mention should be made, however, of general employment laws and regulations that affect all types of businesses. Laws such as those regulat-ing minimum wages and requiring worker's compensation insurance typically apply to multimedia companies. Employers should make sure that they are aware of various labor, tax, and environmental laws that may affect their business.

Discrimination

Multimedia companies need to be concerned with the same anti-discrimination laws that apply in other industries. Federal and state laws prohibit discrimination against applicants and employees on the basis of race, color, gender, religious beliefs, national origin, physical disability, and age (for persons over forty). State and municipal laws may prohibit discrimination on the basis of marital status or sexual orientation.

Employers can hire, fire, and promote employees based on their experience, skills, and performance. Even if an employer doesn't intend to discriminate, appearances, such as when all senior positions are filled with white males or when men consistently earn more than women, can provide damning evidence to the contrary. To avoid even the appearance of discrimination, employers should make every effort to recruit employees by advertising job listings widely so that they will come to the attention of a diverse pool of candidates. Employers should use selection criteria tied to skills and experience needed for the job, eliminating non-essential criteria that might limit the diversity of the applicant pool.

When questioning candidates, employers should avoid asking for information that may violate state and federal laws. Employers, for instance, can ask how long a candidate has lived in the community, but should not ask when and where a candidate was born, as this is likely to produce information as to the person's age and natural origin, factors that should not be considered in hiring. Likewise, it may be proper for an employer to inquire about which languages a candidate can speak if fluency in foreign languages is a skill that might help an employee perform his job; but asking a candidate about his ancestry or religion would rarely be proper.

Civil Liberties

Employees have a right of privacy arising from the United States Constitution. This right is not surrendered because a person accepts a job. Gathering background information on a prospective employee can violate his rights. To avoid liability, employers should obtain prior written consent from candidates before investigating their background. Employees also have rights of free speech and association that an employer cannot restrict.

Privacy and E-Mail

In many workplaces electronic mail is widely used to transmit messages. Employees are often surprised to learn that the law apparently does not protect E-mail to the same extent as that afforded voice and paper mail communications. Congress enacted the Electronic Communications Privacy Act of 1986 (ECPA)[15] to extend the privacy protection covering telephone calls to electronic mail and computer data transfers. While the ECPA prohibits unauthorized access to stored electronic communication,[16] it does not necessarily prevent employers from monitoring the E-mail of their employees. That is because the Act protects the privacy of E-mail messages from access by outsiders, exempting conduct authorized by the provider of the service. Moreover, the Act applies only to messages sent over public, not private, E-mail systems. Under ECPA, businesses with private networks can intercept the employees' electronic messages if the interception is performed as part of system maintenance or is necessary to protect the rights or privacy of the telecommunications service provider.

In at least two instances, California courts have refused to extend privacy rights to E-mail that was monitored by employers. These courts reasoned that since the employers owned the E-mail systems, they were entitled to monitor them.[17] A federal district court, interpreting Pennsylvania law, has held that an employee who made disparaging comments on a corporate E-mail system had no expectation of privacy.[18] In this case the company maintained an internal E-mail system that employees could access from home. The employer assured its employees that E-mail communications would remain confidential and privileged, and messages would not be used against employees as grounds for termination. After an employee fired off a message characterizing management as "back-stabbing bastards," he was fired. The court held that the employee lost any expectation of privacy when he made allegedly unprofessional comments over the corporate E-mail system.[19]

Notwithstanding the aforementioned cases, employers are well advised to take precautions to forestall liability for intercepting employees' E-mail. While ECPA may not presently prohibit an employer from monitoring E-mail, courts could find employers liable on the basis of violation of state or local laws, or on the basis of rights derived from the U.S. Constitution. Moreover, under different facts, an employer could be found to have given employees, either expressly or implicitly, a reasonable expectation of privacy.

Employers should also be concerned about liability arising from employees' acts that might violate the rights of third parties or co-workers. Employees could use an employer's computer network, for example, to defame third parties or to distribute copyrighted material without authorization. An employee downloading pornography from the Internet could create a hostile environment, thereby exposing an employer to liability for sexual harassment. Employees can damage employers by allowing trade secrets and other proprietary information to be disseminated, or by exposing the employer's computer network to viruses.

Employers should take precautions to protect employees' privacy and prevent unauthorized disclosure of company data. Access to personnel databases should be restricted. In an era when traveling employees and telecommuting employees regularly communicate with their employers by modem, and customers are encouraged to obtain information and buy products online, it is easy for company information to get loose. As employers establish Intranets to allow employees to efficiently share information, they should also recognize that these systems have great potential for abuse. Locking a file cabinet provides little protection in the information age. The most important company asset may be its databases. With a few keystrokes, a disgruntled employee can cause irreparable harm. Furthermore, the damage that can result from unauthorized access is multiplied because it is so easy and inexpensive today to disseminate data widely via the Internet.

To preclude liability and damage, employers should adopt detailed written personnel policies, which should be given to all employees. Such a policy might restrict E-mail use to business purposes. Employees should also be informed that their E-mail may be monitored at any time without prior notice. To ensure that all employees are aware of the policy, and to periodically remind them of it, the notice could be programmed to appear on-screen whenever an employee logs on to his computer. The system might require an employee to affirmatively acknowledge reading the notice before allowing him to move on to another screen. Before adoption, a policy should be reviewed in light of any collective-bargaining agreements that might grant workers privacy or other rights. Employees should be informed that violations of company policy are grounds for dismissal.

Companies may want to regularly audit their databases to ensure that they are being used properly and to ensure that the databases do not contain any unauthorized software.

Job Tenure

Unless an employer agrees otherwise, most employment will be considered at will, which means the employer can terminate the employee at any time, for any lawful reason, or for no reason. Conversely, the employee is free to quit at any time. This means a programmer who is critical to the successful and timely delivery of a software program can walk off the job if she gets a better offer elsewhere.

Although an employer may intend to hire workers on an at-will basis, an employer's written and oral statements could be construed as an offer of job security. A statement to an employee that he is assured of employment as long as he works hard could create an enforceable contract, permitting termination only for just cause.[20] Likewise, employer policy manuals that state that employees will be given notice and certain disciplinary procedures will be followed before termination can restrict an employer from discharging an employee without following these rules.

It is often wise for employers to adopt a written policy manual or handbook. These documents clearly set forth the company's policy as to vacations, working hours, and fringe benefits, eliminating ambiguity and ensuring that all employees receive the same information. A policy manual can also set forth a company's policy against sexual harassment or illegal discrimination, statements that could prove useful to management in the event of a lawsuit. To forestall claims of job tenure, employers may want to include statements that employees do not have an employment agreement unless and until it is signed by the company president. Moreover, the employer may want to expressly reserve the right to terminate employees without cause. Employers should ensure that policies set forth in employee handbooks are fair, reasonable, and consistently enforced.

Employers should maintain personnel files containing performance evaluations and notations as to any employee violation of rules. This information can provide evidence that an employee was discharged for poor performance, and refute an employee's allegation that he was discriminated against improperly. On the other hand, if an employee's file is filled with glowing performance reviews, this documentation can be used by the employee to prove that he was wrongfully discharged.

Guild/Union Concerns

The guilds, which represent writers, directors, and actors, hope that the development of interactive programs will provide additional employment for their members. They are concerned, however, that the rights and level of compensation that they have gained from years of difficult negotiations with the movie studios and televisions networks do not erode.

The guilds recognize that interactive programming is still a fledgling market, and the producers of this new form of programming cannot afford to hire guild members on the same terms as an established studio. Moreover, the guilds realize that if hiring their members is too costly, producers will look to non-union talent to fill their needs. Guild members will lose the opportunity to gain experience in the new medium and producers will develop a non-union pool of talent to draw upon. Ultimately, producers may see little reason to become a guild signatory if most of the talent they desire is non-union.

The Screen Actors Guild (SAG), the American Federation of Television and Radio Artists (AFTRA), and the Writers Guild of America (WGA) have adopted a flexible approach that imposes minimal obligations on producers who want to hire their members. They are simply trying to get their foot in the door with the expectation that as the market develops they will be able to win additional benefits for their members. These guilds have developed short, simple agreements for producers to sign.

The WGA allows a production company to become a Guild signatory for one production only by signing a one-page-letter agreement. The agreement does not require the usual WGA minimum payments or compliance with any Guild rules other than requiring the producer to make payments to the writer's pension and health funds. These payments amount to 12.5% of gross compensation.

SAG was the first guild to develop an agreement for minimum compensation rates for the interactive market. The agreement defines the medium as the production of audiovisual material for display on either a home television or a computer screen. Under the agreement, the minimum wage rate for extras is $103 per day. Day performers receive $522 a day for an eight-hour day, which rates remain effective until June 1997. The AFTRA day-player rate is the same. Under the SAG and AFTRA agreements, producers must contribute to the health and pension plans, which amounts to 12.65% of gross compensation. No residual payments are required, although SAG expressly reserves the right to bargain for payment for extended rights to distribute interactive programs as of the contract's renewal on June 30, 1997. The SAG agreement also includes a Most Favored Nations clause, which gives a signatory producer the option of upgrading the agreement to any future SAG agreement that grants a producer more favorable terms.

The Directors Guild of America (DGA) has taken a different approach to interactive programming. The DGA is concerned that its members receive both an up-front payment for their services and that they participate in the success of programs with some kind of back-end payment. A back-end payment can be royalty based upon the number of units sold or tied to a share of the producer's profits. The DGA believes that if it does not insist on some kind of back-end payment now, a bad precedent will be set and it will become difficult for the Guild to win this type of compensation later. Thus, the DGA wants to establish this principle, even though back-end payments would be low today because of limited sales of interactive programming.

In October 1993, the DGA signed its first agreement, a contract with Digital Pictures for production of a live-action interactive film and video games.[21] The DGA declined to disclose the terms of the deal other than to say that it included back-end compensation. The DGA subsequently adopted a tiered approach to their Interactive side-letter agreement: if the budget for the live action segment is under $1,000,000, then the DGA allows its members to negotiate their own deal subject only to Guild shop, pension and health, and arbitration provisions. No minimum salary, residuals, or back-end payment is required. If the live-action budget is for more than $1,000,000, the minimal initial compensation is $44,778 for no more than forty days' directing services. In lieu of residual payments, directors receive bonuses after the Publisher sells 150,000 units of the interactive programs. Both tiers of the DGA side-letter are subject to negotiation.

The DGA has taken the position that its members cannot work on interactive programming unless the producer signs a Guild agreement. While the WGA wants its members to work for companies that sign the WGA letter, for the time being it will allow writers to work for non-signatories under special "waiver" circumstances after the member and the Guild have exhausted all other efforts.

CONTRACTS

As previously mentioned, to resolve any doubts as to ownership of work product, a hiring party is wise to include a clause in the hiring agreement that transfers to the hiring party any rights the hired party may have. Here is one such clause:

RESULTS AND PROCEEDS OF SERVICES CLAUSE

(a) Work Made for Hire: Writer acknowledges that all results and proceeds of Writer's services (including all original ideas in connection therewith) prepared by Writer as an employee of Employer within the scope of Writer's employment shall be considered a "work made for hire" for Employer and, therefore, Employer shall be the author and copyright owner thereof for all purposes throughout the universe. In consideration of the monies paid to Writer hereunder, Employer shall solely and exclusively own throughout the universe in perpetuity, including renewal and extension periods, if any, all rights of every kind and nature, whether now or hereafter known or created, and in connection with such results and proceeds, in whatever stage of completion as may exist from time to time, including: (i) the copyright and all rights of copyright; (ii) all neighboring rights, trademarks, and any and all other ownership and exploitation rights now or hereafter recognized in any territory, including all rental, lending, fixation, reproduction, broadcasting (including satellite transmission), distribution, and all other rights of communication by any and all means, devices, and technology; (iii) the right to adapt, change, delete from and add to such results and proceeds, and to use all or any part thereof in new versions, adaptations, and other motion pictures, including remakes and sequels; (iv) the right to use the title of the Work in connection therewith or otherwise to change such title; and (v) all rights generally known as "moral rights."

(b) Assignment: If any provision in sub-section (a) above does not fully vest in Employer any of the rights set forth in subsection (a) above, Writer hereby grants and assigns to Employer all rights not so vested (and so far as may be appropriate by way of immediate assignment of future copyright) throughout the universe in perpetuity, including renewal and extension periods, if any, whether now or hereafter known or created, free from all restrictions and limitations. To the extent the rights generally known as "moral rights" may not be granted or assigned, then, to the maximum extent possible, Writer hereby irrevocably and unconditionally waives in perpetuity, including renewal and extension periods, if any, all rights under any law relating to "moral rights" or any similar law throughout the universe, or resulting from any alleged violation of such rights. Writer shall not institute any action on the ground that any changes, deletions, additions, or other uses of such results and proceeds violates such rights.

(c) Member of the Public: Nothing in this Agreement (i) shall at any time limit Employer's right to utilize freely, in any creation of production, any story, idea, plot, theme, sequence, scene, episode, incident, name, characterization, dialogue, or other material which may be in the public domain, whether included in the Work or any Writing Step or derived from any other source; or (ii) shall be construed to be prejudicial to or operate in derogation of any rights, licenses, privileges, or property which Employer may enjoy or be entitled to as a member of the public, as if this Agreement were not in existence.

(d) Vesting of Rights: All rights granted or agreed to be granted to Employer shall vest in Employer immediately without reservation, condition, or limitation and shall remain vested whether or not his Agreement is terminated for any reason, and no right of any kind, nature, or description is reserved by Writer subject only to the reservation contained in the current WGA Agreement.

(e) Further Documentation: Writer shall sign additional documentation as Employer may reasonably require in order to effectuate the purposes and intent of this Agreement. Writer irrevocably grants Employer the power coupled with an interest, with rights of substitution and delegation, to sign such further documentation in Writer's name if Writer has not complied with Employer's request within seven (7) days thereafter (or such shorter period of time as Employer shall reasonably require). If Employer signs any documents as Writer's attorney-in-fact, Employer will provide Writer with copies of any such documents.

EMPLOYMENT AGREEMENT

This Employment Agreement ("Agreement") is entered into between _____ ("Employer") and _____ ("Employee").

In consideration of the employment, or continued employment of Employee by Employer, Employer and Employee agree as follows:

1. Employment, Complete Agreement, and Modification: Employer agrees to employ, or continue to employ, Employee and Employee agrees to be employed by Employer on the terms and conditions set forth herein. This Agreement supersedes all previous correspondence, promises, representations, and agreements, if any, either written or oral. No provision of this Agreement may be modified except by a writing signed both by Employer and Employee.

2. Duties and Compensation: Employee shall perform any and all duties now and hereafter assigned to Employee by Employer, or performed by Employee whether or not assigned to Employee, for a salary as may from time to time be fixed by Employer. Employee agrees to abide by Employer's rules, regulations, and practices, including those concerning work schedules, vacation, and sick leave, as they may from time to time be adopted or modified.

3. Salary May Be Changed: Employee understands and agrees that Employee's salary may be adjusted from time to time by Employer at Employer's sole discretion without affecting this Agreement.

4. Termination of Employment: Employer, at Employer's sole option, may terminate Employee at any time with or without cause. Employer, at its option, shall provide Employee either fourteen (14) days' prior written notice of termination or a severance pay in an amount equal to Employee's salary for fourteen (14) days. Employee shall provide Employer fourteen (14) days' prior written notice of his or her termination.

5. Salary Is Full Compensation: Employee understands that Employee's salary will constitute the full and exclusive monetary consideration and compensation for all services performed by Employee and for the performance of all Employee's promises and obligations hereunder.

6. Other Compensation: Employee understands and agrees that any additional compensation to Employee (whether a bonus or other form of additional compensation) shall rest in the sole discretion of Employer and that Employee shall not earn or accrue any right to additional compensation by reason of Employee's employment.

7. Employee Benefits Plan: Employer may adopt or continue in-force benefits plans for the benefit of its employees or certain of its employees. Such benefits plans may include, as examples only, group life insurance or medical insurance. Employer may terminate any or all such plans at any time and may choose not to adopt any additional plans. Employee's rights under any benefits plans now in force or later adopted by Employer shall be governed solely by their terms.

8. Duty To Devote Full Time and To Avoid Conflict of Interest: Employee agrees that during the period of employment, Employee shall devote full-time efforts to his or her duties as an employee of Employer. During the period of employment, Employee further agrees not to (i) solely or jointly with others undertake or join any planning for or organization of any business activity competitive with the business activities of Employer's _____ Division, and (ii) directly or indirectly, engage or participate in any other activities in conflict with the best interests of Employer.

9. Information Disclosed Remains Property of Employer: All ideas, concepts, information, and written material disclosed to Employee by Employer, or acquired from a customer or prospective customer of Employer, are and shall remain the sole and exclusive property and proprietary information of Employer or such customers, and are disclosed in confidence by Employer or permitted to be acquired from such customers in reliance upon Employee's agreement to maintain them in confidence and not to use or disclose them to any other person except in furtherance of Employer's business.

10. Inventions and Creations Belong to Employer: Any and all inventions, discoveries, improvements, or creations (collectively "Creations") which Employee has conceived or made or may conceive or make during the period of employment in any way, directly or indirectly, connected with Employer's _____ Division, shall be the sole and exclusive property of Employer. Employee agrees that all copyrightable works created by Employee, or under Employer's direction in connection with Employer's business, are "works made for hire" and shall be the sole and complete property of Employer and that any and all copyrights to such works shall belong to Employer.

To the extent such works are not deemed to be "works made for hire," Employee hereby assigns all proprietary rights, including copyright, in these works to Employer without further compensation.

Employee further agrees to (i) disclose promptly to Employer all such Creations which Employee has made or may make solely, jointly, or commonly with others, (ii) assign all such Creations to Employer, and (iii) execute and sign any and all applications, assignments, or other instruments which Employer may deem necessary in order to enable it, at its expense, to apply for, prosecute, and obtain copyrights, patents, or other proprietary rights in the United States and foreign countries or in order to transfer to Employer all right, title, and interest in said Creations.

11. Confidentiality:

(a) Definition. During the term of employment with Employer, Employee will have access to and become acquainted with various trade secrets and other proprietary and confidential information which are owned by Employer and which are used in the operation of Employer's business. "Trade secrets and other proprietary and confidential information" could include: (i) software (source and object code), algorithms, computer-processing systems, techniques, methodologies, formulae, processes, compilations of information, drawings, proposals, job notes, reports, records, and specifications; and (ii) information concerning any matters relating to the business of Employer, any of its customers, customer contacts, licenses, the prices it obtains or has obtained for the licensing of its software products and services, or any other information concerning the business of the Employer and Employer's good will.

(b) No Disclosure. Employee shall not disclose or use in any manner, directly or indirectly, any such trade secrets and other proprietary and confidential information, either during the term of this Agreement or at any time thereafter, except as required in the course of employment with Employer.

12. Return of Material: Employee agrees that, upon request of Employer or upon termination of employment, Employee shall turn over to Employer all documents, discs or, other computer media, or other material in his or her possession or under his or her control that (i) may contain or be derived from ideas, concepts, Creations, or trade secrets and other proprietary and confidential information as set forth in paragraphs 9, 10 and 11 above, or (ii) connected with or derived from Employee's services to Employer.

13. Covenant Not To Compete:

(a) Restriction. Employee agrees that he or she will not, during the course of employment or for a period of _____ (___) months commencing upon the expiration of employment, voluntarily or involuntarily, directly or indirectly, anywhere in the United States, develop, or assist others to develop, software product(s) with functionality similar to the functionality of any software product(s) developed or under development by Employer's _____ Division. The term "develop software product(s)" shall mean design, create general or detailed functional or technical specifications for, create or write code for, enhance, debug or otherwise modify code for, or otherwise participate in the creation or modification of software product(s).

(b) Employee's Acknowledgments and Agreements. Employee acknowledges and agrees that the software developed by Employer's _____ Division is or is intended to be marketed and licensed to customers nationally throughout the United States. Employee further acknowledges and agrees to the reasonableness of this covenant not to compete and the reasonableness of the geographic area and duration of time which are a part of said covenant. Employee also acknowledges and agrees that this covenant will not preclude Employee from becoming gainfully employed following termination of employment with Employer.

14. Inducing Employees To Leave Employer; Employment of Employees:
Any attempt on the part of Employee to induce others to leave Employer's employ, or any effort by Employee to interfere with Employer's relationship with its other employees, would be harmful and damaging to Employer. Employee agrees that during the term of employment and for a period of _____ (___) months thereafter, Employee will not in any way, directly or indirectly, (i) induce or attempt to induce any employee of Employer to quit employment with Employer; (ii) otherwise interfere with or disrupt Employer's relationship with its employees; (iii) solicit, entice, or hire away any Employee of Employer; or (iv) hire or engage any employee of Employer or any former employee of Employer whose employment with Employer ceased less than one (1) year before the date of such hiring or engagement.

15. Non-Solicitation of Business:
For a period of _____ (_____) months from the date of termination of employment, Employee will not divert or attempt to divert from Employer any business Employer had enjoyed or solicited from its customers during the _____ (___) months prior to termination of his or her employment.

16. Remedies—Injunction: In the event of a breach or threatened breach by Employee of any of the provisions of this Agreement, Employee agrees that Employer—in addition to and not in limitation of any other rights, remedies, or damages available to Employer at law or in equity—shall be entitled to a permanent injunction in order to prevent or restrain any such breach by Employee or by Employee's partners, agents, representatives, servants, employees, and/or any and all persons directly or indirectly acting for or with Employee.

17. Severability: In the event that any of the provisions of this Agreement shall be held to be invalid or unenforceable in whole or in part, those provisions to the extent enforceable and all other provisions shall nevertheless continue to be valid and enforceable as though the invalid or unenforceable parts had not been included in this Agreement. In the event that any provision relating to the time period or scope of restriction shall be declared by a court of competent jurisdiction to exceed the maximum time period or scope such court deems reasonable and enforceable, then the time period or scope of restriction deemed reasonable and enforceable by the court shall become the maximum time period or scope.

18. Governing Law: This Agreement shall be construed and enforced according to the laws of the State of California. Both Employer and Employee consent to jurisdiction in California.

19. Arbitration: Any controversy or claim arising out of or relating to this agreement or any breach thereof shall be settled by arbitration in accordance with the Rules of the American Arbitration Association; the parties select expedited arbitration using one arbitrator, to be a disinterested attorney, as the sole forum for the resolution of any dispute between them. The venue for arbitration shall be Los Angeles, California. The determination of the arbitrator in such proceeding shall be final, binding, and non-appealable. Judgment upon the award rendered by the arbitrator may be entered in any court having jurisdiction thereof. The prevailing party shall be entitled to reimbursement for costs and reasonable attorneys' fees.

20. Agreement, Read, Understood, and Fair: Employee has carefully read and considered all provisions of this Agreement and agrees that all of the restrictions set forth are fair and reasonable and are reasonably required for the protection of the interests of Employer.

AGREED:

EMPLOYER:

_____
Signature

_____
Name

_____
Title

_____
Address

_____

_____
Date

EMPLOYEE:

_____
Signature

_____
Name

_____
Title

_____
Address

_____

_____
Date

CONSULTANT AGREEMENT

This Software Consultant Agreement ("Agreement") is entered into this _____ day of _____, 199_, by and between ABC, Inc., a corporation organized and existing under the laws of the State of California and having a principal place of business at _____ ("Client"), and XYZ, Inc., a corporation organized and existing under the laws of the State of California and having a principal place of business at _____ ("Consultant").

1. Performance by Consultant: Consultant agrees to provide consulting and software-development services (the "Services") specified in the Statement of Work attached hereto as Appendix A, as amended from time to time by Supplemental Statements of Work.

2. Payment for Services

(a) Fees, Price Protection. Client agrees to pay Consultant for the Services in accordance with the Fee Schedule set forth in the Statement of Work. The fees specified in the Statement of Work are the total fees and charges for the Services and will not be increased during the term of this Agreement except as the parties may agree in writing. Consultant represents that the price stated for the Services performed hereunder is at least as favorable as that charged to any other customer for the same or similar services.

(b) Out-of-Pocket Expenses. Consultant shall be reimbursed for all reasonable out-of-pocket expenses not exceeding a monthly allotment of $_____ per month incurred in performance of the Services. Consultant shall obtain the written approval of Client before incurring expenses in excess of the monthly allotment.

(c) Invoices. Consultant shall invoice Client monthly for Services rendered during the preceding monthly period. The invoice will detail the work performed during such period. Client will pay the invoices within thirty (30) days after receipt.

3. Obligations of Consultant

(a) Work on Client's Premises. Consultant will ensure that its employees and agents will, whenever on Client's premises, obey all reasonable instructions and directions issued by Client.

(b) Key Person. The parties agree that _____ is essential to the Services offered pursuant to this Agreement and should this person no longer be active on Client's account or be employed by Consultant for whatever reason, Client shall have the right to terminate this Agreement on thirty (30) days' written notice.

(c) Consultations, Reports. Consultant agrees to make available Consultant's representative, who shall be mutually agreed upon by Consultant and Client, for monthly meetings to review the progress of all work under this Agreement. Consultant also shall prepare and submit to Client each month a written report setting forth the status of such work in a format to be mutually agreed upon by Consultant and Client.

(d) Regeneration of Lost or Damaged Data. With respect to any data which Consultant has lost or damaged, Consultant shall, at its own expense, promptly replace or regenerate such data from Client's machine-readable supporting material, or obtain, at Consultant's own expense, a new machine-readable copy of lost or damaged data from Client's data sources.

4. Obligations of Client: Client agrees to make available to Consultant, upon reasonable notice, computer programs, data, and documentation required by Consultant to complete the Services.

5. Statements of Work

(a) In General. When required by Client, the parties shall in good faith negotiate Supplemental Statements of Work ("Supplements"), each of which upon signing shall be deemed a part of this Agreement. Supplements, which shall be entered into as required by Client, shall be substantially in the form of Appendix B hereto. Unless otherwise agreed in a Supplement, the following provisions shall govern Supplements generally:

(i) Term. In the absence of an express provision for the duration or early termination of a Supplement, such agreements shall be terminable on thirty (30) days' written notice of either party without cause.

(ii) Payment. Supplements may call for lump sum or periodic payment, or payment against performance milestones, and for compensation based on time and materials or on a fixed price.

(iii) Specifications. Supplements shall include written specifications for any computer programs and documentation to be provided thereunder.

(iv) Costs of Negotiating. In the event that the parties do not conclude negotiations for a specific Supplement, each party shall bear its respective costs relating to the negotiations unless otherwise agreed, and the progress of such efforts and discussions shall not obligate either party to the other.

(v) Other. Each Supplement may contain such additional terms and conditions as may be mutually agreed to by the parties, including by way of example and not limitation, automatic renewal terms, required supplementary documentation, further specifications, or the like.

(b) Installation and Testing. Consultant shall provide reasonable assistance to Client to facilitate Client's installation and testing of all computer programs developed under the Statement of Work or Supplements (i) against previously prepared specifications and (ii) for systems integration ("Acceptance Testing"). Acceptance Testing shall be commenced within ten (10) days of delivery and installation by Consultant of any computer program, and such computer program shall be deemed accepted when it has operated in conformity with specifications for a period of thirty (30) consecutive days ("Acceptance"). In the event that the computer program does not so perform, the period shall be extended on a day-by-day basis until such performance is achieved for thirty (30) consecutive days. If, at any time following sixty (60) days after commencement of Acceptance Testing, the computer program has not met Acceptance Testing standards, Client may terminate the Supplement.

6. Rights in Data and Works

(a) Ownership. Consultant agrees that Client is the owner of all right, title, and interest in all computer programs, including any source code, object code, enhancements and modifications, all files, including input and output materials, all documentation related to such computer programs and files, all media upon which any such computer programs, files, and documentation are located (including tapes, discs, and other storage media) and all related material that are used by, developed for, or paid for by Client in connection with the performance of any Services provided by Consultant before or after the date set forth above.

(b) Proprietary Rights. In no way limiting Section 6(a) above, Consultant agrees that all copyrights and other proprietary rights in computer programs, files, documentation, and related materials that are paid for by Client or developed by Consultant in connection with this Agreement are owned by Client and Consultant hereby assigns to Client all right, title, and interest in such copyrights and other proprietary rights.

(c) Access. Client shall have unrestricted access to all computer media containing Client data from time to time in connection with the performance of the Services. Consultant, at the request of Client, shall promptly deliver to Client all computer programs, including source code, files, media, documentation, and related materials, concerning any services provided by Consultant before or after the date of this Agreement.

7. Recruitment: Consultant and Client agree not to recruit employees who are currently employed (or who were employed in the last six (6) months) by the other party unless written permission is obtained from the other party. This provision shall remain in effect for a period of six (6) months after termination of this Agreement.

8. Warranties: Consultant warrants the following with respect to Services performed:

(a) Compliance with Specifications. Consultant's computer programs, files, documentation, and all other work product will strictly comply with the descriptions and representations as to the Services (including performance capabilities, completeness, specifications, configurations, and function) that appear in the Statement of Work or any Supplemental Statements of Work.

(b) Compliance with Specifications After Acceptance. For a period of 180 days after Acceptance pursuant to Section 5(b), any computer programs developed under this Agreement will operate in conformance with the specifications for such computer programs.

(c) Non-Infringement of Third-Party Rights. The Services will not violate or in any way infringe upon the rights of third parties, including property, contractual, employment, trade secrets, proprietary information and non-disclosure rights, or any trademark, copyright, or patent rights.

9. Termination

(a) Commencement and Renewal. This Agreement shall commence on the date set forth above and shall remain in effect for one (1) year. Thereafter, this Agreement shall be renewed automatically without interruption for successive one (1) month terms on the same terms, conditions, and prices as set forth herein. After the initial one (1) year term, either party may notify the other party, in writing, of its election not to renew, in which event this Agreement will terminate thirty (30) days after receipt of such notice. This Agreement may be renewed with revised terms, conditions, and prices only upon written agreement of both parties.

(b) Termination. Either party, upon giving written notice to the other party, may terminate this Agreement:

(i) if the other party or its employees, consultants or other agents violate any provision of this Agreement and the violation is not remedied within thirty (30) days of the party's receipt of written notice of the violation;

(ii) if at any time after the commencement of the Services, Client, in its reasonable judgment, determines that such services are inadequate, unsatisfactory, or substantially nonconforming to the specifications, descriptions, warranties, or representations contained herein and the problem is not remedied within thirty (30) days of the party's receipt of written notice describing the problem; or

(iii) at any time in the event the other party terminates or suspends its business, becomes subject to any bankruptcy or insolvency proceeding under Federal or state statute, or becomes subject to direct control by a trustee or similar authority.

In the event that any of the above events occurs to a party, that party shall immediately notify the other party of its occurrence.

(c) Obligations Upon Expiration or Termination. Upon expiration or termination of this Agreement, Consultant shall promptly return to Client all computer programs, files, documentation, media, related material, and any other material that, pursuant to Section 6 above, is owned by Client. Expiration or termination of this Agreement shall not relieve either party of its obligations regarding Confidential Information under Section 10 below.

10. Confidential Information

(a) Non-Disclosure. Each party agrees not to use, disclose, sell, license, publish, reproduce, or otherwise make available the Confidential Information of the other party except and only to the extent necessary to perform under this Agreement. Each party agrees to secure and protect the other party's Confidential Information in a manner consistent with the maintenance of the other party's confidential and proprietary rights in the information and to take appropriate action by instruction or agreement with its employees, consultants, or other agents who are permitted access to the other party's Confidential Information to satisfy its obligations under this Section.

(b) Definition. "Confidential Information" means a party's information, not generally known by non-party personnel, used by the party and which is proprietary to the party or the disclosure of which would be detrimental to the party. Confidential Information includes, but is not limited to, the following types of information (whether or not reduced to writing or designated as confidential):

(i) work product resulting from or related to Services performed under this Agreement;

(ii) a party's computer software, including documentation;

(iii) a party's internal personnel, financial, marketing, and other business information and manner and method of conducting business;

(iv) a party's strategic, operations, and other business plans and forecasts;

(v) confidential information provided by or regarding a party's employees, customers, vendors, and other contractors; and

(vi) the existence of a contractual relationship between the parties.

(c) Confidentiality Agreement With Consultant's Employees. All of Consultant's employees or agents who perform services for Client shall sign a confidentiality agreement in a form approved by Client.

11. Indemnification: Consultant agrees to indemnify and shall hold harmless (including payment of reasonable attorneys' fees) Client, its corporate affiliates, and any employee or agent thereof (each of the foregoing being hereinafter referred to individually as "Indemnified Party") against all liability to third parties (other than liability solely the fault of the Indemnified Party) arising from or in connection with the performance of Services under this Agreement. Consultant's obligation to indemnify any Indemnified Party will survive the expiration or termination of this Agreement by either party for any reason. Client shall conduct the defense of any such third-party action arising as described herein unless Consultant and Client shall mutually agree that Consultant will conduct the defense.

12. Limitation of Liability: In no event shall either of the parties hereto be liable to the other for the payment of any consequential, indirect, or special damages, including lost profits. The provisions of this Section, however, shall not apply in any way to Consultant's obligations to replace, regenerate, or obtain lost or damaged data or to indemnify any Indemnified Party.

13. Injunctive Relief: It is hereby understood and agreed that damages shall be an inadequate remedy in the event of a breach by Consultant of this Agreement and that any such breach by Consultant will cause Client great and irreparable injury and damage. Accordingly, Consultant agrees that Client shall be entitled, without waiving any additional rights or remedies otherwise available to Client at law or in equity or by statute, to injunctive and other equitable relief in the event of a breach or intended or threatened breach by Consultant.

14. Assignment

(a) Consent Required. Consultant shall not assign or subcontract the whole or any part of this Agreement without Client's prior written consent.

(b) Subcontracting. Any subcontract made by Consultant with the consent of Client shall incorporate by reference all the terms of this Agreement. Consultant agrees to guarantee the performance of any subcontractor used in performance of the Services.

15. Other Provisions

(a) Status as Independent Contractor. Consultant and Client are contractors independent of one another, and neither party's employees will be considered employees of the other party for any purpose. This Agreement does not create a joint venture or partnership, and neither party has the authority to bind the other to any third party.

(b) Applicable Law and Forum. This Agreement shall be governed and construed in accordance with the laws of the State of California without regard to the conflicts of laws or principles thereof. Any action or suit related to this Agreement shall be brought in the state or federal courts sitting in California.

(c) Notices. Any notice or other communication required or permitted under this Agreement shall be given in writing and delivered by hand or by registered or certified mail, postage prepaid and return receipt requested, to the following persons (or their successors pursuant to due notice):

If to Client: _____

If to Consultant: _____

(d) Waiver. No waiver by Client of any breach by Consultant of any of the provisions of this Agreement shall be deemed a waiver of any preceding or succeeding breach of the same or any other provisions hereof. No such waiver shall be effective unless in writing and then only to the extent expressly set forth in writing.

(e) Entire Agreement. This Agreement, including Appendices A and B, constitutes the entire agreement between Consultant and Client.

(f) Modifications. No modification of this Agreement shall be effective unless in writing and signed by both parties.

(g) Severability. If any provision of this Agreement is invalid or unenforceable under any statute or rule of law, the provision is to that extent to be deemed omitted, and the remaining provisions shall not be affected in any way.

IN WITNESS WHEREOF, and in acknowledgment that the parties hereto have read and understood each and every provision hereof, the parties have executed this Agreement on the date first set forth above.

CLIENT:

_____
Signature

_____
Name

Title
_____

Address
_____

_____

CONSULTANT:

_____
Signature

_____
Name

_____
Title

_____
Address

_____

APPENDIX A

STATEMENT OF WORK

1. Description of Services

2. Fee Schedule

APPENDIX B
SUPPLEMENTAL STATEMENT OF WORK

This Supplemental Statement of Work is entered into as of this _____ day of _____, _____ by and between ABC, Inc. ("Client") and XYZ, Inc. ("Consultant").

1. Relationship to Agreement: This Supplemental Statement of Work is subject to all the terms and conditions of the Software Consulting Agreement ("Agreement").

2. Effective Date and Term: This Supplemental Statement of Work shall be effective as of the date first written above and shall terminate on _____, or earlier, upon no less than _____ (___) days' prior notice of termination given by either party to the other for any reason. Consultant represents that the termination date above reflects its best estimate of the time required to perform under this Supplemental Statement of Work.

3. Services: Consultant shall staff this contract with the equivalent of _____ (___) full-time employees to develop and document, if required, the computer program(s) or perform the other services specified on Schedule 1 hereto. All work delivered hereunder shall meet the specifications (as defined in Schedule 1) and satisfy Acceptance Testing (as defined in the Agreement).

4. Payment: This Supplemental Statement of Work shall be payable on a time and materials or fixed-price basis as indicated in Schedule 2 hereto. Payment shall be against invoices which shall describe in reasonable detail the nature and extent of work performed during the billing period.

5. Other Provisions: Schedule 3 hereto specifies any further terms and conditions made part of this Supplemental Statement of Work.

IN WITNESS WHEREOF, and in acknowledgment that the parties hereto have read and understood each and every provision hereof, the parties have executed this Supplemental Statement of Work on the date first set forth above.

AGREED:

CLIENT:

_____
Signature

_____
Name

_____
Title

_____
Address

CONSULTANT:

_____
Signature

_____
Name

_____
Title

_____
Address

SCHEDULE 1
TO SUPPLEMENTAL STATEMENT OF WORK

SPECIFICATIONS

Specifications of computer program(s) and documentation:

SCHEDULE 2
TO SUPPLEMENTAL STATEMENT OF WORK

PAYMENT SCHEDULE

1. Price

This Supplemental Statement of Work is:

_____ a fixed-price Contract ("FP");
or

_____ a time-and-materials Contract ("T & M").

Check one line above. If FP, such price shall be $_____; if T & M, Consultant agrees that the aggregate time costs shall not exceed $_____ (at the applicable hourly rate), and materials cost will not exceed $_____.

2. Out-of-Pocket Expenses

Consultant shall be reimbursed for all reasonable out-of-pocket expenses not exceeding an allotment of $_____ per month incurred in performance of the Services. Consultant shall obtain the written approval of Client before incurring expenses in excess of this allotment.

SCHEDULE 3
TO SUPPLEMENTAL STATEMENT OF WORK

ADDITIONAL TERMS AND CONDITIONS

WORK FOR HIRE AGREEMENT
WITH INDEPENDENT CONTRACTOR (PROGRAMMER)

I. Introduction

This is a work made for hire agreement in which ABC, Inc. ("Programmer") agrees to provide programming services to XYZ, Inc. ("Company"). Company shall pay Programmer according to the payment schedule set forth in Attachment A of this contract, which is incorporated by reference herein.

II. Definitions

A. "Program" shall mean the computer program described in Attachment B to this contract, which is hereby incorporated by reference.

B. "Software Development Tools" shall mean all compilers, interpreters, linkers, routines, subroutines, and other programs that are used by the programmer to develop the program specified in this contract.

C. (Include other relevant definitions)

III. Duties

Programmer shall create a computer program and complete documentation (Program) for Company as per the specifications set forth in Attachment B to this contract, which is incorporated by reference herein.

Company shall supply Programmer all items listed in Attachment C prior to _____ , 19__.

IV. Ownership

Program is a work made for hire. Company shall be considered the author of Program under the U.S. copyright laws. The program shall be the exclusive property of Company. Consistent with Programmer's recognition of Company's complete ownership rights in Program, Programmer agrees not to use Program or any part of it, except for the material described in Section VII of this agreement, for the benefit of any party other than Company.

V. Completion Date

Programmer agrees to complete all work as per the schedule set forth in Attachment D of this contract, which is hereby incorporated by reference herein. Time is of the essence.

VI. Trade Secrets

Programmer understands that Company considers all programming to be a trade secret belonging to Company. Programmer, therefore, will neither divulge nor discuss with third parties matters relating to programs on which Programmer is working or any other programs belonging to Company without written permission of Company. In addition, Programmer agrees to sign, upon request, non-disclosure agreements relating to any aspect of Company's business.

VII. Mediation and Arbitration

If any dispute arises under the terms of this agreement, the parties agree to select a mutually agreeable, neutral third party to help them mediate it. If the mediation is unsuccessful, the parties agree that the dispute shall be decided by binding arbitration under the rules issued by the American Arbitration Association. The decision of the arbitrator shall be final. Costs and fees (other than attorneys' fees) associated with the mediation or arbitration shall be shared equally by the parties. Each party shall be responsible for his or her attorneys' fees associated with arbitration.

VIII. Property Belonging to Programmer

Company agrees that Programmer owns and retains all rights to the software and software development tools previously owned by Programmer and described in Attachment E, and Programmer agrees that company shall have an unrestricted, non-exclusive worldwide license to use such materials listed on Attachment E that are made part of Program, provided that Company shall make no other commercial use of these materials without written consent of Programmer.

IX. General Provisions

A. Programmer may neither subcontract nor hire persons to aid in the programming work without the prior written consent of Company.

B. Any modifications to this agreement must be in writing and signed by both parties.

_____

ABC, Inc.   Date

_____

XYZ, Inc.   Date

ATTACHMENT A
PAYMENT SCHEDULE

Programmer shall be paid on the first and fifteenth day of each month until the work is completed. Payment shall be $_____ per month.

ATTACHMENT B
PROGRAMMER'S DUTIES

Programmer will be responsible for:

ATTACHMENT C
COMPANY'S DUTIES

Company will be responsible for:

ATTACHMENT D
WORK SCHEDULE

ATTACHMENT E
PROPERTY OWNED BY PROGRAMMER

PRODUCTION AGREEMENT

AGREEMENT dated _____, 1997 (the "Agreement")
between _____, a _____
corporation, with its principal place of business at
_____("Provider") and
_____ a _____ corporation, with its principal place
of business at _____ ("ABC").

The parties hereto agree as follows:

1. Definitions: The following terms used in this Agreement
shall have the meanings hereinafter set forth.

(a) "ABC's Production Advance Commitment": The term
"ABC's Production Advance Commitment" means the maximum
aggregate amount of Production Cost Advances which ABC has
agreed or may agree to make.

(b) "Program": The term "Program" means (a) the specific
program(s) utilizing the Source Materials (as hereinafter defined)
and tentatively entitled "_____," and (b) all laser
interactive optical technology/systems in which the specific
program described herein is produced, converted, ported, manufactured, distributed and promoted as provided in Paragraph
14(a) below.

(c) "Disc": The term "Disc" means the Program physically
embodied on laser optical interactive software.

(d) "Completion Date": The term "Completion Date" means
the date provided in the Production and Delivery Schedule (as
hereinafter defined) for the delivery of the Master Materials (as
hereinafter defined).

(e) "Development Delivery Items": The term "Development
Delivery Items" (also referred to herein as "Blue Phase Milestones") means the items to be delivered to ABC by Provider
pursuant to paragraph 2(a) and 2(b) below, and set forth in
more detail in Exhibit A attached hereto and made a part hereof.

(f) "Development Phase": The term "Development Phase"
means the initial phase of the Production Term with respect to
the Program, sometimes referred to herein as the "Blue Phase,"
during which Provider will prepare and submit the Development
Delivery Items specified in Exhibit A hereto. The Development
Phase shall terminate upon ABC's election to proceed or not to
proceed with the production of the Program pursuant to paragraph 3 below.

(g) "Distributor": The term "Distributor" means ABC and
solely insofar as concerns Provider and Distributor (and without
thereby creating any third party beneficiary rights) any distributor, subdistributor, licensee or sublicensee of ABC.

(h) "Effective Date": The term "Effective Date" means the date of full and complete execution of this Agreement by the parties hereto.

(i) "Master Materials": The term "Master Materials" means (i) the source and object code for the Program; (ii) all audio and visual data in a format specified by ABC (including, without limitation, the Master Materials and the digitized master tapes of the Program); and (iii) all supporting documentation and items required by ABC to properly master the tape disc image as specified in Exhibit B which is attached hereto and made a part hereof. The Master Materials shall also include all rights documentation required by ABC, including, without limitation, the following: (i) All rights and releases for pre-recorded video or stock film; (ii) All rights and permission regarding the use of images scanned or otherwise digitized in the creation of graphics; (iii) Releases from all graphic artists; (iv) Talent release forms—voice and picture; (v) Synchronization rights (if any); (vi) Master music cue sheets (necessary for international distribution); (vii) All rights and releases for Source Materials and any third party characters, trademarks, trade names and/or service marks used in the Program; and (viii) A concise summary of any limitations (whether to time, place or otherwise) in connection with the foregoing rights and releases.

(j) "Production and Delivery Schedule": The term "Production and Delivery Schedule" means the time schedule for completing various steps in developing and producing the Program which schedule has been or will be prepared by Provider and approved in writing by ABC. The Production and Delivery Schedule shall be prepared in form substantially as set forth in Exhibit B which is attached hereto and made a part hereof.

(k) "Production Budget": The term "Production Budget" means the budget of costs for developing and producing the Program, which has been or will be prepared by Provider and approved in writing by ABC. The Production Budget shall be prepared in form substantially as set forth in Exhibit C which is attached hereto and made a part hereof.

(l) "Production Costs": The term "Production Costs" means the actual direct cost of developing and producing the Program and, unless otherwise expressly approved by ABC in writing, (i) shall not include any overhead or general or administrative charges or costs not specifically and directly incurred by Provider in connection with development or production of the Program, (ii) shall not include charges for salaries, payroll taxes or burden or fringe benefits of Provider's executive or managerial personnel who provide supervisorial services to Provider's development and production activities, (iii) shall not include interest, taxes, attorneys' fees, (iv) shall not include charges for rental of Provider's facilities, tools or equipment, but (v) shall include all costs and charges incurred by Provider which directly relate to the Program being produced and which are payable to unaffiliated third parties.

(m)"Production Cost Advances": The term "Production Cost Advances" means the advances of Production Costs made by ABC from time to time with respect to development and production of the Program.

(n) "Production Milestone": The term "Production Milestone" means the satisfaction of the delivery preconditions pursuant to paragraph 4 hereinbelow for each Production Cost Advance hereunder.

(o) "Production Term": The term "Production Term" means the period commencing upon the Effective Date hereof and continuing until the delivery to and acceptance by ABC of all the Master Materials for the Program produced hereunder; provided, however, that the Production Term may be terminated by ABC at the end of the Development Phase if ABC elects not to proceed with further development or production of the Program.

(p) "Program Participants": The term "Program Participants" means those key persons providing creative or production services to the production of the Program, such as producer, director, writer, composer, art director, and any featured artist, actor, actress, narrator, programmer, graphic designer and interactive designer.

(q) "Project": The term "Project" means the development and production effort relative to the Program.

(r) "Reference Rate": The term "Reference Rate" means the daily rate of interest announced by Citibank, N.A. (main New York office) as its "prime" or "reference" interest rate for unsecured loans of less than one (1) year maturity.

(s) "Rights Period": The term "Rights Period" means the period of time during which Distributor may exploit all of its rights in the Program, which period commences upon the Effective Date hereof and shall endure in perpetuity.

(t) "Source Materials": The term "Source Materials" means:

(i) Generally, the sources or subject matter upon which the Program is to be based, more specifically identified in paragraph 1(t)(ii) below.

(ii) In particular, the Source Materials shall be

_____.

(u) "Territory": The term "Territory" means the geographical area (and all political territories, possessions and military bases of the countries included in such geographical area) of the entire universe.

2. Development Phase:

(a) Blue Phase. Provider shall prepare and deliver to ABC the Development Delivery Items for the Blue Phase in accordance with the Development Budget and deliverables folder for the Blue Phase, and in accordance with the delivery and payment schedule for the Blue Phase attached hereto and incorporated herein as Exhibit A. ABC's approval of the Development Delivery Items for the Blue Phase shall not be unreasonably withheld. Unless such Development Delivery Items are approved by ABC in writing within fifteen (15) days after submission thereof to ABC, they shall be deemed disapproved. The Blue Phase shall conclude upon ABC's approval of all of the Development Delivery Items for the Blue Phase. Within sixty (60) days after the conclusion of the Blue Phase, ABC shall advise Provider whether ABC elects to proceed with production of the Program.

(c) Overbudget Costs. Provider shall complete and deliver the Development Delivery Items in strict conformity with the Production Budget as set forth in Exhibit A. Provider shall be solely responsible for any costs in excess of the Production Budget incurred in completing and delivering the Development Delivery Items.

(d) Ownership of Development Delivery Items. All of the Development Delivery Items prepared by Provider and/or Provider's employees and independent contractors shall be owned by ABC as "works made for hire." ABC shall own and Provider hereby assigns to ABC all rights of every kind or nature therein, including, without limitation, all copyrights, patents and trademarks. From time to time upon ABC's request, Provider shall execute and shall cause Provider's employees and independent contractors to execute such documents as ABC may reasonably require to evidence or effectuate ABC's rights in the Development Delivery Items, and Provider hereby irrevocably appoints ABC as its attorney-in-fact to execute on behalf of Provider any such documents which Provider may fail to execute.

3. Production Terms and Conditions:

(a) Production Budget and Delivery Schedule.

(i) Following Provider's delivery and ABC's acceptance of the Development Delivery Items, ABC will advise Provider in writing whether ABC elects to proceed with production of the Program. Before ABC's election to proceed or not to proceed with production, ABC may request Provider to modify the Production Budget and/or the Production and Delivery Schedule. If ABC o requests Provider to modify the Production Budget and/or the Production and Delivery Schedule, Provider shall promptly consult with ABC in order to modify the same to ABC's satisfaction. ABC shall notify Provider no later than thirty (30) days following the submission of any revised Production Budget and/or Production and Delivery Schedule requested by ABC whether ABC elects to proceed with the production of the Program. Upon ABC's written approval, the Production and Delivery Schedule shall become the "Approved Schedule" and the Production Budget shall become the "Approved Budget."

(ii) If ABC does not elect to proceed to production pursuant to paragraph 3(a)(i) above, ABC shall nevertheless retain all ownership of the Development Delivery Items as works made for hire and shall be free to proceed or not to proceed with the further development, production and/or distribution of the Program with no further obligation to Provider in connection therewith, and Provider shall have no obligation to repay any amounts theretofore advanced to Provider by ABC.

(b) Production Funding and Payment Schedule:

(i) ABC's Production Advance Commitment for the Program shall be such sum as ABC may approve in writing following the conclusion of the Development Phase. Provider shall contribute all of the remaining Production Costs contained in the Approved Budget and Provider shall produce the Program in accordance therewith. Subject to the provisions of paragraph 4(c) hereinbelow, the total dollar amount of Production Costs for the Program shall not exceed the Approved Budget and any Production Costs in excess of the Approved Budget shall be borne solely by Provider.

(ii) ABC's Production Cost Advance Commitment pursuant to paragraph 3(b)(i) hereinabove shall be paid to Provider in installments upon the satisfaction of the associated Production Milestones approved in writing by ABC after completion of the Development Phase.

(c) Production Cost Advances: Prior to receipt by Provider of each Production Cost Advance hereunder, Provider shall submit to ABC a complete and itemized written statement of all expenditures in accordance with the Production Budget format incurred or made by Provider constituting the Production Costs of the Program incurred to the date of each Production Milestone in accordance with the Production Budget format. Such statement shall certify that all costs so incurred by Provider have been paid in full and such certificate shall be certified as true and accurate by an officer of the Provider. If the Production Budget includes an allowance for supplies or other consumables or for use of facilities, the cost thereof shall be deemed incurred ratably over the Production Term hereunder.

(d) Program Specifications: The Program shall (i) be fully scored, edited and composed with visuals, text, music, images, graphics, sound and other audio or visual features fully synchronized, (ii) generally, when performed or played, correspond to the approved script, approved interactive design and approved storyboards, and (iii) meet the technical requirements of the designated specifications and shall be of a quality technically satisfactory for formatting on the platform(s) designated by ABC.

(e) Approval of Production Elements: Provider shall develop and submit to ABC for approval, in accordance with the Production and Delivery Schedule, the final script including, without limitation, written text, music, narration, sound effects, storyboards, the user interface, the interactive design, the source and object code, the retrieval software system, artwork and graphic design ("Production Elements") each of which shall, in general, conform to the approved outline. ABC shall have a reasonable right of approval over each Production Element hereunder, provided that if ABC disapproves any of such items and Provider is unwilling to make revisions as requested by ABC, ABC shall have the option, at ABC's sole election, to abandon the development or production of the Program, or to take over the production of the Program, at ABC's sole cost and expense and Provider shall thereupon be excused from any obligation to advance any further Production Costs hereunder. Any Program so completed by ABC shall nevertheless be marketed by ABC pursuant to the terms of this Agreement; provided, however, that the royalty payable to Provider shall be reduced by multiplying the royalties specified hereinbelow by a percentage equal to the percentage of the total production work following completion of the Development Phase successfully completed by Provider before take over or abandonment, as reasonably determined by ABC. Provider shall not be entitled to any royalty on any Program which ABC abandons or takes over before ABC's decision to proceed with production pursuant to paragraph 3(a) above.

(f) Technical Assistance: ABC shall provide Reasonable Technical Assistance required by Provider. "Reasonable Technical Assistance" as used herein means (i) providing Provider with interpretation of the so-called "Green Book" specifications or other specifications reasonably required and (ii) making available for use by Provider any unique authoring tools and/or utilities, if any, developed by or licensed to ABC; provided, however, that such use by Provider shall not violate any license between ABC and a third party.

(g) Abandonment; Postponement; Discontinuance:

(i) Notwithstanding anything to the contrary contained elsewhere in the Agreement but subject only to the provisions of subparagraph (ii) below, ABC shall have the right (in ABC's sole discretion) to abandon and/or postpone the development and/or production of the Program at any time, for any reason. ABC shall have no obligation to make, produce, distribute or exploit the Program, or, if commenced, to continue the production, distribution or exploitation of the Program. ABC shall have no obligation to use the services of Provider hereunder, and if ABC elects (in ABC's sole discretion) to discontinue the services of Provider, ABC may continue the development and/or production of the Program without Provider's further participation.

(ii) In the event of any abandonment, postponement and/or discontinuance of the Program and/or the services of Provider as provided in subparagraph (a) above, ABC will be obligated to pay Provider only for such Milestone(s) or portion(s) thereof which are completed as of the date of abandonment, postponement or discontinuance. With respect to any royalties otherwise payable to Provider pursuant to Paragraph 16 below, in the event that Provider's services are discontinued hereunder for reasons other than default or breach of this Agreement, and if ABC actually produced and distributes the Program using assets created by Provider hereunder, then Provider's royalties for the Program under Paragraph 16 hereof shall vest in the same proportion that the aggregate payments made to Provider with respect to the development and/or production of the Program prior to the date of such discontinuance bear to the total development and production budget for the Program. (For example, if the aggregate of the milestone payments made to Provider amounts to Fifty Percent (50%) to the total budget for the development and production of the Program, then provider will receive Fifty Percent (50%) of the royalties otherwise payable to Provider pursuant to Paragraph 16 below).

(iii)   Neither party shall be liable to the other for any incidental damages, consequential damages or lost profits resulting from any abandonment, postponement or discontinuance of the Program as provided hereunder, and any right to recover such incidental or consequential damages or lost profits is hereby expressly waived by both ABC and Provider.

(iv)   Upon any abandonment, postponement, or discontinuance hereunder, ABC may require Provider to return any assets created by Provider hereunder to ABC, and if ABC so requires, Provider will immediately comply.

(h) Equipment: Any equipment furnished by ABC to Provider in connection with the Production of the Program shall at all times remain the sole and exclusive property of ABC and shall be returned to ABC upon demand.

4. Progress Reports; Delivery; Completion of the Program:

(a) (i) Provider shall, on a monthly basis, provide ABC with progress reports on the development and production effort hereunder, advise ABC of the cumulative costs incurred to that date in the Production Budget Format and advise ABC of any anticipated modifications to the Approved Budget.

(ii) Within ninety (90) days following delivery of the Master Materials for the Program, Provider shall submit to ABC a full, complete, detailed and itemized written statement of all expenditures incurred or made by Provider constituting the Production Costs of the Program hereunder in accordance with the Production Budget Format. Such statement shall be certified as true and accurate by an officer of Provider. ABC shall in no event have any responsibility of any sort for any other costs that may thereafter be alleged to constitute Production Costs hereunder. The final Production Costs shown on such statement, along with the costs incurred by ABC and so certified, shall be used by the parties in determining the Production Costs to be recouped in calculating royalties payable hereunder to Provider.

(b) Provider shall, on or before the Completion Date, deliver to ABC each of the Master Materials. Delivery to ABC shall not be deemed made unless and until each of the Master Materials have been delivered to ABC. Provider shall, at all times, maintain duplicate or safety "back-up" copies of all Master Materials produced from time to time, and after proper delivery hereunder shall continue to store a duplicate of all Master Materials so delivered until advised by ABC that duplicates of such Master Materials have been made by or for ABC's benefit.

(c) Provider hereby agrees to the completion of production and delivery of the Program (hereinafter "Completion of the Program") on or before the Completion Date (subject to "Force Majeure" as specified in paragraph 8 below) in accordance with the Approved Budget and the Approved Schedule hereunder. Provider may perform Provider's obligations with respect to the Production Budget, at Provider's option, either (i) by assuming all costs in excess of the Approved Budget required to meet the costs of Completion of the Program, or (ii) by abandoning production of the Program and refunding to ABC within five (5) days of such abandonment all Production Cost Advances previously advanced, less the value of materials delivered by Provider to ABC in connection with the Program (such value to be based on Production Costs which ABC reasonably anticipates that ABC will save by using such materials in completing the Program), together with interest thereon at the Reference Rate from the date of such advance to the date of repayment of such advance, and (iii) turning over to ABC, if ABC so desires, all items necessary to complete production of the Program.

5. Accounting Records Relating to Production of Program:

(a) Provider shall keep or cause to be kept at Provider's principal place of business full and proper books of accounts, records, and contracts, together with vouchers and receipts representing production charges for the Project, which books shall be kept in accordance with generally accepted monthly accounting principles.

(b) ABC shall have the right, during reasonable business hours, until the expiration of twenty-four (24) months from delivery of the Master Materials hereunder, at ABC's expense, to examine and take excerpts from the accounts, vouchers, receipts, records and contracts maintained by Provider for the purpose of inquiring into any records or transactions relating to credits or charges, at the place where Provider maintains such books and records. In addition, all such accounts, records, contracts, vouchers and receipts shall be kept by Provider for a time period of not less than three (3) years, and ABC and all appropriate tax authorities, with ABC's consent, shall have access to such documents during such time period.

6. Confidentiality of Information: ABC and Provider shall treat all proprietary data and other information received by one from the other relating to laser optical hardware systems, software for such systems and procedures for developing such systems and software (collectively "Information"), as confidential and proprietary to such other party. Moreover, neither party shall duplicate or use any Information received from the other hereunder for any purpose other than for the Project. In addition, neither party shall disclose any Information to any party that is not specifically authorized by the other party to receive it and who has not agreed to the same obligations specified in this paragraph 6. Each party, respectively, further agrees that it will disclose the Information only on a need-to-know basis to persons known to it to be under the same obligations as set forth herein with respect to that Information. After Provider has delivered the Master Materials to ABC, Provider shall return to ABC all tangible Information provided to Provider by ABC in connection with the Project, and ABC shall return to Provider all tangible Information provided to ABC by Provider in connection with the Project.

7. Insurance:

(a) Provider shall, before the commencement of development of any Program and until delivery to ABC of the Master Materials hereunder, insure the Program against fire, theft, vandalism or other malicious mischief and other insurable risks generally covered by an extended coverage casualty policy. The cost of such insurance shall be paid by Provider, subject to reimbursement to the extent of the sum included in respect thereof in the Approved Budget.

(b) Provider shall obtain and maintain all required worker's compensation insurance, meeting the laws of the various states or countries in which Provider may have employees furnishing services with regard to the Project, for the benefit of all employees directly engaged by Provider, as well as public liability and property damage insurance relative to the acts or omissions of such employees and the condition of the premises and facilities maintained by Provider. None of the premium costs (or deductibles) of such insurance policies shall be included in the Production Costs of the Program. Provider shall indemnify, defend and hold ABC harmless from and against any and all damages, claims, actions, obligations, liabilities and expenses which may be asserted by or on behalf of any person engaged directly by Provider in connection with the Project by reason of injury or death arising out of and in the course of his/her employment, or by or on behalf of any person by reason of accident, injury, death, or property damage resulting from any negligence or fault of Provider or which is in any way connected with the preproduction or production of the Program.

(c) ABC shall obtain (or at ABC's election may request of Provider, and if Provider is so requested, Provider shall obtain) producer's errors and omission insurance against third party claims, including claims for damages for infringement of copyrights or other literary property rights, libel, slander, or any other forms of defamation, invasion of rights of privacy, unauthorized use of names, plagiarism, and similar matters. Such insurance shall be in the amount specified by ABC up to Five Million Dollars ($5,000,000.00) for any claim arising out of a single occurrence and Five Million Dollars ($5,000,000.00) for all claims in the aggregate, and shall have no exclusions and no deductible greater than Ten Thousand Dollars ($10,000.00). The premium cost of such insurance shall be charged as a Production Cost of the Program. If ABC has blanket insurance policies in force at the time of commencement of the Project and if the insurer is willing to extend coverage thereof to a Program, Provider shall accept such coverages in such amounts, with such limits of liability, and upon such terms and conditions as ABC may consider reasonable or necessary. If Provider shall desire or require insurance in excess of, or in addition to, any such insurance, Provider shall have the right (but shall not be obligated) to apply for and to procure the same at Provider's sole cost and expense and without any portion of the cost thereof being charged to ABC or Production Costs hereunder. Provider and ABC shall comply with the requirements of such insurance regarding the giving of notices and cooperating with the carrier in the defense of claims under the policy, and Provider shall maintain such insurance policy for the period ending at least five (5) years after the delivery of the Master Materials.

(d) All insurance obtained by Provider or ABC hereunder shall be for the benefit of ABC and Provider as their respective interests may appear. All policies, endorsements, and certificates relating to any insurance obtained pursuant to this Paragraph 7, shall provide for losses to be adjusted with and (with the exception of Worker's Compensation) be payable to ABC.

8. Force Majeure: Provider shall not be deemed in default hereunder and shall not be liable to ABC if and to the extent Provider is unable to commence or complete production of the Program at the times herein required by reason of fire, earthquake, flood, hurricanes, tornados (but not including any other weather conditions), epidemic, accident, explosion, casualty, strike, lockout, labor controversy, riot, civil disturbance, act of public enemy, embargo, war, act of God, any municipal, county, state or national ordinance or law, any executive or judicial order enacted or in effect, any failure of any electrical equipment of any laboratory or production facility or any failure beyond Provider's control to obtain material or power, or any other essential thing required to produce the Program or similar causes beyond Provider's control and without fault of Provider. The Completion Date may, at Provider's option, be postponed for a period equal to the period the production of the Program is prevented or delayed by reason of the occurrence of any event referred to in the foregoing sentence. If completion of production of the Program is prevented or delayed for a period of ninety (90) days or more by reason of any events referred to hereinabove, ABC may, at ABC's option, at any time thereafter, terminate any or all of ABC's obligations hereunder with respect to furnishing or causing to be furnished Production Cost Advances.

9. Defaults and Termination:

(a) Each of the following events shall constitute an "event of default" for the purposes hereof:

(i) Any material breach or default by Provider (or any affiliated person or entity); or

(ii) If the Program or any of the Master Materials relating thereto is attached or levied upon by a creditor or claimant of Provider or an affiliated person or entity of Provider, and such attachment or levy is not released within five (5) days after such levy; or

(iii) If any representation or warranty made by Provider in this Agreement proves to be false or misleading in any material manner and is not cured within ten (10) days following notice by ABC to Provider.

(b) If any event of default shall occur, ABC may (but shall not be obligated to):

(i) Suspend, or require any other party to suspend, any or all of its obligations with respect to the furnishing of Production Cost Advances;

(ii) Take over production of the Program;

(iii) Terminate any or all of ABC's obligations hereunder including, but not limited to, the furnishing of Production Cost Advances;

(iv) Offset against any sums which may then or there-after be due Provider and/or any affiliated person or entity, under this Agreement or any other agreement the full amount of such liability or any part thereof;

(v) Exercise any other available right or remedy; and/or

(vi) Enter upon any premises where the physical elements of the Program may be and take possession thereof; demand and receive possession from anyone who has possession thereof; remove, keep, and store the Program, Master Materials or any portion thereof, or put a custodian in charge thereof; and take such other measures as ABC may deem appropriate for the protection thereof including, but not limited to, the right to complete the Program and to cause it to be delivered for distribution.

(vii) All costs incurred by ABC in proceeding under this Paragraph 9 (including, without limitation, reasonable attorneys' fees) shall be added to any sums due ABC by Provider.

(c) If ABC breaches this Agreement, Provider's rights and remedies shall be limited to Provider's rights, if any, to recover damages in an action at law, and Provider shall not be entitled by reason of such breach to terminate, revoke, or rescind this Agreement or any of the rights granted to ABC, or to enjoin or restrain ABC or ABC's licensees from exercising any of the rights granted to ABC.

(d) If this Agreement is terminated, or production of the Program is abandoned for Provider's default, ABC shall be released and discharged from any liability whatsoever to Provider hereunder with respect to such Program.

(e) With respect to any breach by ABC, Provider may not exercise any remedy other than suspension of Provider's performance unless ABC fails to fully cure the breach within twenty (20) days after Provider gives written notice thereof.

(f) Neither party shall be liable to the other for any consequential damages or lost profits resulting from a breach or default, and any right to recover lost profits or consequential damages is hereby expressly waived by both ABC and Provider.

10. Right of Termination: If ABC exercises a right of termination of this Agreement pursuant to paragraph 9 hereinabove before the completion of the Production Term, then all funds advanced by ABC to Provider in connection with the development and production of the Program shall be immediately repayable by Provider to ABC, except as otherwise provided hereunder.

11. Exclusive Rights in Physical Materials: As between Distributor and Provider and subject to this Agreement, Distributor shall have full rights to use, possess and enjoy all pre-mastering and Master Materials utilized in creating the Program.

12. Publicity Rights: Provider hereby grants to Distributor for and during the Rights Period and throughout the Territory, the right to advertise and publicize and authorize others to advertise and publicize and to use, reproduce, transmit, broadcast, exploit, publicize, exhibit and control in connection with the distribution, publication, advertisement and exploitation of the Program and the Discs, the names, photographs, likenesses, voices and other sound effects (as well as recordings, transcriptions, films and other reproductions thereof) of all Program Participants appearing in or providing creative services to the production of the Program and the right to broadcast, transmit or exhibit excerpts of the Source Materials, the Program or the Discs by any means or media now known or hereafter devised including, but not limited to, radio, television, cable, videodisc, videocassette, audiodisc, whether by living actors, electrical transcriptions, film, tape, disc, cassette or otherwise in any language for the purpose of advertising, publicizing and exploiting the Program or the Discs.

13. Credits: On each Disc or unit of the Program, ABC's "bumper" (i.e., animated logo presentation sequence) and the following credits shall appear in the main titles or opening credits and the packaging of each Disc or unit of the Program: "Produced by _____ in Association with _____ Interactive Media" and "Distributed by _____ Interactive Media." The packaging of each Disc or unit of the Program may contain additional or substitute distribution credits as determined by ABC. Upon Provider's request, ABC will consult with Provider regarding credits accorded in connection with the Program and will give good faith consideration to Provider's reasonable requests. No casual or inadvertent failure by ABC or any failure by any third party to accord credit in compliance with the credit provisions hereunder shall constitute a breach of this Agreement.

14. Grant of Rights; Copyright Ownership, Protection and Enforcement:

(a) Provider acknowledges that as between ABC and Provider, (i) Provider owns all right, title and interest in and to the Source Materials, including, without limitation, the copyrights therein throughout the world; and (ii) ABC shall own all right, title and interest in and to all Development Delivery Items and all tools, utilities, design processes, software systems, source and object codes, program logic, interactive program structures, retrieval software systems, user interface designs and other procedures and methods of operation which are utilized in connection with the Program, including, without limitation, the copyrights therein throughout the world. Provider hereby grants to ABC a non-exclusive, perpetual license throughout the Territory to any and all components, routines, sub-routines, mathematical techniques, programs, modules and effects currently owned by Provider and used in the development and production of the Development Delivery Items described herein. ABC shall further own all right, title and interest in and to the Program including, without limitation, the copyrights therein throughout the world. Without limiting the foregoing, Provider grants to ABC the exclusive right during the Rights Period to develop, produce, reproduce, manufacture, convert, distribute, perform, display, promote, advertise, market, sell, rent and exploit the Program, the Discs or the Source Materials (and any foreign and/or dual language versions, edited versions and other derivative or new versions of the Program or Discs) in all configurations in all languages for all laser interactive optical technology/systems, and all forms of interactive television and/or video-on-demand, whether such configurations and/or technology/systems are now known or hereafter developed throughout the Territory under whatever title(s) ABC may designate and the right, license and authority to sub-license any of the aforementioned rights.

(b) ABC shall own all right, title and interest in and to the results and proceeds of the services of Provider and Provider's employees and independent contractors in connection with the Program (including, without limitation, the copyright thereof as a "work made for hire" within the meaning of the 1976 Copyright Act of the United States). Provider hereby waives any so-called "moral rights" of authors which are now or may hereafter be recognized by custom, usage or law. Provider shall cause all of Provider's employees and independent contractors who render services in connection with the Program to execute written "work made for hire" agreements in a form satisfactory to ABC and shall deliver copies of such agreements to ABC together with the Master Materials.

(c) ABC shall cause the due and timely registration of

copyright throughout the Territory of the Program. Copyright registration of the Program and notices on each unit of Disc or Program shall be in ABC's name unless such registration and/or notices are customarily done in the name of the individual distributor or licensee in such territory. Distributor and ABC agree to take all reasonable action to instruct third party licensees, subdistributors and others authorized to exploit the Program to comply with all copyright notice and registration requirements and further agree to refrain from taking any action and from authorizing others to take action, which would cause or allow the Program to become part of the public domain in the United States or in any other country of the world adhering to either or both the Berne Convention or the Universal Copyright Convention, provided that ABC shall have no liability arising from any inadvertent failure to take such action.

(d) Distributor shall have full and complete authority, either in the name of ABC and Provider or otherwise as Distributor deems appropriate, to take such steps (including but not limited to the placement on the Program and/or the packaging thereof a warning that piracy of the Program is prohibited under local law) as Distributor (or Distributor's licensee) deems appropriate by action at law, or otherwise, to prevent unauthorized replication, manufacture and/or distribution of the Program in the Territory or any infringement upon the rights of ABC or Provider in the Program; and Distributor or Distributor's nominee may, as ABC's and Provider's attorney-in-fact, execute, acknowledge, verify and deliver all pleadings and/or instruments pertaining thereto in the name of and on behalf of ABC and Provider as Distributor deems appropriate. Distributor may (but shall not be obligated to) take such steps as Distributor shall deem appropriate, by action at law, or otherwise, to recover monies due with respect to the distribution or exhibition of the Discs or Program. Any and all recoveries from any such action shall be applied first to recover all expenses incurred in such action and the balance (after paying to the licensee for such territory such amount as Distributor is contractually obligated to pay such licensee) shall be divided equally between ABC and Provider.

15. Sales Policies:

(a) Distributor may exploit and distribute the Discs or Program and exercise any and all rights herein granted, in accordance with such sales or rental methods, policies, practices and terms as it may determine in its discretion. Distributor may adjust and increase or decrease any allowances to any published prices; allow reasonable "free goods" whether on a regular or special promotion basis; permit reasonable returns for any reason; license the distribution of the Discs or Program for a particular country (other than the United States, Canada, Great Britain, France, Germany, Spain, Italy, Japan or Australia) on a flat sum basis; license the distribution of the Discs or Program upon a percentage of receipts, royalty, or flat amount per unit; bundle, sell or license the Discs or Program together with other discs or separately, as it shall deem desirable; and refrain from distribution in any place at any time, as Distributor, in Distributor discretion, may elect. Distributor shall be obligated to deal with related persons and entities on a good faith, arm's-length basis.

(b) Distributor has not made any express or implied representation, warranty, or agreement as to the amount of royalties or receipts which shall be derived from the distribution of the Discs or Program, nor has Distributor made any express or implied representation, warranty, or agreement that there will be any royalties or other sums payable to Provider, or that the Discs or Program will be favorably received by retailers or the public. Neither party shall incur any liability hereunder based upon any claim that either party has failed to realize revenues or to effectuate sales which should have been realized.

(c) Provider acknowledges that ABC may distribute other discs in competition with the Discs or Program and shall be under no duty to avoid competing products, or to expend the same promotional efforts for and on behalf of the Discs or Program as Distributor's expends for other discs, irrespective of the similarity of potential market. Whenever a licensee pays for the right to manufacture and distribute a number of discs, including the Discs or Program, under an agreement which does not specify what portion of the license payments apply to each of the respective discs in the group, Distributor may, in good faith, allocate to the Discs or Program for the purpose hereof, such portion of such total license payment as Distributor may in good faith consider proper. ABC has no obligation to actually produce or release the Program or to actually use any of the Source Materials in connection therewith.

16. Royalties:

(a) In full consideration of all services rendered and expenses incurred by Provider hereunder and all rights granted to ABC by Provider hereunder, and conditioned upon Provider's full performance of Provider's material obligations, and provided Provider is not in material breach or default of this Agreement, ABC agrees to pay Provider the following royalties in connection with the marketing and distribution of Discs or Program:

(i)   ABC shall pay to Provider, as full compensation for the rights granted herein, a royalty of ____ Percent (_%) of the Wholesale Price (as hereinafter defined) with respect to each Disc sold by ABC and/or its designees, paid for and not returned in the United States ("U.S. Royalty").

(ii) The foreign royalty payable to Provider for the Discs or Program sold outside the United States shall be equal to the published price to dealer (net of "free goods") in the applicable country of the Territory outside the United States multiplied by one-half (1/2) of the applicable U.S. royalty rate provided in sub-paragraph 16(a)(i) above.

(iii) ABC shall have the right hereunder to sell each Disc "bundled" with the sale of ABC's or other hardware manufacturer's players. If ABC negotiates an agreement to "bundle" the Discs or Program with players, Provider and ABC shall be entitled to a royalty equal to one-half (1/2) of the otherwise applicable royalty.

(iv) If ABC exercises ABC's right to rent the Discs or Program hereunder, or to exploit the Program in any form of interactive television or video-on-demand, ABC and Provider shall negotiate in good faith the royalties payable to Provider with respect thereto; provided, however, that Provider hereby agrees to accept a royalty arrangement which provides that Provider shall receive no less than a percentage of the net revenues retained by ABC from the rental or other exploitation of the Discs or Program hereunder equal to the percentage royalty which would have been applicable in the event of a sale.

(v) Provider hereby agrees that Provider shall be solely responsible for all accountings and payments to any and all third party royalty participants with whom Provider has contracted and who are entitled to compensation based on exploitation of the Program out of Provider's share of royalties hereunder.

(vi) Notwithstanding any of the foregoing, in the event of Scrap, Budget, or Mid-Priced sales of Discs hereunder, the applicable percentage royalty rate as defined in Paragraph 16(a) hereof shall be modified as follows:

Reduction in Paragraph 16(a)
Rate Scrap Sales 100%
Budget Sales 50%
Mid-Price Sales 25%

Scrap or Budget sales will only be made in order to liquidate existing inventory or in the event that continuing sales of the Discs are less than 100 units per month.

For purposes of the foregoing table, "Scrap Sales" shall mean Discs furnished free to users or sold as scrap or "cut-outs" at prices equal to or less than 33-1/3% of the Wholesale Price, and on Discs furnished on a so-called "no charge" basis to distributors, subdistributors, dealers or others; "Budget Sales" shall mean the sale or license of Discs at prices equal to or less than 50% (but more than 33-1/3%) of the Wholesale Price; and "Mid-Price Sales" shall mean the sale or license of Discs at prices equal or less than 66-2/3% (but more than 50%) of the Wholesale Price.

(b) The term "Wholesale Price" as used herein shall mean the published price to dealer (net of "free goods") for the Discs or Program sold to dealers.

17. Royalty Statements: Within sixty (60) days after the end of each calendar quarter, subject to delay on account of events or circumstances beyond ABC's control, ABC shall send Provider statements showing, in summary form, (i) the net number of the units of the Program reported to ABC during the period as having been sold (whether or not actually sold during that accounting period), and (ii) the royalties, if any, due with respect to such units of the Program for the accounting period covered by such statement. All statements may be submitted on a billings or collections basis as ABC may from time to time elect, and if such statements are changed from one basis to another, such statements may thereafter be amended to reflect adjustments by reason thereof. If the statements are submitted on a billings basis, ABC may either establish reasonable reserves (as established by Distributor) for unpaid units, or charges against sales and bad debts as they are recognized. Should ABC make any overpayment for any reason, ABC shall have the right to deduct and retain an amount equal to any such overpayment from any sums that may thereafter become due or payable to Provider or for Provider's account, and/or may demand repayment from Provider, in which event Provider agrees to repay the same when such demand is made. No royalties shall be payable on employee sales. Any amounts payable to Provider pursuant to any such statement shall be payable simultaneously with the rendering of such statement, subject to any provision in this Agreement relieving ABC from such obligation; provided, however, that all amounts payable to Provider hereunder shall be subject to all laws and regulations now or hereafter in existence requiring or permitting the deduction or withholding of payment for taxes or other amounts payable by, or assessable against, Provider. Provider shall make and prosecute any and all claims which it may have with respect to the same directly with the governmental agency having jurisdiction in the premises. Notwihstanding any sub-license or distribution arrangement, Provider will look solely to ABC to perform all obligations undertaken by ABC or its designee pursuant to this Agreement, including the payment of all royalties. At ABC's election, however, ABC may cause a third party to perform its obligation to account to Provider as provided in paragraphs 17, 18 and 19 hereof.

18. Accounting Records and Audit Rights Relating to Distribution of Discs or Program: ABC shall keep reasonably adequate books of account relating to the distribution of the Discs or Program. With twenty (20) days written notice to ABC, Provider may, at Provider's own expense, audit the applicable records at the place where ABC maintains the same in order to verify royalty statements hereunder. Any such audit shall be conducted only by a certified public accountant during business hours and in such manner as not to interfere with ABC's normal business activities. A copy of all reports made by Provider's accountant pursuant to any such audit shall be delivered to ABC at the same time such reports are delivered to Provider. No audit with respect of any royalty statements shall commence later than twelve (12) months from the date of the royalty statement on which the audited matter is initially reflected; nor shall any audit continue for longer than such time reasonably necessary to complete it; nor shall audits be made hereunder more frequently than once in any year; nor shall the records supporting any royalty statement be audited more than once. Provider shall be forever barred from maintaining or instituting any action or proceeding in any way relating to any transactions had by Distributor in connection with the Discs or Program and the accounting embraced in any statement or account delivered hereunder, and such statements and accounts shall be final and binding on Provider, unless written objection thereto is given to ABC within said twelve (12) month period and such action or proceeding is commenced within twenty-four (24) months after the date of the subject statement. The right to examine books of account and other documents herein granted to Provider may only be exercised by Provider with respect to the Discs or Program, and Provider shall have no right to inspect or examine the books of account or any other documents with respect to any other discs distributed by ABC.

19. Foreign Currency: Foreign receipts shall be converted to United States Dollars at the same rate at which such funds were actually converted into and received by ABC in the United States in U.S. dollars. Provider's pro rata portion of foreign currency conversion and transmission charges will be deducted from the royalty otherwise payable.

20. Supplemental Documents; Power of Attorney: Provider will execute, acknowledge and deliver such instruments as ABC may request to evidence, maintain, effectuate, or defend any and all of the rights granted to ABC under this Agreement. If Provider shall fail to execute, acknowledge or deliver to ABC any such instrument, ABC is irrevocably appointed Provider's attorney-in-fact, with full right and authority to execute, acknowledge and deliver the same in the name and on behalf of Provider. Provider agrees that such authority and agency is a power coupled with a pecuniary interest and shall survive the dissolution or other cessation of existence of Provider.

21. Representations and Warranties:

(a) ABC and Provider each represent and warrant that it is duly organized, validly existing and in good standing under the laws of its state of incorporation and is qualified to do business in any state or country where such qualification is necessary; that it has full right, power, and authority to enter into and perform this Agreement, and to grant all of the rights granted and agreed to be granted pursuant hereto; that it has taken all necessary action to authorize the execution and performance of this Agreement; and that the same does not and will not violate or require any consent under any provision of its charter documents, or of any agreement or instrument to which it is a party or by which a material part of its assets are bound, nor will such execution or performance violate any judgment or decree by which it is bound.

(b) Provider further represents and warrants to ABC as follows:

(i) That Provider has not assigned or otherwise transferred and will not assign or otherwise transfer to any person or entity, any right, title or interest in or to the Source Materials, the Program, the Discs or any part thereof;

(ii) That Provider shall, on or before the Completion Date have paid or made adequate provision for payment of all known bills and other sums payable or due as a result of the production of the Program including, without limitation, all contributions made to any collective bargaining unit, or health or welfare fund administered by any such entity, except to the extent that Provider is contesting such obligation in good faith and no lien or security interest has attached or will attach to the Program or the Discs as a consequence of non-payment, nor will ABC be deemed to have assumed any legal responsibility for payment of such sums by ABC's exercise of the rights granted hereunder;

(iii) That Provider owns all necessary rights, including, without limitation, all such rights in all applicable copyrights, trademarks, trade names, titles and similar rights, in and to the Source Materials furnished by Provider to grant ABC the rights granted to it under this Agreement, without payment of any additional sums therefor by Provider or ABC;

(iv) That there are and shall be no claims, demands, liens, encumbrances or rights of any kind in the Source Materials furnished by Provider, Program, the Discs or any part thereof, or the copyright therein resulting from any act or omission by Provider, which can or will impair or interfere with the rights of ABC and that nothing contained in the Source Materials furnished by Provider nor any use thereof by ABC permitted hereunder will violate any right of any third party;

(v) That Provider owns all necessary rights in all music and lyrics used in the Program, including, without limitation, not less than a good and valid synchronization license in customary form issued by the copyright proprietor of such music and/or lyrics, or his/her agent or trustee, in each case together with the nonexclusive, irrevocable right to publicly perform such music and lyrics in the advertising, display or promotion of the Program or the Discs and the right to make and sell copies of the Program or the Discs in the United States without payment of any additional sums by Provider or Distributor and the right to perform publicly such music and lyrics outside the United States, subject only to clearance by applicable performing rights societies in accordance with their customary practices and payment of their customary fees and the right to produce and sell copies of the Program or the Discs without payment of any additional sums by Provider or Distributor;

(vi) That Provider owns all necessary rights in (or licenses to) all previously trademarked characters, logos, captions or slogans, used in or appearing on the Program and/or the Discs or its packaging, without payment of any additional sums therefor by Provider or ABC.

22. Indemnity: Each party shall indemnify, defend and hold harmless the other party from and against any and all loss, cost, damage, liability, expense, claim, demand, suit or action (including reasonable attorneys' fees) (collectively "Claims") arising in connection with a breach by it of this Agreement. If any claim, suit, action or demand shall be asserted, made or brought against the indemnitee alleging facts which, if true, would constitute a breach by the indemnitor hereunder, or involving any matter connected with the Program caused by or under the control of the indemnitor, the indemnitor shall, at its expense, cause counsel reasonably satisfactory to the indemnitee to defend such claim or action. If ABC is the indemnitee, ABC shall have the right at its election to withhold payment of any monies otherwise payable to Provider in an amount reasonably related to the claim and potential liability, provided that ABC shall not withhold such monies, if and to the extent that Provider provides ABC with a surety bond issued by a company and in a form satisfactory to ABC. Any amount withheld shall be released if a proceeding with respect to the subject claim is not commenced within eighteen (18) months following the commencement of the applicable withholding. The foregoing does not limit ABC's right to recommence withholding at any time if a proceeding is subsequently commenced. No settlement of any such action shall be made by the indemnitor without the indemnitee's express approval. The foregoing indemnification shall not diminish rights set forth elsewhere in this Agreement relative to a default or breach.

23. Notices:

(a) All notices and accounting statements delivered hereunder shall be given in writing and sent to the other party at the addresses specified below:

TO PROVIDER: TO ABC:

(b) Any notice to be served hereunder shall be deemed to have been served in the case of delivery on the day of delivery; in the case of service by certified mail within ten (10) working days from the day it was posted; and in the case of a telex or facsimile transmission on the date of transmission of the notice. Any notice given in any other manner shall be effective only when actually received.

24. Assignment: Neither party hereto shall assign or otherwise transfer all or any of its rights hereunder without the consent of the other party, except that ABC shall have the right to assign or otherwise transfer all or any of ABC's rights hereunder to any parent, affiliate, subsidiary or successor to substantially all of its capital stock or business assets, or company into which ABC merges, all without the consent of Provider. Provider shall not have the right to and shall not sell, assign, transfer or hypothecate (collectively "assign") all or any part of Provider's right to receive royalties, at any time, while Provider is indebted to ABC or while any advances hereunder including, without limitation, Production Cost Advances, have not as of yet been recouped by ABC pursuant to the terms of this Agreement. In all events, any assignment shall be subject to all of ABC's rights hereunder. No assignment shall relieve Provider of any obligation to ABC pursuant to this Agreement. ABC's obligation to pay royalties to an assignee in accordance with any such assignment shall be further conditioned upon receipt of written notice of irrevocable authority in form satisfactory to ABC and executed by Provider. ABC's payment in accordance with any such assignment shall be deemed to be the equivalent of payment to Provider hereunder. Subject to the foregoing, this Agreement shall be binding upon and inure to the benefit of the parties hereto and their respective legal successors and assigns.

25. Arbitration: With respect to any dispute or disagreement between the parties arising out of or in connection with this Agreement, the parties shall make a good faith effort to resolve that dispute by discussions between them. If they are unable to resolve that dispute or disagreement within forty-five (45) calendar days after one party has given the other notice of such dispute or disagreement, then the dispute or disagreement may, upon written demand of either party, be settled by binding arbitration pursuant to the Rules of the Southern California

Chapter of the American Arbitration Association. Arbitration shall take place in Los Angeles County, California and both parties consent to the in personam jurisdiction of the federal and state courts of such County. An award of arbitration may be entered as a judgment in any court having jurisdiction in the matter, or application may be made to such a court for acceptance of the award and for an order of enforcement as the case may require. Each party shall bear its own costs and expenses of the arbitration and one-half (1/2) of the arbitrator's fees and costs, subject to such a different award as the arbitrator may make.

26. Miscellaneous: Nothing contained herein shall constitute a partnership between or joint venture by the parties or constitute either party the agent of the other. Neither party shall hold itself out contrary to the terms of this Paragraph 26 and neither party shall become liable by any representation, act or omission of the other contrary to the provisions hereof. This Agreement is not entered into for the benefit of any third party and shall not be deemed to give any right or remedy to any such party whether or not referred to herein. No waiver by either party hereto of any breach of this Agreement shall be deemed to be a waiver of any preceding or succeeding breach of the same or any other provision hereof. The exercise of any right granted to either party hereunder shall not operate as a waiver. No remedy or election hereunder shall be deemed exclusive but shall, whenever possible, be cumulative with all other remedies at law or in equity. This Agreement shall be construed and interpreted pursuant to the laws of the State of California applicable to agreements entered into and fully performed in California. If any provision hereof is deemed to be unenforceable as written it shall be modified so as to make it in its general interest, enforceable and as so modified shall form part of this Agreement. Nothing contained herein shall be construed to require the commission of any act contrary to law, and whenever there is any conflict between any provision of this Agreement and any material statute, law or ordinance the latter shall prevail, but in such event the provision of this Agreement affected shall be curtailed and limited only to the extent necessary to bring it within the legal requirements. This Agreement and the schedules, exhibits and attachments hereto constitute the entire Agreement and supersedes and cancels all prior negotiations, undertakings and agreements, both oral and written, between the parties with respect to the subject matter hereof and shall be binding only when executed by bot parties hereto. No officer, employee or representative of either party has any authority to make any representation or promise not contained in this Agreement and neither party has executed this Agreement in reliance on any such representation or promise. No waiver, modification or cancellation of any term or condition of this Agreement shall be effective unless executed in writing by an authorized representative of the party charged therewith. If this Agreement is executed in counterparts, such counterparts shall constitute one and the same instrument.

IN WITNESS WHEREOF, the parties hereto have executed this Agreement by their respective officers, thereunto duly authorized, as of the day and year first above written.

_____

("Provider")

By: _____

Its: _____

_____

ALPHA BETA COMPANY ("ABC")

By: _____

Its: _____

EXHIBIT A

EXHIBIT B

EXHIBIT C

PRODUCTION BUDGET FORMAT

Attached is a Production Budget which ABC has created to monitor and track the production of the Program. ABC requests that you use this format.

This budget is not all encompassing in terms of every single item that may go into the production of the Program. However, the major categories and budget items are listed. Each program has specific and unique requirements and this particular budget model is designed so that it can be used as a template which can be molded to meet the exact needs of the Program.

This budget has been integrated into a computer spreadsheet type program and this software template is available from ABC. This particular budget style was adopted because it can provide an easy to use format that can be readily updated and monitored.

In addition to the standard type of budget tracking, this format also includes the following features:

• Comparison of the amount budgeted for a given category vs. the actual amount spent in that category by month.

• Summary of the cumulative budget as a percentage of the total budget.

• Summary of the actual amount of cumulative dollars spent as a percentage of the total budget.

ABC will also be adding another component to this format which will allow for a comparison of the cumulative amount of money spent versus progress in the production as expressed by the Production Milestones noted in the Exhibit B, Production and Delivery Schedule.

CHAPTER 4

SUBMISSION OF MATERIAL

When submitting ideas, proposals, or other information of value to others, multimedia producers should take care to protect their rights in the material. Conversely, there are dangers to avoid when accepting material from others.

PROTECTING YOUR INTERESTS WHEN SUBMITTING MATERIALS

There are several measures you can take to protect your rights before submitting material. First and foremost, you should study the company or person you are considering submitting material to. Is this an appropriate company to submit to? If you have developed a children's CD-ROM program, is this a publisher in that business? If yes, does the company have a directly competing product that might pose a conflict of interest? What is the reputation of the company? Have developers complained of being "ripped off?" Has this company been repeatedly sued for infringing the rights of others? Does the company require you to sign a submission release with onerous terms?

If your material is a story or other material eligible for a copyright, you should register the work with the copyright office before you submit it to others.

If you want to protect an invention eligible for a patent, you should apply for one. You will need to file an application within one year from the date that the invention is either in public use, on sale in the U.S.A., described in a printed publication, or patented in a foreign country. Trade secrets can be protected by having the person to whom you are submitting material sign a non-disclosure or confidentiality agreement.[1] Chapter 7 provides details as to how to protect your rights under copyright, trademark, patent, and trade secret law.

You can also protect your rights under the principles of contract law. Material not protected under copyright, trademark, patent, or trade secret law, can be protected if parties enter into an agreement that provides protection to the submitting party. The most enforceable type of contract is one that is in writing, signed by both parties. However, a fledgling developer who approach a successful publisher may not have the clout to insist upon a written agreement. Indeed, a fledgling developer may have difficulty gaining access to a large publisher under any conditions, and the publisher may insist on a submission release before it is willing to accept material for review. Some companies have a policy of not accepting unsolicited materials.[2]

A more viable alternative might be for the developer to protect himself with an oral agreement. The developer would begin the meeting stating, "Before I present my proposal, I want to make sure you understand that I am presenting this proposal with the understanding that if you decide you want to use it, I expect to receive reasonable compensation for it." If the publisher responds by nodding his head "Yes," or saying "Of course," the parties have a deal. If the publisher does not agree to those terms, the developer should not submit the proposal. If a developer communicates with a publisher by correspondence, he can enter into the same agreement with a properly worded submission letter. A sample submission letter is printed at the end of this chapter.

A major drawback of an oral contract is that the party seeking to enforce the contract may have difficulty proving the terms of the agreement.[3] That is why it is a good idea to have a witness or some documentation as evidence of what the parties agreed to. The developer could bring a colleague, agent, or associate along to a meeting. After the meeting, the developer could mail a letter to the publisher that reiterates the oral understanding. The letter could simply state, "It was a pleasure meeting with you to discuss my proposal about. . . . As we agreed, if you decide you would like to publish this material, you agree to pay me reasonable compensation." If the terms set forth in the developer's letter are not disavowed by the publisher, the letter could be used as evidence of an agreement.[4]

But what if a publisher doesn't steal your proposal but discloses it to a third party who uses it? You can protect yourself against this eventuality by saying, "I am presenting my proposal with the understanding that you will keep it confidential and will not tell it to anyone else without my prior permission." If the publisher agrees, you have a deal, and you can sue for breach of contract if he discloses it to another.

PROTECTING YOURSELF WHEN ACCEPTING MATERIAL TO REVIEW

For a moment, let us wear the other hat. Now you are the recipient of information. You are concerned that by reviewing some third party's proposal you may obligate yourself. What if a proposed program is remarkably similar to one you are already developing? What if you like the proposal but do not have confidence that the person submitting it can successfully execute it? What if the terms demanded are unacceptable?

Now you want to qualify prospective submissions. Is this person who wants to submit material to you someone you might want to do business with? What is his track record? Can he fulfill his end of the bargain in a timely manner? Will a meeting with him, or reviewing his proposal, be a waste of time and expose you to a potential lawsuit for misappropriation?

To protect yourself, you may want to screen your mail and return unsolicited proposals without opening the envelopes they arrive in. Or you may require people who want to submit material to you to sign a written submission release, making it more difficult for them to claim infringement. A sample release is printed at the end of this chapter.

SUBMISSION LETTER

[Date]

ABC Publisher
39 Electronic Way
Any City, CA

Re:

Dear Ms. _____:

The enclosed proposal "_____ ," is being submitted to you with the understanding that if you further develop and/or publish it, I will receive reasonable and customary compensation as the developer of the program.

Moreover, the material is being submitted in confidence with the understanding that it will not be disclosed to others without my prior permission.

Thank you.

Sincerely,

Diane Developer

SUBMISSION RELEASE

_____ , 199__

David Developer
12 Development Lane
Hollywood, CA

Dear Mr. Developer:

I am submitting the enclosed material ("said material")
_____ to you.

The material is submitted on the following conditions:

1.   I acknowledge that because of your position in the enter-
tainment/multimedia industry you receive numerous unsolicited
submissions of ideas, formats, stories, suggestions, and the like
and that many such submissions received by you are similar to
or identical to those developed by you or your employees or
otherwise available to you. I agree that I will not be entitled to
any compensation because of the use by you of any such similar
or identical material.

2.   I further understand that you would refuse to accept and
evaluate said material in the absence of my acceptance of each
and all of the provisions of this agreement. I shall retain all rights
to submit this or similar material to persons other than you. I
acknowledge that no fiduciary or confidential relationship now
exists between you and me, and I further acknowledge that no
such relationships are established between you and me by
reason of this agreement or by reason of my submission to you
of said material.

3.   I request that you read and evaluate said material with a
view to deciding whether you will undertake to acquire it.

4.   I represent and warrant that I am the author of said material, having acquired said material as the employer-for-hire of all
creators thereof; that I am the present and sole owner of all
right, title, and interest in and to said material; that I have the
exclusive, unconditional right and authority to submit and/or
convey said material to you upon the terms and conditions set
forth herein; that no third party is entitled to any payment or
other consideration as a condition of the exploitation of said
material.

5.   I agree to indemnify you from and against any and all
claims, expenses, losses, or liabilities (including, without limitation, reasonable attorneys' fees and punitive damages) that may

be asserted against you or incurred by you at any time in connection with said material, or any use thereof, including without limitation those arising from any breach of the warranties and promises given by me herein.

6.   You may use, without any obligation or payment to me, any of said material which is not protected as literary property under the laws of plagiarism, or which a third person would be free to use if the material had not been submitted to him or had not been the subject of any agreement with him, or which is in the public domain. Any of said material which, in accordance with the preceding sentence, you are entitled to use without obligation to me is hereinafter referred to as "unprotected material." If all or any part of said material does not fall within the category of unprotected material, it is hereinafter referred to as "protected material."

7.   You agree that if you use or cause to be used any protected material provided and it has not been obtained from, or independently created by, another source, you will pay or cause to be paid to me an amount which is comparable to the compensation customarily paid for similar material.

8.   I agree to give you written notice by registered mail of any claim arising in connection with said material or arising in connection with this agreement, within 60 calendar days after I acquire knowledge of such claim, or of your breach or failure to perform the provisions of this agreement, or if it be sooner, within 60 calendar days after I acquire knowledge of facts sufficient to put me on notice of any such claim, or breach or failure to perform; my failure to so give you written notice will be deemed an irrevocable waiver of any rights I might otherwise have with respect to such claim, breach, or failure to perform. You shall have 60 calendar days after receipt of said notice to attempt to cure any alleged breach or failure to perform prior to the time that I may file a Demand for Arbitration.

9.   In the event of any dispute concerning said material or concerning any claim of any kind or nature arising in connection with said material or arising in connection with this agreement, such dispute will be submitted to binding arbitration. Each party hereby waives any and all rights and benefits which he or it may otherwise have or be entitled to under the laws of the State of _____ to litigate any such dispute in court, it being the intention of the parties to arbitrate all such disputes. Either party may commence arbitration proceedings by giving the other party written notice thereof by registered mail and proceeding thereafter in accordance with the rules and procedures of the American Arbitration Association. The arbitration shall be conducted in the County of _____ , State of _____ ,

and shall be governed by and subject to the laws of the State of
_____ and the then-prevailing rules of the Ameri-
can Arbitration Association. The arbitrators' award shall be final
and binding and a judgment upon the award may be enforced
by any court of competent jurisdiction.

10. I have retained at least one copy of said material, and I
release you from any and all liability for loss or other damage to
the copies of said material submitted to you hereunder.

11. Either party to this agreement may assign or license its or
their rights hereunder, but such assignment or license shall not
relieve such party of its or their obligations hereunder. This
agreement shall inure to the benefit of the parties hereto and
their heirs, successors, representatives, assigns and licensees,
and any such heir, successor, representative, assign or licensee
shall be deemed a third-party beneficiary under this agreement.

12. I hereby acknowledge and agree that there are no prior or
contemporaneous oral agreements in effect between you and
me pertaining to said material, or pertaining to any material
(including, but not limited to, agreements pertaining to the
submission by me of any ideas, formats, plots, characters, or the
like). I further agree that no other obligations exist or shall exist
or be deemed to exist unless and until a formal written agreement has been prepared and entered into by both you and me,
and then your and my rights and obligations shall be only such
as are expressed in said formal written agreement.

13. I understand that whenever the word "you" or "your" is
used above, it refers to (1) you, (2) any company affiliated with
you by way of common stock ownership or otherwise, (3) your
subsidiaries, (4) subsidiaries of such affiliated companies, (5)
any firm, person, or corporation to whom you are leasing
production facilities, (6) clients of any subsidiary or affiliated
company of yours, and (7) the officers, agents, servants, employees, stockholders, clients, successors, and assigns of you, and of
all such person and corporations referred to in (1) through (6)
hereof. If said material is submitted by more than one person,
the word "I" shall be deemed changed to "we," and this agreement will be binding jointly and severally upon all the persons
so submitting said material.

14. Should any provision or part of any provision be void or
unenforceable, such provision or part thereof shall be deemed
omitted, and this agreement with such provision or part thereof
omitted shall remain in full force and effect.

15. This agreement shall be governed by the laws of the State of _____ applicable to agreements executed and to be fully performed therein.

16. I have read and understand this agreement, and no oral representations of any kind have been made to me, and this agreement states our entire understanding with reference to the subject matter hereof. Any modification or waiver of any of the provisions of this agreement must be in writing and signed by both of us.

Sincerely,

_____
Signature
Paul Programmer

_____
Address

_____
Telephone Number

ACCEPTED AND AGREED TO:

_____
David Developer

SUBMISSION RELEASE

(another form)

_____ , 199__

Dear Gentleman:

Thank you for your interest in _____ (the "Company") and your offer to submit your material or idea called _____ (the "Idea") to us for evaluation. This agreement sets forth the terms and conditions under which we will accept your material for review and evaluation. We will return to you all material which you have provided to the Company upon completion of our evaluation or upon your earlier request. Please understand that the Company receives a great deal of material for evaluation and that our employees and consultants are engaged in a continuous program of internal development of new ideas. We may, from time to time, receive submissions of material similar to yours, or we may be developing similar ideas ourselves. As a result, we cannot agree to treat as confidential your idea or any information which you may choose to disclose to us during the course of our evaluation, whether or not marked as "confidential" or "proprietary." Please read the following numbered paragraphs carefully, and if you agree to them, sign in the space provided at the end of this Agreement and return the original executed and dated Agreement to the Company, to the attention of _____.

I ACKNOWLEDGE AND AGREE AS FOLLOWS:

1. The information submitted by me at any time which relates to the Idea (including any sample or model) is not confidential and that, in accepting such information, the Company is not incurring any obligation of any kind to keep secret or confidential such information;

2. The Company will not incur any obligation whatsoever to me or to any other person or entity as a result of my submission or disclosure of information concerning the Idea or the Company's examination or consideration of such information, regardless of how the Company may use (or not use) such information;

3. The Company makes no express or implied promise to pay me or any other person or entity any compensation whatsoever for any use or disclosure of any information concerning the Idea;

4. The use, if any, to be made of the information submitted by me is a matter resting fully and completely in the Company's exclusive discretion;

5. If the information submitted by me concerning the Idea appears to have value to the Company and is original and not already known, the Company may elect to compensate me for use of such information in such amount as the Company may determine in the Company's exclusive discretion, and I will not make any claim or demand whatsoever against the Company with respect to any or all such information;

6. I understand that the Company acknowledges and agrees this release shall not constitute a waiver or transfer of any protected intellectual-property rights held by me, including, but not limited to: copyright, trademark, patent, or trade secret elements of the Idea. The foregoing shall in no way obligate the Company to treat as confidential any information or material disclosed by me.

7. I represent and warrant that all of the terms and conditions above are binding on me and any other person or entity who may have an interest in the information and/or ideas submitted by me to the Company;

8. All of the terms and conditions above shall apply to all additional disclosure(s) submitted incidental to my original submission.

I UNDERSTAND THAT THIS DOCUMENT INVOLVES LEGAL ISSUES. I HAVE CONSULTED AND/OR HAVE HAD THE OPPORTUNITY TO CONSULT A LAWYER, AND FULLY UNDERSTAND THE MEANING AND CONSEQUENCES OF THIS DOCUMENT. I ALSO ACKNOWLEDGE THAT THIS DOCUMENT DESCRIBES THE ENTIRE AGREEMENT BETWEEN _____ AND ME, AND I HAVE NOT RELIED ON ANY OTHER STATEMENTS OR ASSURANCES, WRITTEN OR ORAL, IN SIGNING THIS DOCUMENT.

PLEASE NOTE: If the submitted materials and information (or any portion thereof) are the property of more than one individual, all the persons having an interest in such subject matter must sign this agreement and attach a statement of the name, address, and telephone number of each such person. Any submitter who is younger than 21 years old must have his or her parent or legal guardian also sign this Agreement in the space provided below. If the submitter is a corporation, a corporate officer empowered to enter into agreements on behalf of such corporation must sign this agreement.

ACCEPTED:

By: _____

Signature

_____

Printed Name

_____

Date

_____

Address

_____

Phone Number

Complete if applicable:

I certify that I am the parent or legal guardian of the submitter indicated above:

_____

Signature

_____

Print Name

CHAPTER 5

PUBLICATION AND DISTRIBUTION

The creators of multimedia programming, such as developers, content providers, and producers, often do not distribute their own work. They may contract with publishers and/or distributors to deliver their work to end users. The terms of these agreements vary depending on how the parties share the financial risks of creating and selling a program, and how they allocate marketing and distribution chores.

A number of publishers develop some or all of their own programs. A publisher could hire employees or independent contractors to create programming. As an employer, the publisher will own the copyright to work created by its employees within the scope of their employment. In the case of work created by independent contractors, the copyright can be assigned to the publisher, or certain rights can be licensed to a publisher for a term of years. See Chapter 3 to review how parties structure these deals. The Production Agreement reprinted at the end of Chapter 3 is used when a publisher funds development of a program that the publisher will own.

This chapter primarily addresses works created by developers on their own. These independent developers seek to arrange publication and distribution of their work by contracting with a publisher. Here, the developer may retain ownership of the copyright to the work. The developer could license certain publication and distribution rights to a publisher for a term of years. Alternatively, the developer could assign the entire copyright to a publisher. A publisher might insist on owning the copyright if the publisher funded much of the development. As the cost of creating product has increased, fewer developers are able to finance development of a product without an advance from a publisher.

There are several ways to distribute multimedia programming. One method is packaged media, such as computer floppy discs, video-game cartridges, CD-ROMs, and Digital Video Discs (DVDs). Another method is electronic distribution over land-lines, for example via the Internet or the cable networks, or by broadcasting a signal terrestrially or by satellite. A third means is a hybrid of the first two, namely electronic distribution of data to a site, such as movie theaters or retail music stores, where consumers can view the transmitted program or purchase it as packaged media. Distribution can be based on one-way delivery of a program to the end user or on a two-way system that allows interactive communication.

PACKAGED MEDIA

At the present time, the platforms available to display packaged media include player devices connected to televisions (game consoles such as those used to display Nintendo game cartridges), CD-ROM devices connected to computers, CD-ROM-based game consoles (Sega Saturn and Sony PlayStation),[1] and newly introduced Digital Video Discs (DVDs).

Video-game platforms have incompatible formats, so software from one does not operate on another. With the exception of Nintendo, video-game companies are shifting from video cartridges to CD-ROMs because of the CD-ROM's larger storage capacity and lower manufacturing cost. Making a CD-ROM can cost less than one dollar per disc, compared to the $30 it can cost to make a Nintendo 64 cartridge.

As mentioned in Chapter 1, CD-ROMs can store an enormous amount of information. Each disc can hold an amount of information that would require hundreds of high-density floppy discs. A single CD-ROM can store the equivalent of 350,000 pages of text, or an hour of full-motion video images, or 2.4 hours of stereo music, or 8,000 photos. Most of the top CD-ROMs are PC-based, while a smaller number are Macintosh compatible or dual format. As DVD grows, disc storage capacity will increase dramatically. DVDs can store seven times as much as CD-ROMs.

CD-ROMs are inexpensive to manufacture. The cost of pressing a CD-ROM and preparing the packaging is about $2 per unit. Retail prices generally range from $29 to $59 per title.

Once consumers are wired into the electronic superhighway with large-bandwidth fiber optic or coaxial cable connections, and faster modems, program developers will be able to deliver large programs quickly and directly into the home without reliance on packaged media like CD-ROMs. Computer discs could be relegated to off-line computing uses, or more likely, used in conjunction with online services. For example, a program could provide an encyclopedia on CD-ROM combined with an online service to update the information.

CD-ROM sales have increased as the number of computers with CD-ROM drives has grown, title prices have dropped, and retail outlets have expanded. Mass merchandisers such as Wal-Mart and bookstore chains have begun to sell CD-ROM titles. The Blockbuster Video retail chain will rent CD-ROM game titles, allowing consumers to take a test drive. Many titles are included with CD-ROM upgrade kits or the purchase of a new computer with a CD-ROM drive. These "bundling" sales have boosted distribution of titles while encouraging consumers to purchase CD-ROM hardware and software.

THE DISTRIBUTION CHAIN

The person or company that takes an idea and creates a product is called the developer. This person or company may also be referred to as the programmer, software author, content provider, or creator. A content provider, like a stock photo house, could be an entity that merely provides some or all of the content—such as text or photos—that a developer incorporates into a finished product. The term might also refer to the person who develops the final product, known as the "gold master," from which copies will be made.

Developers should prepare for international, as well as domestic, distribution. Code should be written so that the language text and audio files that need to be modified for foreign versions can be readily translated without affecting the other modules. Preparing foreign versions is generally referred to as "localization."

A publisher packages the product, conceives a marketing strategy, creates a marketing campaign and marketing materials, determines the optimal suggested retail price, and arranges for distribution of the product. Marketing includes promoting the product with advertising, publicity, and exhibition at trade shows. Arranging for distribution may include negotiating with mass-market distributors for retail sales, equipment manufacturers for bundling deals, and catalog companies for mail-order sales. Publishers are often involved in the development of a product, especially if the publisher is paying an advance that is funding development.

A distributor warehouses the product, ships it to retailers, offers co-op marketing programs to publishers, and invoices and collects accounts receivable from retailers. There are two types of distributors: computer specialty (e.g., Ingram-Micro, Merisel) and entertainment distributors (e.g., Baker & Taylor, Navarre). The entertainment distributors grew from businesses that distributed other products such as books or videocassettes. They expanded into the multimedia arena using their existing distribution infrastructure. They will place product in a variety of different types of retail stores, including software-only stores, computer superstores, home-video outlets, and music and bookstores. Major software retailers include Best Buy, Comp USA, Wal-Mart, Computer City, Sam's Clubs, and Fry's Electronics. Note that many top publishers sell directly to retailers as well as to distributors.

The publisher bears the risk of the product not selling. Typically, retailers have 100% return privileges. Essentially, the retailer is taking the product on consignment. If it does not sell quickly, it may be returned to the publisher. The distributor takes some financial risk since the publisher is usually paid 60 days after receipt of goods, although the distributor may not collect money from retailers for 90 to 120 days—and not at all if the retailer defaults.

Companies may perform more than one function. A developer may self-publish its titles, acting as a developer/publisher. Likewise, some companies that are primarily publishers of the work of others may choose to develop their own products. Similarly, some publishers choose to distribute their own products.

As a publisher/distributor, a company like Electronic Arts or GT Interactive will press, package, market, and distribute a title. If the product was acquired from an outside developer, the developer will receive a royalty of approximately 10% to 15% of the publisher's net revenue, which is generally defined as the wholesale price, less cost of goods, returns, markdowns, taxes, freight, and credits. For games developed for game-console systems, the publisher may also pay and deduct royalties to game-console owners such as Sony PlayStation and Nintendo.

DISTRIBUTION CHANNELS

Retail sales account for most publisher sales. While the retail channel is important, other channels may be more profitable, such as direct selling. A publisher might maintain a mailing list of customers and sell directly to them. By asking customers who purchase at retail to mail in their name and address, and by giving them an incentive to do so, a publisher can build a valuable mailing list to sell upgrades and ancillary products.

Another vehicle for sales can be catalogs that market CD-ROM titles. Publishers may have to buy advertising space in catalogs to gain entry.

Bundling is the practice of selling a product with another product—for example, selling a computer with pre-installed software or selling a number of CDs at a reduced price. A purchaser might receive ten free CDs upon purchase of a computer. Publishers do not make much money per product (as little as fifty cents to a dollar per disc for special, limited, or demo versions), but the volume of sales may be large. In addition, these sales will build public awareness of the product and may help sell other products in a series, or upgrades.[2]

MARKETING CALENDAR

The most important sales period for packaged media is the Christmas selling season. More than 40% of yearly sales occur in the fourth quarter, which includes Christmas. In order to have one's product on store shelves by Christmas, sales need to be finalized the prior summer. Product needs to be shipped to retailers the week prior to Thanksgiving. The trade show E3 in May is used by publishers to introduce new products to retailers. Publishers prepare packaging prototypes, a marketing plan, and a budget for co-op advertising. Distributors and retailers expect to see packaging designs, some playable level of the product, and information on the amount of marketing dollars the publisher plans to spend.

TYPES OF RETAIL OUTLETS

HOME VIDEOCASSETTE STORES
BOOKSTORES
COMPUTER SOFTWARE
COMPUTER SUPERSTORES
MUSIC
CONSUMER ELECTRONIC
OFFICE AND WAREHOUSE
MASS MERCHANTS
DEPARTMENT STORES
SUPERMARKETS
TOY STORES

A public relations campaign should begin in June in order to ensure that reviews are published before Christmas. Lead times for magazines are often two to three months, and reviewers need time to evaluate a product.

Because of the lead time needed to market CD-ROMs, developers should approach prospective publishers early in the calendar year, when publishers begin planning their product lines for the following Christmas.

NEGOTIATING THE PUBLISHING AGREEMENT

When entering into an agreement with another company, developers should be certain to have all essential terms set forth in a written contract with clear and unequivocal language. Handshake deals and private understandings are unwise, even if they are with an executive you trust and who is a close friend. Tomorrow, the executive could lose his job, and his replacement may not honor your understanding. Indeed, the entire company could be sold and the management replaced.

Before entering an agreement, a developer should carefully research the background and reputation of a potential publisher. What products has the publisher distributed, what platforms does the publisher use, and what methods does the publisher utilize to distribute its products? If the publisher is a start-up company, it may be undercapitalized and could fold after it has acquired rights to your product. A developer may have difficulty regaining publishing/distribution rights from a publisher in bankruptcy. Moreover, the delay in regaining rights, and reissuing the product with another publisher, may doom the product, as the market for software changes quickly.

MARKETING AND DISTRIBUTION TERMS

GOLD MASTER: The finished product as delivered by the developer. From the gold master, duplicates are made for sale.

STREET PRICES: The price the end user pays at retail, often less than SRP (Suggested Retail Price).

SRP: Suggested Retail Price.

SKU: Similar Stockkeeping Unit.

Nowadays, it can be difficult to obtain a publishing partner unless you have a top-quality product. Brand names, such as a game based on a famous character or trademark, have also become important.

One should always read contracts carefully, including any addendum of standard terms and conditions. Never assume that a publisher's "standard" terms are non-negotiable. The terms one can obtain will vary depending on how desirable your product is. An experienced multimedia attorney will know which terms are negotiable and which are not.

Conflict of Interest

When a publishing company develops some of its own products, it may favor products developed in-house over those acquired outside. Outside developers should be aware of this inherent conflict of interest, which may become pronounced if the internally developed product is more profitable to the publisher than outside-acquired products. A developer should

---

THE PLAYERS

CONTENT PROVIDER: A CONTENT PROVIDER, SUCH AS A STOCK PHOTO HOUSE, PROVIDES SOME OR ALL OF THE CONTENT, WHICH A DEVELOPER INCORPORATES INTO A FINISHED PRODUCT. SOMETIMES THE TERM REFERS TO THE PERSON WHO DEVELOPS THE PRODUCT.

DEVELOPER: THE DEVELOPER IS THE PERSON OR COMPANY THAT CREATES A PRODUCT FROM AN IDEA. THIS PERSON MIGHT BE CALLED A PROGRAMMER, SOFTWARE AUTHOR, PRODUCER, CONTENT PROVIDER, OR CREATOR.

PUBLISHER: THE PUBLISHER PACKAGES AND MARKETS THE PRODUCT AND ARRANGES FOR ITS DISTRIBUTION. THE PUBLISHER PROMOTES THE PRODUCT WITH ADVERTISING, PUBLICITY AND EXHIBITION AT TRADE SHOWS. THE PUBLISHER ARRANGES FOR DISTRIBUTION TO RETAIL OUTLETS, MAKES BUNDLING DEALS WITH EQUIPMENT MANUFACTURERS, AND NEGOTIATES FOR SALES THROUGH MAIL-ORDER CATALOGS. SOMETIMES PUBLISHERS PARTICIPATE IN THE DEVELOPMENT OF A PROGRAM.

DISTRIBUTOR: THE DISTRIBUTOR WAREHOUSES PRODUCT, SHIPS IT TO RETAILERS, AND INVOICES AND COLLECTS ON ACCOUNTS WITH RETAILERS. DISTRIBUTORS MAY OFFER CO-OP MARKETING PROGRAMS TO PUBLISHERS.

not enter into an agreement with a publisher whose principal motivation is to fill out its productn line.

The contract can state that the publisher will use its "best efforts" to market the product, although the term "best efforts" is a somewhat vague standard by which to judge the publisher's performance. Alternatively, the publisher could agree to promote the program on a no-less-favorable basis than its other programs.[3] Likewise, the publisher could agree to spend minimum amounts of money to advertise and promote the product. If the latter course is chosen, make sure that the agreement carefully defines advertising and marketing expenses to exclude the publisher's general overhead, legal fees, staff costs and office rent. It is best to define advertising expenses so that they only include direct out-of-pocket expenditures made to promote the particular product.

Another way to motivate a publisher to aggressively sell a product is to obtain a large advance against future royalties. Publishers generally expend effort in proportion to their investment in a program. If a publisher has given a large advance, it will want to recoup it. Alternatively, a provision for minimum royalty payments will give the publisher a strong incentive to sell the program.

Grant of Rights

The developer of a program can license limited rights, or all rights, to a publisher. If the program is custom-made, the company that commissions it will often insist on copyright ownership. Here, the developer may only be entitled to receive payment for creating the program. Agreeing to forego copyright ownership may not be much of a concession if the program is so unique that there is no outside market for it anyway.[4]

Developers who use their own resources to create a program may not want to sell all rights to one publisher. Rights can be divided by time, platform or geography. One publisher may not have the ability to market the product on all platforms in all territories.[5] A developer could grant one publisher the right to distribute by CD-ROM and computer discs but reserve game cartridge and other rights, including the right to distribute the program over the Internet. Publishers usually desire a broad grant of rights. Since the marketplace is developing, they are concerned that platforms popular today could be superseded by new ones in the near future.

Merchandising and book publishing rights should be considered. Spin-off products from a hot video game, such as a toy or motion picture, can generate substantial revenue. The right to make sequels can be an issue. If the publisher helps make the program a hit, it will want to continue to reap the rewards by publishing sequels. The developer, on the other hand, may want to reserve these rights, or limit the publisher to a right of last refusal on sequel rights. As explained later, a Right of Last Refusal gives the publisher the right to match the best offer given the developer by a third party.

Publishers usually will insist on exclusive rights for whatever markets and media are within their grant of rights. Therefore, the developer would not be able to contract with another publisher for the same markets and media. Moreover, publishers will want developers to agree not to develop any products that directly compete with the product given the publisher. Distributors, on the other hand, may be willing to accept products on a non-exclusive basis, and may distribute competing products.

A developer can grant only those rights he possesses. If a multimedia program incorporates a software engine or a component borrowed from another program, the developer may only have the right to use it on a one-time basis in his own program. The developer cannot assign a copyright to components he does not own but merely has a limited license to use.

MARKETING "DOOM"

ID, THE DEVELOPER OF THE HIT COMPUTER GAME "DOOM," MARKETED ITS PRODUCT BY GIVING AWAY THE FIRST LEVEL OF ITS GAME FOR FREE. THE GAME COULD BE DOWNLOADED FROM THE INTERNET OR ORDERED DIRECT FROM ID FOR A $5.00 SHIPPING CHARGE. ADVANCED LEVELS OF THE GAME COULD BE PURCHASED DIRECTLY FROM ID, THEREBY BYPASSING THE RETAIL CHANNEL. BECAUSE OF THE ADDICTIVE NATURE OF THE GAME, *WIRED* MAGAZINE LIKENED THIS FIRST-TASTE FREE MARKETING SCHEME TO THAT USED BY DRUG DEALERS TO BUILD UP A LOYAL CLIENTELE.[13]

Reserved Rights

If the developer wants to use portions of his work in future work, he should reserve that right. For instance, the developer may want to use characters created for one program in another program. Or, the developer may want to reuse certain development tools, routines, or underlying technology in other programs. When a developer reserves the right to use portions of a program again, the publisher receives non-exclusive rights to those portions of the program.

Reserved rights may be subject to a Right of First Negotiation or a Right of Last Refusal. A Right of First Negotiation would require the developer to negotiate with the publisher before negotiating a license for designated rights with a third party. A Right of Last Refusal may be combined with, or used as an alternative to, the Right of First Negotiation. With the Right of Last Refusal, the publisher has the right to acquire a reserved right under the same terms and conditions as the best offer made by a third party. If Publisher A has a Right of Last Refusal, then a developer is free to offer the right to Publisher B. Before closing the deal, however, the developer must offer Publisher A the right to license these rights on the same terms as Publisher B's best offer.[6]

Compensation

Compensation is typically in the form of royalties, often with an advance payment made to the developer. The advance counts against the royalties earned. If the advance is non-refundable, as is common, the developer will not have to repay it, even if the royalties do not pay back the advance.

Often a developer wants an advance that is payable before completion of the program because the money is needed to create or finish the program.[7] A publisher is unlikely to give such an advance unless it is fairly confident that the developer can deliver the final product. If such an advance is given, it will be refundable in the event that the developer fails to deliver the program. In many instances, the advance is paid in increments as certain "milestones" are reached during the development of the product.

While the size of the royalty is important, the manner in which it is calculated is critical. A royalty could be based on gross revenues with no deductions for the publisher's marketing and shipping costs. More likely, the royalty will be based on net revenues (also called net receipts) where certain costs are deducted from gross revenues, and what is left, if anything, is the base on which the royalty is paid.

Publishers prefer a royalty based on net revenues because they want to be able to deduct some expenses before sharing revenue with the developer. They will argue that it is not fair to ask them to pay royalties before they recoup their manufacturing and shipping expenses.

Developers are concerned that publishers will deduct so many expenses, some of questionable merit, that no payments will be received. In the movie business, studios have a history of "creative accounting." Distribution agreements define "net profits" so that a studio is allowed to deduct substantial distribution fees, overhead, and interest. As a result, profit participants rarely receive any profits.[8]

In multimedia publishing, royalties are typically based on "net revenue," and the term is defined so that taxes, freight, discounts, returns and markdowns are deducted, but no deduction is allowed for distribution fees, marketing, or overhead. The definition may, or may not, allow a deduction for manufacturing costs.

A publisher can expect to receive from resellers—such as distributors, wholesalers, and retailers—about 50% to 60% of the retail price. Thus, a program selling for $100 retail might return $50 to the publisher. After deductions for discounts, returns, and other allowable expenses, net revenue may amount to $40 per product. If the developer is entitled to a 10% royalty, the developer will get $4.00 per product sold. If the developer received a $40,000 advance, royalties from the first 10,000 sales will be retained by the publisher to recoup the advance.[9] Note that revenue may decline if the publisher discounts the product to spur sales or reduce old inventory. Moreover, by

1996 the retail price of many CD-ROM programs had dropped to the $29 to $39 range.

The parties might agree to a fixed royalty, which is a royalty that is a fixed sum, perhaps payable in installments. The developer, for example, could be paid $100,000, payable in four $25,000 installments. Here, the developer is guaranteed a fixed amount, regardless of how many units the publisher sells. Publishers willing to pay a fixed royalty accept the risk of paying the royalty despite poor sales, but they also stand to retain a larger share of revenue if the product is a hit because the royalty does not increase as sales grow.

Publishers will want to set fixed royalties low. Developers may be unhappy with a modest fixed royalty because they will not share in the product's "upside" potential. A better solution, from the developer's point of view, may be a non-refundable advance payment against royalties. The advance amount is a guaranteed, set amount that applies against a royalty on sales. This way, the developer is assured of receiving the advance and can share in revenues from a hit product.

Royalties are often from 5% to 20% of net receipts, with most deals falling in the 10% to 15% range. Royalties can be payable according to a sliding scale, with the percentage changing as sales increase. For example, a 10% royalty might be payable on the first 10,000 copies sold, with a 15% royalty thereafter. A different royalty often applies to direct sales through mail-order catalogs, foreign sales, and sales of product on a different platform.

If the publisher has worldwide rights, the publisher may sub-license publishing rights to foreign publishers. Thus, a U.S. publisher could arrange for a Japanese publisher to market and distribute the product in Japan. The Japanese distributor may bear all the costs of translating and marketing the product in Japan. There is little financial risk to the U.S. publisher. Royalty payments received by the U.S. publisher go straight to the bottom line since the U.S. publisher does not incur the cost of foreign marketing. Therefore, a developer is justified in seeking a larger share of these royalty payments. A one-third to one-half share of foreign royalties is reasonable.[10]

Bundling Deals

If the product is "bundled," calculation of net revenue may become problematical. "Bundled" software accompanies the sale of other hardware or software. If one buys a computer, for instance, Windows may be installed on the hard disc. The software is included as part of the purchase price of the computer. When a program is bundled, sales may increase dramatically since the software is being sold in volume with another product. The publisher, however, will likely receive a modest payment for each copy sold. Since different publishers' software products may be bundled, allocation of revenue among the programs may be difficult. A potential conflict of interests exists if a publisher is willing to give away a product as a premium or to build market share. This strategy may be beneficial to the publisher but may not be desirable for the developer.

The publishing agreement should address how the developer will be paid for bundling deals. Often the developer will simply receive a fixed-dollar amount per copy rather than a royalty.

Audits and Accounting

The agreement should provide for monthly, quarterly, or semi-annual payment of royalties with an accompanying accounting statement. The developer should have a reasonable length of time to challenge statements. A developer will not want to incur the expense of an audit until he believes enough money is at stake to make an audit worthwhile. Since revenue may dribble in over an extended period,[11] developers should not be forced to audit early or waive their rights.

The agreement may provide for reimbursement of audit costs and attorneys' fees if the developer successfully recovers payments due as a result of accounting errors. If the publisher maintains several offices, the developer should specify that the audit take place at a convenient location.

The agreement may permit the publisher to establish a reserve for returns. This allows a publisher to withhold some of the royalty due the developer, because returns may reduce the amount of royalty due. The publisher will argue that it should not have to pay a timely royalty on all copies sold because retailers often return product and receive a refund. The reserve for returns should fall within the range of 10% to 25% of sales.

Interest and Security

Late payments due the developer should be subject to an interest charge. The higher the interest rate, the less incentive there is for the publisher to delay payment. Although publishers will resist paying interest on late payments, developers should request such a provision. In the event the developer must sue to recover payments due, courts usually cannot grant interest before a judgment is received. Such pre-judgment interest may only be recoverable if a contract between the parties provides for it. Since a plaintiff may have to pursue litigation for years before recovering a judgment, a provision for pre-judgment interest is important.

Developers can also request, in any distribution agreements, a lien or security interest on the monetary proceeds from sale of the progran. This could give the developer preference over unsecured creditors in the event that a publisher goes bankrupt. Security interests in copyrightable works should be recorded with the Copyright Office at the Library of Congress in Washington, D.C. You cannot record such a security interest in a work or a distribution contract until the work itself is registered with the Copyright Office. Use a Document Cover Sheet to record the security interest. The secured party needs a written and signed agreement that grants the security interest. One should also register the security interest under state law in the state where the publisher has its principal office. Registration is accomplished by filing a financing statement under the Uniform Commercial Code, form UCC-1.

Warranties and Indemnification

As mentioned in Chapter 2, a warranty is a promise. Indemnification means reimbursement.

A publisher will want the developer to warrant that he has good and complete title to the property or the rights he is licensing, that the property does not infringe on anyone else's rights (including rights of defamation, invasion of privacy, right of publicity, trademark, and copyright), and that there are no claims or litigation outstanding in regard to the property. The developer if often asked to warrant that the developer has not granted any rights to the property to another party, and that no money is owed to any creators of the property.

The publisher will prefer that the warranties be absolute. Under such a warranty, if the developer's promise is broken, the developer will be liable, notwithstanding any excuses he may have. The fact that the developer made a promise in good faith, honestly believing his promise to be true, does not relieve him of liability. Thus, if the developer thought that his program did not infringe anyone's copyright because he mistakenly believed a film clip in the program was in the public domain, he would nevertheless be liable for breaching his warranty. If the publisher is entitled to indemnification, then the publisher can have the developer reimburse the publisher for the expense of defending against a lawsuit and paying any court judgment.

A lesser warranty is one that is limited to the best of one's knowledge and belief. Under such a warranty, if the promisor has a good-faith belief that his work does not infringe the rights of others, he will not be liable for breaching his warranty, even if the work is infringing. That is because the developer has only promised that as far as he knew, he did not infringe another's rights. Developers should try to avoid giving absolute warranties. If the publisher objects, the developer can point out that E & O insurance is available to protect against potential liability, and the insurance carrier's assets are more substantial than the developer's. If the publisher insists that you give an absolute warranty, try to limit it to those matters of which you have first-hand knowledge. For example, warranting that you have not licensed publishing rights to another is something that you should know, and therefore there is less danger in warranting that fact absolutely.

Developers may want the publisher to warrant certain facts as well. The publisher may be asked to warrant that it is solvent, not in bankruptcy, and has authority to enter into the agreement. The developer may want the publisher to warrant that materials or program tools provided by the publisher to developer will not infringe any third-party rights.

Delivery Requirements

The agreement will specify when a fully functional copy of the program must be delivered to the publisher. Publishers often want delivery to be in object code (machine-readable code) with documented source code (human-readable code). Developers may want to retain source code, delivering only object code. With access to source code, the publisher could conceivably create its own version of the program. Consequently, developers often guard their source code carefully. If source code is delivered, the publisher may or may not have the right to use it. If a publisher requires delivery of source code, a developer may insist on a more lucrative deal.

A newly written computer program is likely to contain errors or "bugs." Upon integration of all elements of the program, it will undergo alpha testing, which is usually done by professional testers employed by the developer or publisher. Next is beta testing, or live-environment testing, where test copies are given to users to test the program outside the laboratory in a real-life context. When a product successfully completes testing, the publisher will often certify in writing that the product appears to meet its performance requirements.

The developer may nevertheless have a continuing obligation to fix any "bugs" that surface later and promptly deliver a corrected version. If the developer does not supply a corrected version in a timely manner, the publisher may have the right to prepare a corrected version and charge the developer for the expense. The agreement could provide that the developer will fix any bugs for six months after delivery, for no additional fee. Alternatively, the developer could agree to provide a certain number of hours to fix any bugs after the program has been accepted. After that, the publisher may be required to pay the developer for time and materials to fix bugs. Besides fixing bugs, the publisher may want the developer to enhance the program. For this service, the publisher should pay the developer a fee.

Source-Code Escrow

Publishers want to ensure that a developer will be able to meet its obligations to complete the program, as well as provide updates and fix bugs. Without access to source code, a publisher cannot modify a program should the developer go out of business.[12] The publisher may have invested a substantial amount of money into the development of a project, either by giving the developer an advance, or if the developer is employed on a work-for-hire basis, in the form of compensation. Moreover, the publisher's reputation with distributors and retailers will suffer if the publisher is unable to deliver an acceptable product because of a developer's default.

The concerns of both the developer and publisher can often be met by putting the source code and other proprietary information into escrow. A source-code escrow agreement provides that a neutral third party holds the source code, subject to instructions mutually agreed upon by the parties. Typically, the agreement allows the source code to be released to the publisher under certain conditions, such as the bankruptcy of the developer, its failure to make timely delivery of a program, or if a developer declines to provide a sequel when the publisher has the right to one.

A professional escrow firm should be used. Source code should be stored in vaults designed to protect magnetic media. The firm should have the expertise to confirm that the source code is accurate and complete.

Technical Support of End Users

Either the developer or publisher may provide technical support. This may be a considerable burden and a continuing expense that developers should not undertake lightly. Placing this responsibility on the developer makes sense because the developer has much more intimate knowledge of the product than the publisher, and thus, is in a better position to answer technical inquiries. On the other hand, many developers may not have the financial wherewithal to provide technical support to the public. A publisher may want to handle this function itself because of concern that the developer might go out of business, and because inadequate or no technical support could hurt the publisher's reputation. Nowadays, publishers usually provide technical support.

When the publisher agrees to provide technical support, the developer will be expected to help train the publisher's personnel and to consult with the publisher to resolve technical problems.

Upgrades

New versions, or upgrades of the program, are important because software products can become obsolete quickly. Upgrades may be prepared by the developer or publisher. If the developer has the responsibility for preparing the upgrade, the publisher may be required to pay the developer a non-refundable advance against royalties. The contract might specify how many lines of code are required for each upgrade and when the upgrades need to be done. The obligation to do an upgrade may be tied to time, for example, once a year, or tied to the amount of sales, for example, in the event that less than 10,000 units are sold in a quarter.

If the publisher takes responsibility for preparing upgrades, the developer's royalties may be scaled back as future versions are released. A reduced royalty may be reasonable because at some point a subsequent version may contain little or no code from the developer's original program.

Trademarks

The name of a program may become a valuable trademark. Sequel products may rely on this brand-name to help the public identify a product. Publishers often insist on owning the trademarks to the programs they sell. The publisher will want to own all rights to advertising and promotional materials as well. The developer may want to have its company's trademark placed on packaging material and in advertising.

Confidentially

Both parties may want to protect various trade secrets, technology, financial information, and marketing plans from disclosure to outsiders. Particular care must be taken to protect trade secrets, which cannot be protected once they are no longer secret.

Termination

In the event a developer defaults, a publisher will want the right to terminate the agreement, retain rights to the work-in-progress, and recoup any advances paid. A developer may default if he fails to meet performance milestones, breaches his representations and warranties, or goes into bankruptcy.

Publishers may insist on language that allows the publisher to terminate without cause. In such an event, the publisher typically compensates the developer for work completed, and the publisher relinquishes all its rights to the product. The publisher may have the right to have its advances reimbursed in the event that the developer finishes the product and publishes it through another company.

Developers should also ask for a termination clause in their publishing agreements. In the event that a publisher breaches the contract, this provision may allow the developer to recover all money due him as well as regain all rights to his program. The publisher will want to limit grounds for termination to a "material" breach, and will want a requirement that the developer give the publisher notice of any alleged breach, and time to cure it, before the developer can terminate the agreement. The developer's right to regain rights to the product might be contingent on the developer reimbursing the publisher for costs it has incurred.

ARBITRATION

Arbitration is usually preferable to litigation. This is especially the case when the other party is better able to finance a protracted court struggle. Arbitration is a much quicker, more informal, and less expensive method of resolving disputes. Conflicts can be settled within a matter of months, rules of evidence do not apply, and costs are reduced.

An arbitration clause should provide that the prevailing party is entitled to reimbursement for costs and reasonable attorneys' fees. Without such a provision, the prevailing party in litigation or arbitration usually cannot recoup these expenses.

Binding arbitration awards are difficult to overturn. The grounds for appeal are quite limited. If the losing party does not voluntarily comply with the arbitration award, the prevailing party can go to court to seek confirmation of the award. Once confirmed, the award is no different from any court judgment. A judgment creditor can have the sheriff seize the judgment debtor's assets to satisfy the award.

A novel pilot program has been established to resolve certain disputes online. The "Virtual Magistrate" program (http://mag.low.vill.edu:8080/) is a joint project of the American Arbitration Association, the Cyberspace Law Institute, the National Center for Automated Information Research, and the Villanova Center for Information Law and Policy. Disputes are submitted by electronic mail and resolved under the rules of the American Arbitration Association. The program attempts to resolve complaints within three business days of acceptance. The Virtual Magistrate will consider complaints about messages, postings, copyright and trademark infringement, and other wrongful conduct. The project will not resolve billing questions between users and system operators, nor consider disputes considered unsuitable for this type of dispute resolution.

SOFTWARE PUBLISHING AGREEMENT CHECKLIST

PARTIES:
    DEVELOPER:
    PUBLISHER:

ENTITY: IS THE PUBLISHER AN INDIVIDUAL, PARTNERSHIP, CORP.?

DUE DILIGENCE: IS PUBLISHER REPUTABLE?

DOES PUBLISHER HANDLE THIS TYPE OF PRODUCT?

WHAT IS THE TRACK RECORD OF PUBLISHER?

GRANT OF RIGHTS: OWNERSHIP OF COPYRIGHT: IS THE LICENSE
    EXCLUSIVE OR NON-EXCLUSIVE?

TERM:

PLATFORMS:
    CD-ROM FOR IBM COMPATIBLE
    CD-ROM FOR GAME CONSOLE
    GAME CARTRIDGE:
    ONLINE:

TERRITORIES:

ANCILLARY RIGHTS:

MERCHANDISING:

BOOK PUBLISHING:

SEQUEL PROGRAM/CONVERSIONS TO OTHER PLATFORMS:

RESERVED RIGHTS:
    RIGHT TO USE PORTIONS OF WORK IN OTHER PRODUCTS
    RIGHT OF FIRST NEGOTIATION
    RIGHT OF LAST REFUSAL

COMPENSATION:
    ADVANCE:
    NON-RECOUPABLE:
    AGAINST ROYALTIES:
    MINIMUM ROYALTY PAYMENTS:

[CONTINUED]

SOFTWARE PUBLISHING AGREEMENT CHECKLIST
[CONTINUED]

GUARANTEE:

RIGHT TO TERMINATE IF SHORTFALL:

ROYALTIES:

PERCENT OF NET REVENUES:

AMOUNTS PAID:

AMOUNTS INVOICED:

DEDUCTIONS ALLOWED: TAXES, FREIGHT, DISCOUNTS, RETURNS

DEDUCTIONS NOT ALLOWED DISTRIBUTION FEE, OVERHEAD

DEDUCTIONS NEGOTIABLE: COST OF MANUFACTURING, CO-OP ADS

FIXED ROYALTY:

TIME OF PAYMENT:

INSTALLMENTS:

SLIDING SCALE ROYALTIES:

____% OF FIRST _____ COPIES SOLD

____% OF NEXT _____ COPIES SOLD

____% THEREAFTER

ROYALTY ON SUB-LICENSES:

CONFLICTS OF INTEREST: CONFLICTS WITH OTHER PRODUCTS

BEST EFFORTS CLAUSE

FAVORED NATION'S CLAUSE

MINIMUM ADVERTISING & PROMOTION:

LIMITED TO DIRECT OUT-OF-POCKET COSTS?

BUNDLING DEALS:

FIXED DOLLAR AMOUNT PER COPY:

AUDITS AND ACCOUNTING:

ACCOUNTING:
   MONTHLY, QUARTERLY, YEARLY

[CONTINUED]

SOFTWARE PUBLISHING AGREEMENT CHECKLIST
[CONTINUED]

AUDIT RIGHTS:
　　LOCATION OF AUDIT:
　　TIME LIMIT?

REIMBURSEMENT OF AUDIT FEES IF UNDERPAYMENT?

RESERVE FOR RETURNS: (10% TO 25%)

INTEREST ON LATE PAYMENTS:

DELIVERY REQUIREMENTS:

OBJECT CODE ONLY:

DATE FOR DELIVERY:

DEVELOPER'S CONTINUING OBLIGATION FOR TESTING AND CORRECTION:

TECHNICAL SUPPORT OF END USERS:

PUBLISHER:

DEVELOPER:
　　DIRECT TO END USER OR
　　CONSULT WITH PUBLISHER

SECURITY INTEREST:

WARRANTIES:
　　ABSOLUTE
　　BEST OF KNOWLEDGE AND BELIEF

E & O INSURANCE:
　　NAMED INSURED:

SECURITY INTEREST:

TERMINATION CLAUSE:
　　FOR BREACH:
　　FOR SHORTFALL:

ARBITRATION:
　　VENUE:
　　FORUM:
　　REIMBURSEMENT OF ATTORNEYS' FEES:

CHOICE OF LAW:

SOFTWARE PUBLISHING AGREEMENT

This SOFTWARE PUBLISHING AGREEMENT is entered into this _____ day of _____, _____, by and between _____, a _____ corporation ("Publisher"), and _____, a resident of _____ ("Developer").

IN CONSIDERATION of the promises, agreements, covenants, representations, and warranties herein contained, Publisher and Developer hereby agree as follows:

1. DEFINITIONS: For purposes of this Agreement, the following terms will have the meanings set forth:

(a) "Software": The term "Software" will mean Developer's entertainment computer software program for the _____ computer [or ____ platform], currently known as: "_____" as described in Exhibit A attached hereto and incorporated herein, in object form only, in existence as of the Effective Date (as defined below) as well as any version of _____ that is delivered pursuant to this Agreement.

(b) "Software Package": The term "Software Package" will mean the standard stock-keeping unit intended for retail marketing, comprising an individual copy of the Software, together with any user manual and other supplementary materials, as determined in the sole discretion of Publisher.

(c) "User Documentation": The term "User Documentation" will mean the documentation accompanying the Software in Software Packages for the purposes of instructing end users in the use and operation of the Software.

(d) "Nonconformity": The term "Nonconformity" will mean a design error, design defect, functional defect, programming error or anomaly, and/or deviation from the specifications in the Exhibit A.

(e) "Alpha Acceptable": The term "Alpha Acceptable" will mean suitability of a software product acceptance for alpha testing by Publisher's Test Department based upon the Test Department's determination that such product appears to have substantially all of its intended functionality and performance, such that the predominant development task to be completed is the correction of Nonconformities.

(f) "Product Certification": The term "Product Certification" will mean the issuance of a written certificate of an officer of Publisher that the testing of the first product has been successfully concluded and that such product is ready for manufacture for commercial distribution, based upon Publisher's determination that such product appears to have substantially all of its intended functionality and performance, that it appears to perform all functions described in the functional specifications in the manner described, that it appears to be reasonably free from Nonconformities and Nonconformities which cause operational failure and/or premature termination of the product.

(g) "Corrected Version": The term "Corrected Version" will mean a version of the Software prepared solely for the purpose of correcting Nonconformities (as defined above) in the Software.

(h) "Translated Version" [Localized Version]: The term "Translated Version" [Localized Version] will mean a foreign-language translation of the Software.

(i) "Effective Date": The term "Effective Date" will mean the date first set forth above, which, upon execution of this Agreement by both parties, will be the effective date of this Agreement.

(j) "Includes"; "Including": Except where followed directly by the word "only," the terms "includes" or "including" will mean "includes, but is not limited to" and "including, but not limited to," respectively, it being the intention of the parties that any enumeration following thereafter is illustrative and not exhaustive.

2. GRANT OF RIGHTS:

(a) Grant: Developer hereby grants to Publisher the exclusive right during the term of this Agreement to prepare, manufacture, market, and distribute throughout the world, in all languages, copies of the Software in object-code form only.

(b) Publisher To Determine Marketing: Publisher will determine, in its sole discretion, the manner and method of marketing and distributing the Software, including marketing expenditures, advertising and promotion, packaging, channels of distribution, and the suggested retail license fee of the Software.

(c) Minimum Royalty: Commencing upon the date on which Software Packages are first shipped for commercial exploitation, the license granted hereunder will be subject to Publisher's fulfillment of the annual minimum royalty levels set forth in Exhibit B attached hereto and incorporated herein (the "Minimum Royalty").

(i) Publisher's Right To Make Up Shortfall: In the event that Publisher's sales of the Software do not generate sufficient revenues for the Minimum Royalty to be satisfied, Publisher may, but will not be obligated, to pay Developer an amount equal to the difference between the actual royalties earned by the Software during the period in question and the Minimum

Royalty in effect for such period (the "Shortfall Amount"). If Publisher pays the Shortfall Amount, Publisher will be deemed for all purposes of this Agreement to have fulfilled the Minimum Royalty for such period. All amounts paid as Shortfall Amounts will be deemed to be non-refundable advances against royalties.

(ii) Remedy for Publisher's Failure To Fulfill Minimum Royalty: In the event that the Minimum Royalty is not satisfied by sales of the Software and Publisher does not pay the Shortfall Amount, Developer's sole remedy will be to terminate the license granted to Publisher under this Agreement. Any such Termination will be in accordance with the following procedures:

Not later than sixty (60) days after the end of the annual period for which the Minimum Royalty was not fulfilled, Developer will give Publisher notice of termination.

Publisher will have ten (10) days from receipt of such notice in which to pay Developer the Shortfall Amount.

If Publisher does not pay the Shortfall Amount within such ten (10) day period, the termination will become effective immediately.

If Developer does not give notice of termination within the foregoing sixty (60) day period set forth in Section 2(c)(ii) above, Developer will be conclusively deemed to have waived its right to terminate with respect to the annual period for which the Minimum Royalty was not fulfilled.

(d) Publisher To Bear Costs: Except as expressly set forth herein, Publisher will bear all costs of manufacturing, marketing, and distributing Software Packages containing the Software.

(e) Further Assurances of Developer: Developer agrees to execute such documents as Publisher may reasonably request from time to time to vest in Publisher any and all of the rights granted or transferred by Developer hereunder. Developer will take all reasonable steps to have each of those persons who has or will have participated on behalf of Developer execute any such agreements.

(f) Reserved Rights: All rights not specifically and expressly granted by Developer to Publisher are hereby reserved by Developer.

3. DELIVERY: Not later than _____, _____, Developer will deliver to Publisher two (2) Alpha Acceptable copies on CD-ROM discs of the fully functional object-code version of the Software ("Delivery") [or refer to milestone schedule].

4. CONTINUING OBLIGATIONS OF DEVELOPER:

(a) Product Testing, Correction, and Certification: Following Delivery and the commencement of alpha testing by Publisher's

Test Department, Publisher will promptly advise Developer of the discovery of any Nonconformity. Developer will promptly correct all Nonconformities. Developer will deliver Corrected Versions once weekly. All Nonconformities will be corrected on or before _____ 199_. In the event that the Software fails to achieve Product Certification by _____, 199_ (other than as a result of a delay caused by Publisher's Test Department), Publisher may, without limiting any of its other remedies, terminate this Agreement at any time, effective immediately upon notice to Developer.

(b) Corrected Versions: Following Product Certification, Developer will prepare and deliver to Publisher, at no charge to Publisher, Corrected Versions of the Software within thirty (30) days from each date upon which Developer discovers or is otherwise apprized of a Nonconformity. If Developer fails for any reason to promptly deliver to Publisher a Corrected Version when required under this Clause 4(b) and upon demand by Publisher, Publisher may make other arrangements to prepare such Corrected Version (including, if Developer fails to deliver source code of the Software to Publisher in a timely manner, recompiling, disassembling, or otherwise reverse-engineering the Software), and may charge the reasonable costs of doing so to sums accruing to Developer hereunder. Upon notice by Publisher of its intention to prepare such Corrected Version in the manner aforesaid, Developer will deliver to Publisher whatever materials are reasonably necessary to produce the Corrected Version, including the source code of the Software. Publisher's chargeable costs may be (i) a reasonable amount of fees paid to a third party for preparing such Corrected Version(s); (ii) Publisher's internal staff costs and out-of-pocket expenses if Publisher prepares such Corrected Version(s); or (iii) a combination of (i) and (ii) if both a third party and Publisher prepare such Corrected Version(s).

(c) Translated Versions: At Publisher's request, Developer will provide reasonable assistance to Publisher (or to third parties commissioned or licensed by Publisher) in connection with the preparation of Translated Versions. [Developer will provide translated versions in accordance with the milestones set forth in Exhibit A.]

(d) Training: At Publisher's request, Developer will provide one (1) day of training to Publisher's Product Assurance and Software Support departments and will provide reasonable assistance to Publisher's software support personnel in connection with Publisher's technical support of end users of the Software Packages. Publisher will reimburse Developer its reasonable coach-class travel expense in connection with rendering training services at sites other than Publisher's headquarters facility.

(e) No Competitive Products: During the term of this Agreement (or the duration of the copyright in the Software, if shorter), Developer will not develop, for any party other than Publisher, products directly competitive to the Software,[14] including any product containing any of the same characters or characterizations or any product which is or might reasonably be considered to be a sequel to the Software, and also including any add-on products such as new scenarios or scenery discs.

5. UPGRADES: In the event that either Publisher or Developer desires to market an upgraded version of the Software (an "Upgrade"), Publisher and Developer will negotiate in good faith the specifications for such Upgrade, the amount Developer will charge Publisher for preparing such Upgrade, which amount will be paid to Developer by Publisher as a non-refundable, fully recoupable advance against royalties, provided that neither party will be obligated to negotiate at all if the number of Software Packages sold in the twelve (12) months preceding the negotiation is less than _____ units.

6. END-USER TECHNICAL SUPPORT: Publisher will provide end-user technical support to all end users of the Software. Developer will provide reasonable telephone consultation to Publisher with respect to any questions or problems concerning the Software or the use of the Software.

7. CONSIDERATION:

(a) Advance Against Royalties: Publisher will pay to Developer a non-refundable, fully recoupable advance against royalties in the amount of _____ Dollars ($_____), payable as follows:[15]

(i) _____ Dollars ($_____) upon Delivery; and

(ii) _____ Dollars ($_____) upon Product Certification.

(b) Net Receipts: For purposes of this Agreement, "Net Receipts" will mean amounts actually received by Publisher in connection with the licensing, sale, or other commercial exploitation of the Software, less (i) promotional, refund, or similar credits against amounts invoiced; (ii) returns; and (iii) any federal, state, or foreign sales, excise, or other taxes or tariffs imposed on Software Packages (not including any tax based on Publisher's net income).

(c) Royalties: Provided that Developer will perform all the terms and covenants of this Agreement and in consideration of the rights granted by Developer to Publisher hereunder, Publisher will pay to Developer an amount equal to _____ percent (____%) of the Net Receipts derived from marketing and distribution of copies of the Software, with no minimum royalty per copy.[16] There will be no minimum distribution commitment by Publisher.

(d) Royalties On Sublicenses: In the event that Publisher sublicenses the right to publish the Software such that the sublicensee bears the cost of manufacturing and marketing the copies of the Software sold by such sublicensee, the royalties payable to Developer with respect to such sublicense will be an amount equal to thirty-three and one-third percent (33 1/3%) of the Net Receipts actually received from such sublicensee with respect to copies of the Software, with no minimum royalty per copy.

(e) Evaluation Copies: Without limiting the generality of Clause 7(b), Publisher may, in its sole discretion, distribute copies of the Software at no charge for the purpose of demonstrating the Software or for other promotional purposes ("Evaluation Copies"). No royalties will be due to Developer with respect to any use or distribution of Evaluation Copies.

(f) Overpayment: In the event that Developer receives an overpayment, including royalties paid on Software Packages that are subsequently returned, other than any unearned advance, Developer agrees that Publisher may deduct the amount of such overpayment from any further royalties accruing to Developer's account.

(g) Payment of Royalties; Reports; Audits: Within thirty (30) days following the end of each calendar quarter during the term of this Agreement, Publisher will submit to Developer a royalty report that will specify the royalties earned by Developer during the previous quarter and the calculation thereof, together with the royalty fee due for such previous quarter. The report will include a detailed listing of the number of units sold, the price per unit, the deductions taken, and the amount of reserves held. The information contained in a royalty report will be conclusively deemed correct and binding upon Developer, resulting in the loss of all further audit rights with respect to such report, unless specifically challenged by written notice from Developer within three (3) years from the date such report was delivered by Publisher. Publisher agrees to allow Developer's representatives, and/or independent auditors at Developer's sole expense, to admit and analyze appropriate and relevant accounting records of Publisher at Publisher's premises to verify accurate and full accounting for and payment of all moneys due Developer hereunder. Any such audit will be permitted during business hours within seven (7) days of receipt of Developer's written request. No audit (other than the first audit) may be conducted less than six (6) months after the previous audit. [A copy of the audit will be provided to Publisher within 30 days of its delivery to Developer.]

(h) All monies due Developer shall be paid in a timely manner in accordance with this agreement. Publisher shall pay Developer interest at the legal rate of interest on any amounts past due for ten (10) days or more.

(i) Security Interest: As security for payment of Developer's share of Net Receipts hereunder, Publisher hereby grants and assigns a lien and security interest in all of Publisher's right title and interest in and to (i) all rights granted to Publisher in the Software and its underlying elements, (ii) all Software elements, content, code, and other physical materials of any kind to be used in the exploitation of the Software by Publisher, (iii) all proceeds realized by Publisher from the exploitation of the Software, to which Developer is entitled as Developer's share of Net Receipts hereunder. With respect to said security interest, Developer shall have all the rights, power, and privileges of a secured party under the _____ Uniform Commercial Code as the same may be amended from time to time. Publisher agrees to sign and deliver to Developer all such financing statements and other instruments as may be legally necessary for Developer to file, register, and/or record such security interests.

(j) No additional Amounts Due: Except as herein expressly provided, no other royalties or monies will be payable or paid to Developer.

8. PRODUCT NAME; PACKAGING:

(a) Ownership of Product Packaging: Publisher will own all components of the Software Packages other than the Software and any other materials delivered by Developer. Without limiting the generality of the foregoing, Publisher will own all packaging designs, logos, slogans, advertising materials, and promotional materials, and Developer will have no rights thereto under any circumstances whatsoever.

(b) Ownership of Product Name: Publisher will determine, in its sole discretion, the name under which the Software will be marketed (the "Product Name"). Publisher will own all right, title, and interest in and to the Product Name, including copyright and trademark rights. Developer will not have, under any circumstances whatsoever, any right to use such Product Name, notwithstanding any reconveyance, rescission, or any other circumstance whatsoever, if any, under which Developer is or becomes entitled to market the Software.

9. SERIES AND SEQUEL PRODUCT RIGHTS:

(a) "Product Series"; "Series Identifier"; "Sequel Product": For purposes of this Clause 9, the term "Product Series" will mean two or more products published in such fashion as to create a common identity between the products through use of a Series Identifier. A "Series Identifier" includes, but is not limited to, a common series name or logo, a common marketing theme, common packaging elements, or any other characteristic suggestive of a common identity. For purposes of this Clause 9, the term "Sequel Product" will mean a product that is based upon the Software and/or that concerns the same characters or characterizations as the Software or that is an add-on to the Software, whether it is marketed under the same name as the software, under a similar name, or a different name. A product may be a Sequel Product under this Agreement, even though it might not be considered a sequel in a literary sense.

(b) Ownership of Series Identifiers: In the event that the Software is published as part of a Product Series (including where the Software is the first product published in such Product Series), or where subsequent to the publication of the Software, Publisher establishes a Product Series which includes the Software, Publisher will own all right, title, and interest in and to any Series Identifiers. Developer will not be entitled to any royalty or other payments with respect to such Product Series or Series Identifiers other than with respect to the Software and as set forth in this Agreement.

(c) Publisher Right To Create Sequel Products: Publisher may, in its sole discretion, create one or more Sequel Products, provided that such Sequel Product is created without infringing any of Developer's copyright, trade secret, or other proprietary rights (except where such Sequel Product is prepared by Developer). This Clause 9 will not be construed as giving Publisher any license or other right to incorporate any portion of the Software except as may be permitted by law.

(i) Sequel Product Using Name "_____": In the event that a Sequel Product is prepared by any party other than Developer, and published using the name "_____," provided that Developer will perform all the terms and covenants of this Agreement and in consideration of the rights granted by Developer to Publisher hereunder, Publisher will pay to Developer an amount equal to _____ percent (____%) of the Net Receipts derived from marketing and distribution of copies of the Software, with no minimum royalty per copy. There will be no minimum distribution commitment by Publisher.

(ii) Sequel Product Not Using Name "_____": In the event that a Sequel Product is published using a name other than the name "_____," Developer will not be entitled to receive any royalty or other payments with respect to such Sequel Product.[17]

(iii) Sequel By Developer: In the event that Publisher and Developer agree that Developer will prepare a Sequel

Product, and Developer does prepare such Sequel Product (a "Developer Sequel Product"), the Developer Sequel Product will be deemed to be the Software, and will be subject to all the terms and conditions of this Agreement as though it were the original version of the Software, except that Section 7(a) will not apply. In addition, Clauses 9(c)(i) and 9(c)(ii) will not apply to any Developer Sequel Product.

(iv) No Royalty: Except as expressly set forth in this Clause 9, Developer will not be entitled to any royalty or other payments with respect to such Sequel Product.

(d) Section Does Not Supersede Law: This Clause 9 is intended to follow and be governed by, and not to supersede, United States copyright and trademark laws and applicable common law, and will not enlarge the proprietary rights of Developer or of Publisher beyond applicable laws.

10. NO OBLIGATION TO PUBLISH OR TO CONTINUE PUBLISHING:

(a) No Obligation To Publish or Continue Publishing: Developer acknowledges that there is no assurance that the market opportunity for the Software presently believed by the parties to exist will, in Publisher's sole determination, continue to exist at a commercially reasonable level. Accordingly, Publisher will have no obligation to market the Software or to continue marketing the Software, and the determination whether or not to market or continue marketing the Software, for any reason whatsoever, will be made by Publisher in its sole discretion.

(b) No Representation as to Success: Developer acknowledges that Publisher has made no representation as to the possible or expected success of or perceived need for the Software. Developer understands and acknowledges that no officer of Publisher or any other person is authorized to make any such representation on Publisher's behalf. Developer further acknowledges that in entering into this Agreement it is not relying upon any representations by Publisher (including any Publisher employee or independent contractor) except for representations, if any, expressly set forth herein.

11. TERM AND TERMINATION:

(a) Term: This Agreement will become effective on the Effective Date and will continue until terminated by either party as set forth in this Clause 11. Except as expressly set forth, this Agreement may not be terminated by either party except in accordance with this Clause 11.

(b) Termination For Cause: Either party may terminate this Agreement at any time effective upon written notice of termination to the other party in the event that such other party materially fails to perform any of its material obligations hereunder and such failure continues unremedied for a period of thirty (30) days after written notice of such failure from the party alleging such failure.

(c) Termination for Inadequate Sales: Either party may terminate this Agreement by written notice to the other within fourteen (14) days after the anniversary of the Effective Date if during the preceding four (4) calendar quarters the aggregate royalties payable as a result of the marketing and distribution of the Software (whether such royalties are actually paid to Developer or are charged against advances on royalties) are less than _____ Dollars ($_____), except that Publisher may, at its sole option, pay to Developer an amount equal to _____ Dollars ($_____), less the royalties actually earned by the Software during such calendar quarters, which amount will be treated as a non-refundable advance against royalties. Such amount will be paid to Developer not later than thirty (30) days after receipt by Publisher from Developer of notice of intention to terminate this Agreement.

(d) Clearance of Inventory: Notwithstanding termination or expiration of this Agreement for any reason whatsoever, Publisher will have the continuing right to market and distribute copies of the Software manufactured prior to the effective date of termination or expiration. In addition, in the event that the Software is listed in any catalog as of the effective date of termination or expiration, Publisher may continue to accept and fulfill orders for the Software from any such catalog until the last such catalog is out of print.

(e) No Damages for Termination: Neither party to this Agreement will be liable to the other by reason of termination of this Agreement for compensation, reimbursement, or damages on account of any loss of prospective profits on anticipated sales or on account of expenditures, investments, leases, or other commitments relating to the business or goodwill of either party, notwithstanding any law to the contrary. No termination of this Agreement will release Publisher from its obligation to pay Developer any royalties that accrued prior to such termination or that will accrue to Developer after the effective date of such termination.

(f) No Effect on End User: Upon an end user entering into the End-User License Agreement with Publisher with respect to a Software Package, the end-user licensor will be entitled to use that Software Package including the Software for the term and in the manner provided for in the End-User License Agreement. The end-user rights set forth therein are independent of this Agreement and will survive any termination of this Agreement for any reason whatsoever.

(g) Right to Use Software for Support: No termination of

this Agreement for any reason whatsoever will limit in any way Publisher's right to use the Software for its own purposes and for the purpose of providing technical support to end users of the Software, but Publisher may not manufacture or distribute copies of the Software except as expressly provided herein.

12. CONFIDENTIALITY:

(a) Confidential Information: For purposes of this Agreement, "Confidential Information" will mean any information or material that is proprietary to the disclosing party or designated as Confidential Information by the disclosing party and not generally known other than by the disclosing party. Confidential Information also includes any information that the disclosing party obtains from any third party that the disclosing party treats as proprietary or designates as Confidential Information, whether or not owned by the disclosing party. "Confidential Information" does not include the following:

(i) information that is known by the receiving party at the time of receipt from the disclosing party that is not subject to any other non-disclosure agreement between the parties;

(ii) information that is now or that hereafter becomes generally known to the industry through no fault of the receiving party, or that is later published or generally disclosed to the public by the disclosing party; or

(iii) information that is otherwise lawfully developed by the receiving party, or lawfully acquired from a third party without any obligation of confidentiality.

(b) No Disclosure: The receiving party agrees to hold in confidence and not to disclose or reveal to any person or entity any Confidential Information disclosed hereunder without the clear and express prior written consent of a duly authorized representative of the disclosing party. The receiving party further agrees not to use or disclose any of the Confidential information for any purpose at any time, other than for the limited purpose(s) of this confidence. In the event that either party is directed to disclose any portion of any Confidential Information of the other party or any other materials proprietary to the other party in conjunction with a judicial proceeding or arbitration, the party so directed will immediately notify the other party both orally and in writing. Each party agrees to provide the other with reasonable cooperation and assistance in obtaining a suitable protective order and in taking any other steps to preserve confidentiality.

(c) Published Reports: Without limiting the generality of the foregoing, the parties specifically agree that any reports concerning Confidential Information that are not made or authorized by the disclosing party and that appear in any publication prior to the disclosing party's official disclosure of such Confidential Information will not release the receiving party from its obligations hereunder with respect to such Confidential Information.

(d) No Confidential Information of Other Parties: Developer represents and warrants that it will not use in the course of its performance hereunder, and will not disclose to Publisher, any Confidential Information of any third party (including competitors of Publisher or Developer) unless Developer is expressly authorized in writing by such third party to do so.

13. DEVELOPER REPRESENTATIONS AND WARRANTIES:

(a) Proprietary and Other Rights Warranty: Developer hereby warrants, represents, and covenants as follows: Developer has the full right, power, and authority to enter into and perform this Agreement and to grant to and vest in Publisher all rights herein set forth, free and clear of any and all claims, rights, and obligations whatsoever; the rights hereunder, and any and all of the results of proceeds of the services of Developer hereunder, are and will be new and original; Developer will be the creator of the Software and no part of the Software will be an imitation or copy of, or will infringe upon, any other material, or will violate or infringe upon any common law or statutory rights of any person or entity, including rights relating to defamation, contractual rights, copyrights, trade secret rights, and rights of privacy or publicity; and Developer has not sold, assigned, leased, or in any other way disposed of or encumbered said rights herein granted to Publisher, nor will Developer sell, assign, lease, license, or in any other way dispose of or encumber said rights.

(b) Product Operation: Developer warrants that the Software as delivered to Publisher is or will be free from any material Nonconformities, and will operate and run in a reasonable and efficient manner as described in, and in conformance with, the specifications and instructions set forth in the User Manual. Should any material Nonconformity be detected, Developer will, at its sole expense, promptly either correct such Nonconformity or provide a work-around suitable for relatively unsophisticated end users.

14. LIABILITY LIMITATION: Limitation of Liability and exclusion of consequential damages: NOTWITHSTANDING ANYTHING TO THE CONTRARY CONTAINED HEREIN, EXCEPT AS EXPRESSLY PROVIDED, NEITHER PARTY WILL, UNDER ANY CIRCUMSTANCES, BE LIABLE TO THE OTHER PARTY FOR CONSEQUENTIAL, INCIDENTAL, OR SPECIAL DAMAGES, INCLUDING BUT NOT LIMITED TO LOST PROFITS, EVEN IF SUCH PARTY HAS BEEN APPRIZED OF THE LIKELIHOOD OF SUCH DAMAGES OCCURRING.

15. INDEMNITY:

(a) Indemnification: Developer will defend, at its sole expense, any suit or proceeding brought against Publisher insofar as such suit or proceeding will be based upon a claim that (i) the Software infringes or constitutes wrongful use of any patent, copyright, trade secret, or other right of any third party, or (ii) the Software is in any way defective or does not conform to published specifications, provided Publisher gives Developer such reasonable cooperation and assistance as Developer may request from time to time in the defense thereof. Developer will pay any damages and costs assessed against Publisher (or paid or payable by Publisher pursuant to a settlement agreement) in connection with such a suit or proceeding. Developer agrees to indemnify and hold Publisher harmless from and with respect to any such loss or damage (including, but not limited to, reasonable attorneys' fees and costs).

(b) Cessation of Distribution: In the event that Publisher ceases to distribute the Software as provided in this Clause 15 (other than by reason of a temporary restraining order), Developer will either (i) modify the Software so that Publisher's distribution as permitted hereunder ceases to be infringing or wrongful, or (ii) procure for Publisher the right to continue distributing the Software. If, after reasonable efforts, Developer is unable to achieve either (i) or (ii) above, Publisher may terminate this Agreement. Notwithstanding the limitations on liability contained in Clause 14 above, in the event that Publisher is required to replace copies of the Software that have been distributed to end users with copies that do not contain infringing matter, or to refund any part of the fee paid by end users for copies of the Software, Developer will reimburse Publisher for all reasonable costs incurred in replacing copies of the Software or for all refunds given, as well as all reasonable costs of removing all infringing copies of the Software from the channels of distribution. Publisher will be entitled to offset any royalty or other payments due to Developer under this Agreement against any sums owed by Developer to Publisher pursuant to this Clause 15. Following the earlier of the presentation of any demand or claim or the commencement of any litigation covered by this Clause 15 in which Publisher is named as a defendant, Publisher will be entitled to withhold royalty payments to Developer pending the outcome of such litigation.

16. ACTIONS:
Publisher will have the right, in its absolute discretion, to employ attorneys and to institute or defend any action or proceeding and to take any other appropriate steps to protect all rights and interest in and to the Software and every portion thereof and, in that connection, to settle, compromise in good faith, or in any other manner dispose of any matter, claim, action, or proceeding and to satisfy any judgment that may be

rendered, in any manner as Publisher in its sole discretion may determine. In the event of any claim, action, or proceeding against Publisher based upon allegations that if true would constitute a breach of any of the representations, covenants, or warranties made by Developer hereunder, Publisher will have the right to defend any such claim, action, or proceeding through counsel of its own choice and to make Developer a party to such action or proceeding. Developer will be entitled to participate in any such proceeding at its own expense. In the event that Publisher actually recovers any amounts hereunder from a third party, Publisher will keep all sums so recovered.

17. NOTICES: Except as specifically provided herein, all notices required hereunder will be in writing and will be given by personal delivery, national overnight courier service, or by U.S. mail, certified or registered, postage prepaid, return receipt requested, to the party to whom it is given at the address set forth below, or at such other address as either party hereto may direct by notice given in accordance with the terms and conditions of this Clause 17.

To Developer: _____

To Publisher: _____

All notices will be deemed effective upon personal delivery, or three (3) days following deposit in the United States mail in accordance with this Clause 17, or one (1) business day following deposit with any national overnight courier service in accordance with this Clause 17.

18. MISCELLANEOUS:

(a) Entire Agreement: This Agreement constitutes the entire understanding and agreement between the parties hereto and supersedes any and all prior or contemporaneous representations, understandings, and agreements between Publisher and Developer with respect to the subject matter hereof, all of which are merged herein. Notwithstanding the foregoing, the parties understand and agree that any confidentiality agreements between the parties are separate from this Agreement, and, except as may be expressly stated herein, nothing contained in this Agreement will be construed as affecting the rights or obligations of either party set forth in any such agreement. It is expressly understood and agreed that no employee, agent or other representative of Publisher has any authority to bind Publisher with regard to any statement, representation, warranty, or other expression unless the same is specifically set forth or incorporated by reference herein. It is expressly understood and agreed that, there being no expectation to the contrary between the parties hereto, no usage of trade or custom and practice within the industry, and no regular practice or method of dealing between the parties hereto, will be used to modify, supplement, or alter in any manner the express terms of this Agreement or any part hereof. This Agreement will not be modified, amended, or in any way altered except by an instrument in writing signed by Developer and an officer of Publisher.

(b) Independent Parties: Nothing contained herein will be deemed to create or construed as creating a joint venture or partnership between Publisher and Developer. Neither party is, by virtue of this Agreement or otherwise, authorized as an agent or legal representative of the other party. Neither party is granted any right of authority to assume or to create any obligation or responsibility, express or implied, on behalf of or in the name of the other party or to bind such other party in any manner.

(c) Waiver: No waiver of any provision of this Agreement or any rights or obligations of either party hereunder will be effective, except pursuant to a written instrument signed by the party or parties waiving compliance, and any such waiver will be effective only in the specific instance and for the specific purpose stated in such writing.

(d) Amendments: All amendments or modifications of this Agreement will be binding upon the parties, despite any lack of consideration so long as the same will be in writing and executed by the parties hereto in accordance with the other terms of this Agreement regarding modification.

(e) Severability of Provisions: In the event that any provision hereof is found invalid or unenforceable pursuant to judicial decree or decision, the remainder of this Agreement will remain valid and enforceable according to its terms. Without limiting the generality of the foregoing, this Agreement is intended to follow and be governed by, and not to supersede, the trademark and copyright laws and judicial decisions of the United States and the State of _____, and in the event of any irreconcilable conflict, such laws and judicial decisions will prevail.

(f) Assignment:

(i) Developer: Developer may not assign or transfer this Agreement or any of its obligations hereunder, without the prior written consent of Publisher, which consent may be granted or withheld by Publisher in its sole discretion. Any attempted assignment without such consent will be null and void. The sale, transfer, or encumbrance of fifty percent (50%) or more of the ownership interest in, or outstanding voting stock of, Developer, or the merger of Developer into or with any other third party or entity, will be deemed an assignment for purposes of this Clause 19(f)(i).

(ii) Publisher: Publisher will have the right to assign or transfer this Agreement or any interest herein (including rights and duties of performance to any entity), (A) that owns more than fifty percent (50%) of Publisher's issued and outstanding voting stock, (B) in which Publisher owns more than fifty percent (50%) of the issues and outstanding voting stock, (C) that acquires all or substantially all of Publisher's operating assets, or (D) into which Publisher is merged or reorganized pursuant to any plan of merger or reorganization.

(iii) Binding: This Agreement will be binding upon and inure to the benefit of each of the parties hereto and their respective legal successors and permitted assigns.

(g) Arbitration: This Agreement was entered into in the State of _____, and its validity, construction, interpretation and legal effect will be governed by the laws and judicial decisions of the State of _____, applicable to contracts entered into and performed entirely within the State of _____. Any controversy or claim arising out of or relating to this agreement or any breach thereof shall be settled by arbitration in accordance with the Rules of the American Arbitration Association; the parties select expedited arbitration using one arbitrator, to be a disinterested attorney, as the sole forum for the resolution of any dispute between them. The venue for arbitration shall be the city of _____, State of _____. The arbitrator may make any interim order, decision, determinations, or award he deems necessary to preserve the status quo until he is able to render a final order, decision, determination, or award. The determination of the arbitrator in such proceeding shall be final, binding, and non-appealable. Judgment upon the award rendered by the arbitrator may be entered in any court having jurisdiction thereof. The prevailing party shall be entitled to reimbursement for costs and reasonable attorneys' fees.

(h) Force Majeure: Neither Publisher nor Developer will be deemed in default if its performance or obligations hereunder are delayed or become impossible or impractical by reason of any act of God, war, fire, earthquake, labor dispute, sickness, accident, civil commotion, epidemic, act of government or governmental agency or officers, or any other cause beyond such party's control.

(i) Counterparts: This Agreement may be executed in counterparts, each of which will be deemed an original and all of which together will constitute one and the same instrument.

IN WITNESS WHEREOF, the parties have executed this Agreement as of the date first set forth above.

Publisher   Developer

By: _____   By: _____

Name: _____   Name: _____

Title: _____   Title: _____

EXHIBIT A

SPECIFICATIONS

[This page would include such information as design and technical specifications, milestone schedule, and the composition of the development team.]

_____ (Initial)

EXHIBIT B

MINIMUM ANNUAL ROYALTY LEVELS

First Year:

$_____, prorated by the number of weeks left in the year after the release date.

Second Year:

$_____

Third Year:

$_____

There shall be no minimum annual royalty level required after the end of the third year.

_____ (Initial)

ESCROW AGREEMENT

THIS AGREEMENT by and between _____ ,
a _____ corporation, having an office and principal
place of business at _____
(hereinafter referred to as "Depositor"), and _____
a _____ corporation, having an office and principal place of business at _____
(hereinafter referred to as "Licensee"), and _____ a _____
corporation, having an office and principal place of business at
_____ (hereinafter referred to as "Escrow Agent").

W I T N E S S E T H

WHEREAS, Depositor has entered into an License Agreement
with Licensee dated _____, pursuant to which Depositor
has licensed the use of certain materials in connection with the
development and maintenance of certain CD-ROM multimedia
products listed in Exhibit A (the "Products") to Licensee (such
agreement hereinafter referred to as the "License", a copy of
which is attached hereto as Exhibit B);

WHEREAS, Depositor wishes to provide to Licensee the uninter-
rupted availability of such materials; and

WHEREAS, in connection with the Products, Depositor wishes to
deposit such materials in escrow to be held by Escrow Agent in
accordance with the terms and conditions of this Agreement.

NOW, THEREFORE, for good and valuable consideration, the
receipt of which is hereby acknowledged, and in consideration
of the promises, mutual covenants, and conditions contained
herein, the parties hereto agree as follows:

1. Appointment of Escrow Agent: The Escrow Agent is hereby
appointed as escrow agent to hold and distribute the Deposit (as
defined herein) in accordance with the terms hereof, and Escrow
Agent hereby agrees to act in such capacity.

2. Deposit of Escrow; Revision:

2.1. Deposit: Depositor hereby agrees to deposit or to cause to
have deposited with Escrow Agent, segregated by Product: (1)
one copy of the Product in CD-ROM format; (2) one data file
copy, in the machine-readable format specified on Exhibit C, of
all of the constituent elements of the Product including but not
limited to text, data, images, photographs, illustrations, animation, graphics, video, and audio segments; and (3) source and
object code and user and system documentation, in the machine-readable format specified on Exhibit C (or in the case of
documentation, in hard-copy form), of all software used in the
creation of the Product, and any software which is embodied in

the Product, including without limitation driver or run-time modules (collectively, the "Deposit").

2.2. Revisions: From time to time any Product or version thereof may be corrected, updated, improved, modified, or otherwise revised by Depositor. As of the time any Product or version thereof is so revised, Depositor shall deposit or shall cause to have deposited with Escrow Agent, in accordance with Section 2.1 hereof, one (1) complete revised Deposit for such revised Product or version thereof that is made available to Licensees (the "Revised Deposit"), and such Revised Deposit shall be considered part of the Deposit hereunder. Upon delivery of such Revised Deposit and written notice from Licensee, Escrow Agent shall immediately return to Depositor the Deposit being replaced by such Revised Deposit.

3. Term of Agreement: This Agreement shall remain in full force and effect so long as the License remains in full force and effect, unless terminated earlier in accordance with the terms and provisions of this Agreement.

4. Delivery of Deposit by Escrow Agent:

4.1. Triggering Events: The occurrence of any of the following events (hereinafter referred to as "Triggering Events") shall give rise to a right on Licensee's part to request that Escrow Agent deliver to Licensee the Deposit:

(a) Depositor ceases to do business as a going concern;

(b) Depositor makes a general assignment for the benefit of its creditors;

(c) Depositor is unable or admits in writing its inability to pay its debts as they become due;

(d) Depositor is insolvent, bankrupt, or the subject of receivership;

(e) Depositor authorizes, applies for, or consents to the appointment of a trustee or liquidator of all or a substantial part of its assets or has proceedings seeking such appointment commenced against it which are not dismissed within sixty (60) days of such commencement;

(f) Depositor files a voluntary petition under title 11 of the United States Code or under any bankruptcy, insolvency, or any similar law of any jurisdiction or has proceedings under any such law instituted against it, which, if such proceedings are instituted against Depositor, are not terminated within sixty (60) days of such commencement;

(g) Any substantial part of Depositor's property is or becomes subject to any levy, seizure, assignment, or sale for or by any creditor or governmental agency without being released or satisfied within sixty (60) days thereafter;

(h) Depositor gives notice of termination of this Agreement to Licensee pursuant to Article 5; or

(i) Depositor commits a breach of the License.

4.2. Notice by Licensee: Upon the occurrence of any of the Triggering Events, if Licensee wishes to request Escrow Agent to deliver to it the Deposit, Licensee shall give written notice thereof simultaneously to Escrow Agent and Depositor, which notice shall specify the nature of the Triggering Event. Upon receipt of such notice, Escrow Agent shall deliver to Licensee the Deposit.

5. Termination: In the event Depositor wishes to terminate this Agreement, it shall give written notice of such termination simultaneously to Escrow Agent and to Licensee. Following the expiration of thirty (30) days from the giving of such notice, this Agreement shall terminate; provided, however, that if within such thirty (30) day period Licensee shall file with Escrow Agent an objection to such termination executed by an officer of Licensee, this Agreement shall remain in full force and effect. If at the conclusion of such thirty (30) day period Licensee has not filed with Escrow Agent an objection to termination of this Agreement, or if subsequent to such thirty (30) day period Licensee files with Escrow Agent a withdrawal of its objection, this Agreement shall terminate and Escrow Agent shall return to Depositor the Deposit in accordance with the written instructions given by Depositor.

6. Indemnification of Escrow Agent: Escrow Agent shall not, by reason of its execution of this Agreement, assume any responsibility or liability for any transaction between Depositor and Licensee and shall have no liability hereunder except for its negligence, misconduct, bad faith or fraud. In the absence of Escrow Agent's negligence, misconduct, bad faith, or fraud, Licensee and Depositor shall indemnify and hold harmless Escrow Agent from any and all liability, damages, costs, or expenses, including reasonable attorneys' fees, which shall be sustained or incurred by Escrow Agent as a result of taking such action.

7. Confidentiality: Except as provided in this Agreement, Escrow Agent agrees that neither it nor any of its directors, officers, employers, agents, or designees will divulge or otherwise make available to any third party whatsoever, or make any use whatsoever, of the Deposit without the express prior written consent of Depositor and Licensee. Escrow Agent further agrees that it will take such further steps as may be reasonably necessary or desirable to preserve the confidentiality of the Deposit and to prevent unauthorized disclosure thereof, including without limitation, storing the Deposit in such a manner as to restrict disclosure of and access to the Deposit only to those of its employees who require such disclosure and/or access in order to effectuate the purposes of this Agreement and obtaining from any such employee, prior to any such disclosure or access, an agreement of non-disclosure.

8. Compensation of Escrow Agent: As compensation for the services to be performed by Escrow Agent hereunder, Depositor shall pay to Escrow Agent a monthly escrow fee and pickup and delivery fees as specified in Exhibit D attached hereto. As a condition precedent to Escrow Agent's obligation pursuant to this Agreement to deliver to Licensee the Deposit, Licensee will tender to Escrow Agent an amount equal to the cost as well as all taxes, if any, applicable to such delivery. In the event of non-payment to Escrow Agent's fees or the inability of Escrow Agent and Depositor to consummate negotiations of fees for subsequent years, Escrow Agent shall give Depositor and Licensee sixty (60) days notice of default in payment or inability to renegotiate. In the event the sixty (60) day notice period elapses without Escrow Agent having received payment from any party or consummated negotiations of fees for subsequent years, Escrow Agent then shall have the option, without further notice to any party and without any liability to any party, to terminate this Escrow Agreement, in which event Escrow Agent shall destroy the Deposit or, at Licensee's option, deliver all such material to Licensee.

9. Amendments to Exhibits: Licensee may from time to time and at any time during the term of this Agreement deliver to Escrow Agent revised exhibits of this Agreement, together with copies of any amendments to the License or any other licenses or agreements entered into by the parties which are to be added to Exhibit B of this Agreement. Upon receipt by Escrow Agent of such revised exhibits, each shall be incorporated herein by this reference and made a part hereof.

10. Notices: Any notices required by this Agreement shall be given by confirmed facsimile transmission or by mailing same by certified or registered mail, return receipt requested, to the affected parties at their respective addresses recited at the beginning of this Agreement or at such other address as shall be specified hereafter by notice as provided herein.

11. General:

11.1. Supplementary to License: This Agreement shall be considered an agreement supplementary to the License for purposes of Section 365(n) of the U.S. Bankruptcy Code.

11.2. Assignment: This Agreement shall be binding on the parties hereto and their respective legal successors and permitted assigns; provided, however, that neither Depositor nor Escrow Agent shall assign any of its rights or obligations hereunder, nor delegate any obligations hereunder, without Licensee's prior written consent.

11.3. Entire Agreement: This Agreement, all Exhibits attached hereto, and the License constitute the entire agreement between the parties and supersedes all previous agreements, promises, representations, understandings, and negotiations, whether written or oral, between the parties in connection with the subject matter hereof. No modification, amendment, supplement to or waiver of this Agreement or any of its provisions shall be binding upon the parties unless made in writing and duly signed by all parties to this Agreement.

11.4. No Waiver: A failure or delay by any party to enforce at any time any of the provisions of this Agreement or to require at any time performance of any of the provisions hereof shall in no way be construed to be a waiver of such provisions of this Agreement, and no waiver of any breach hereunder shall be deemed a waiver of any subsequent breach.

11.5. New York Law: The validity of this Agreement, the construction and enforcement of its terms, and the interpretation of the rights and duties of the parties shall be governed by the laws of the State of _____.

IN WITNESS WHEREOF, the parties hereto, each acting with proper authority, have executed this Agreement as of the date hereof.

_____   _____
DEPOSITOR, INC.   LICENSEE

By: _____   By: _____

Title: _____   Title: _____

_____
ESCROW AGWNT

By: _____

Title: _____

CHAPTER 6

VENTURING INTO CYBERSPACE

Communication over the Internet has raised a host of new legal issues. Technology has enabled people to engage in activities not contemplated by lawmakers when they enacted most of our laws. Courts are likely to conclude that many existing laws, such as those prohibiting theft, false advertising, defamation, and copyright infringement, should apply to cyberspace activities. There may be considerable uncertainty, however, as to how to apply these laws. Other issues arise because of conflicting local, state, federal, and international laws. When a message crosses territorial boundaries, it may be unclear which jurisdiction's laws apply.

THE INTERNET

The Internet, or Net, is a loose collection of computer networks worldwide. By 1996, it had grown to a network comprised of more than 9.4 million host systems, which are computers directly connected via the Internet Protocol (IP). By passing data from one computer to another, computer users can communicate with each other quickly and inexpensively. An estimated 18 to 30 million people currently use the Internet, and those numbers are expected to grow rapidly.

No one oversees the Internet as a whole, although the networks that comprise the Internet are controlled by their owners. Certain universities and private organizations have taken the responsibility for handling various administrative and technical tasks to keep the Internet operational. Since there is no "gatekeeper" that decides what can be transmitted over the Internet, anyone could transmit anything in digital form to anyone else on the network.

The decentralized nature of the Internet is a result of its predecessor, the ARPANet. This network was designed by the Defense Department so that research centers could collaborate. A decentralized system was established to ensure that a single bomb or act of sabotage could not disable the entire system. Thus, there is no central hub on the Internet through which all messages must past. Messages can travel through any number of alternative paths to reach their destination.

In the 1980s, the National Science Foundation (NSF), desiring to extend the benefits of computer networking to academic research, linked various networks

NETIQUETTE

HERE ARE SOME GUIDELINES TO HELP NOVICE COMPUTER USERS AVOID BAD MANNERS, A BREACH OF NETWORK ETIQUETTE:

OFF-TOPIC POSTING: DO NOT POST MESSAGES IRRELEVANT TO A NEWSGROUP.

BREVITY: KEEP MESSAGES SHORT AND TO THE POINT. KEEP YOUR SIGNATURE SHORT, TOO.

REPEAT QUESTIONS: DO NOT REPEAT QUESTIONS THAT HAVE ALREADY BEEN ANSWERED AND CAN BE FOUND IN THE FREQUENTLY ASKED QUESTIONS (FAQ) FILE.

PRIVATE MESSAGES: DO NOT POST PRIVATE MESSAGES ON A PUBLIC FORUM.

CONTEXT: WHEN REPLYING, SUMMARIZE THE PRIOR MESSAGE.

ALL CAPS: CAPITAL LETTERS ARE CONSIDERED SHOUTING! USE THEM ONLY IF YOU WISH TO RESPOND TO ANOTHER USER IN THAT MANNER. YOU WILL FIND THAT IT MAY ELICIT A NEGATIVE RESPONSE.

COPYRIGHT: DO NOT POST ANOTHER'S COPYRIGHTED MATERIAL UNLESS YOU HAVE PERMISSION TO DO SO.

FLAMING: DO NOT INSULT OTHERS OR USE RUDE OR VULGAR LANGUAGE. BE POLITE.

to form the Internet. Five universities became prime points of connection. The network was principally used by academic and government researchers. Since government funds were used to establish the network, it was limited to non-commercial uses. Individual networks established Acceptable Use Policies (AUP) that restricted use.

By the 1990s, the NSF opened the Internet to commercial use. Access providers began to offer Internet access to anyone desiring it. A flood of new computer users, "Newbies," invaded the Net community, antagonizing some veteran users. With the floodgates open, it was only a matter of time before people devised methods to make money utilizing the Net.

Communicating over the Net offers many advantages over traditional media. A thirty-second local television spot in prime time can cost $2,500 to reach 190,000 viewers. A piece of direct mail costs about $330 for printing and postage to reach 1,000 people. Internet advertising, on the other hand, costs about $1,000 a month to lease a computer and a full-access line. This equipment enables one to reach 30 million computer users. Thus, while television costs $26.32 per thousand viewers per minute, and mailing costs $330 per thousand pieces, Internet communication might cost as little as three cents per thousand recipients per month.[1]

Internet communication provides other benefits. E-mail is delivered much faster than traditional mail. Recipients can reply immediately if they wish to order merchandise or request additional information. Lengthy product descriptions can be sent inexpensively without the inherent limitations of a thirty-second television spot or the increased printing and postage cost of a mailer. Internet advertisers need not stuff envelopes or sort mail by zip code. The sender can compose the advertisement on a computer and, using an electronic mailing list, he or she can zap the message to millions of people with a few key strokes. The economies are even greater when one considers that half of all Internet users reside outside the U.S.A. To reach them with traditional media, senders would need to pay international postage or telephone rates.

The Internet allows users access to a tremendous amount of information. Users can access Newsgroups on a wide variety of topics. Many are devoted to technical and computer topics, while others are socially oriented, functioning as electronic personal ads. There are groups that discuss such topics as cellular biology, beer, and Italian culture. No subject appears too arcane to merit its own group. There are many sex-related groups, some of which allow users to engage in sexually explicit communications, download pornographic images, or locate individuals with complementary sexual fetishes.

Access providers do not necessarily provide access to all Newsgroups. They choose those of most interest to their subscribers. Some Newsgroups are moderated. Here, someone screens messages and decides which are acceptable to be posted. Most Newsgroups, however, are not moderated. Communication is uncensored, and at times, messages may be vulgar, defamatory, and sexually explicit.

The Internet permits individuals with similar interests to form a community across vast distances at a nominal expense. It can widely disseminate information about the government and encourage citizens to organize and express their own views. At the same time, it allows persons with unpopular, racist, and antisocial views to easily communicate their message to millions of others.

The Internet is a fairly democratic media. While most individuals cannot afford newspaper ads or television spots to air their views, anyone with access to a computer can communicate to millions of computer users via the Internet. Electronic publications can be widely disseminated for minimal cost. The unrestricted nature of the Internet allows users to bypass the media gatekeepers that control other forms of mass media. Those with fringe or eccentric views have just as much access as those with mainstream views. Of course, those who cannot afford a computer with a modem are shut out, which at the present time is the vast majority of the world.

ADVERTISING ON THE NET

There is considerable controversy over the appropriateness of advertising on the Net. In April 1994, two immigration attorneys in Scottsdale, Arizona, advertised their services to approximately 6,000 Newsgroups. The attorneys reportedly obtained 25,000 inquiries, and $100,000 worth of business, from the transmission. The attorneys were also subjected to a fierce backlash. Many Internet aficionados were outraged that someone would indiscriminately post ads to Newsgroups, most of which were devoted to topics unrelated to immigration. The attorneys received numerous "flames," or E-mailed insults and threats. Subsequent postings by the attorneys were canceled by a Norwegian computer user who forged the attorneys' names. Someone sent a death threat to the President of the United States under the attorneys' forged names. Complaints were made to the Tennessee and Arizona Bar Associations. The attorneys' home addresses were published on the Net with the suggestion that their residences be burned.[2]

Opponents of advertising on the Net are vehemently against the practice of off-topic posting. Many consider it bad manners, a breach of "Netiquette," to post a message announcing a sale of cars to a Newsgroup about cats. By posting irrelevant messages, the sender is sending electronic junk mail. Recipi-

INTERNET TERMS

AUP: ACCEPTABLE USE POLICIES. RULES THAT GOVERN THE USE OF A NETWORK.

AUTOMATIC RESPONSE ROBOT: A PROGRAM THAT AUTOMATICALLY REPLIES TO INTERNET INQUIRIES WHEN THE SENDER INCLUDES IN HIS OR HER MESSAGE KEY WORDS SUCH AS "SEND INFO."

BBS: BULLETIN BOARD SERVICES. AN ELECTRONIC BULLETIN BOARD THAT ALLOWS USERS TO POST MESSAGES. MANY ARE DEVOTED TO SPECIALIZED TOPICS AND ARE RUN BY INDIVIDUALS. SOMETIMES THERE IS A CHARGE FOR ACCESS. OTHER TIMES, THE SYSTEM OPERATOR (SYSOP) OPERATES IT AS A HOBBY. THERE ARE AN ESTIMATED 60,000 PUBLIC BBSS IN THE UNITED STATES.

CHAT: LIVE OR "REAL-TIME" COMMUNICATION OR "TALK" BY COMPUTER. ALSO KNOWN AS "INTERNET RELAY CHAT" (IRC). THE COMPUTER USER TYPES A MESSAGE, WHICH IMMEDIATELY APPEARS ON THE SCREEN OF ALL COMPUTER USERS LOGGED ONTO THE CHANNEL AND ALLOWS MULTIPLE PARTIES TO CONVERSE SIMULTANEOUSLY. SOME SYSTEMS ALLOW FOR "PRIVATE ROOMS" FOR INTIMATE CONVERSATIONS BETWEEN SELECTED PEOPLE.

[CONTINUED]

ents are forced to wade through messages that do not interest them. Although an unwanted message can easily be deleted with a few keystrokes, if recipients receive a flood of such mail, the Newsgroup will become a less attractive forum for networking. Unlike magazines, newspapers, billboards, mail, television, and radio, the Net is one of the few mediums not saturated by commercial advertising, although this is changing as advertiser web sites increase. One can understand why Net aficionados do not want their domain invaded by the mercantile interests that dominate other media.

At present, there does not appear to be any law against advertising on Usenet.[3] Some access providers have Acceptable Use Policies (AUP) that prohibit their subscribers from engaging in commercial (i.e., money-making) activities. Because advertising on the Net is so inexpensive, however, one can foresee a time when the Net may be immersed in it. A significant restrain on traditional advertising is the enormous cost of mass mailings and television spots. However, by using the Net, any individual with a computer and a modem could generate millions of unwanted messages. How will

---

INTERNET TERMS [Continued]

DOMAIN NAME: Electronic address of a computer, such as http://www.laig.com/law/entlaw.

FTP: File Transfer Protocol is a simple, widely used method for examining and transferring files on the Internet.

FREENET (Free Internet access): usually offered by a government entity to local residents.

HANDLE: Assumed name or pseudonym.

HTTP: Hypertext Transfer Protocol. The standard for communication between browser software and servers on the World Wide Web.

HYPERTEXT LINKS: A document with words or graphics that contain links to other documents, which usually may be accessed by simply clicking a highlighted word.

ISP: Internet Service Provider. An entity that provides access to the Internet.

ISDN: Integrated Services Digital Network. ISDN lines are digital phone lines that can transmit data much faster than a high-speed modem communicating over traditional phone lines.

[Continued]

computer users react when they log onto a Newsgroup about health care and have to wade through 200 messages from drug companies in order to find the content that they are looking for? Under such a scenario, participation in Newsgroups can be expected to plummet.

There are several possible solutions to this problem. The government could attempt to restrict advertising on the Net. Perhaps all ads should be identified as such in the title of their message so that computer users can readily delete them without reading an unwanted message. Or perhaps Newsgroups will restrict access, limiting participation to subscribers who pay a fee.

Restricting access to Newsgroups, however, will not prevent the transmission of unsolicited E-mail. Messages can be sent anonymously, or senders' addresses can be forged as their addresses are on their E-mail messages. In order to rectify such annoyances, computer programs have been developed that will block out unwanted messages in a manner similar to caller blocking or the identification programs that some phone companies offer.

Naturally, there is less opposition to ad-

INTERNET TERMS [Continued]

LISTSERVE MAILING LISTS: Electronic mailing lists, each of which concerns an interest or organization the subscribers have in common. Every computer user on a list receives all messages posted to the list via E-mail.

NETIQUETTE: The unofficial code of manners for Internet users.

USENET: A collection of 10,000 "Newsgroups" devoted to a wide variety of topics. These forums for public discussion allow users to post messages to one another.

TELNET: A program that allows those on distant computers to access and operate another computer on the network as if they were sitting at the terminal at that distant site.

WAIS: Wide Area Information Server is a tool to search databases that have been indexed with keywords.

WORLD WIDE WEB: Also known as the Web, an interactive, multimedia portion of the Internet.

ZINES: Electronic periodicals.

vertising when ads are posted to relevant Newsgroups. One Newsgroup is misc.forsale, which is the second most popular Newsgroup on Usenet. This group reaches 250,000 computer users. Those who log onto this electronic classified-ad forum, as would be expected, are looking to peruse ads.

Most computer users do not object to indirect advertising. Here, the advertiser does not indiscriminately send out unsolicited ads. Instead, computer users must log onto an information site and request information. Many companies have established such sites to provide in-depth information to potential customers. Virtual shopping malls have been established, allowing computer users to shop in the convenience of their homes. Using the Net to market a business requires creativity and a well-designed web site. The trend is toward "pushing" information out to users who want to receive it. A user visits a web site and signs up as a subscriber of information that will be sent to them on a periodic basis.

INTERNET WEB SITES

The World Wide Web (WWW or the Web) is home to a number of virtual malls. The Web is a hypertext-based system that allows users to move easily from one cyberspace location to another by clicking on highlighted text or an icon. A Web site allows anyone to log on and view the data located there. Users need a graphic web-browser program such as Netscape Navigator or Microsoft Internet Explorer.

Advertising through banners on web sites generated an estimated $138 million in revenues for the first three quarters of 1996. Total 1996 revenue, including non-Web publishers such as America Online, is estimated to be more than $300 million for the full year, according to the market research firm Jupiter Communications. Forrester Research estimates that Internet advertising will top $2 billion by the year 2000. The online retail market is estimated to grow from $500 million in 1996 to more than $6 billion in the year 2000.

Most computer users today access the Internet through standard telephone lines, which do not have the bandwidth capacity for quickly transmitting large volumes of audio and video signals. While the Web is easy to use, downloading audio and video signals takes a long time for those with the relatively slow modems common today.

Another alternative method of communicating over the Net is with File Transfer Protocol (FTP). FTP can be used by anyone who is able to send or receive E-mail. FTP is a quick way for computer users to retrieve computer files from anywhere in the world. FTP sites are easier to establish than Web or Gopher sites. The principal drawback to FTP sites is that the contents of a file cannot be viewed online. After the file is downloaded it can be examined.

FREEDOM OF EXPRESSION IN CYBERSPACE

In America everyone is entitled to their opinion, no matter how bizarre or unpopular. If someone makes a statement you disagree with, your remedy is to refute it by offering a countervailing opinion. The underlying philosophy is to let everyone freely express themselves with the expectation that citizens, not government officials, will be the judge of which statements are cogent and which are nonsense.

The First Amendment of the U.S. Constitution restricts the government from infringing on citizens' freedom of speech. Similarly, the Fourteenth Amendment has been interpreted to bar state and local governments from infringing on citizens' speech. Thus, with limited exceptions, the government cannot censor or restrict speech. In our democracy, we simply do not allow the government to pick and choose which ideas will be disseminated and which will be banished.

Keep in mind that while these Constitutional protections are important, they do not stop private system operators from censoring speech on their own networks. Since most of the Internet is comprised of private networks, each operator may exercise editorial discretion, just as newspaper editors choose what to publish in their papers. The First and Fourteenth Amendments restricts the government, not private citizens, from infringing speech.[4]

While the government generally cannot punish speech because it does not like its content, it can punish behavior. Granted, the line between speech and conduct can easily blur. Some speech, such as a conversation among criminal conspirators, is speech as well as illegal conduct, and is punishable. Likewise, when speech is defamatory, invades another person's privacy, is obscene, comprises false advertising, or infringes copyrighted material, liability may be imposed. As is often said, the right to freedom of speech does not give one the right to falsely shout "fire" in a crowded theater.

Speech that advocates illegal or violent actions may be restricted if it poses a clear and present danger. Thus, posting a message that calls for the violent overthrow of the government could, in some instances, be punished. The test is whether the speech is directed at inciting imminent lawless action and whether it is likely to incite or produce such action.[5] A speaker inciting a crowd to riot could be punished. On the other hand, a bulletin board message simply advocating the overthrow of the government, without urging immediate and specific action, would likely be considered protected speech.

OBSCENITY

There is a great deal of sexually oriented material transmitted on the Net. The material ranges from swimsuit pictures to hard-core pornography. Material may be in the form of sexually explicit stored text, sexually explicit contemporaneous text (Hot Chat), digitized images, or animated sequences.

The First Amendment does not protect obscene works. The courts have had great difficulty, however, in defining precisely what is obscene and what is not. Perhaps it is impossible to articulate a useful definition. In *Miller v. California*,[6] the U.S. Supreme Court put forth the following definition:

(1) Whether the average person, applying contemporary community standards, would find that the work, taken as a whole, appeals to prurient interest;

(2) Whether the work depicts or describes, in a patently

offensive way, sexual conduct specifically defined by the applicable state law; and

(3) Whether the work, taken as a whole, lacks serious literary, artistic, political, or scientific value.

If all three of the above criteria are met, the work is considered obscene and is not protected under the First Amendment. If the material does not meet the above test, it may be declared indecent and in bad taste, but nevertheless, courts have considered it a protected form of expression.

Congress attempted to change the law when it enacted the Communications Decency Act (CDA), part of the Telecommunications Act of 1996.[7] The CDA attempts to prohibit the transmission of "indecent" or "patently offensive" material to minors. The American Civil Liberties Union (ACLU) and nineteen other groups successfully contested the "indecent" and "patently offensive" provisions on the grounds that they were unconstitutional. The Justice Department appealed. U.S. Supreme Court affirmed the decision.

Those who transmit obscene material through cyberspace may be particularly vulnerable to prosecution. The community standard test in *Miller v. California* allows a jury to take into account local mores. Thus, in determining whether communication is obscene, the court can consider that residents of Manhattan may be more tolerant of sexually explicit material than people living in a small town in the Bible belt. But how is "community" defined when information is transmitted far and wide over the Internet? Should the community be considered the online community, those who log onto a sexually explicit BBS, or the community in which any recipient resides?

In July 1994, Robert and Carleen Thomas were convicted for transmitting pictures portraying bestiality and sexual fetishes from a computer board in their California home. Internet users in Tennessee complained, and the Thomases were prosecuted there and convicted of eleven counts of transmitting obscenity over phone lines. Each count carried a jail term of up to five years and a fine of $250,000.[8] The Thomases argued that they should be held to the standard of what is obscene in California, the source of the transmission, rather than Tennessee, where the materials were downloaded. On appeal the Thomases lost, the court holding that Tennessee was a proper venue for prosecution because the defendants had approved of distribution of their pornographic materials to Tennessee.

Federal law prohibits the interstate transportation of obscene material.[9] Another federal statute outlaws interstate and international obscene communications over telephone lines.[10] Although this law was designed with 1-900 telephone services in mind, it may apply to computer users who log onto the Internet via telephone lines. State laws also prohibit communication of obscene materials and may prohibit the distribution of non-obscene material to minors if it is deemed to be harmful to them. As a result, it would be wise for system operators who deal in sexually explicit material to prohibit minors from participating.

Note that, while laws which prohibit the transmission of obscene material are constitutional, the Supreme Court has held that the government cannot prohibit mere possession of such materials at home.[11] Thus, the existence and viewing of obscene material in one's computer would not, by itself, be grounds for prosecution. The government may, however, prohibit importation, transportation, and receipt of such obscene material.[12]

CHILD PORNOGRAPHY

Different rules govern child pornography, which is the depiction of minors in a sexually explicit manner. Here, the government's interest extends beyond the effect such material may have on those who view it. The government has an important interest in protecting minors from participating in such activities. Consequently, depiction of minors in a sexually explicit fashion may be outlawed, even if such material is not legally obscene. The material must, however, involve the visual depiction of a minor. Text stories about minors involved in sex would not suffice unless there were pictures or imagesof children engaged in sexual activities accompanying the text. Likewise, depiction of an adult who looked like a minor would not be sufficient.[13]

Unlike obscene material, people do not have a right to even possess child pornography in the privacy of their home. Federal law specifically prohibits the computer transmission of child pornography.[14] Advertising child pornography is illegal as well.[15] Courts have upheld child pornography statutes against constitutional challenges. The United States Supreme Court[16] upheld a law that made it a crime for any non-parent to possess a nude photo of a minor except for medical, scientific, or other "proper purpose."[17]

LIABILITY OF ACCESS PROVIDERS

Courts have struggled with the question of whether an online access provider, such as America Online (AOL), should be liable for the cyberspace torts of its subscribers. Is AOL responsible, for instance, if one of its subscribers defames another on an AOL bulletin board, or transmits obscene material to minors via E-mail?

Traditionally, the courts have imposed liability on newspaper and magazine publishers, even if they merely republished content created by others. As publishers, they were presumed to exercise editorial discretion over their publications. They were liable for defamation, although they didn't intend to defame anyone or know that the published material was defamatory. On the other hand, courts treated news vendors, libraries, and bookstores as distributors entitled to a greater degree of protection under the First Amendment. Distributors would not be liable unless they knew or had reason to know that they were disseminating defamatory matter. Only a few courts have addressed the question of whether an online service provider should be treated like a publisher or a distributor.

In *Cubby, Inc. v. CompuServe, Inc.*,[18] CompuServe was sued for defamation and unfair competition after a subscriber posted allegedly defamatory statements on one of its bulletin boards. In a 1991 decision, a federal district court ruled that CompuServe was entitled to the same First Amendment protection as a distributor rather than the lower level of protection accorded a publisher.

In the 1995 decision of *Stratton Oakmont v. Prodigy Services, Inc.*,[19] a New York lower court held that the online service provider Prodigy Services (Prodigy) was entitled only to the limited First Amendment protection accorded publishers. The court likened Prodigy to a newspaper publisher because it had exercised editorial control over the content of messages on its bulletin boards. Prodigy had attempted to regulate communications with content guidelines and by using software that automatically screened postings for offensive language. Prodigy filed an appeal but the case was settled before the appeal was resolved.

Stratton Oakmont was a controversial decision. It penalized Prodigy for taking limited measures to control online activities. As an online service provider who made an effort to curb offensive language, Prodigy was held to the standard of a publisher. Providers who made no attempt to regulate communications, however, would be accorded the higher level of protection of a news vendor, as in the *Cubby* decision. If this were the law of the land, it would certainly discourage online service providers from making any attempt to curb the transmission of offensive material.

Congress recognized the dilemma posed by the *Stratton Oakmont* decision, and expressly overruled it when enacting the Telecommunications Act of 1996. The Act states:

No provider or user of an interactive computer service shall be held liable on account of:

(a) any action voluntarily taken in good faith to restrict access to or availability of material that the provider or user considers to be obscene, lewd, lascivious, filthy, excessively violent, harassing, or otherwise objectionable, whether or not such material is constitutionally protected; or

(b) any action taken to enable or make available to information content providers or others the technical means to restrict access to material. . . .[20]

This act does not immunize online service providers; it accords them the same First Amendment protections given distributors, such as news vendors and bookstores, when the online service providers merely transmit content created by others. Distributors can be liable for defamation, however, when they have actual or imputed knowledge of a defamatory communication and they nevertheless disseminate it.

The act does nothing to protect online providers from liability arising from the transmission of material that infringes another's trademark or copyright,[21] though online providers are no better able to police the transmission of material that may violate another's copyright or trademark than they are able to monitor offensive language.

In the 1995 case of *Religious Technology Center v. Netcom On-Line Communication Services, Inc.*,[22] Netcom, a bulletin-board service (BBS) operator and an Internet access provider, was sued when a subscriber of the BBS, using Netcom as his access provider, posted portions of the copyrighted work of Scientology founder L. Ron Hubbard. The subscriber was a vocal critic of Scientology, and his posting was too extensive to be considered a fair use. The plaintiff attempted to stop the distribution of the copyrighted material by demanding that the BBS operator and Netcom drop the subscriber from their systems. The defendants refused.

The court found that Netcom could not be held directly liable for the subscriber's copyright infringement. The court concluded that Netcom had acted as a conduit for the data of others, not unlike the photocopy machine owner who lets the public make copies.[23] While the court found that Netcom could not be liable for direct infringement, it also held that Netcom could be liable on the theory of contributory infringement or vicarious liability. If an access provider was found to have induced, caused, or materially contributed to the primary infringer's conduct, the access provider could be liable as a contributory infringer. Alternatively, if the access provider had the right and ability to control the infringer's acts, and received a direct financial benefit from the infringement, the provider could be vicariously liable for the infringement.

The court's decision not to impose direct liability on Netcom was based on the fact that Netcom had not taken any direct action that resulted in the copying of plaintiff's work. Netcom's system automatically forwarded data at the request of a third party.

There are several other cases, however, where courts, under slightly different facts, have imposed liability on providers. In one case, a BBS operator was held directly liable for allowing subscribers to download Playboy photos.[24] In another case, a court enjoined operation of a BBS because it had facilitated the downloading of pirated video games. Here, the court held that the BBS operator could be liable as a contributory infringer, although he did not know when the copying was taking place.[25]

PRIVACY CONCERNS

E-mail messages must pass through numerous computers on their way to their destination, making them susceptible to interception. E-mail is more like a post card than a sealed letter.

The basis for protecting citizens' rights to privacy can be found in decisions interpreting the United States Constitution as well as a variety of federal and state statutes. In 1968, Congress enacted the Omnibus Crime Control and Safe Street Act, which governed telephone wiretaps. In 1986, those provisions were expanded to cover digital electronic communications.[26] More recently, the Electronic Communications Privacy Act (ECPA)[27] was passed. Under this Act, any government agent or private individual who intentionally intercepts any electronic communication, or intentionally uses or discloses such communication, violates the law. Thus, a computer system operator generally cannot disclose a message to someone other than the intended recipient without the consent of the message sender. There are several exceptions to this rule. For instance, the system operator may divulge the communication if necessary to forward it, and may report it to law enforcement authorities if it pertains to the commission of a crime.[28]

In addition to prohibiting unauthorized interceptions, the ECPA prohibits unauthorized access to computers, so-called hacking. If committed for the purpose of commercial advantage or malicious destruction, the hacker is liable for a fine of up to $250,000 and imprisonment for up to one year. The penalties become more severe for subsequent offenses.[29]

In summary, the ECPA prohibits unauthorized interception, access, and disclosure of electronic communications. Moreover, a person whose privacy rights have been violated may bring a civil suit against the infringer under state common law.

As mentioned in Chapter 2, there are several types of invasion of privacy actions: intrusion, appropriation, public disclosure of private facts, and false light. Several of these types of privacy actions could be readily committed on the Internet. Reading another's E-mail, for instance, could be considered an intrusion. Disclosing intimate facts about another on a BBS could be a public disclosure of private facts. Likewise, portraying another in a false light in an electronic communication might give rise to liability.[30] Considering how easily one can widely disseminate information on the Internet, damages could be substantial.

ANONYMOUS COMMUNICATIONS

Computer users can, and often do, communicate anonymously. Many users adopt fictitious names, or handles, under which they send messages. Using an assumed name, by itself, does not appear to be illegal. Using a misleading name that misrepresents a user's identity could, however, serve as a basis for a fraud action.

The United States Supreme Court has held that at least some forms of speech can be communicated anonymously.[31] Indeed, the founding fathers published the *Federalist Papers* under a pseudonym.[32] System operators may be able to prevent the government from gaining access to their subscriber lists on the grounds that the government's access to this information might violate the subscribers' constitutional right of association.[33]

THE PRIVACY PROTECTION ACT OF 1980

The Privacy Protection Act of 1980[34] protects publishers against government seizure of documents in their possession. Law-enforcement agents are required to subpoena documents, rather than seize them under a search warrant, if they are intended to be published. When a publisher is served with a subpoena, the publisher has the opportunity to object in court before the government seizes the documents. The restriction does not apply, however, when the publisher is the target of a criminal investigation.

It is not clear whether the act applies to electronic publishers and bulletin-board operators. The recent case of *Steve Jackson Games v. United States Secret Service*[35] implies that it does apply.

COPYRIGHT ISSUES

As explained in Chapter 2, copyright law protects works of authorship such as literary works, musical works, paintings, and photographs.[36] Works that are original, an "expression of an author," non-utilitarian, and fixed in a tangible medium of expression are eligible for copyright protection.[37] Just about anything a person writes beyond a bare idea is copyrighted when it is created, regardless of whether the author registers his copyright. In other words, if a writer composes a letter, that letter is immediately copyrighted once the author puts it on paper or on a computer disc. If the letter is then placed on the Internet, the unauthorized downloading of it by another may be copyright infringement.

Thus, communicating over the Internet may pose a trap for the unwary. Unlike phone conversations, data transmitted over the Internet is often protected under copyright law. Telephone conversations are not copyrightable because ordinarily they are not fixed in a tangible medium. Electronic communications, such as E-mail, however, are fixed, and therefore an unauthorized copying or distribution could violate the copyright owner's rights. Dissemination of the contents of a book via the Internet, for instance, should be considered as much a copyright infringement as the duplication and distribution of a hard copy of the book.

Scanning a copyrighted work, including copyrighted graphic images, may comprise copyright infringement. Likewise, reposting a message from one bulletin board to another may be copyright infringement. Of course, if the reposting is authorized by the copyright owner, or is considered a fair use, there would be no infringement. Giving proper credit to the author of copyright material is good scholarship and polite, but it does not immunize the copier from liability.

Computer programs are copyrightable material. Unauthorized copying, except for archival copies or copies necessary to execute a program, may be an infringement. Some software is distributed for free on the Internet. Other software, known as shareware, may be given away with the understanding that it can be used for free during a trial period, but after that, the user is required to send in a registration fee for continued use. Of course, as a practical matter, it may be difficult for a copyright owner to discover whether his work has been copied onto someone else's computer.

There are few reported cases dealing with copyright infringement in cyberspace. As mentioned in Chapter 2, a court has held that loading a computer program from a disc into the random-access memory (RAM) of a computer is a "copying" and therefore a violation of copyright unless otherwise privileged.[38]

In another previously mentioned case, the operator of a computer bulletin board in Florida was sued by Playboy Enterprises when subscribers downloaded some Playboy photos. The photos had been uploaded by subscribers to the bulletin board, but the system operator had no knowledge that the photos were being disseminated over his BBS. The court found that the transmission of the photos was a public "display" and thus a violation of Playboy's copyright.[39] The fact that the operator was unaware of the infringement was no defense since intent or knowledge is not required for one to infringe another's copyright.

Copyright law provides for criminal as well as civil penalties for infringement. An infringer is subject to criminal prosecution if the infringement is conducted "willfully and for pur-poses of commercial advantage or private financial gain."[40] In a recent case, the United States Government prosecuted David LaMacchia, an MIT student, after he set up a bulletin board and encouraged correspondents to upload and download popular copyrighted software programs. Because LaMacchia did not derive any personal benefit from the scheme, he was not liable for criminal copyright infringement. Instead, LaMacchia was charged with wire fraud,[41] which does not require that a defendant be shown to have sought to personally profit from a scheme to defraud.[42]

A U.S. District Court, however, dismissed the case against LaMacchia.[43] The court stated that it appeared that Congress did not intend the wire-fraud statutes to apply to copyright infringement. Therefore, criminal prosecutions for copyright infringement are limited to those crimes specified in the Copy-right Act. This "loophole" in the criminal law may be closed by Congress. For the time being, however, it appears that hackers like LaMacchia who gratuitously distribute copyrighted pro-grams on BBSs without any financial gain are not subject to criminal prosecution. They could, nevertheless, be held liable in a civil action.

VIRTUAL SHOPPING MALL
ADVERTISER AGREEMENT

AGREEMENT dated _____ between _____,a _____ corporation having an office at _____ ("Web Site Owner"), and _____ ("Advertiser"), having an office at _____.

This agreement sets forth the terms and conditions for Advertiser to advertise on Web Site Owner's _____ cyberspace shopping mall found on the World Wide Web at: http://www_____ ("The Web Site").

TERM OF AGREEMENT:

DATE SERVICE TO BEGIN:

INSTALLATION FEE:

MONTHLY PAYMENT:

DESCRIPTION OF PRODUCT(S):

1. Advertiser agrees to provide responsive customer service to all Web Site shoppers and fulfill all orders in a prompt and diligent manner. At any time, Web Site Owner reserves the right to remove Advertiser's ads from the Web Site if Web Site Owner determines, in its sole discretion, that Advertiser is not providing responsive, prompt, and diligent customer service to Web Site shoppers.

2. Advertiser will provide in the Advertisement either (a) a telephone number, (b) a section for electronic messaging, or (c) a mailing address (if all Products are offered free of charge) in order to permit Shoppers to communicate with Advertiser. Web Site Owner may, as it deems appropriate, otherwise make available to Shoppers the Advertiser's telephone number and mailing address.

3. If Advertiser elects to receive Shopper Orders by electronic transmission, Advertiser will check for and download such Shopper Orders at least every hour and confirm the receipt of each Shopper Order within _____ business days of the time such Shopper Order is available for downloading. Advertiser will send Shopper an order confirmation with any products ordered.

4. If Advertiser elects to receive messages from Shoppers, Advertiser will check for messages received at least once each business day and will respond to or acknowledge all messages relating to Products or the Advertisement within two business

days of receipt. Upon Web Site Owner's request, Advertiser will promptly provide Web Site Owner with copies of all such messages and responses.

5. If there is a charge for a Product, Advertiser will either provide information on the Web Site permitting calculation of the final charge for the Shopper Order, or will afford Shoppers the right to cancel their orders or return the Product ordered for a full refund, free of any penalty or fee.

6. Advertiser will provide warranties and customer services for Products offered or ordered from the Web Site equivalent to those it otherwise provides for the same or similar Products.

Except for Web Site Owner software used for accessing the Web Site, any software which Web Site Owner provides to Advertiser, its Agency, or any other agent of the Advertiser to further the purposes of the provisions of this Agreement ("Producer Software" or "Support Software") is provided subject to the following (all terms are as defined in the General Terms and Conditions):

(a) Web Site Owner grants Advertiser a royalty-free, non-exclusive, personal, revocable license to use the Producer Software (and the accompanying user documentation) provided by Web Site Owner solely for the purpose, and in the manner, stated in such user documentation.

(b) Advertiser may provide the Producer Software and documentation (or permitted copies thereof) to Agency or other agent upon written notice to Web Site Owner. If Advertiser or Web Site Owner provides the Producer Software (and documentation) to an Agency or other agent, Advertiser warrants and represents that Agency or other agent shall use the Producer Software and documentation solely in accordance with the provisions of this license.

(c) Advertiser may, upon written notice to Web Site Owner, make copies of the Producer Software only as necessary to fulfill the purpose of the license granted above. Such notice shall specify the number of copies to be made, and Web Site Owner, in its sole discretion, may limit the number of copies. Any and all other use, copying, transfer, or modification of the Producer Software is a breach of the provisions of this license and a violation of applicable law.

(d) Unless terminated earlier in writing by either party, the term of the license granted herein shall begin on the date of delivery of the Producer Software to Advertiser by Web Site Owner and shall end on the date of termination of display of the Advertisement, at which time this license shall terminate and all rights of Advertiser in connection with the Producer Software (and documentation) shall cease, and Advertiser shall return all copies of the Producer Software and any documentation, or destroy same when requested to do so by Web Site Owner. In the event of a temporary take-down of the Advertisement, the license shall be deemed suspended during the temporary take-down and automatically renewed when the Advertisement is again displayed on the Web Site and shall continue for such period of display. Advertiser may retain the Producer Software during the temporary take-down. If the license is terminated during the period of display, or the Producer Software becomes unavailable due to a claim that it infringes a third party's rights, the parties shall negotiate in good faith to identify substitute software or a procedure for accomplishing the same objectives.

(e) The Producer Software (and any accompanying documentation) are provided "as is," and Web Site Owner makes no warranties, express or implied, including, without limitation, warranties of merchantability or fitness for a particular purpose or intended use, concerning any aspect of the use, operation, or performance of the Producer Software (and documentation). Web Site Owner's sole liability for defective Producer Software shall be replacement of the program discs. In no event will Web Site Owner be liable to Advertiser, Agency, or other agent for incidental, special, or consequential damages of any kind (including damages for lost profits).

(f) Web Site Owner shall indemnify and hold Advertiser harmless against any claim, action, liability, loss, and expense (including reasonable attorneys' fees) relating to or arising out of any claim that the Producer Software infringes any copyright, patent, or trade secret of any third party.

(g) Advertiser, Agency, and any other agent shall indemnify and hold Web Site Owner harmless against any claim, action, liability, loss, and expense (including attorneys' fees) relating to or arising out of any breach of the terms of the license granted above.

(h) Subject to the foregoing terms, Advertiser shall abide by any and all additional terms provided by Web Site Owner regarding the Producer Software.

GENERAL TERMS AND CONDITIONS

1. The following definitions shall apply to this Agreement:

(a) "Advertisement": Any advertisement of any nature whatsoever (including any music and/or sound, if applicable) displayed on or sent via the Web Site, including, but not limited to, Standard Advertising Units, Premium Positions, Priority Exposures, Web Site Owner Direct Mail ("PDMs"), and any and all Optional Enhancements described in this Agreement.

(b) "Agency": Advertiser's advertising agency, if any, as specified in the Insertion Order or as designated by Advertiser in a manner prescribed by Web Site Owner.

(c) "Shopper": Any person or entity authorized by Web Site Owner to have access to the Web Site.

(d) "Shopper Order": Any order for a Product, and any response or request made by a Shopper to Advertiser, by means of the Service. Any such order, response or request sent via the electronic-mail function of the Web Site will be deemed a Shopper Order only if Advertiser accepts orders for Products sent in such fashion.

(e) "Product": Any product, service, or information which Advertiser makes available to consumers, whether by sale or otherwise.

2. The installation fee is payable upon execution of this agreement. Monthly fees are payable in advance. All fees are due and payable in U.S. dollars. Advertiser and Agency shall be jointly and severally liable for any amounts due and payable to Web Site Owner and for all taxes other than taxes based on Web Site Owner's net income. If any amount is not paid when due, Web Site Owner may, on fifteen (15) days' prior written notice, discontinue any or all services if such amount is not paid within ten (10) days of such notice. If it should become necessary for Web Site Owner to initiate collection proceedings, then Advertiser and/or Agency shall be liable for all costs and expenses incurred by Web Site Owner in collecting such overdue amounts including, but not limited to, reasonable attorneys' fees.

3. Web Site Owner accepts any Advertisement only upon the representation that Advertiser and/or Agency have the right (including all necessary approvals) to publish on the Web Site as described herein the entire contents and subject matter thereof. Submission (including electronic transmission) of any material for display or sending on the Web Site constitutes approval to display or send it in the form submitted.

4. Web Site Owner will not display in the Advertisement any material relating to Advertiser or the products or services to be advertised without Advertiser's or Agency's approval. Approval of display of any material on the Web Site also entitles Web Site Owner to use such material for research, demonstration, testing, promotion, and Web Site operation. Following display of the Advertisement,. Web Site Owner may use such material for any internal use and for research, demonstration, or promotion, but may use promotional or demonstrational materials only until replaced or the supply is exhausted. Advertiser's approval shall not be necessary for any Web Site Owner promotion (whether or not on the Web Site) or any Web Site function enabling Shoppers to access Advertisements. Web Site Owner will not use Advertiser's name or Advertisements in general media advertising without Advertiser's or Agency's written approval. Web Site Owner shall not be required to retain or recreate any Advertisement or related material.

5. Advertiser and Agency, jointly and severally, assume all responsibility for the content and subject matter of Advertisements and related material (including text, illustrations, and music) and shall indemnify and hold Web Site Owner harmless against any claim, action, liability, loss, and expense (including reasonable attorneys' fees) relating to or arising out of the display, sending, or use of such Advertisements or related material by Web Site Owner in accordance with the provisions of this Agreement.

6. Web Site Owner shall use reasonable efforts to meet the display dates listed on the Insertion Order, but Web Site Owner does not guarantee any specific display or mailing date.

7. Web Site Owner reserves the right to reject or remove any Advertisement from the Web Site for any reason at any time, regardless of any prior acceptance, display, or sending of any such Advertisement. Web Site Owner will have no liability if it fails for any reason to create or produce any Advertisement or screen by any scheduled date or to display or send any Advertisement on, or removes any Advertisement from, the Web Site or if, for any reason beyond Web Site Owner's control, the Web Site is not available when or where it is scheduled to be available; except that the Display Fee for any Advertisement except PDMs will be prorated if the Advertisement is not displayed for the period stated on the Insertion Order.

8. Except for supplying any applicable payment information as provided by the Shopper in each Shopper Order that Web Site Owner makes available to Advertiser, Web Site Owner shall have no other responsibility whatsoever, and Advertiser shall bear all risk, with respect to payment for such Shopper Order. Advertiser will be solely responsible for the collection and payment of any federal, state, or local tax of any nature whatsoever (except taxes based upon Web Site Owner's net income) relating to any Shopper Order.

9. Web Site Owner shall have absolutely no responsibilities or obligations whatsoever regarding any Product offered or ordered on the Web Site. Any service provided by Web Site Owner to any person or entity other than Advertiser and Agency and in connection with any Product or Shopper Order is voluntary on Web Site Owner's part, and shall create no obligation or responsibility of Web Site Owner to Advertiser or Agency. Advertiser shall indemnify and hold Web Site Owner harmless against any claim, action, liability, loss, and expense (including reasonable attorneys' fees) relating to or arising out of any Product offered by, or ordered or requested from, Advertiser by means of the Web Site.

10. Web Site Owner shall indemnify and hold Advertiser harmless against any claim, action, liability, loss, and expense (in-

cluding reasonable attorneys' fees) relating to or arising out of Web Site Owner's display or sending of any Advertisement other than as approved by Advertiser or Agency under the provisions of this Agreement; provided that Advertiser shall notify Web Site Owner in writing within ten (10) days of the display or sending of the Advertisement other than as approved by Advertiser. In no event will Web Site Owner be liable to Advertiser or Agency for incidental, special, or consequential damages of any kind (including damages for lost profits).

11. Advertiser shall abide by all applicable portions of the Direct Marketing Association's then-current Guidelines for Ethical Business Practices, and all federal, state, and local laws and regulations, applicable to any advertisements, promotions, or offers made by Advertiser over or relating to the Web Site, or any Products offered, ordered, or requested through the Web Site.

12. Web Site Owner will have sole discretion to determine all aspects of the operation of the Web Site, and, except where otherwise expressly provided in this Agreement, all matters relating to the content, structure, and sequence of material appearing on the Web Site. Web Site Owner reserves the right to change the layout of any editorial feature and the position of any Advertisement within any editorial feature. Web Site Owner reserves the right to display the word "advertisement" (or a similar notice) in any Advertisement which, in Web Site Owner's judgment, resembles editorial material.

13. Web Site Owner makes no warranties, express or implied ,including, without limitation, warranties of merchantability or fitness for a particular purpose or intended use, concerning any aspect of the performance, capacity, or quality of the Web Site, the personnel of Web Site Owner or any Web Site Owner agent or contractor, or any materials, information, or services which may be used by or furnished to Advertiser or Agency. Web Site Owner will have no liability for any action or representation of any person using the Web Site.

14. Advertiser may not keep records of any personal information about any Shopper ascertained solely as a result of advertising on the Web Site (including, but not limited to, the fact that the individual is a Shopper of the Web Site) other than information specifically provided to the Advertiser by the Shopper. Web Site Owner may record, use, and disclose information relating to Advertisements viewed or sent, and Shopper orders placed, but Web Site Owner will not identify that particular Advertisements viewed or sent or Shopper Orders placed were Advertiser's in any disclosure other than to Advertiser, Agency, and Web Site Owner's independent auditor and authorized agents and contractors.

15. Advertiser and Agency shall use any reports provided by Web Site Owner at their own risk, and may not distribute or

disclose them to any third party without Web Site Owner's prior written consent.

16. If Agency executes and/or submits the Insertion Order, Agency does so as Advertiser's agent. If an Agency is designated by Advertiser, whether on the Insertion Order or subsequent to the effective date of the Insertion Order in a manner prescribed by Web Site Owner, Advertiser and Agency represent that Agency has full authority to act on Advertiser's behalf in connection with all matters arising under the provisions of this Agreement including, without limitation, authority to:

(a) provide, and approve of displaying or sending on the Web Site, any material intended for use in connection with the Advertisement, and

(b) receive and pay all invoices.

Nothing contained herein shall in any way release Advertiser from its obligations, and Web Site Owner may look to Advertiser for performance of any and all such obligations. Web Site Owner Services Company shall be entitled to rely on Agency's authority until expressly rescinded by written notice.

17. Advertiser and Agency shall use the Web Site Owner software and the Web Site only in accordance with Web Site Owner's then-current Shopper Agreement (e.g., the agreement between Web Site Owner and Shoppers) and shall not use them to solicit orders and/or responses or to send unsolicited messages, without Web Site Owner's prior written consent.

18. No terms and conditions other than as set forth in this Agreement, including any terms and conditions printed or appearing on order forms or other documents which conflict with the provisions of this Agreement, will be binding on Web Site Owner unless specifically agreed to in writing by a duly authorized official of Web Site Owner. No Insertion Order will be binding on Web Site Owner until it is countersigned by such an official or expressly acknowledged in writing by such an official. If so acknowledged, the acknowledgment shall govern unless the Advertiser notifies Web Site Owner otherwise in writing. No verbal agreements will be binding on Web Site Owner or Advertiser. Until an order is accepted by Web Site Owner, all rates, terms, and conditions are subject to change without notice. After an Order has been accepted by Web Site Owner, all rates, terms and conditions are subject to change on _____ (__) days' prior written notice.

19. The Insertion Order (i.e., the order placing an advertisement) and this Agreement set forth the entire agreement of the parties regarding the subject matter hereof, and supersede any and all prior agreements or understandings, whether written or oral, with respect thereto. The Insertion Order and this Agreement shall be construed in accordance with and governed by the

laws of the State of _____, without regard to its conflict of laws rules. If any provision of this Agreement is held to be invalid, the remainder will remain in full force and effect.

20. Any controversy or claim arising out of or relating to this agreement or any breach thereof shall be settled by arbitration in accordance with the Rules of the American Arbitration Association; the parties select expedited arbitration using one arbitrator, to be a disinterested attorney, as the sole forum for the resolution of any dispute between them. The venue for arbitration shall be _____. The arbitrator may make any interim order, decision, determinations, or award he deems necessary to preserve the status quo until he is able to render a final order, decision, determination, or award. The determination of the arbitrator in such proceeding shall be final, binding, and non-appealable. Judgment upon the award rendered by the arbitrator may be entered in any court having jurisdiction thereof. The prevailing party shall be entitled to reimbursement for costs and reasonable attorneys' fees.

21. _____ and _____ Mall are service marks of the Web Site Owner. Web Site Owner's prices are subject to change.

AGREED TO AND ACCEPTED:

_____
on behalf of
WEB SITE OWNER

_____
ADVERTISER

AGREEMENT FOR ONLINE DISTRIBUTION OF MULTIMEDIA PROGRAM

This Agreement is made on _____, 199_, by and between _____ Inc., a _____ corporation having its principal place of business at _____ (hereinafter referred to as "Multimedia Producer"), and _____ Inc., a _____ corporation having its principal place of business at _____ (hereinafter referred to as "Online Company").

WHEREAS, Multimedia Producer owns or controls certain rights, title, and interest in the Materials as defined herein and listed on Exhibit A (collectively, the "Materials") and is engaged in the business of designing, producing, and distributing multimedia products and has created an interactive multimedia product based, in part, on the Material; and

WHEREAS, Online Company is the owner and operator of the "Service" as defined herein;

NOW THEREFORE, the parties hereto agree as follows:

1. Definitions:

1.1. Service: As used herein, the term "Service" shall mean an online computerized interactive information-retrieval system, as further described in Exhibit B, which is offered to consumers on a commercial basis.

1.2. Access: As used herein, the term "Access" shall mean the electronic connection through standardized procedures established by Online Company to its computer network, hardware programs, and databases designated by it to constitute the Service.

1.3. Materials: As used herein, "Materials" shall mean the entire contents of the Materials, including, but not limited to, text, data, images, photographs, illustrations, animation and graphics, video or audio segments of any nature as published by Multimedia Producer in CD-ROM format.

1.4. Product: As used herein, the term "Product" shall mean the CD-ROM product developed by Multimedia Producer based on the Materials in CD-ROM format.

1.5. Interactive Retrieval: As used herein, the term "Interactive Retrieval" shall mean transmission of items of the information contained in the Product in response to a contemporaneous request on the Service.

1.6. Subscriber: "Subscriber" shall mean any person or entity which has entered into an agreement with, or has made any payment to, Online Company by reason of which such person or entity has become entitled to receive information from the Product by Interactive Retrieval.

1.7. Fees: "Fees" shall mean any and all monies received by Online Service from Subscribers for the Access to the Service.

2. The Grant:

2.1. Grant: Multimedia Producer hereby grants Online Company a non-exclusive license to extract data from the Product for storage in a central processing unit under Online Company's Control for the sole purpose of permitting Subscribers to extract information incorporated in the Product by means of Interactive Retrieval. Online Company shall be responsible for reviewing the Product provided on the Service and maintaining its accuracy at all times. Online Company will report problems and errors it discovers in the Product to Multimedia Producer, who will take such action as it deems necessary for correction in a subsequent update of the Product.

2.2. Proprietary Rights: All Materials shall remain the sole and exclusive property of Multimedia Producer or its licensors. All rights not explicitly granted to Online Company, whether now existing or which may hereafter come into existence, including without limitation, print publication, electronic publication in all media and formats other than those addressed herein, and the right to make any derivatives thereof, are reserved to Multimedia Producer or its licensors. Without limiting the foregoing, and except as provided herein, Multimedia Producer reserves all rights to make any derivative works of the Materials, transmit, broadcast, or download the Materials through electronic, telephonic, optical, or other means, alter or modify the Materials, or publicly perform or display or exhibit the Materials or any derivative works thereof.

2.3. Product Contents and Modifications: Multimedia Producer agrees to manage, review, create, delete, edit and otherwise control the contents of the Product in accordance with editorial standards and conventions of style for published materials suitable for general public consumption.

Online Company shall have the right under this Agreement to use all or any portion of the Materials on the Online Company Service and shall have general editorial supervision of the Materials; provided, however, that any deletions, modifications, or revisions to the Materials or any portion thereof shall be subject to the prior written approval of Publisher. Online Company shall by notice advise Multimedia Producer when the Materials have been incorporated into the Service, and Publisher shall have fifteen (15) business days from such notice to review the information as it has been incorporated from the Product for the Service. Such review shall be made by a Multimedia Producer representative on Online Company's premises during regular business hours. Multimedia

Producer shall have final approval over the use of all material from the Materials, such approval not to be unreasonably withheld. In the event Multimedia Producer requests changes to be made and/or Online Company makes additional changes to the material in the Materials for the Service, Online Company shall submit any such changes to Multimedia Producer for approval. Multimedia Producer shall then have five (5) days to approve or disapprove such changed material. Online Company shall make any additional changes required by Multimedia Producer or shall remove such changed material from the Service upon notice from Multimedia Producer.

2.4. Trademarks, Legends, and Notices: Multimedia Producer grants Online Company the right to use the trademarks set forth on Exhibit C (the "Licensed Marks"), but only in the format and manner approved by Multimedia Producer, and only in accordance with the terms of this Agreement. The Licensed Marks are trademarks of Multimedia Producer and/or Multimedia Producer's licensor, and all right, title, and interest therein and the goodwill pertaining thereto belong exclusively to them. Multimedia Producer hereby authorizes Online Company to use the Trademarks in connection with the promotion and offering of the Service provided the requirements herein are met.

Prior to the initial use and distribution of the Service which contains the Materials and the Licensed Marks and prior to the initial release or distribution of any and all advertising or promotional materials bearing the Licensed Marks relating to the promotion of the Service, Online Company shall submit to Multimedia Producer, for Multimedia Producer's approval, a sample of each such use so that Multimedia Producer may ascertain the correctness of all legends, markings, and notices in the form and manner in which the Licensed Marks are displayed, and to determine whether the Service, art work, and plans for advertising are consistent with the quality and prestige associated with the Licensed Marks. Five (5) business days shall be allowed for Multimedia Producer to exercise such approval. Upon Multimedia Producer's approval of the sample or samples submitted in connection with this Section, Online Company represents that it shall maintain the quality and appearance of the submitted materials in all respects at the same level approved in writing by Multimedia Producer. The Materials used for the Service and all advertisements and promotional materials relating thereto shall bear the Licensed Marks and shall include an appropriate legend as reasonably requested by Multimedia Producer. Online Company hereby acknowledges the ownership of the Licensed Marks and agrees not to contest such ownership. All use of Licensed Marks by Online Company shall inure to the benefit of Multimedia Producer. All the rights in the Licensed Marks other than those specifically granted in this Agreement are reserved by Multimedia Producer.

Multimedia Producer acknowledges that Online Company is the owner of all other trademarks and trade names associated with the Service.

3. Obligations of Online Company:

(a) Online Company will (i) use reasonable efforts to promote Subscriber Access to the Service and (ii) will meet periodically with Multimedia Producer to determine ways to promote such Subscriber Access. At its discretion, Online Company may produce and publish promotional or instructional literature or information relating to the Product. All promotional and instructional material pertaining to the Product must be approved by Multimedia Producer.

(b) Except as otherwise provided herein, Online Company shall not assign, whether by direct transfer, by sublicense, by distribution agreement, or by any other arrangement desired to make the Product available to others, all or any portion of the Product to any other person without the express prior written consent of Multimedia Producer, and any such unauthorized assignment shall be null and void.

(c) Online Company has the right to add text, data, images, photographs, illustrations, animation and graphics, video or audio segments of any nature to the Product with the consent of Multimedia Producer.

(d) Without limiting Multimedia Producer's rights to the Product, all programs, documents, data, inventions, discoveries, and improvements to the Service provided by Online Company are, and shall remain, the sole and exclusive property of Online Company.

4. Delivery of Materials: Multimedia Producer shall be solely responsible for the delivery of the Product in CD-ROM format within ten (10) days of the execution of this Agreement.

5. Confidential Materials::

(a) Multimedia Producer and Online Company agree to keep confidential all confidential and proprietary information and materials (i) prepared or developed by or for it (including the financial terms of this Agreement), and (ii) supplied by one party to the other under this Agreement, provided that information and materials intended to be held in confidence are (A) designated as "Confidential" and (B) are not available in the public domain.

(b) Confidential information may be disclosed as necessary to enforce a party's rights under this Agreement and to comply with any legal or governmental action. In the event of legal or governmental action, the disclosing party shall promptly notify the other and shall cooperate in any reasonable manner with the other in contesting such disclosure.

6. Warranties and Disclaimers:

(a) Multimedia Producer warrants that:

(i) it has full power and authority to enter into this Agreement;

(ii) it has all rights to the Materials necessary to grant the rights hereunder;

(iii) to the best of Multimedia Producer's knowledge and belief, the use of the Materials by Online Company hereunder will not violate or infringe any copyright, trademark, United States patent, or any right of privacy or publicity; and

(iv) there are no pending lawsuits or claims asserted with respect to the Materials or any portion thereof which may materially affect Multimedia Producer's ability to perform under this Agreement, and Multimedia Producer will promptly notify Online Company in the event any such suit or proceeding is instituted or claim asserted.

(b) THE MATERIALS AS USED FOR THE SERVICE ARE LICENSED ON AN "AS IS" BASIS. EXCEPT AS PROVIDED HEREIN, MULTIMEDIA PRODUCER MAKES NO OTHER WARRANTIES WITH RESPECT TO FITNESS FOR A PARTICULAR PURPOSE OR MERCHANTABILITY, AND NO SUCH WARRANTIES ARE TO BE IMPLIED WITH RESPECT TO THE LICENSE GRANTED HEREUNDER.

(c) Online Company warrants that:

(i) it has the full power and authority to enter this Agreement;

(ii) it will include any and all copyrights and trademark notices reasonably requested by Multimedia Producer as necessary to protect and preserve Multimedia Producer's proprietary interests in and to the Materials;

(iii) any deletions, modifications, or revisions made by Online Company to the Materials pursuant to the terms of this Agreement will not change the substantive meaning of the information contained in the Materials and displayed on the Service;

(iv) no person or entity has, or will have at any time during the term of this Agreement, any right, title, or interest in or to the Service which would in any way impair or derogate from any rights granted by Multimedia Producer herein, and Online Company shall not do anything which may impair or derogate from the rights granted by Multimedia Producer hereunder or fail to do anything necessary to maintain and preserve such rights;

(v) there are no lawsuits or proceedings pending in any forum or any claims asserted concerning any aspect of the Service or which could materially affect Online Company's ability to perform its obligations under this Agreement, and Online Company will promptly notify Multimedia Producer in the event that any such suit or proceeding is instituted or claim asserted.

(vi) it is technically possible to completely purge or remove the Materials from the Service upon the expiration or earlier termination of this Agreement.

7. Indemnifications:

(a) Multimedia Producer shall defend and indemnify Online Company from all damages, costs, and expenses which they may incur as a result of a breach of the warranties set forth in Paragraph 6. Notwithstanding the foregoing, Multimedia Producer shall not be liable for any matter not specifically contained in the original Materials and the Product.

(b) Online Company shall indemnify Multimedia Producer for all damages, costs, and expenses which it may incur as a result of a breach of the warranties set forth in Paragraph 5 as well as any claim, suit, loss, or damage arising in connection with the Service. With respect to any suit, claim, demand, or action against Multimedia Producer for which Multimedia Producer is indemnified by Online Company pursuant to this Section, Multimedia Producer may elect either to undertake the defense thereof with counsel of its own choosing or to notify Online Company to undertake the defense. In either case, Online Company shall bear the costs and expenses of the settlement and/or defense thereof. Should Multimedia Producer undertake the defense, and should Online Company nevertheless wish to be represented in the matter by attorneys of its own choosing, Online Company shall bear the expenses of its own attorney. Online Company may in any case and at any time settle any such claim provided, however, that Online Company shall in no event impose any obligations on Multimedia Producer as part of any such settlement. Any settlement by Multimedia Producer of a claim hereunder shall be subject to the approval of Online Company, such approval not to be unreasonably withheld.

(c) in the event of an indemnification obligation arising from Section 6(a) herein, Online Company shall not have the rights to withhold Payment of any amounts otherwise due nor may Online Company otherwise attempt to defray any costs and expenses it may incur against any sums due to Multimedia Producer.

8. Term:

(a) This Agreement shall continue in force for an initial term of one (1) year from the time the Product is made available to Subscribers, or eighteen (18) months from the date of the signing of this Agreement, whichever is earlier.

(b) In the event of termination or expiration of the term of this Agreement, each party shall, within (30) days after receipt of written request from the other party, return or destroy (as the requesting party may direct) all confidential and proprietary information of the other party (including computer-readable media containing the Product delivered by Multimedia Producer to Online Company) then in its possession and control.

(c) The terms of Section 7 of this Agreement shall survive the termination of this Agreement.

9. Marketing and Promotion:

(a) Online Company will provide reasonable feedback to Multimedia Producer on use of the Product by Online Company Subscribers.

(b) Multimedia Producer will cooperate with Online Company in the development and production of promotional or instructional literature or information relating to the Product; provided, however, that such materials shall be subject to Multimedia Producer's written approval.

10. Royalties: Online Company shall pay to Multimedia Producer a royalty of __ percent (__%) of the fees received by Online Company from Subscriber Access to the Product.

11. Force Majeure: Neither party shall be liable to the other or deemed to be in default hereunder for non-performance or delays due to fire, boycott, lock-out, war, labor or civil disturbance, riots, acts of God, insurrection, government orders or regulations, or any other cause beyond the reasonable control of the party delayed or prevented from performing. If, however, a party's non-performance or delay continues for a period of three (3) months, then the other party may terminate this Agreement for convenience upon thirty (30) days' prior written notice to the other party; provided, however, that if performance resumes within said thirty (30) day period, then this Agreement shall continue in full force and effect as though no such notice had been given.

12. Notices: All notices under this Agreement shall be given in writing via confirmed facsimile transmission, or by first-class mail, certified, return receipt request, to the addresses set forth above or such other address as either party may substitute by notice hereunder and all such notices given in accordance hereunder shall be deemed given on the date of the facsimile transmission or within three (3) days of the date of mailing as applicable.

13. Assignments:

Neither this Agreement nor any rights or obligations hereunder may be transferred, assigned, or sublicensed by Online Company without the prior written consent of Multimedia Producer except that Online Company may assign the Agreement to its parent or "affiliate," as that term is defined in the Rules and Regulations promulgated under the Securities & Exchange Act of 1934, provided that in the event of any such assignment allowed by this paragraph, Online Company shall continue to remain responsible for all of its obligations and liabilities under this Agreement. Any transfer, assignment, or sublicense in contravention hereof shall be null and void.

14. Arbitration:

This Agreement shall be governed by and construed under the laws of the State of _____ applicable to agreements made and fully performed therein. Any controversy or claim arising out of or relating to this agreement or any breach thereof shall be settled by arbitration in accordance with the Rules of the American Arbitration Association; the parties select expedited arbitration using one arbitrator as the sole forum for the resolution of any dispute between them. The venue for arbitration shall be _____. The arbitrator may make any interim order, decision, determinations, or award he deems necessary to preserve the status quo until he is able to render a final order, decision, determination, or award. The determination of the arbitrator in such proceeding shall be final, binding and non-appealable. Judgment upon the award rendered by the arbitrator may be entered in any court having jurisdiction thereof. The prevailing party shall be entitled to reimbursement for costs and reasonable attorneys' fees.

15. Entire Agreement:

This agreement constitutes the sole and entire agreement between the parties concerning the subject matter hereof and supersedes all proposals, oral or written, and all negotiations, conversations, and other communications and contracts between the parties relating to the subject matter herein. No waiver, alteration, or modification of any of the provisions hereof shall be binding unless in writing and signed by duly authorized representatives of the parties.

WITNESS WHEREOF, the parties have executed this Agreement as of the date hereof.

ONLINE COMPANY, INC.   MULTIMEDIA PRODUCER, INC.

By: _____   By: _____

Title: _____   Title: _____

CHAPTER 7

PROTECTING MULTIMEDIA WORKS FROM INFRINGEMENT

Multimedia producers will want to take steps to ensure that their work is not pirated by others. Protection can be obtained under copyright, trademark, patent, and trade secret laws.

COPYRIGHT

The Copyright Office has taken the position that the screen display of a computer program is protected by the copyright in the program. Thus, one need not register the screen display separately as an audiovisual work. While some decisions have expressed the view that screen images should be separately registered to fully protect them,[1] the Copyright Office announced in June 1988 that the screen display of a computer program is protected as part of the program.[2]

A multimedia work comprising a series of images could be classified, for copyright purposes, as either a motion picture (if the images are moving) or an audiovisual work.[3] Video games are considered audiovisual works.[4] A virtual-reality display might be considered a motion picture.

Although copyright registration is not required, it is desirable. Registration for U.S. authors is necessary before instituting an infringement action,[5] and only authors who register their works in a timely manner can recover statutory damages and attorneys' fees. While a copyright notice ("©"), name of the author, the year of publication is optional after March 1, 1989,[6] placing a notice on all work is recommended. The notice will prevent infringers from claiming that they did not know the work was copyrighted. The amount of damages recoverable from innocent infringers is less than from willful infringers.[7]

A multimedia work may be registered by completing one application, or each of the elements may be registered separately. Individual registrations are required if any element is published separately or if the copyright to various elements are held by different persons.[8]

The elements of the multimedia work will determine which form or forms are appropriate. Form PA should be

REGISTRATION OF MULTIMEDIA WORKS

SELECTION OF THE APPROPRIATE COPYRIGHT APPLICATION FORM DEPENDS ON THE ELEMENTS OF THE MULTIMEDIA WORK. USE FORM:

PA: IF THE WORK CONTAINS AN AUDIOVISUAL ELEMENT, SUCH AS SLIDES, FILM, OR VIDEOTAPE, REGARDLESS OF WHETHER THERE ARE ANY SOUNDS.

SR: IF THE WORK DOES NOT CONTAIN AN AUDIOVISUAL ELEMENT BUT CONTAINS AN AUDIOTAPE OR DISC IN WHICH SOUND-RECORDING AUTHORSHIP IS CLAIMED.

TX: IF THE WORK CONTAINS ONLY TEXT, SUCH AS A COMPUTER PROGRAM THAT PRODUCES A TEXTUAL SCREEN DISPLAY.

SINGLE REGISTRATION: ALL COPYRIGHTABLE ELEMENTS OF A MULTIMEDIA WORK MAY BE REGISTERED BY COMPLETING ONE APPLICATION, DEPOSITING A COPY, AND PAYING THE REGISTRATION FEE. THIS SINGLE REGISTRATION WILL ONLY BE ACCEPTED IF (1) THE ELEMENTS ARE NOT PUBLISHED, OR IF PUBLISHED, THEY ARE PUBLISHED AS A SINGLE UNIT, AND (2) THE COPYRIGHT CLAIMANT IS THE SAME FOR EACH ELEMENT (I.E., ONE PERSON OR COMPANY OWNS ALL THE ELEMENTS).

SEPARATE REGISTRATION: ELEMENTS MAY BE SEPARATELY REGISTERED. SEPARATE REGISTRATION IS REQUIRED WHEN ANY ELEMENT IS PUBLISHED SEPARATELY OR WHEN THERE ARE DIFFERENT COPYRIGHT OWNERS OF THE ELEMENTS.

PROTECTING
MULTIMEDIA
WORKS
FROM
INFRINGEMENT

255

used for audiovisual elements, such as slides, film or video-tape. Form SR should be used if the work doesn't contain an audiovisual element but contains an audiotape or disc in which sound-recording authorship is claimed. Form TX is used if the work is comprised solely of text.

To prevail in a copyright infringement suit, one must prove ownership of the copyright in question, and that the protected expression was copied. Copying is usually proven by circumstantial evidence since copyright infringers generally operate out of the view of witnesses. The fact that the defendant had access to the original work and the fact that the works are substantially similar can be used as evidence of copying.

Treatments and scripts for multimedia works may be registered with the Writers Guild of America (WGA). Registration is evidence of the completion date of the registered material. In a plagiarism dispute, a key issue may be which party created the work and which party copied the other. The party who can prove first creation is presumed to be the creator, the other the copier. Thus, registration creates key evidence that may help a writer protect his work. If a work

WHAT CAN BE COPYRIGHTED
LITERARY WORKS
MUSICAL WORKS
DRAMATIC WORKS
PANTOMIMES
PHOTOGRAPHS
GRAPHIC DESIGN
SCULPTURE
MOTION PICTURES
SOUND RECORDINGS
CHOREOGRAPHY
COMPUTER PROGRAMS

WHAT CANNOT BE COPYRIGHTED
INVENTIONS
IDEAS
THEMES
INDUSTRIAL DESIGN
TYPEFACE DESIGN
TITLES
HISTORICAL EVENTS
ANYTHING IN THE PUBLIC DOMAIN

is registered with the Copyright Office, that registration is evidence of authorship; therefore, registration with the WGA is less important. Copyright registration also grants the author additional protections such as statutory damages and reimbursement

COPYRIGHT OWNERSHIP

(1) SELF-EMPLOYED INDIVIDUALS: THEY WILL OWN THE COPYRIGHT TO WORK THEY CREATE AS LONG AS THE WORK MEETS THE CRITERIA FOR A COPYRIGHT.

(2) COLLABORATORS: WORKS CREATED BY THE COLLABORATIVE EFFORT OF SEVERAL AUTHORS MAY BE JOINT WORKS. A JOINT WORK IS PREPARED BY TWO OR MORE AUTHORS WITH THE INTENTION THAT THEIR CONTRIBUTIONS ARE MERGED INTO INSEPARABLE OR INTERDEPENDENT PARTS OF A UNITARY WHOLE. IT IS IMPORTANT THAT THE AUTHORS INTEND AT THE TIME OF CREATION THAT THEIR RESPECTIVE LABORS ARE INTEGRATED INTO ONE WORK.

(3) EMPLOYEES: ALL WORKS PREPARED BY EMPLOYEES WITHIN THE SCOPE OF THEIR EMPLOYMENT ARE PRESUMED TO BE WORKS FOR HIRE UNLESS THE PARTIES HAVE EXPRESSLY AGREED OTHERWISE IN A WRITTEN INSTRUMENT SIGNED BY THEM. THE EMPLOYER IS CONSIDERED THE COPYRIGHT OWNER OF WORKS MADE FOR HIRE. THE EMPLOYEE HAS NO OWNERSHIP RIGHTS AT ALL.

(4) FREELANCE ARTISTS AND INDEPENDENT CONTRACTORS: CERTAIN WORKS[9] THAT ARE SPECIALLY MADE OR COMMISSIONED FROM INDEPENDENT CONTRACTORS ARE CONSIDERED WORKS FOR HIRE IF THE PARTIES EXPRESSLY AGREE SO IN WRITING. AS EXPLAINED IN CHAPTER 3, THE AGREEMENT MUST BE SIGNED BY BOTH PARTIES AND MUST CONSIST OF EXPLICIT WORDING THAT THE WORK IS A WORK FOR HIRE. OTHERWISE, THE ARTIST/CONTRAC-TOR WILL OWN THE COPYRIGHT. IF YOU ARE EMPLOYING AN ARTIST, AND YOU WANT TO OWN THE COPYRIGHT TO HIS OR HER WORK PRODUCT, IT IS IMPORTANT THAT A WRITTEN CONTRACT BE SIGNED BY THE ARTIST BEFORE ANY WORK BEGINS. OTHERWISE, THE INITIAL COPYRIGHT WILL VEST IN THE ARTIST. IF WORK HAS BEGUN WITHOUT A SIGNED CONTRACT, YOU SHOULD ALSO HAVE THE ARTIST SIGN AN ASSIGNMENT AGREEMENT THAT TRANSFERS THE COPYRIGHT TO YOU.

(5) SUBSEQUENT OWNERS: LIKE OTHER PROPERTY, COPYRIGHTS CAN BE SOLD AND TRANSFERRED. TO BE EFFECTIVE, TRANSFERS OF COPYRIGHT MUST BE IN WRITING AND SIGNED BY THE TRANSFER-RING COPYRIGHT OWNER. THIS REQUIREMENT DOES NOT APPLY TO A NON-EXCLUSIVE LICENSE (I.E., GIVING SOMEONE PERMIS-SION TO USE YOUR WORK ON A NON-EXCLUSIVE BASIS).

of attorneys' fees if the registration is timely. One advantage of WGA registration is that the deposited work is sequestered and is not available to the public. WGA registration lasts five years and may be renewed for an additional five-year period.

COPYRIGHT NOTICE
FOR MULTIMEDIA WORKS

The copyright notice should contain three elements:

(1) The symbol ©, or word "copyright" or abbreviation "copr." This should be placed on copies of the work that are visually perceptible, either with the naked eye or with the use of a machine, or the symbol should be placed on phonorecords of sound recordings.

(2) The year of first publication of the work.

(3) The name of the copyright owner.

Although a separate notice may be placed on each element of a multimedia work, one notice is sufficient. Where a sound recording is included, however, the notice should be placed on the phonorecord.

DURATION OF COPYRIGHT

BEFORE 1978: COPYRIGHT LASTS FOR TWENTY-EIGHT YEARS AND CAN BE RENEWED FOR ONE ADDITIONAL TWENTY-EIGHT-YEAR TERM. FOR WORKS PUBLISHED BEFORE 1978, THE 1909 ACT'S TWO TWENTY-EIGHT-YEAR-TERM SCHEME CONTINUES TO APPLY. HOWEVER, THE SECOND TERM HAS BEEN EXTENDED TO FORTY-SEVEN YEARS. THE FIRST TERM IS MEASURED FROM THE DATE OF PUBLICATION.

AFTER 1978: THE COPYRIGHT FOR WORKS CREATED AFTER JANUARY 1, 1978, WILL LAST FOR THE LIFETIME OF THE AUTHOR PLUS FIFTY YEARS.[10] FOR ANONYMOUS WORKS AND WORKS MADE FOR HIRE, COPYRIGHT GENERALLY LASTS 75 YEARS FROM FIRST PUBLICATION OR 100 YEARS FROM CRE-ATION, WHICHEVER EXPIRES FIRST.

ADDITIONAL COPYRIGHT INFORMATION

Copyright Office
Library of Congress
Washington, DC 20559
(202) 707-3000

To order publications, write to "Publications Section, LM-455" at the above address, or call the Copyright Office forms and circulars hotline at: (202) 707-9100. Orders are recorded automatically and then mailed to you. Publications are free. Some publications of particular interest to multimedia producers:

Copyright Basics: Circular 1

Publications on Copyright: Circular 2

Copyright Fees: Circular 4

Copyright Registration for Multimedia Works: Circular 55

Copyright Registration for Computer Programs: Circular 61

Registration for Video Games and Other Machine-Readable Audiovisual Works: Circular 49

Copyright Law of the United States: Circular 92

How to Investigate the Status of a Work: Circular 22

Fair Use: Information Kit 102

Computer Programs: Information Kit 113

Multi-Media Kits: Information Kit 112

Games: Information Kit 108

Some copyright documents are available by fax. Call (202) 707-2600 from a touchtone telephone to order documents you would like faxed back to you. Note that copyright application forms are not available by fax.

All copyright application forms and frequently requested circulars, announcements, and proposed regulations are available via the Internet. They may be downloaded and printed for use. The Copyright Office home page is http://www.loc.gov/copyright. You need Adobe Acrobat Reader

[Continued]

PROTECTING
MULTIMEDIA
WORKS
FROM
INFRINGEMENT

259

ADDITIONAL COPYRIGHT INFORMATION
[CONTINUED]

INSTALLED ON YOUR COMPUTER TO VIEW OR PRINT THE FORMS.
IT IS AVAILABLE FOR FREE AT THE SAME INTERNET SITE.

COPYRIGHT OFFICE RECORDS, INCLUDING REGISTRATION
INFORMATION AND RECORDED DOCUMENTS, FROM JANUARY 1,
1978, TO THE PRESENT CAN BE EXAMINED OVER THE
INTERNET. THE COPYRIGHT OFFICE DOES NOT CHARGE FOR
ACCESS TO ITS INTERNET RESOURCES.

REGISTRATION PROCEDURES

THE FOLLOWING SHOULD BE SENT IN ONE ENVELOPE:

(1) A PROPERLY COMPLETED APPLICATION FORM. USE FORM:

TX: FOR PUBLISHED AND UNPUBLISHED NONDRAMATIC
LITERARY WORKS.

PA: FOR PUBLISHED AND UNPUBLISHED WORKS OF THE
PERFORMING ARTS (MUSICAL AND DRAMATIC WORKS,
PANTOMIMES, CHOREOGRAPHY, MOTION PICTURES).

VA: FOR PUBLISHED AND UNPUBLISHED WORKS OF THE
VISUAL ARTS (PICTORIAL, GRAPHIC, AND SCULPTURAL
WORKS).

SR: FOR PUBLISHED AND UNPUBLISHED SOUND RECORD-
INGS.

(2) A NON-REFUNDABLE FEE (CURRENTLY $20.00) AND,

(3) A DEPOSIT COPY.

(4) SEND THE ENVELOPE TO:
REGISTER OF COPYRIGHTS
LIBRARY OF CONGRESS
WASHINGTON, DC 20559-6000

REGISTRATION IS EFFECTIVE ON THE DATE OF RECEIPT IN THE
COPYRIGHT OFFICE.

✐ Filling Out Application Form TX

Detach and read these instructions before completing this form.
Make sure all applicable spaces have been filled in before you return this form.

BASIC INFORMATION

When to Use This Form: Use Form TX for registration of published or unpublished nondramatic literary works, excluding periodicals or serial issues. This class includes a wide variety of works: fiction, nonfiction, poetry, textbooks, reference works, directories, catalogs, advertising copy, compilations of information, and computer programs. For periodicals and serials, use Form SE.

Deposit to Accompany Application: An application for copyright registration must be accompanied by a deposit consisting of copies or phonorecords representing the entire work for which registration is to be made. The following are the general deposit requirements as set forth in the statute:

Unpublished Work: Deposit one complete copy (or phonorecord).

Published Work: Deposit two complete copies (or one phonorecord) of the best edition.

Work First Published Outside the United States: Deposit one complete copy (or phonorecord) of the first foreign edition.

Contribution to a Collective Work: Deposit one complete copy (or phonorecord) of the best edition of the collective work.

The Copyright Notice: For works first published on or after March 1, 1989, the law provides that a copyright notice in a specified form "may be placed on all publicly distributed copies from which the work can be visually perceived." Use of the copyright notice is the responsibility of the copyright owner and does not require advance permission from the Copyright Office. The required form of the notice for copies generally consists of three elements: (1) the symbol "©," or the word "Copyright," or the abbreviation "Copr."; (2) the year of first publication; and (3) the name of the owner of copyright. For example: "© 1995 Jane Cole." The notice is to be affixed to the copies "in such manner and location as to give reasonable notice of the claim of copyright." Works first published prior to March 1, 1989, **must** carry the notice or risk loss of copyright protection.

For information about notice requirements for works published before March 1, 1989, or other copyright information, write: Information Section, LM-401, Copyright Office, Library of Congress, Washington, D.C. 20559-6000.

LINE-BY-LINE INSTRUCTIONS
Please type or print using black ink.

1 SPACE 1: Title

Title of This Work: Every work submitted for copyright registration must be given a title to identify that particular work. If the copies or phonorecords of the work bear a title or an identifying phrase that could serve as a title, transcribe that wording *completely* and *exactly* on the application. Indexing of the registration and future identification of the work will depend on the information you give here.

Previous or Alternative Titles: Complete this space if there are any additional titles for the work under which someone searching for the registration might be likely to look or under which a document pertaining to the work might be recorded.

Publication as a Contribution: If the work being registered is a contribution to a periodical, serial, or collection, give the title of the contribution in the "Title of this Work" space. Then, in the line headed "Publication as a Contribution," give information about the collective work in which the contribution appeared.

2 SPACE 2: Author(s)

General Instructions: After reading these instructions, decide who are the "authors" of this work for copyright purposes. Then, unless the work is a "collective work," give the requested information about every "author" who contributed any appreciable amount of copyrightable matter to this version of the work. If you need further space, request Continuation sheets. In the case of a collective work such as an anthology, collection of essays, or encyclopedia, give information about the author of the collective work as a whole.

Name of Author: The fullest form of the author's name should be given. Unless the work was "made for hire," the individual who actually created the work is its "author." In the case of a work made for hire, the statute provides that "the employer or other person for whom the work was prepared is considered the author."

What is a "Work Made for Hire"? A "work made for hire" is defined as (1) "a work prepared by an employee within the scope of his or her employment"; or (2) "a work specially ordered or commissioned for use as a contribution to a collective work, as a part of a motion picture or other audiovisual work, as a translation, as a supplementary work, as a compilation, as an instructional text, as a test, as answer material for a test, or as an atlas, if the parties expressly agree in a written instrument signed by them that the work shall be considered a work made for hire." If you have checked "Yes" to indicate that the work was "made for hire," you must give the full legal name of the employer (or other person for whom the work was prepared). You may also include the name of the employee along with the name of the employer (for example: "Elster Publishing Co., employer for hire of John Ferguson").

"Anonymous" or "Pseudonymous" Work: An author's contribution to a work is "anonymous" if that author is not identified on the copies or phonorecords of the work. An author's contribution to a work is "pseudonymous" if that author is identified on the copies or phonorecords under a fictitious name. If the work is "anonymous" you may: (1) leave the line blank; or (2) state "anonymous" on the line; or (3) reveal the author's identity. If the work is "pseudonymous" you may: (1) leave the line blank; or (2) give the pseudonym and identify it as such (for example: "Huntley Haverstock, pseudonym"); or (3) reveal the author's name, making clear which is the real name and which is the pseudonym (for example, "Judith Barton, whose pseudonym is Madeline Elster"). However, the citizenship or domicile of the author **must** be given in all cases.

Dates of Birth and Death: If the author is dead, the statute requires that the year of death be included in the application unless the work is anonymous or pseudonymous. The author's birth date is optional but is useful as a form of identification. Leave this space blank if the author's contribution was a "work made for hire."

Author's Nationality or Domicile: Give the country of which the author is a citizen or the country in which the author is domiciled. Nationality or domicile **must** be given in all cases.

Nature of Authorship: After the words "Nature of Authorship," give a brief general statement of the nature of this particular author's contribution to the work. Examples: "Entire text"; "Coauthor of entire text"; "Computer program"; "Editorial revisions"; "Compilation and English translation"; "New text."

3 SPACE 3: Creation and Publication

General Instructions: Do not confuse "creation" with "publication." Every application for copyright registration must state "the year in which creation of the work was completed." Give the date and nation of first publication only if the work has been published.

Creation: Under the statute, a work is "created" when it is fixed in a copy or phonorecord for the first time. Where a work has been prepared over a period of time, the part of the work existing in fixed form on a particular date constitutes the created work on that date. The date you give here should be the year in which the author completed the particular version for which registration is now being sought, even if other versions exist or if further changes or additions are planned.

Publication: The statute defines "publication" as "the distribution of copies or phonorecords of a work to the public by sale or other transfer of ownership, or by rental, lease, or lending"; a work is also "published" if there has been an "offering to distribute copies or phonorecords to a group of persons for purposes of further distribution, public performance, or public display." Give the full date (month, day, year) when, and the country where, publication first occurred. If first publication took place simultaneously in the United States and other countries, it is sufficient to state "U.S.A."

4 SPACE 4: Claimant(s)

Name(s) and Address(es) of Copyright Claimant(s): Give the name(s) and address(es) of the copyright claimant(s) in this work even if the claimant is the same as the author. Copyright in a work belongs initially to the author of the work (including, in the case of a work made for hire, the employer or other person for whom the work was prepared). The copyright claimant is either the author of the work or a person or organization to whom the copyright initially belonging to the author has been transferred.

Transfer: The statute provides that, if the copyright claimant is not the author, the application for registration must contain "a brief statement of how the claimant obtained ownership of the copyright." If any copyright claimant named in space 4 is not an author named in space 2, give a brief statement explaining how the claimant(s) obtained ownership of the copyright. Examples: "By written contract"; "Transfer of all rights by author"; "Assignment"; "By will." Do not attach transfer documents or other attachments or riders.

5 SPACE 5: Previous Registration

General Instructions: The questions in space 5 are intended to show whether an earlier registration has been made for this work and, if so, whether there is any basis for a new registration. As a general rule, only one basic copyright registration can be made for the same version of a particular work.

Same Version: If this version is substantially the same as the work covered by a previous registration, a second registration is not generally possible unless: (1) the work has been registered in unpublished form and a second registration is now being sought to cover this first published edition; or (2) someone other than the author is identified as copyright claimant in the earlier registration, and the author is now seeking registration in his or her own name. If either of these two exceptions apply, check the appropriate box and give the earlier registration number and date. Otherwise, do not submit Form TX; instead, write the Copyright Office for information about supplementary registration or recordation of transfers of copyright ownership.

Changed Version: If the work has been changed and you are now seeking registration to cover the additions or revisions, check the last box in space 5, give the earlier registration number and date, and complete both parts of space 6 in accordance with the instructions below.

Previous Registration Number and Date: If more than one previous registration has been made for the work, give the number and date of the latest registration.

6 SPACE 6: Derivative Work or Compilation

General Instructions: Complete space 6 if this work is a "changed version," "compilation," or "derivative work" and if it incorporates one or more earlier works that have already been published or registered for copyright or that have fallen into the public domain. A "compilation" is defined as "a work formed by the collection and assembling of preexisting materials or of data that are selected, coordinated, or arranged in such a way that the resulting work as a whole constitutes an original work of authorship." A "derivative work" is "a work based on one or more preexisting works." Examples of derivative works include translations, fictionalizations, abridgments, condensations, or "any other form in which a work may be recast, transformed, or adapted." Derivative works also include works "consisting of editorial revisions, annotations, or other modifications" if these changes, as a whole, represent an original work of authorship.

Preexisting Material (space 6a): For derivative works, complete this space and space 6b. In space 6a identify the preexisting work that has been recast, transformed, or adapted. An example of preexisting material might be: "Russian version of Goncharov's 'Oblomov'." Do not complete space 6a for compilations.

Material Added to This Work (space 6b): Give a brief, general statement of the new material covered by the copyright claim for which registration is sought. **Derivative work** examples include: "Foreword, editing, critical annotations"; "Translation"; "Chapters 11-17." If the work is a **compilation**, describe both the compilation itself and the material that has been compiled. Example: "Compilation of certain 1917 Speeches by Woodrow Wilson." A work may be both a derivative work and compilation, in which case a sample statement might be: "Compilation and additional new material."

7 SPACE 7: Manufacturing Provisions

Due to the expiration of the Manufacturing Clause of the copyright law on June 30, 1986, this space has been deleted.

8 SPACE 8: Reproduction for Use of Blind or Physically Handicapped Individuals

General Instructions: One of the major programs of the Library of Congress is to provide Braille editions and special recordings of works for the exclusive use of the blind and physically handicapped. In an effort to simplify and speed up the copyright licensing procedures that are a necessary part of this program, section 710 of the copyright statute provides for the establishment of a voluntary licensing system to be tied in with copyright registration. Copyright Office regulations provide that you may grant a license for such reproduction and distribution solely for the use of persons who are certified by competent authority as unable to read normal printed material as a result of physical limitations. The license is entirely voluntary, nonexclusive, and may be terminated upon 90 days notice.

How to Grant the License: If you wish to grant it, check one of the three boxes in space 8. Your check in one of these boxes together with your signature in space 10 will mean that the Library of Congress can proceed to reproduce and distribute under the license without further paperwork. For further information, write for Circular 63.

9,10,11 SPACE 9,10,11: Fee, Correspondence, Certification, Return Address

Deposit Account: If you maintain a Deposit Account in the Copyright Office, identify it in space 9. Otherwise leave the space blank and send the fee of $20 with your application and deposit.

Correspondence (space 9) This space should contain the name, address, area code, and telephone number of the person to be consulted if correspondence about this application becomes necessary.

Certification (space 10): The application can not be accepted unless it bears the date and the handwritten signature of the author or other copyright claimant, or of the owner of exclusive right(s), or of the duly authorized agent of author, claimant, or owner of exclusive right(s).

Address for Return of Certificate (space 11): The address box must be completed legibly since the certificate will be returned in a window envelope.

FORM TX

For a Literary Work
UNITED STATES COPYRIGHT OFFICE

REGISTRATION NUMBER

TX	TXU

EFFECTIVE DATE OF REGISTRATION

Month	Day	Year

DO NOT WRITE ABOVE THIS LINE. IF YOU NEED MORE SPACE, USE A SEPARATE CONTINUATION SHEET.

1

TITLE OF THIS WORK ▼

PREVIOUS OR ALTERNATIVE TITLES ▼

PUBLICATION AS A CONTRIBUTION If this work was published as a contribution to a periodical, serial, or collection, give information about the collective work in which the contribution appeared. **Title of Collective Work ▼**

If published in a periodical or serial give: **Volume ▼**   **Number ▼**   **Issue Date ▼**   **On Pages ▼**

2

a

NAME OF AUTHOR ▼

DATES OF BIRTH AND DEATH
Year Born ▼   Year Died ▼

Was this contribution to the work a "work made for hire"?
☐ Yes
☐ No

AUTHOR'S NATIONALITY OR DOMICILE
Name of Country
OR { Citizen of ▶
     Domiciled in ▶

WAS THIS AUTHOR'S CONTRIBUTION TO THE WORK
Anonymous?   ☐ Yes ☐ No
Pseudonymous?   ☐ Yes ☐ No
If the answer to either of these questions is "Yes," see detailed instructions.

NATURE OF AUTHORSHIP Briefly describe nature of material created by this author in which copyright is claimed. ▼

NOTE

Under the law, the "author" of a "work made for hire" is generally the employer, not the employee (see instructions). For any part of this work that was "made for hire" check "Yes" in the space provided, give the employer (or other person for whom the work was prepared) as "Author" of that part, and leave the space for dates of birth and death blank.

b

NAME OF AUTHOR ▼

DATES OF BIRTH AND DEATH
Year Born ▼   Year Died ▼

Was this contribution to the work a "work made for hire"?
☐ Yes
☐ No

AUTHOR'S NATIONALITY OR DOMICILE
Name of Country
OR { Citizen of ▶
     Domiciled in ▶

WAS THIS AUTHOR'S CONTRIBUTION TO THE WORK
Anonymous?   ☐ Yes ☐ No
Pseudonymous?   ☐ Yes ☐ No
If the answer to either of these questions is "Yes," see detailed instructions.

NATURE OF AUTHORSHIP Briefly describe nature of material created by this author in which copyright is claimed. ▼

c

NAME OF AUTHOR ▼

DATES OF BIRTH AND DEATH
Year Born ▼   Year Died ▼

Was this contribution to the work a "work made for hire"?
☐ Yes
☐ No

AUTHOR'S NATIONALITY OR DOMICILE
Name of Country
OR { Citizen of ▶
     Domiciled in ▶

WAS THIS AUTHOR'S CONTRIBUTION TO THE WORK
Anonymous?   ☐ Yes ☐ No
Pseudonymous?   ☐ Yes ☐ No
If the answer to either of these questions is "Yes," see detailed instructions.

NATURE OF AUTHORSHIP Briefly describe nature of material created by this author in which copyright is claimed. ▼

3

a

YEAR IN WHICH CREATION OF THIS WORK WAS COMPLETED   This information must be given ◀ Year in all cases.

b

DATE AND NATION OF FIRST PUBLICATION OF THIS PARTICULAR WORK
Complete this information ONLY if this work has been published.   Month ▶   Day ▶   Year ▶   ◀ Nation

4

See instructions before completing this space.

COPYRIGHT CLAIMANT(S) Name and address must be given even if the claimant is the same as the author given in space 2. ▼

TRANSFER If the claimant(s) named here in space 4 is (are) different from the author(s) named in space 2, give a brief statement of how the claimant(s) obtained ownership of the copyright. ▼

DO NOT WRITE HERE — OFFICE USE ONLY

APPLICATION RECEIVED

ONE DEPOSIT RECEIVED

TWO DEPOSITS RECEIVED

FUNDS RECEIVED

MORE ON BACK ▶ • Complete all applicable spaces (numbers 5-11) on the reverse side of this page.
• See detailed instructions.   • Sign the form at line 10.

DO NOT WRITE HERE

Page 1 of _____ pages

EXAMINED BY	**FORM TX**
CHECKED BY	
☐ CORRESPONDENCE Yes	FOR COPYRIGHT OFFICE USE ONLY

DO NOT WRITE ABOVE THIS LINE. IF YOU NEED MORE SPACE, USE A SEPARATE CONTINUATION SHEET.

PREVIOUS REGISTRATION Has registration for this work, or for an earlier version of this work, already been made in the Copyright Office?

☐ **Yes** ☐ **No** If your answer is "Yes," why is another registration being sought? (Check appropriate box) ▼

a. ☐ This is the first published edition of a work previously registered in unpublished form.

b. ☐ This is the first application submitted by this author as copyright claimant.

c. ☐ This is a changed version of the work, as shown by space 6 on this application.

If your answer is "Yes," give: **Previous Registration Number** ▼   **Year of Registration** ▼

5

DERIVATIVE WORK OR COMPILATION Complete both space 6a and 6b for a derivative work; complete only 6b for a compilation.

a. Preexisting Material Identify any preexisting work or works that this work is based on or incorporates. ▼

b. Material Added to This Work Give a brief, general statement of the material that has been added to this work and in which copyright is claimed. ▼

6

See instructions before completing this space.

—space deleted—

7

REPRODUCTION FOR USE OF BLIND OR PHYSICALLY HANDICAPPED INDIVIDUALS A signature on this form at space 10 and a check in one of the boxes here in space 8 constitutes a non-exclusive grant of permission to the Library of Congress to reproduce and distribute solely for the blind and physically handicapped and under the conditions and limitations prescribed by the regulations of the Copyright Office: (1) copies of the work identified in space 1 of this application in Braille (or similar tactile symbols); or (2) phonorecords embodying a fixation of a reading of that work; or (3) both.

a ☐ Copies and Phonorecords   b ☐ Copies Only   c ☐ Phonorecords Only

8

See instructions.

DEPOSIT ACCOUNT If the registration fee is to be charged to a Deposit Account established in the Copyright Office, give name and number of Account.
Name ▼   **Account Number** ▼

9

CORRESPONDENCE Give name and address to which correspondence about this application should be sent.   Name/Address/Apt/City/State/ZIP ▼

Area Code and Telephone Number ▶

Be sure to give your daytime phone ◀ number

CERTIFICATION* I, the undersigned, hereby certify that I am the

Check only one ▶
{
☐ author
☐ other copyright claimant
☐ owner of exclusive right(s)
☐ authorized agent of _____
}

of the work identified in this application and that the statements made by me in this application are correct to the best of my knowledge.

Name of author or other copyright claimant, or owner of exclusive right(s) ▲

10

Typed or printed name and date ▼ If this application gives a date of publication in space 3, do not sign and submit it before that date.

_____ Date ▶ _____

Handwritten signature (X) ▼

MAIL CERTIFICATE TO

Name ▼

Number/Street/Apt ▼

City/State/ZIP ▼

Certificate will be mailed in window envelope

YOU MUST:
• Complete all necessary spaces
• Sign your application in space 10
SEND ALL 3 ELEMENTS IN THE SAME PACKAGE:
1. Application form
2. Nonrefundable $20 filing fee in check or money order payable to *Register of Copyrights*
3. Deposit material
MAIL TO:
Register of Copyrights
Library of Congress
Washington, D.C. 20559-6000

11

⊘Filling Out Application Form SR

Detach and read these instructions before completing this form.
Make sure all applicable spaces have been filled in before you return this form.

BASIC INFORMATION

When to Use This Form: Use Form SR for copyright registration of published or unpublished sound recordings. It should be used when the copyright claim is limited to the sound recording itself, and it may also be used where the same copyright claimant is seeking simultaneous registration of the underlying musical, dramatic, or literary work embodied in the phonorecord.

With one exception, "sound recordings" are works that result from the fixation of a series of musical, spoken, or other sounds. The exception is for the audio portions of audiovisual works, such as a motion picture soundtrack or an audio cassette accompanying a filmstrip; these are considered a part of the audiovisual work as a whole.

Deposit to Accompany Application: An application for copyright registration of a sound recording must be accompanied by a deposit consisting of phonorecords representing the entire work for which registration is to be made.

Unpublished Work: Deposit one complete phonorecord.

Published Work: Deposit two complete phonorecords of the best edition, together with "any printed or other visually perceptible material" published with the phonorecords.

Work First Published Outside the United States: Deposit one complete phonorecord of the first foreign edition.

Contribution to a Collective Work: Deposit one complete phonorecord of the best edition of the collective work.

The Copyright Notice: For sound recordings first published on or after March 1, 1989, the law provides that a copyright notice in a specified form "may be placed on all publicly distributed phonorecords of the sound recording." Use of the copyright notice is the responsibility of the copyright owner and does not require advance permission from the Copyright Office. The required form of the notice for phonorecords of sound recordings consists of three elements: (1) the symbol "Ⓟ" (the letter "P" in a circle); (2) the year of first publication of the sound recording; and (3) the name of the owner of copyright. For example "Ⓟ 1996 XYZ Record Co." The notice is to be "placed on the surface of the phonorecord, or on the label or container, in such manner and location as to give reasonable notice of the claim of copyright." Notice was required under the 1976 Copyright Act. This requirement was eliminated when the United States adhered to the Berne Convention, effective March 1, 1989. Although works published without notice before that date could have entered the public domain in the United States, the Uruguay Round Agreements Act restores copyright in certain foreign works originally published without notice.

For information about notice requirements for works published before March 1, 1989, or other copyright information, write: Publications Section, LM-455, Copyright Office, Library of Congress, Washington, D.C. 20559-6000.

LINE-BY-LINE INSTRUCTIONS

Please type or print neatly using black ink. The form is used to produce the certificate.

1 SPACE 1: Title

Title of This Work: Every work submitted for copyright registration must be given a title to identify that particular work. If the phonorecords or any accompanying printed material bear a title (or an identifying phrase that could serve as a title), transcribe that wording completely and exactly on the application. Indexing of the registration and future identification of the work may depend on the information you give here.

Previous, Alternative, or Contents Titles: Complete this space if there are any previous or alternative titles for the work under which someone searching for the registration might be likely to look, or under which a document pertaining to the work might be recorded. You may also give the individual contents titles, if any, in this space or you may use a Continuation Sheet. Circle the term that describes the titles given.

2 SPACE 2: Author(s)

General Instructions: After reading these instructions, decide who are the "authors" of this work for copyright purposes. Then, unless the work is a "collective work," give the requested information about every "author" who contributed any appreciable amount of copyrightable matter to this version of the work. If you need further space, request additional Continuation Sheets. In the case of a collective work such as a collection of previously published or registered sound recordings, give information about the author of the collective work as a whole. If you are submitting this Form SR to cover the recorded musical, dramatic, or literary work as well as the sound recording itself, it is important for space 2 to include full information about the various authors of all of the material covered by the copyright claim, making clear the nature of each author's contribution.

Name of Author: The fullest form of the author's name should be given. Unless the work was "made for hire," the individual who actually created the work is its "author." In the case of a work made for hire, the statute provides that "the employer or other person for whom the work was prepared is considered the author."

What is a "Work Made for Hire"? A "work made for hire" is defined as: (1) "a work prepared by an employee within the scope of his or her employment"; or (2) "a work specially ordered or commissioned for use as a contribution to a

collective work, as a part of a motion picture or other audiovisual work, as a translation, as a supplementary work, as a compilation, as an instructional text, as a test, as answer material for a test, or as an atlas, if the parties expressly agree in a written instrument signed by them that the work shall be considered a work made for hire." If you have checked "Yes" to indicate that the work was "made for hire," you must give the full legal name of the employer (or other person for whom the work was prepared). You may also include the name of the employee along with the name of the employer (for example: "Elster Record Co., employer for hire of John Ferguson").

"Anonymous" or "Pseudonymous" Work: An author's contribution to a work is "anonymous" if that author is not identified on the copies or phonorecords of the work. An author's contribution to a work is "pseudonymous" if that author is identified on the copies or phonorecords under a fictitious name. If the work is "anonymous" you may: (1) leave the line blank; or (2) state "anonymous" on the line; or (3) reveal the author's identity. If the work is "pseudonymous" you may: (1) leave the line blank; or (2) give the pseudonym and identify it as such (for example: "Huntley Haverstock, pseudonym"); or (3) reveal the author's name, making clear which is the real name and which is the pseudonym (for example: "Judith Barton, whose pseudonym is Madeline Elster"). However, the citizenship or domicile of the author **must** be given in all cases.

Dates of Birth and Death: If the author is dead, the statute requires that the year of death be included in the application unless the work is anonymous or pseudonymous. The author's birth date is optional, but is useful as a form of identification. Leave this space blank if the author's contribution was a "work made for hire."

Author's Nationality or Domicile: Give the country in which the author is a citizen, or the country in which the author is domiciled. Nationality or domicile **must** be given in all cases.

Nature of Authorship: Sound recording authorship is the performance, sound production, or both, that is fixed in the recording deposited for registration. Describe this authorship in space 2 as "sound recording." If the claim also covers the underlying work(s), include the appropriate authorship terms for each author, for example, "words," "music," "arrangement of music," or "text."

Generally, for the claim to cover both the sound recording and the underlying work(s), every author should have contributed to both the sound recording **and** the underlying work(s). If the claim includes artwork or photographs, include the appropriate term in the statement of authorship.

3 SPACE 3: Creation and Publication

General Instructions: Do not confuse "creation" with "publication." Every application for copyright registration must state "the year in which creation of the work was completed." Give the date and nation of first publication only if the work has been published.

Creation: Under the statute, a work is "created" when it is fixed in a copy or phonorecord for the first time. Where a work has been prepared over a period of time, the part of the work existing in fixed form on a particular date constitutes the created work on that date. The date you give here should be the year in which the author completed the particular version for which registration is now being sought, even if other versions exist or if further changes or additions are planned.

Publication: The statute defines "publication" as "the distribution of copies or phonorecords of a work to the public by sale or other transfer of ownership, or by rental, lease, or lending"; a work is also "published" if there has been an "offering to distribute copies or phonorecords to a group of persons for purposes of further distribution, public performance, or public display." Give the full date (month, date, year) when, and the country where, publication first occurred. If first publication took place simultaneously in the United States and other countries, it is sufficient to state "U.S.A."

4 SPACE 4: Claimant(s)

Name(s) and Address(es) of Copyright Claimant(s): Give the name(s) and address(es) of the copyright claimant(s) in the work even if the claimant is the same as the author. Copyright in a work belongs initially to the author of the work (including, in the case of a work made for hire, the employer or other person for whom the work was prepared). The copyright claimant is either the author of the work or a person or organization to whom the copyright initially belonging to the author has been transferred.

Transfer: The statute provides that, if the copyright claimant is not the author, the application for registration must contain "a brief statement of how the claimant obtained ownership of the copyright." If any copyright claimant named in space 4a is not an author named in space 2, give a brief statement explaining how the claimant(s) obtained ownership of the copyright. Examples: "By written contract"; "Transfer of all rights by author"; "Assignment"; "By will." Do not attach transfer documents or other attachments or riders.

5 SPACE 5: Previous Registration

General Instructions: The questions in space 5 are intended to show whether an earlier registration has been made for this work and, if so, whether there is any basis for a new registration. As a rule, only one basic copyright registration can be made for the same version of a particular work.

Same Version: If this version is substantially the same as the work covered by a previous registration, a second registration is not generally possible unless: (1) the work has been registered in unpublished form and a second registration is now being sought to cover this first published edition; or (2) someone other than the author is identified as copyright claimant in the earlier registration and the author is now seeking registration in his or her own name. If either of these two exceptions apply, check the appropriate box and give the earlier registration number and date. Otherwise, do not submit Form SR; instead, write the Copyright Office for information about supplementary registration or recordation of transfers of copyright ownership.

Changed Version: If the work has been changed, and you are now seeking registration to cover the additions or revisions, check the last box in space 5, give the earlier registration number and date, and complete both parts of space 6 in accordance with the instructions below.

Previous Registration Number and Date: If more than one previous registration has been made for the work, give the number and date of the latest registration.

6 SPACE 6: Derivative Work or Compilation

General Instructions: Complete space 6 if this work is a "changed version," "compilation," or "derivative work," and if it incorporates one or more earlier works that have already been published or registered for copyright, or that have fallen into the public domain, or sound recordings that were fixed before February 15, 1972. A "compilation" is defined as "a work formed by the collection and assembling of preexisting materials or of data that are selected, coordinated, or arranged in such a way that the resulting work as a whole constitutes an original work of authorship." A "derivative work" is "a work based on one or more preexisting works." Examples of derivative works include recordings reissued with substantial editorial revisions or abridgments of the recorded sounds, and recordings republished with new recorded material, or "any other form in which a work may be recast, transformed, or adapted." Derivative works also include works "consisting of editorial revisions, annotations, or other modifications" if these changes, as a whole, represent an original work of authorship.

Preexisting Material (space 6a): Complete this space **and** space 6b for derivative works. In this space identify the preexisting work that has been recast, transformed, or adapted. For example, the preexisting material might be: "1970 recording by Sperryville Symphony of Bach Double Concerto." Do not complete this space for compilations.

Material Added to This Work (space 6b): Give a brief, general statement of the additional new material covered by the copyright claim for which registration is sought. In the case of a derivative work, identify this new material. Examples: "Recorded performances on bands 1 and 3"; "Remixed sounds from original multitrack sound sources"; "New words, arrangement, and additional sounds." If the work is a compilation, give a brief, general statement describing both the material that has been compiled **and** the compilation itself. Example: "Compilation of 1938 Recordings by various swing bands."

7,8,9 SPACE 7,8,9: Fee, Correspondence, Certification, Return Address

Deposit Account: If you maintain a Deposit Account in the Copyright Office, identify it in space 7a. Otherwise leave the space blank and send the fee of $20 with your application and deposit.

Correspondence (space 7b): This space should contain the name, address, area code, telephone number, and fax number (if available) of the person to be consulted if correspondence about this application become necessary.

Certification (space 8): This application cannot be accepted unless it bears the date and the **handwritten signature** of the author or other copyright claimant, or of the owner of exclusive right(s), or of the duly authorized agent of the author, claimant, or owner of exclusive right(s).

Address for Return of Certificate (space 9): The address box must be completed legibly since the certificate will be returned in a window envelope.

MORE INFORMATION

"Works": "Works" are the basic subject matter of copyright; they are what authors create and copyright protects. The statute draws a sharp distinction between the "work" and "any material object in which the work is embodied."

"Copies" and "Phonorecords": These are the two types of material objects in which "works" are embodied. In general, **"copies"** are objects from which a work can be read or visually perceived, directly or with the aid of a machine or device, such as manuscripts, books, sheet music, film, and videotape. **"Phonorecords"** are objects embodying fixations of sounds, such as audio tapes and phonograph disks. For example, a song (the "work") can be reproduced in sheet music ("copies") or phonograph disks ("phonorecords"), or both.

"Sound Recordings": These are "works," not "copies" or "phonorecords." "Sound recordings" are "works that result from the fixation of a series of musical, spoken, or other sounds, but not including the sounds accompanying a motion picture or other audiovisual work." Example: When a record company issues a new release, the release will typically involve two distinct "works": the "musical work" that has been recorded, and the "sound recording" as a separate work in itself. The material objects that the recorded company sends out are "phonorecords": physical reproductions of both the "musical work" and the "sound recording."

Should You File More Than One Application?

If your work consists of a recorded musical, dramatic, or literary work and if both that "work" and the sound recording as a separate "work" are eligible for registration, the application form you should file depends on the following:

File Only Form SR if: The copyright claimant is the same for both the musical, dramatic, or literary work and for the sound recording, and you are seeking a single registration to cover both of these "works."

File Only Form PA (or Form TX) if: You are seeking to register only the musical, dramatic, or literary work, not the sound recording. Form PA is appropriate for works of the performing arts; Form TX is for nondramatic literary works.

Separate Applications Should Be Filed on Form PA (or Form TX) and on Form SR if: (1) The copyright claimant for the musical, dramatic, or literary work is different from the copyright claimant for the sound recording; or (2) You prefer to have separate registrations for the musical, dramatic, or literary work and for the sound recording.

FORM SR

For a Sound Recording
UNITED STATES COPYRIGHT OFFICE

REGISTRATION NUMBER

_____

SR   SRU

EFFECTIVE DATE OF REGISTRATION

_____

Month   Day   Year

DO NOT WRITE ABOVE THIS LINE. IF YOU NEED MORE SPACE, USE A SEPARATE CONTINUATION SHEET.

1

TITLE OF THIS WORK ▼

PREVIOUS, ALTERNATIVE, OR CONTENTS TITLES (CIRCLE ONE) ▼

2 a

NAME OF AUTHOR ▼

DATES OF BIRTH AND DEATH
Year Born ▼   Year Died ▼

Was this contribution to the work a "work made for hire"?
☐ Yes
☐ No

AUTHOR'S NATIONALITY OR DOMICILE
Name of Country
OR { Citizen of ▶ _____
Domiciled in ▶ _____

WAS THIS AUTHOR'S CONTRIBUTION TO THE WORK
Anonymous? ☐ Yes ☐ No
Pseudonymous? ☐ Yes ☐ No
If the answer to either of these questions is "Yes," see detailed instructions.

NATURE OF AUTHORSHIP Briefly describe nature of material created by this author in which copyright is claimed. ▼

NOTE

Under the law, the "author" of a "work made for hire" is generally the employer, not the employee (see instructions). For any part of this work that was "made for hire," check "Yes" in the space provided, give the employer (or other person for whom the work was prepared) as "Author" of that part, and leave the space for dates of birth and death blank.

b

NAME OF AUTHOR ▼

DATES OF BIRTH AND DEATH
Year Born ▼   Year Died ▼

Was this contribution to the work a "work made for hire"?
☐ Yes
☐ No

AUTHOR'S NATIONALITY OR DOMICILE
Name of Country
OR { Citizen of ▶ _____
Domiciled in ▶ _____

WAS THIS AUTHOR'S CONTRIBUTION TO THE WORK
Anonymous? ☐ Yes ☐ No
Pseudonymous? ☐ Yes ☐ No
If the answer to either of these questions is "Yes," see detailed instructions.

NATURE OF AUTHORSHIP Briefly describe nature of material created by this author in which copyright is claimed. ▼

c

NAME OF AUTHOR ▼

DATES OF BIRTH AND DEATH
Year Born ▼   Year Died ▼

Was this contribution to the work a "work made for hire"?
☐ Yes
☐ No

AUTHOR'S NATIONALITY OR DOMICILE
Name of Country
OR { Citizen of ▶ _____
Domiciled in ▶ _____

WAS THIS AUTHOR'S CONTRIBUTION TO THE WORK
Anonymous? ☐ Yes ☐ No
Pseudonymous? ☐ Yes ☐ No
If the answer to either of these questions is "Yes," see detailed instructions.

NATURE OF AUTHORSHIP Briefly describe nature of material created by this author in which copyright is claimed. ▼

3 a

YEAR IN WHICH CREATION OF THIS WORK WAS COMPLETED
_____ ◀ Year
This information must be given in all cases.

b
Complete this information ONLY if this work has been published.

DATE AND NATION OF FIRST PUBLICATION OF THIS PARTICULAR WORK
Month ▶ _____ Day ▶ _____ Year ▶ _____
_____ ◀ Nation

4 a

COPYRIGHT CLAIMANT(S) Name and address must be given even if the claimant is the same as the author given in space 2. ▼

See instructions before completing this space.

b
TRANSFER If the claimant(s) named here in space 4 is (are) different from the author(s) named in space 2, give a brief statement of how the claimant(s) obtained ownership of the copyright. ▼

DO NOT WRITE HERE
OFFICE USE ONLY

APPLICATION RECEIVED

ONE DEPOSIT RECEIVED

TWO DEPOSITS RECEIVED

FUNDS RECEIVED

MORE ON BACK ▶
• Complete all applicable spaces (numbers 5-9) on the reverse side of this page.
• See detailed instructions.   • Sign the form at line 8.

DO NOT WRITE HERE

Page 1 of _____ pages

DO NOT WRITE ABOVE THIS LINE. IF YOU NEED MORE SPACE, USE A SEPARATE CONTINUATION SHEET.

PREVIOUS REGISTRATION Has registration for this work, or for an earlier version of this work, already been made in the Copyright Office?

☐ Yes ☐ No If your answer is "Yes," why is another registration being sought? (Check appropriate box) ▼

a. ☐ This work was previously registered in unpublished form and now has been published for the first time.

b. ☐ This is the first application submitted by this author as copyright claimant.

c. ☐ This is a changed version of the work, as shown by space 6 on this application.

If your answer is "Yes," give: **Previous Registration Number** ▼   **Year of Registration** ▼

5

DERIVATIVE WORK OR COMPILATION Complete both space 6a and 6b for a derivative work; complete only 6b for a compilation.

a. Preexisting Material Identify any preexisting work or works that this work is based on or incorporates. ▼

b. Material Added to This Work Give a brief, general statement of the material that has been added to this work and in which copyright is claimed. ▼

6

See instructions before completing this space.

DEPOSIT ACCOUNT If the registration fee is to be charged to a Deposit Account established in the Copyright Office, give name and number of Account.

Name ▼   Account Number ▼

a

7

CORRESPONDENCE Give name and address to which correspondence about this application should be sent.   Name/Address/Apt/City/State/ZIP ▼

b

Area code and daytime telephone number ▶   Fax number ▶

CERTIFICATION* I, the undersigned, hereby certify that I am the

Check only one ▼

☐ author

☐ other copyright claimant

☐ owner of exclusive right(s)

☐ authorized agent of _____

Name of author or other copyright claimant, or owner of exclusive right(s) ▲

8

of the work identified in this application and that the statements made by me in this application are correct to the best of my knowledge.

Typed or printed name and date ▼ If this application gives a date of publication in space 3, do not sign and submit it before that date.

Date ▶ _____

☞ Handwritten signature (X) ▼

Mail certificate to:	Name ▼	**YOU MUST:** • Complete all necessary spaces • Sign your application in space 8
	Number/Street/Apartment Number ▼	**SEND ALL 3 ELEMENTS IN THE SAME PACKAGE:** 1. Application form 2. Nonrefundable $20 filing fee in check or money order payable to *Register of Copyrights* 3. Deposit material
Certificate will be mailed in window envelope	City/State/ZIP ▼	**MAIL TO:** Register of Copyrights Library of Congress Washington, D.C. 20559-6000

9

⬭Filling Out Application Form PA

Detach and read these instructions before completing this form.
Make sure all applicable spaces have been filled in before you return this form.

BASIC INFORMATION

When to Use This Form: Use Form PA for registration of published or unpublished works of the performing arts. This class includes works prepared for the purpose of being "performed" directly before an audience or indirectly "by means of any device or process." Works of the performing arts include: (1) musical works, including any accompanying words; (2) dramatic works, including any accompanying music; (3) pantomimes and choreographic works; and (4) motion pictures and other audiovisual works.

Deposit to Accompany Application: An application for copyright registration must be accompanied by a deposit consisting of copies or phonorecords representing the entire work for which registration is made. The following are the general deposit requirements as set forth in the statute:

Unpublished Work: Deposit one complete copy (or phonorecord).

Published Work: Deposit two complete copies (or one phonorecord) of the best edition.

Work First Published Outside the United States: Deposit one complete copy (or phonorecord) of the first foreign edition.

Contribution to a Collective Work: Deposit one complete copy (or phonorecord) of the best edition of the collective work.

Motion Pictures: Deposit *both* of the following: (1) a separate written description of the contents of the motion picture; and (2) for a published work, one complete copy of the best edition of the motion picture; or, for an unpublished work, one complete copy of the motion picture or identifying material. Identifying material may be either an audiorecording of the entire soundtrack or one frame enlargement or similar visual print from each 10-minute segment.

The Copyright Notice: For works first published on or after March 1, 1989, the law provides that a copyright notice in a specified form "may be placed on all publicly distributed copies from which the work can be visually perceived." Use of the copyright notice is the responsibility of the copyright owner and does not require advance permission from the Copyright Office. The required form of the notice for copies generally consists of three elements: (1) the symbol "©", or the word "Copyright," or the abbreviation "Copr."; (2) the year of first publication; and (3) the name of the owner of copyright. For example: "© 1995 Jane Cole." The notice is to be affixed to the copies "in such manner and location as to give reasonable notice of the claim of copyright." Works first published prior to March 1, 1989, **must** carry the notice or risk loss of copyright protection.

For information about requirements for works published before March 1, 1989, or other copyright information, write: Information Section, LM-401, Copyright Office, Library of Congress, Washington, D.C. 20559-6000.

LINE-BY-LINE INSTRUCTIONS
Please type or print using black ink.

1 SPACE 1: Title

Title of This Work: Every work submitted for copyright registration must be given a title to identify that particular work. If the copies or phonorecords of the work bear a title (or an identifying phrase that could serve as a title), transcribe that wording *completely* and *exactly* on the application. Indexing of the registration and future identification of the work will depend on the information you give here. If the work you are registering is an entire "collective work" (such as a collection of plays or songs), give the overall title of the collection. If you are registering one or more individual contributions to a collective work, give the title of each contribution, followed by the title of the collection. For an unpublished collection, you may give the titles of the individual works after the collection title.

Previous or Alternative Titles: Complete this space if there are any additional titles for the work under which someone searching for the registration might be likely to look, or under which a document pertaining to the work might be recorded.

Nature of This Work: Briefly describe the general nature or character of the work being registered for copyright. Examples: "Music"; "Song Lyrics"; "Words and Music"; "Drama"; "Musical Play"; "Choreography"; "Pantomime"; "Motion Picture"; "Audiovisual Work."

2 SPACE 2: Author(s)

General Instructions: After reading these instructions, decide who are the "authors" of this work for copyright purposes. Then, unless the work is a "collective work," give the requested information about every "author" who contributed any appreciable amount of copyrightable matter to this version of the work. If you need further space, request additional Continuation Sheets. In the case of a collective work, such as a songbook or a collection of plays, give the information about the author of the collective work as a whole.

Name of Author: The fullest form of the author's name should be given. Unless the work was "made for hire," the individual who actually created the work is its "author." In the case of a work made for hire, the statute provides that "the employer or other person for whom the work was prepared is considered the author."

What is a "Work Made for Hire"? A "work made for hire" is defined as: (1) "a work prepared by an employee within the scope of his or her employment"; or (2) "a work specially ordered or commissioned for use as a contribution to a collective work, as a part of a motion picture or other audiovisual work, as a translation, as a supplementary work, as a compilation, as an instructional text, as a test, as answer material for a test, or as an atlas, if the parties expressly agree in a written instrument signed by them that the work shall be considered a work made for hire." If you have checked "Yes" to indicate that the work was "made for hire," you must give the full legal name of the employer (or other person for whom the work was prepared). You may also include the name of the employee along with the name of the employer (for example: "Elster Music Co., employer for hire of John Ferguson").

"Anonymous" or "Pseudonymous" Work: An author's contribution to a work is "anonymous" if that author is not identified on the copies or phonorecords of the work. An author's contribution to a work is "pseudonymous" if that author is identified on the copies or phonorecords under a fictitious name. If the work is "anonymous" you may: (1) leave the line blank; or (2) state "anonymous" on the line; or (3) reveal the author's identity. If the work is "pseudonymous" you may: (1) leave the line blank; or (2) give the pseudonym and identify it as such (example: "Huntley Haverstock, pseudonym"); or (3) reveal the author's name, making clear which is the real name and which is the pseudonym (for example: "Judith Barton, whose pseudonym is Madeline Elster"). However, the citizenship or domicile of the author **must** be given in all cases.

Dates of Birth and Death: If the author is dead, the statute requires that the year of death be included in the application unless the work is anonymous or pseudonymous. The author's birth date is optional, but is useful as a form of identification. Leave this space blank if the author's contribution was a "work made for hire."

Author's Nationality or Domicile: Give the country of which the author is a citizen, or the country in which the author is domiciled. Nationality or domicile **must** be given in all cases.

Nature of Authorship: Give a brief general statement of the nature of this particular author's contribution to the work. Examples: "Words"; "Coauthor of Music"; "Words and Music"; "Arrangement"; "Coauthor of Book and Lyrics"; "Dramatization"; "Screen Play"; "Compilation and English Translation"; "Editorial Revisions."

3 SPACE 3: Creation and Publication

General Instructions: Do not confuse "creation" with "publication." Every application for copyright registration must state "the year in which creation of the work was completed." Give the date and nation of first publication only if the work has been published.

Creation: Under the statute, a work is "created" when it is fixed in a copy or phonorecord for the first time. Where a work has been prepared over a period of time, the part of the work existing in fixed form on a particular date constitutes the created work on that date. The date you give here should be the year in which the author completed the particular version for which registration is now being sought, even if other versions exist or if further changes or additions are planned.

Publication: The statute defines "publication" as "the distribution of copies or phonorecords of a work to the public by sale or other transfer of ownership, or by rental, lease, or lending"; a work is also "published" if there has been an "offering to distribute copies or phonorecords to a group of persons for purposes of further distribution, public performance, or public display." Give the full date (month, day, year) when, and the country where, publication first occurred. If first publication took place simultaneously in the United States and other countries, it is sufficient to state "U.S.A."

4 SPACE 4: Claimant(s)

Name(s) and Address(es) of Copyright Claimant(s): Give the name(s) and address(es) of the copyright claimant(s) in this work even if the claimant is the same as the author. Copyright in a work belongs initially to the author of the work (including, in the case of a work made for hire, the employer or other person for whom the work was prepared). The copyright claimant is either the author of the work or a person or organization to whom the copyright initially belonging to the author has been transferred.

Transfer: The statute provides that, if the copyright claimant is not the author, the application for registration must contain "a brief statement of how the claimant obtained ownership of the copyright." If any copyright claimant named in space 4 is not an author named in space 2, give a brief statement explaining how the claimant(s) obtained ownership of the copyright. Examples: "By written contract"; "Transfer of all rights by author"; "Assignment"; "By will." Do not attach transfer documents or other attachments or riders.

5 SPACE 5: Previous Registration

General Instructions: The questions in space 5 are intended to show whether an earlier registration has been made for this work and, if so, whether there is any basis for a new registration. As a general rule, only one basic copyright registration can be made for the same version of a particular work.

Same Version: If this version is substantially the same as the work covered by a previous registration, a second registration is not generally possible unless: (1) the work has been registered in unpublished form and a second registration is now being sought to cover this first published edition; or (2) someone other than the author is identified as copyright claimant in the earlier registration, and the author is now seeking registration in his or her own name. If either of these two exceptions apply, check the appropriate box and give the earlier registration number and date. Otherwise, do not submit Form PA; instead, write the Copyright Office for information about supplementary registration or recordation of transfers of copyright ownership.

Changed Version: If the work has been changed, and you are now seeking registration to cover the additions or revisions, check the last box in space 5, give the earlier registration number and date, and complete both parts of space 6 in accordance with the instructions below.

Previous Registration Number and Date: If more than one previous registration has been made for the work, give the number and date of the latest registration.

6 SPACE 6: Derivative Work or Compilation

General Instructions: Complete space 6 if this work is a "changed version," "compilation," or "derivative work," and if it incorporates one or more earlier works that have already been published or registered for copyright or that have fallen into the public domain. A "compilation" is defined as "a work formed by the collection and assembling of preexisting materials or of data that are selected, coordinated, or arranged in such a way that the resulting work as a whole constitutes an original work of authorship." A "derivative work" is "a work based on one or more preexisting works." Examples of derivative works include musical arrangements, dramatizations, translations, abridgments, condensations, motion picture versions, or "any other form in which a work may be recast, transformed, or adapted." Derivative works also include works "consisting of editorial revisions, annotations, or other modifications" if these changes, as a whole, represent an original work of authorship.

Preexisting Material (space 6a): Complete this space **and** space 6b for derivative works. In this space identify the preexisting work that has been recast, transformed, or adapted. For example, the preexisting material might be: "French version of Hugo's 'Le Roi s'amuse'." Do not complete this space for compilations.

Material Added to This Work (space 6b): Give a brief, general statement of the **additional** new material covered by the copyright claim for which registration is sought. In the case of a derivative work, identify this new material. Examples: "Arrangement for piano and orchestra"; "Dramatization for television"; "New film version"; "Revisions throughout; Act III completely new." If the work is a compilation, give a brief, general statement describing both the material that has been compiled **and** the compilation itself. Example: "Compilation of 19th Century Military Songs."

7,8,9 SPACE 7, 8, 9: Fee, Correspondence, Certification, Return Address

Deposit Account: If you maintain a Deposit Account in the Copyright Office, identify it in space 7. Otherwise leave the space blank and send the fee of $20 with your application and deposit.

Correspondence (space 7): This space should contain the name, address, area code, and telephone number of the person to be consulted if correspondence about this application becomes necessary.

Certification (space 8): The application cannot be accepted unless it bears the date and the **handwritten signature** of the author or other copyright claimant, or of the owner of exclusive right(s), or of the duly authorized agent of the author, claimant, or owner of exclusive right(s).

Address for Return of Certificate (space 9): The address box must be completed legibly since the certificate will be returned in a window envelope.

MORE INFORMATION

How to Register a Recorded Work: If the musical or dramatic work that you are registering has been recorded (as a tape, disk, or cassette), you may choose either copyright application Form PA (Performing Arts) or Form SR (Sound Recordings), depending on the purpose of the registration.

Form PA should be used to register the underlying musical composition or dramatic work. Form SR has been developed specifically to register a "sound recording" as defined in the Copyright Act—a work resulting from the "fixation of a series of sounds," separate and distinct from the underlying musical or dramatic work. Form SR should be used when the copyright claim is limited to the sound recording itself. (In one instance, Form SR may also be used to file for a copyright registration for both kinds of works—see (4) below.) Therefore:

(1) File **Form PA** if you are seeking to register the musical or dramatic work, not the sound recording, even though what you deposit for copyright purposes may be in the form of a phonorecord.

(2) File **Form PA** if you are seeking to register the audio portion of an audiovisual work, such as a motion picture soundtrack; these are considered integral parts of the audiovisual work.

(3) File **Form SR** if you are seeking to register the "sound recording" itself, that is, the work that results from the fixation of a series of musical, spoken, or other sounds, but not the underlying musical or dramatic work.

(4) File **Form SR** if you are the copyright claimant for both the underlying musical or dramatic work and the sound recording, *and* you prefer to register both on the same form.

(5) File both forms **PA and SR** if the copyright claimant for the underlying work and sound recording differ, or you prefer to have separate registration for them.

"Copies" and "Phonorecords":
To register for copyright, you are required to deposit "copies" or "phonorecords." These are defined as follows:

Musical compositions may be embodied (fixed) in "copies," objects from which a work can be read or visually perceived, directly or with the aid of a machine or device, such as manuscripts, books, sheet music, film, and videotape. They may also be fixed in "phonorecords," objects embodying fixations of sounds, such as tapes and phonograph disks, commonly known as phonograph records. For example, a song (the work to be registered) can be reproduced in sheet music ("copies") or phonograph records ("phonorecords"), or both.

FORM PA

For a Work of the Performing Arts
UNITED STATES COPYRIGHT OFFICE

REGISTRATION NUMBER

PA	PAU

EFFECTIVE DATE OF REGISTRATION

Month   Day   Year

DO NOT WRITE ABOVE THIS LINE. IF YOU NEED MORE SPACE, USE A SEPARATE CONTINUATION SHEET.

1

TITLE OF THIS WORK ▼

PREVIOUS OR ALTERNATIVE TITLES ▼

NATURE OF THIS WORK ▼ See instructions

2

a

NAME OF AUTHOR ▼

DATES OF BIRTH AND DEATH
Year Born ▼   Year Died ▼

Was this contribution to the work a "work made for hire"?
☐ Yes
☐ No

AUTHOR'S NATIONALITY OR DOMICILE
Name of Country
OR { Citizen of ▶
Domiciled in ▶

WAS THIS AUTHOR'S CONTRIBUTION TO THE WORK
Anonymous? ☐ Yes ☐ No
Pseudonymous? ☐ Yes ☐ No
If the answer to either of these questions is "Yes," see detailed instructions.

NATURE OF AUTHORSHIP Briefly describe nature of material created by this author in which copyright is claimed. ▼

NOTE

Under the law, the "author" of a "work made for hire" is generally the employer, not the employee (see instructions). For any part of this work that was "made for hire" check "Yes" in the space provided, give the employer (or other person for whom the work was prepared) as "Author" of that part, and leave the space for dates of birth and death blank.

b

NAME OF AUTHOR ▼

DATES OF BIRTH AND DEATH
Year Born ▼   Year Died ▼

Was this contribution to the work a "work made for hire"?
☐ Yes
☐ No

AUTHOR'S NATIONALITY OR DOMICILE
Name of Country
OR { Citizen of ▶
Domiciled in ▶

WAS THIS AUTHOR'S CONTRIBUTION TO THE WORK
Anonymous? ☐ Yes ☐ No
Pseudonymous? ☐ Yes ☐ No
If the answer to either of these questions is "Yes," see detailed instructions.

NATURE OF AUTHORSHIP Briefly describe nature of material created by this author in which copyright is claimed. ▼

c

NAME OF AUTHOR ▼

DATES OF BIRTH AND DEATH
Year Born ▼   Year Died ▼

Was this contribution to the work a "work made for hire"?
☐ Yes
☐ No

AUTHOR'S NATIONALITY OR DOMICILE
Name of Country
OR { Citizen of ▶
Domiciled in ▶

WAS THIS AUTHOR'S CONTRIBUTION TO THE WORK
Anonymous? ☐ Yes ☐ No
Pseudonymous? ☐ Yes ☐ No
If the answer to either of these questions is "Yes," see detailed instructions.

NATURE OF AUTHORSHIP Briefly describe nature of material created by this author in which copyright is claimed. ▼

3

a
YEAR IN WHICH CREATION OF THIS WORK WAS COMPLETED This information must be given ◀ Year in all cases.

b
DATE AND NATION OF FIRST PUBLICATION OF THIS PARTICULAR WORK
Complete this information ONLY if this work has been published.
Month ▶   Day ▶   Year ▶   ◀ Nation

4

COPYRIGHT CLAIMANT(S) Name and address must be given even if the claimant is the same as the author given in space 2. ▼

See instructions before completing this space.

TRANSFER If the claimant(s) named here in space 4 is (are) different from the author(s) named in space 2, give a brief statement of how the claimant(s) obtained ownership of the copyright. ▼

DO NOT WRITE HERE OFFICE USE ONLY

APPLICATION RECEIVED

ONE DEPOSIT RECEIVED

TWO DEPOSITS RECEIVED

FUNDS RECEIVED

MORE ON BACK ▶
• Complete all applicable spaces (numbers 5-9) on the reverse side of this page.
• See detailed instructions.
• Sign the form at line 8.

DO NOT WRITE HERE
Page 1 of _____ pages

DO NOT WRITE ABOVE THIS LINE. IF YOU NEED MORE SPACE, USE A SEPARATE CONTINUATION SHEET.

PREVIOUS REGISTRATION Has registration for this work, or for an earlier version of this work, already been made in the Copyright Office?

☐ Yes ☐ No If your answer is "Yes," why is another registration being sought? (Check appropriate box) ▼

a. ☐ This is the first published edition of a work previously registered in unpublished form.

b. ☐ This is the first application submitted by this author as copyright claimant.

c. ☐ This is a changed version of the work, as shown by space 6 on this application.

If your answer is "Yes," give: **Previous Registration Number ▼**   **Year of Registration ▼**

5

DERIVATIVE WORK OR COMPILATION Complete both space 6a and 6b for a derivative work; complete only 6b for a compilation.

a. Preexisting Material Identify any preexisting work or works that this work is based on or incorporates. ▼

b. Material Added to This Work Give a brief, general statement of the material that has been added to this work and in which copyright is claimed. ▼

6

See instructions before completing this space.

DEPOSIT ACCOUNT If the registration fee is to be charged to a Deposit Account established in the Copyright Office, give name and number of Account.

Name ▼   **Account Number ▼**

7

CORRESPONDENCE Give name and address to which correspondence about this application should be sent.   Name/Address/Apt/City/State/ZIP ▼

Area Code and Telephone Number ▶

Be sure to give your daytime phone ◀ number

CERTIFICATION* I, the undersigned, hereby certify that I am the

Check only one ▼

☐ author

☐ other copyright claimant

☐ owner of exclusive right(s)

☐ authorized agent of _____
Name of author or other copyright claimant, or owner of exclusive right(s) ▲

of the work identified in this application and that the statements made by me in this application are correct to the best of my knowledge.

Typed or printed name and date ▼ If this application gives a date of publication in space 3, do not sign and submit it before that date.

Date ▶

☞ **Handwritten signature (X) ▼**

8

9

*17 U.S.C. § 506(e): Any person who knowingly makes a false representation of a material fact in the application for copyright registration provided for by section 409, or in any written statement filed in connection with the application, shall be fined not more than $2,500.

May 1995—300,000   ♲ PRINTED ON RECYCLED PAPER   ☆U.S. GOVERNMENT PRINTING OFFICE: 1995-387-237/46

TRADEMARK

Multimedia producers may want to adopt a company or product trademark to distinguish their goods from those manufactured by others. A trademark or service mark is a brand name that can be a word, a symbol, or a device used by a business to distinguish its goods or services from those of others. "Microsoft" and "Windows" are trademarks, as is "IBM," "Disney," and thousands of other marks used to identify the source of goods or services. Before selecting a trademark, a trademark search should be undertaken to ensure that there are no conflicting state or federal trademarks.

Trademarks can be registered in a state where the mark is used or registered with the federal Patent and Trademark Office if the mark is used on goods or services that are located in more than one state. Registration of a trademark is not required, but will entitle the holder to certain benefits. For example, federal registration makes the mark presumptively valid and incontestable after five years.[11] Registration also enables the trademark owner to obtain triple damages and reimbursement of attorneys' fees.

Trademarks can last indefinitely as long as they are used to distinguish the source of goods or services. They can be abandoned by non-use or can fall into the public domain if they become the generic term for a type of a product. For example, the former trademarks "zipper," "thermos," "aspirin," and "brassiere" have become generic names for all products of each kind, regardless of who manufactures them.

Federal trademark law provides for a registration system administered by the U.S. Trademark Office. You are not re-

---

TRADEMARK SEARCH FIRMS

THOMPSON & THOMPSON
1750 K ST., N.W., STE. 200
WASHINGTON, DC 20006-2305.
TEL: (800) 822-8823, (202) 835-0240
FAX: (202) 728-0744

GOVERNMENT LIAISON SERVICES, INC.
3030 CLARENDON BLVD., STE. 209
ARLINGTON, VA 22201.
TEL: (703) 524-8200, (800) 642-6564
FAX: (703) 525-8451

quired to register a trademark to establish your right to use it. Simply using a particular mark to distinguish your multimedia product from those manufactured by others may establish rights and prevent others from using your mark.

To federally register a mark, one must submit an application. An examiner in the Trademark Office reviews the application to verify:

(1) that the mark is not deceptive;

(2) that the mark is not confusingly similar to another mark; and

(3) that the mark is not merely descriptive or misdescriptive of goods, or is primarily a surname.

Whether one mark infringes another is determined by whether the use of the two marks would cause consumers to be mistaken or confused about the origin of manufacture.

Creation of Federal Trademark Rights

Trademark rights arise from use of the mark or a bona fide intention to use a mark along with the filing of an application to federally register that mark.

Therefore, before a trademark owner may file an application for federal registration, the owner must:

(1) use the mark on goods that are shipped or sold, or services that are rendered in interstate commerce (or commerce between the U.S. and a foreign country), or

(2) have a bona fide intention to use the mark in such commerce in relation to specific goods or services.

The Federal Registration Process

When an application has been filed, an Examining Attorney in the Patent and Trademark Office will review the application and decide whether the mark may be registered. The Office will make an initial determination approximately three months after the application has been filed. The applicant must respond to any objections within six months or the application will be deemed abandoned.

Once the Examining Attorney approves a mark, the mark is published in the *Trademark Official Gazette*. Thirty days are allowed for anyone to object to the registration. If no opposition is filed, the registration will be issued about twelve weeks later for marks in use in commerce. For applications based on intent to use, a notice of allowance will be issued about twelve weeks after publication. The applicant then has six months to either use the mark in commerce or request a six-month extension of time to file a statement of use.

Benefits of Federal Registration

The benefits of federal registration include the following:

(1) The right to sue in federal court for trademark infringement;

(2) The right to recover profits, damages and costs from an infringer, and to recover up to triple damages and attorneys' fees;

(3) Gives others constructive notice of your mark;

(4) Allows the use of the federal registration symbol "®" with the mark;

(5) Allows one to deposit copies of the registration with the Customs Service to stop importation of goods bearing an infringing mark;

(6) Permits one to sue for counterfeiting the mark, providing civil and criminal penalties; and,

(7) Enables one to file a corresponding application in many foreign countries.

State registration gives one important additional benefit. It prevents another from registering the same mark within the state.

Grounds for Refusing Federal Registration

PROTECTING
MULTIMEDIA
WORKS
FROM
INFRINGEMENT

275

(1) The mark is scandalous or disparaging.

(2) The mark is an insignia of a governmental entity.

(3) Without consent, the mark identifies a living individual or a deceased President during the life of his widow.

(4) The mark is confusingly similar to a previously registered mark or to a mark previously used in the United States by another and the mark is not abandoned.

(5) The mark is merely descriptive or deceptively misdescriptive of goods or services. Or it is primarily a surname, and is not distinctive of such goods or services.

Maintenance of the Mark

Continued use of the mark is necessary to avoid abandonment of the mark. Federal registrations must be renewed every ten years. Moreover, between the fifth and sixth year after the date of the registration, you must file an affidavit stating that the mark is currently in use in commerce. If no affidavit is filed, the registration will be canceled.

TRADEMARK/SERVICE MARK APPLICATION, PRINCIPAL REGISTER, WITH DECLARATION	MARK (Word(s) and/or Design)	CLASS NO. (If known)

TO THE ASSISTANT COMMISSIONER FOR TRADEMARKS:

APPLICANT'S NAME:

APPLICANT'S MAILING ADDRESS:

(Display address exactly as it should appear on registration)

_____

_____

_____

APPLICANT'S ENTITY TYPE: (**Check one** and supply requested information)

Individual - Citizen of (Country):

Partnership - State where organized (Country, if appropriate): _____
Names and Citizenship (Country) of General Partners: _____

Corporation - State (Country, if appropriate) of Incorporation:

Other (Specify Nature of Entity and Domicile):

GOODS AND/OR SERVICES:

Applicant requests registration of the trademark/service mark shown in the accompanying drawing in the United States Patent and Trademark Office on the Principal Register established by the Act of July 5, 1946 (15 U.S.C. 1051 et. seq., as amended) for the following goods/services (**SPECIFIC GOODS AND/OR SERVICES MUST BE INSERTED HERE**):

_____

_____

_____

_____

_____

BASIS FOR APPLICATION: (Check boxes which apply, **but never both the first AND second boxes,** and supply requested information related to each box checked.)

[ ] Applicant is using the mark in commerce on or in connection with the above identified goods/services. (15 U.S.C. 1051(a), as amended.) Three specimens showing the mark as used in commerce are submitted with this application.
- Date of first use of the mark in commerce which the U.S. Congress may regulate (for example, interstate or between the U.S. and a foreign country): _____
- Specify the type of commerce: _____
  (for example, interstate or between the U.S. and a specified foreign country)
- Date of first use anywhere (the same as or before use in commerce date): _____
- Specify intended manner or mode of use of mark on or in connection with the goods/services: _____

(for example, trademark is applied to labels, service mark is used in advertisements)

[ ] Applicant has a bona fide intention to use the mark in commerce on or in connection with the above identified goods/services. (15 U.S.C. 1051(b), as amended.)
- Specify manner or mode of use of mark on or in connection with the goods/services: _____

(for example, trademark will be applied to labels, service mark will be used in advertisements)

[ ] Applicant has a bona fide intention to use the mark in commerce on or in connection with the above identified goods/services, and asserts a claim of priority based upon a foreign application in accordance with 15 U.S.C. 1126(d), as amended.
- Country of foreign filing: _____   • Date of foreign filing: _____

[ ] Applicant has a bona fide intention to use the mark in commerce on or in connection with the above identified goods/services and, accompanying this application, submits a certification or certified copy of a foreign registration in accordance with 15 U.S.C 1126(e), as amended
- Country of registration: _____   • Registration number: _____

NOTE: Declaration, on Reverse Side, MUST be Signed

DECLARATION

The undersigned being hereby warned that willful false statements and the like so made are punishable by fine or imprisonment, or both, under 18 U.S.C. 1001, and that such willful false statements may jeopardize the validity of the application or any resulting registration, declares that he/she is properly authorized to execute this application on behalf of the applicant; he/she believes the applicant to be the owner of the trademark/service mark sought to be registered, or if the application is being filed under 15 U.S.C. 1051(b), he/she believes the applicant to be entitled to use such mark in commerce; to the best of his/her knowledge and belief no other person, firm, corporation, or association has the right to use the above identified mark in commerce, either in the identical form thereof or in such near resemblance thereto as to be likely, when used on or in connection with the goods/services of such other person, to cause confusion, or to cause mistake, or to deceive; and that all statements made of his/her own knowledge are true and that all statements made on information and belief are believed to be true.

_____   _____
DATE   SIGNATURE

_____   _____
TELEPHONE NUMBER   PRINT OR TYPE NAME AND POSITION

INSTRUCTIONS AND INFORMATION FOR APPLICANT

TO RECEIVE A FILING DATE, THE APPLICATION <u>MUST</u> BE COMPLETED AND SIGNED BY THE APPLICANT AND SUBMITTED ALONG WITH:

1. The prescribed **FEE ($245.00)** for each class of goods/services listed in the application;
2. A **DRAWING PAGE** displaying the mark in conformance with 37 CFR 2.52;
3. If the application is based on use of the mark in commerce, **THREE (3) SPECIMENS** (evidence) of the mark as used in commerce for each class of goods/services listed in the application. All three specimens may be the same. Examples of good specimens include: (a) labels showing the mark which are placed on the goods; (b) photographs of the mark as it appears on the goods, (c) brochures or advertisements showing the mark as used in connection with the services.
4. An **APPLICATION WITH DECLARATION** (this form) - The application must be signed in order for the application to receive a filing date. Only the following persons may sign the declaration, depending on the applicant's legal entity: (a) the individual applicant; (b) an officer of the corporate applicant; (c) one general partner of a partnership applicant; (d) all joint applicants.

SEND APPLICATION FORM, DRAWING PAGE, FEE, AND SPECIMENS (IF APPROPRIATE) TO:

Assistant Commissioner for Trademarks
Box New App/Fee
2900 Crystal Drive
Arlington, VA 22202-3513

Additional information concerning the requirements for filing an application is available in a booklet entitled **Basic Facts About Registering a Trademark**, which may be obtained by writing to the above address or by calling: (703) 308-HELP.

ALLEGATION OF USE FOR INTENT-TO-USE APPLICATION, WITH DECLARATION (Amendment To Allege Use/Statement Use)	MARK (Identify the mark)
	SERIAL NO.

TO THE ASSISTANT COMMISSIONER FOR TRADEMARKS:

APPLICANT NAME:

Applicant requests registration of the above-identified trademark/service mark in the United States Patent and Trademark Office on the Principal Register established by the Act of July 5, 1946 (15 U.S.C. §1051 *et seq.*, as amended). Three specimens per class showing the mark as used in commerce and the prescribed fees are submitted with this statement.

Applicant is using the mark in commerce on or in connection with the following goods/services (CHECK ONLY ONE):

☐ (a) those in the application or Notice of Allowance; **OR**

☐ (b) those in the application or Notice of Allowance **except** (if goods/services are to be deleted, list the goods/services to be **deleted**): _____

_____

_____

Date of first use in commerce which the U.S. Congress may regulate:_____

Specify type of commerce: _____

(for example, interstate and/or commerce between the U.S. and a foreign country)

Date of first use anywhere: _____

Specify manner or mode of use of mark on or in connection with the goods/services: (for example, trademark is applied to labels, service mark is used in advertisements):_____

_____

_____

The undersigned, being hereby warned that willful false statements and the like so made are punishable by fine or imprisonment, or both, under 18 U.S.C. §1001, and that such willful false statements may jeopardize the validity of the application or any resulting registration, declares that he/she is properly authorized to execute this Amendment to Allege Use or Statement of Use on behalf of the applicant; he/she believes the applicant to be the owner of the trademark/service mark sought to be registered; the trademark /service mark is now in use in commerce; and all statements made of his/her own knowledge are true and all statements made on information and belief are believed to be true.

_____   _____
Date   Signature

_____   _____
Telephone Number   Type or Print Name and Position

☐　　**Check here if Request to Divide is being submitted with this statement** (if Applicant wishes to proceed to publication or registration with certain goods/services on or in connection with which it has used the mark in commerce and retain an active application for any remaining goods/services, a divisional application and fee are required. 37 C.F.R. §2.87)

PLEASE SEE REVERSE FOR MORE INFORMATION

INSTRUCTIONS AND INFORMATION FOR APPLICANT

In an application based upon a bona fide intention to use a mark in commerce, **the Applicant must use its mark in commerce before a registration will be issued.** After use begins, the applicant must file the Allegation of Use. If the Allegation of Use is filed before the mark is approved for publication in the *Official Gazette* it is treated under the statute as **an Amendment to Allege Use (AAU).** If it is filed after the Notice of Allowance is issued, it is treated under the statute as **a Statement of Use (SOU).** The Allegation of Use cannot be filed during the time period between approval of the mark for publication in the *Official Gazette* and the issuance of the Notice of Allowance. The difference between the AAU and SOU is the time at which each is filed during the process.

Additional requirements for filing this Allegation of Use:

1) the fee of $100.00 per class of goods/services **(please note that fees are subject to change, usually on October 1 of each year);** and
2) three (3) specimens of the mark as used in commerce for each class of goods/services (for example, photographs of the mark as it appears on the goods, labels for affixation on goods, advertisements showing the mark as used in connection with services).

• The Applicant may list dates of use for one item in each class of goods/services identified in the Allegation of Use. The Applicant must have used the mark in commerce on all the goods/services in the class, however, it is only necessary to list the dates of use for one item in each class.

• Only the following persons may sign the verification on this form: (a) the individual applicant; (b) an officer of a corporate applicant; (c) one general partner of a partnership applicant; (d) all joint applicants.

• The goods/services in the Allegation of Use must be the same as those specified in the application or Notice of Allowance. The Applicant may limit or clarify the goods/services, but cannot add to or otherwise expand the identification specified in the application or Notice of Allowance. If goods/services are deleted, they may **not** be reinserted at a later time.

• Amendments to Allege Use are governed by Trademark Act §1(c), 15 U.S.C. §1051(c) and Trademark Rule 2.76, 37 C.F.R. §2.76. Statements of Use are governed by Trademark Act §1(d), 15 U.S.C. §1051(d) and Trademark Rule 2.88, 37 C.F.R. §2.88.

MAIL COMPLETED FORM TO:

ASSISTANT COMMISSIONER FOR TRADEMARKS
BOX AAU/SOU
2900 CRYSTAL DRIVE
ARLINGTON, VIRGINIA 22202-3513

Please note that the filing date of a document in the Patent and Trademarks Office is the date of receipt in the Office, not the date of deposit of the mail. 37 C.F.R. §1.6. To avoid lateness due to mail delay, use of the certificate of mailing set forth below, is encouraged.

COMBINED CERTIFICATE OF MAILING/CHECKLIST

Before filing this form, please make sure to complete the following:

☐ three specimens, per class have been enclosed;
☐ the filing fee of $100 (subject to change as noted above), per class has been enclosed; and
☐ the declaration has been signed by the appropriate party

CERTIFICATE OF MAILING

I do hereby certify that the foregoing are being **deposited** with the United States Postal Service as first class mail, postage prepaid, in an envelope addressed to the Assistant Commissioner for Trademarks, 2900 Crystal Drive, Arlington, VA 22202-3513, on _____ (date).

_____   _____
Signature   Date of Deposit

_____
Print or Type Name of Person Signing Certificate

This form is estimated to take 15 minutes to complete including time required for reading and understanding instructions, gathering necessary information, record keeping and actually providing the information. Any comments on the amount of time you require to complete this form should be sent to the Office of Management and Organization, U.S. Patent and Trademark Office, U.S. Department of Commerce, Washington, D.C. 20231. Do not send forms to this address.

REQUEST FOR EXTENSION OF TIME TO FILE A STATEMENT OF USE, WITH DECLARATION	MARK (Identify the mark)
	SERIAL NO.

TO THE ASSISTANT SECRETARY AND COMMISSIONER OF PATENTS AND TRADEMARKS:

APPLICANT NAME:

NOTICE OF ALLOWANCE MAILING DATE:

Applicant requests a six-month extension of time to file the Statement of Use under 37 CFR 2.89 in this application.

Applicant has a continued bona fide intention to use the mark in commerce on or in connection with the following goods/services: (Check One below)

☐ Those goods/services identified in the Notice of Allowance.

☐ Those goods/services identified in the Notice of Allowance except: (Identify goods/services to be **deleted** from application)

_____

_____

_____

This is the_____ request for an Extension of Time following mailing of the Notice of Allowance.
(Specify: First - Fifth)

If this is not the first request for an Extension of Time, check one box below. If the first box is checked explain the circumstance(s) of the non-use in the space provided:

☐ Applicant has not used the mark in commerce yet on all goods/services specified in the Notice of Allowance; however, applicant has made the following ongoing efforts to use the mark in commerce on or in connection with each of the goods/services specified above:

_____

_____

If additional space is needed, please attach a separate sheet to this form

☐ Applicant believes that it has made valid use of the mark in commerce, as evidenced by the Statement of Use submitted with this request; however, if the Statement of Use does not meet minimum requirements under 37 CFR 2.88(e), applicant will need additional time in which to file a new statement.

The undersigned being hereby warned that willful false statements and the like so made are punishable by fine or imprisonment, or both, under 18 U.S.C. 1001, and that such willful false statements may jeopardize the validity of the application or any resulting registration, declares that he/she is properly authorized to execute this Request for an Extension of Time to File a Statement of Use on behalf of the applicant; and that all statements made of his/her own knowledge are true and all statements made on information and belief are believed to be true.

_____
Date

_____
Signature

_____
Telephone Number

_____
Type or Print Name and Position

☐ **Check here if Request to Divide is being submitted with this statement** (if Applicant wishes to proceed to publication or registration with certain goods/services on or in connection with which it has used the mark in commerce and retain an active application for any remaining goods/services, a divisional application and fee are required. 37 C.F.R. §2.87)

INSTRUCTIONS AND INFORMATION FOR APPLICANT

Applicant must file a Statement of Use within six months after the mailing of the Notice of Allowance based upon a bona fide intention to use a mark in commerce, UNLESS, within that same period, applicant submits a request for a six-month extension of time to file the Statement of Use. The written request **must**:

(1) be received in the PTO within six months after the issue date of the Notice of Allowance,

(2) include applicant's verified statement of continued bona fide intention to use the mark in commerce,

(3) specify the goods/services to which the request pertains as they are identified in the Notice of Allowance, and

(4) include a fee of $100 for each class of goods/services (**please note that fees are subject to change, usually on October 1 of each year).**

Applicant may request four further six-month extensions of time. No extensions may extend beyond 36 months from the issue date of the Notice of Allowance. Each further request must be received in the PTO within the previously granted six-month extension period and must include, in addition to the above requirements, a showing of **GOOD CAUSE**. This good cause showing must include:

(1) applicant's statement that the mark has not been used in commerce yet on all the goods or services specified in the Notice of Allowance with which applicant has a continued bona fide intention to use the mark in commerce, **and**

(2) applicant's statement of ongoing efforts to make such use, which may include the following: (a) product or service research or development, (b) market research, (c) promotional activities, (d) steps to acquire distributors, (e) steps to obtain required governmental approval, or (f) similar specified activity.

Applicant may submit one additional six-month extension request during the existing period in which applicant files the Statement of Use, unless the granting of this request would extend the period beyond 36 months from the issue date of the Notice of Allowance. As a showing of good cause for such a request, applicant should state its belief that applicant has made valid use of the mark in commerce, as evidenced by the submitted Statement of Use, but that if the Statement is found by the PTO to be defective, applicant will need additional time in which to file a new statement of use.

Only the following person may sign the declaration of the Request for Extension of Time: (a) the individual applicant; (b) an officer of corporate applicant; (c) one general partner of partnership applicant; (d) all joint applicants.

MAILING INSTRUCTIONS

MAIL COMPLETED FORM TO:

ASSISTANT COMMISSIONER FOR TRADEMARKS
BOX ITU
2900 CRYSTAL DRIVE
ARLINGTON, VIRGINIA 22202-3513

Please note that the filing date of a document in the Patent and Trademarks Office is the date of receipt in the Office, not the date of deposit of the mail. 37 C.F. R. §1.6. To avoid lateness due to mail delay, use of the certificate of mailing set forth below is encouraged.

CERTIFICATE OF MAILING

I do hereby certify that this correspondence is being **deposited** with the United States Postal Service as first class mail, postage prepaid, in an envelope addressed to the Assistant Commissioner for Trademarks, 2900 Crystal Drive, Arlington, VA 22202-3513, on _____ (date).

_____
Signature

Date of Deposit

_____
Print or Type Name of Person Signing Certificate

This form is estimated to take 15 minutes to complete including time required for reading and understanding instructions, gathering necessary information, record keeping and actually providing the information. Any comments on the amount of time you require to complete this form should be sent to the Office of Management and Organization. U.S. Patent and Trademark Office, U.S. Department of Commerce, Washington, D.C. 20231. Do not send forms to this address.

DOMAIN NAMES

A domain name is the address for a computer server on the Internet. It is a real or fanciful word, or letters, separated by periods (called "dots"), such as http://www.laig.com/law/entlaw, which is the domain name for a web site. A suffix to the name indicates the kind of entity is at the address, for example, .com for commercial, .edu for educational, and .gov for government. A "www" in a name indicates a World Wide Web site.

Domain names have been assigned by Network Solutions, Inc. ("NSI"), under contract to the National Science Foundation. In April 1997, the National Science Foundation announced that it would not renew its contract with NSI the following March, thereby removing the government from the domain-name registration business. NSI is expected to compete with other companies to register domain names.

Domain names have traditionally been assigned on a first-come, first-served basis. There have been considerable controversy, and several lawsuits, as a result of individuals choosing domain names that may mislead the public and prevent organizations from subsequently registering domain names similar to their trademarks. The domain name "mtv.com" was registered by a former MTV personality, "kaplan.com" was registered by Princeton Review, a competitor of the Stanley Kaplan test-preparation service, and "McDonald.com" was registered by a person unaffiliated with the famous hamburger chain. These cases were all settled or resolved in arbitration.[12]

Obviously, people and businesses want a memorable domain name, and often prefer one that is very similar to the name of an existing trademark. Domain names had been available free of charge, and without any requirement that the applicant establish any trademark rights to the use of a proposed name. There have been enterprising individuals who have registered well-known trademarks of others as domain names in the hope that they could hold these names hostage and eventually sell them for a profit.

In order to avoid being drawn into domain-name disputes, the NSI has a revised its policy concerning registration of domain names. Registrants must certify that to their knowledge

PROTECTING
MULTIMEDIA
WORKS
FROM
INFRINGEMENT

283

the use of a name does not violate trademark or other laws. NSI can withdraw a registered name if it has received an order from a U.S. Court or arbitration award, finding that the name belongs to another. The InterNIC's dispute policy is posted on the Web at http://rs.internic.net/domain-info/internic-domain-6.html.

A new remedy to help trademark owners control the use of their marks in cyberspace is available under the Federal Trademark Dilution Act of 1995,[13] which was signed into law on January 16, 1996. The law provides a federal cause of action against anyone who makes commercial use of a "famous" trademark in such a manner that it dilutes the distinctive qualities of that mark. Many states have their own anti-dilution statutes that may provide a remedy as well. Several suits concerning domain names were filed soon after enactment of the new federal law. In *Avon Products v. Carnetta Wong Associates*,[14] the Avon cosmetics company filed suit against a defendant who had registered "avon.com" and successfully reclaimed this domain name. In *Hasbro, Inc. v. Entertainment Group Ltd.*,[15] the famous toy company sued when its "Candyland" game title was being used as a domain name for an adult web site. Hasbro obtained a preliminary injunction, preventing the adult web site from using the name "Candyland" until the case can be heard.

For additional information on registering domain names, contact: Network Solutions, Inc., InterNIC Registry Services, 505 Huntmar Park Drive, Herndon, Virginia 20170. E-mail: hostmaster@internic.net, telephone: (703) 742-4777 or (703) 742-0400. The Present charge for Domain name registration is $100. for the first two years, $50. a year thereafter.

PATENT

Both computer software and computer machinery may be eligible for patent protection.[16] Patent law protects the "useful arts," meaning any new and useful process or machinery.[17] Thus, software-based inventions (the process or method), and the hardware (the machine or apparatus), are patentable. Not all inventions, however, are sufficiently innovative to merit patent protection. Computer software that is based on common principles, for instance, may not qualify for patent protection, although the software may be quite valuable. Mathematical algorithms and laws of nature, standing alone, are not patentable, although they may be incorporated in a patentable invention.

Remember, computer software may also be protected under copyright and trade secret law, even if it is not eligible for patent protection. Once a patent is applied for, however, the workings of the invention are revealed to the public and secrecy is lost. Furthermore, competitors might be able to use this information to design around the patent, producing a new product that accomplishes the same result, and negate the value of the patent.

A patent must be applied for and granted by the federal government (the Patent and Trademark Office in the United States) after a determination has been made that the applicant is eligible for the patent. There are several types of patents: utility patents, plant patents, and design patents. Only utility patents and design patents are relevant to the protection of multimedia works. A utility patent can protect computer software and a design patent can protect computer-screen icons.

If your invention is eligible for patent protection, and you do not apply for it in a timely manner, you may lose the exclusive right to control the use of your invention. Inventors need to file an application within one year from the date that the invention is first in public use, on sale in the U.S.A., described in a printed publication, or patented in a foreign country. While private use does not start the clock ticking, beta testing outside the inventor's workplace could be considered a public use.

The process of applying for and receiving a patent can be time-consuming and expensive. Moreover, enforcing a patent can be an arduous task and may require the expenditure of substantial legal fees. Software inventors need to carefully consider whether their invention is sufficiently valuable to justify the cost of seeking a patent. If other existing software can accomplish the same result, or if your invention is likely to be surpassed soon by technological developments, applying for a patent may only produce a mountain of legal bills. If you obtain a patent, there is no guarantee that it will produce a profit for the patent's owner. The owner may not have the financial backing to exploit the patent, and others may not be interested in licensing it.

Pursuing patent infringers can be problematical. If infringement is widespread, and the damages from each infringement are small, it may not be cost-effective to take legal action. On the other hand, if there is a single infringer and the damages are substantial, a suit may be remunerative because a patent owner may obtain as damages all the profits made from the unauthorized use of the invention. And, in certain instances, a court can award triple damages and the reimbursement of attorneys' fees.

Patents can be contested in court after the Patent and Trademark Office (PTO) grants a patent. If an infringer can prove that the patent should not have been granted in the first place, the judge can determine that the patent is not valid. Obtaining patents to software is particularly troublesome because the PTO often has difficulty determining whether software is patentable. Patent examiners may lack the expertise needed to evaluate software, and records are often incomplete regarding what prior software exists. A patent cannot be granted when the subject matter sought to be patented is obvious to people with ordinary skill in that art.[18] A "prior art search" determines the state of the prior art in the field of the invention.

The PTO was the subject of considerable criticism when it awarded Compton's New Media a broad patent on multimedia search-and-retrieval technology widely used by other companies. The PTO later reexamined the validity of the patent and invalidated it on the grounds that the patent examiner who had awarded it was not aware of certain prior art. Compton's appealed the decision.

If the patent is granted, the inventor receives a monopoly on using, making, or selling the invention.[19] Utility patents last for seventeen years and design patents last for fourteen years. The United States grants patents to the first inventor, not the first person to file a patent application. Therefore, if two parties contest ownership to an invention, the first inventor is entitled to the patent.[20]

Patent rights to an invention generally reside in the inventor not the inventor's employer. When software is developed by an employee or an outsider contractor, it is important to have a written agreement between the parties specifying who owns the patent. The agreement may be required as a condition of employment. If the agreement is signed after employment begins, however, additional consideration may be needed to ensure that the contract is binding. In other words, the employer must give the employee something of value, other than just the hiring of the employee, to contractually acquire the patent. Even if the patent rights to an invention reside in an employee, the employer may have the right to use the invention without royalty, in perpetuity. This is known as the "shop rights" doctrine. Under this principle, the employer may only use the invention in the course of its business and may not license it to others. The employee may, however, freely market the invention to others.

While there is no requirement that inventions bear a patent notice, such a notice is advisable. Without the notice, the infringer may only be liable for damages incurred from the date the infringer received notice of the patent. A patent notice comprises the word "patent" or the abbreviation "pat." followed by the number of the patent. If the patent is pending, the notice should state "patent pending."

TRADE SECRET

One of the most famous trade secrets is the formula for Coca-Cola. This secret is reportedly locked in a safe that can only be opened by a few trusted employees. As long as the formula is kept secret, it will remain a trade secret. But if the information is publicly disclosed, it can no longer be protected as a trade secret. Coca-Cola has maintained this trade secret for more than 100 years.

A trade secret is any formula, pattern, device, or compilation of information used in a business and treated confidentially and which provides its owner a competitive advantage. To maintain a trade secret, one must treat the information like a secret. It should only be disclosed to those who agree to keep it confidential. Those who steal trade secrets can be liable for civil damages and criminal penalties.

Unlike a copyright or patent, there is no registration mechanism for trade secrets. The very nature of trade secrets requires that the information be kept secret and not be publicly registered. Trade secrets are protected by keeping the information confidential. This may mean locking it away in a safe place and entering into non-disclosure or confidentiality agreements with employees. Under such agreements, unauthorized disclosure of confidential information will be a breach of contract, as well as a possible violation of various statutes.

Trade secrets are generally protected under state law as there is no federal trade-secret law. State laws vary, although many states have based their laws on the model Uniform Trade Secrets Act. This model legislation provides for a three-year statute of limitation. This means that a trade secret misappropriation claim must be filed within three years of when the theft is discovered. The remedy for theft of a trade secret can be monetary damages and/or an injunction ordering the return of the trade secret information.

TRADE SECRETS

REQUIREMENTS:

(1) INFORMATION NOT GENERALLY AVAILABLE (I.E., THE INFORMATION IS A SECRET)

(2) THE INFORMATION HAS ECONOMIC VALUE

(3) THE OWNER TAKES REASONABLE MEASURES TO MAINTAIN SECRECY

EXAMPLES:

MARKETING STRATEGIES, PLANS, AND FORECASTS

CUSTOMER LISTS

MANUFACTURING PROCESSES

COMPUTER SOFTWARE

Trade secrets are protectable under state law whether or not the information is patentable. Disclosure of information in patent applications does not make the information public. When the patent is issued and published, however, trade secret protection will terminate for the published information.

Regardless of whether information is copyrightable or not, it can be protected as a trade secret. Ideas, facts, and procedures, for example, are not copyrightable. However, they can be protected as trade secrets as long as the information is kept confidential. Computer software often contains elements that are not generally known in the computer industry, and thus is protectable as a trade secret.

Trade secret law does not prevent third parties from independently creating or inventing the same information that you consider to be your trade secret. Thus, third parties can examine your software or other proprietary information and, through "reverse-engineering," create their own identical work. That is why software is usually distributed only in object code, which is hard to reverse-engineer. Because of the difficulty in reverse-engineering object code, it can qualify as a trade secret unless it is actually reverse-engineered. Moreover, the owner of software may ask users to sign licensing agreements in which the licensees agree not to disclose any trade secrets incorporated in the program.

If you attempt, through reverse-engineering, to create work similar to another, you should protect yourself from a claim that you improperly infringed on another's rights. You should document your efforts to create the work independently. This can be done by having your designers work in a so-called "clean room" environment where the information disclosed to them is carefully monitored. In a "clean room," designers are only given publicly available information.

Trade secrets that are developed by an employee within the scope of his employment usually will belong to the employer. Trade secrets developed by an employee on his own time may, however, belong to the employee. To avoid an ambiguity as to ownership of any trade secret developed by employees, it is highly advisable for employers to have a written employment agreement that assigns to the employer any trade secrets developed by the employee.

Employment agreements may also contain a "Covenant Not to Compete," also referred to as a Restrictive Covenant. Such a provision prevents an employee from competing against his employer within a certain geographical area and within certain time limits after termination of the employee's employment. Thus, an employee might be prevented from establishing a competing business within two years of termination. Some states will enforce such covenants if the terms are reasonable. Other states, such as California, refuse to enforce these Covenants on the grounds that they are against the public policy of permitting competition. See Chapter 3 for a detailed discussion of employment contracts.

In addition to including non-disclosure provisions in employment contracts, companies should use care in disclosing trade secrets to outsiders such as beta testers, independent contractors, and potential business partners. A written non-disclosure agreement can be used in each of these cases to prevent unauthorized disclosure. A sample agreement follows.

PROTECTING
MULTIMEDIA
WORKS
FROM
INFRINGEMENT

289

NON-DISCLOSURE AGREEMENT

Gentlemen:

Our business has, in the past, required frequent contact with representatives of business concerns such as your own. In many cases, those contacts have involved the disclosure of confidential information.

If we (the "Company") should supply you with such Confidential Information, the information is being given to you with the understanding that you (the "Recipient") shall not disclose or make any use whatsoever of any Confidential Information or Notes, except disclosures to those parties we permit (the "Permitted Parties") for the purposes of evaluating the "Transaction" (defined below) and who have been advised of, and agree in writing to be bound by, the restrictions set forth in this letter. Recipient shall not disclose, and shall require Permitted Parties not to disclose, the existence, content, or status of any negotiations or communications regarding the Transaction.

We further agree as follows:

1.   "Confidential Information" means information disclosed or made available by Company, its employees, agents, and professional representatives, to Recipient (whether orally, in writing, in the form of computer data, or by inspection) concerning the present or contemplated business, operations, or financial condition of Company, including, but not limited to, financial statements, tax returns, cost and expense data, contracts, client, employee, and marketing data and other information not generally available to the public.

2.   "Notes" means any notes, summaries, analyses, or other material derived by any of the Permitted Parties from evaluation or discussion of Confidential Information. "Permitted Parties" means the Recipient, its or his employees, agents, and professional representatives and such other persons as may be designated in writing by Company.

3.   "Transaction" means the sale of all or part of Company's assets or all or part of Company's outstanding shares, some other form of business combination resulting in an exchange of all or part of Company's outstanding shares, a contemplated co-venture, or contract for services.

4.   "Company" means ABC Consultants, Inc., or any of its affiliated corporations, including those entities listed on the attached Exhibit A.

5.   Upon demand of Company, Recipient shall promptly deliver, and shall cause Permitted Parties promptly to deliver, to

Company all Confidential Information and all Notes which are in a format capable of delivery. All Confidential Information shall remain the property of Company.

6. Any Confidential Information disclosed or made available to any of the Permitted Parties prior to or after the date of this letter shall be subject to the restrictions set forth herein.

7. Neither Company nor any of its directors, officers, employees, agents, or professional representatives shall be deemed to make any representation or warranty as to the accuracy or completeness of any Confidential Information.

8. Any failure or delay (full or partial) of the Company to exercise its rights or remedies hereunder shall not operate as a waiver thereof.

9. The non-disclosure obligations imposed hereunder shall continue for a term of five years from the date of this Agreement.

10. Recipient agrees that the Company's remedies at law for any violation of the restrictions set forth in this Agreement shall be inadequate and that the Company shall be entitled to injunctive relief in any proceeding brought to enforce this Agreement, without proof of actual damage and without a bond.

11. Recipient acknowledges that if Recipient fails to comply with the restrictions set forth in this Agreement, the amount of damages to the Company would be impossible to determine with any reasonable accuracy. Therefore, Recipient shall pay to the Company as liquidated damages, and not as a penalty, an amount equal to fifty thousand dollars ($50,000). This provision for liquidated damages is not intended to be in any way exclusive or restrictive of the right to specific performance or injunctive relief to which the Company may be entitled.

12. The parties acknowledge that the restrictions and damages set forth in this Agreement are reasonable, based upon the facts and circumstances existing as of the date of this Agreement and with due regard to future expectations. However, if any provision of this paragraph shall be held invalid or unenforceable, the remainder shall nevertheless remain in full force and effect.

13. Any controversy or dispute arising out of or relating to this Agreement shall be settled by arbitration in the State of _____, according to the rules of the American Arbitration Association and judgment upon the award rendered by the arbitrator may be entered in any court having jurisdiction thereof. The prevailing party in any such arbitration shall be entitled to recover from the other party reasonable attorneys' fees and costs incurred in connection with it. The determination of the arbitrator in such proceeding shall be final, binding, and non-appealable. Nothing contained in this clause shall preclude any party from seeking and obtaining any injunctive relief or other provisional remedy available in a court of law.

PROTECTING
MULTIMEDIA
WORKS
FROM
INFRINGEMENT

291

14. The covenants and agreements contained herein shall be binding upon and inure to the benefit of the representatives, successors, and assigns of the respective parties.

15. This Agreement shall be governed by, and construed according to, the laws of the State of _____.

IN WITNESS WHEREOF, the parties have executed this Agreement as of the date written below.

RECIPIENT:

By: _____ Date: _____
    Authorized Signatory

Agreed by COMPANY:

By: _____ Date: _____
    Authorized Signatory

APPENDIX

Rights & Permissions Agencies

BZ/Rights & Permissions, Inc.
125 W. 72nd St.
New York, NY 10023
(212) 580-0615; Fax: (212) 769-9224

Copyright Clearinghouse, Inc.
405 Riverside Dr.
Burbank, CA 91506
(818) 558-3480; Fax: (818) 558-3474

Suzanne R. Vaughan Clip Clearance
2029 Century Park East, Ste. 450
Los Angeles, CA 90067
(310) 556-2730; Fax: (310) 556-1312

Business Resources

Commerce.Net
  http://www.commerce.net/

Commercial Sites Index
  http://www.directory.net/

Corporate Finance Network
  http://www.corpfinet.com/

Dun & Bradstreet
  http://dbisna.com/

Federal Express Tracking
  http://www.fedex.com/cgi-bin/track_it

Guide to Financial Info
  http://www.euro.net/innovation/Web_Word_Base/TWW1-html/
    FinTOC1.html

Internet Blacklist
http://www.cco.caltech.edu/~cbrown/BL/

Investment Banks on the Web
http://www.catalog.com/interof/finance/invbanks.html

Motley Fool
http://fool.web.aol.com//fool_mn.htm

Wall Street Net
http://www.netresource.com/wsn/

Distributors (Mail-Order)

BRE Software
http://www.cybergate.com/~bre

Buy Rite Games
http://www.buyrite1.com

CD-Rom Access
http://www.cdaccess.com

Chips & Bits, Inc.
http://www.cdmag.com/chips.html

Cutting Edge Entertainment
http://www.sunmarkinc.com/products/flashback

Funco
http://www.funcoland.com

Gamex
http://www.gamex.com

Game Station, Inc.
http://www.hooked.net/users/gamest

Gecko Games
http://angelfire.com/free/geckogames.html

Distributors (Wholesale)

ABCO Distributors
http://www.abcodist.com/

American Software & Hardware Distributors
http://www.ashd.com/suppliers.htm/

Beamscope Distribution
http://www.beamscope.com/

BRE Software
http://www.cybergate.com/~bre

Buy Rite Videogames
http://www.buyrite1.com/

The Channel
   http://www.thechannel.com/

Cutting Edge Entertainment
   http://www.cuttingedgeent.com/

Gamex
   http://www.gamex.com

Mecca Electronic Industries, Inc.
   http://www.mecca1.com

MS Distributing Company
   http://www.msdist.com

Rentrak Corporation
   http://www.rentrak.com

Strata Distributing
   http://www.stratadist.com/

Telegames
   http://www.telegames.com

United CD-Rom
   http://www.unitedcdrom.com/

Video Game Discounters
   http://www.hc.net/~rosebud/vgd/main.html

Entertainment Industry Web Sites

Most of this list provided courtesy of Steve Arbuss. The list is available on line at http://www.paranoia.com/~ebola/newhot.html

ABC
   http://www.abctelevision.com/

BBC
   http://www.bbcnc.org.uk/

CBS
   http://www.cbs.com/

Cinemania
   http://204.255.247.120/Cinemania/

Court TV
   http://www.courttv.com/

David Letterman
   http://www.cbs.com:80/lateshow/lateshow.html

Disney
   http://www.disney.com/

E! Online
   http://www.eonline.com/

Entertainment Links
http://www.minyos.its.rmit.edu.au/~mraja/tv.htm

ESPN
http://espnet.sportszone.com/

Film Zone
http://www.filmzone.com/

Film.com
http://www.film.com/

Fox
http://www.foxnetwork.com

Gigaplex
http://www.directnet.com/wow/

HBO
http://www.homebox.com

HitsWorld
http://www.hitsworld.com/daily.html

Hollywood Insider
http://www.hollywoodonline.com/hn/hollynews/index.html

Hollywood Online
http://www.hollywood.com/

Hollywood Reporter
http://www.hollywoodreporter.com/m.shtml

Internet Entertainment Network
http://www.hollywoodnetwork.com:80/hn/index.html

Internet Movie Database
http://www.imdb.com

Internet Underground Music Archives
http://www.iuma.com/

MCA
http://www.mca.com

Mr. Showbiz
http://web3.starwave.com/showbiz/

MTV
http://www.mtv.com

NBC
http://www.nbc.com/

NPR
http://npr.org

Pathfinder
http://www.pathfinder.com

PBS
http://www.pbs.org

Paramount
  http://www.paramount.com

Radio & Records
  http://www.rronline.com/

Reuters Entertainment News
  http://www.yahoo.com/headlines/entertainment

Rolling Stones Voodoo Lounge
  http://www.stones.com/

Species
  http://www.digiplanet.com:80/species/

Starwave
  http://www.starwave.com/

Teen Movie Critic
  http://www.dreamagic.com/roger/alphabet.html

The Biz
  http://www.bizmag.com/

TV Guide
  http://www.tvguide.com

Tonight Show
  http://www.nbctonightshow.com/

TV Net
  http://tvnet.com/TVnet.html

Universal Cyberwalk
  http://www.mca.com/index.html

Viacom
  http://www.viacom.com/

Virtual Headbook
  http://www.xmission.com/~wintmx/virtual.html

Virtual Vegas
  http://www.virtualvegas.com/

Warner
  http://www.warnerbros.com

What's on Tonight?
  http://tvnet.com/WhatsOnTonite/pacidays.html

Finding an Internet Service Provider

CyberToday ISP List—L.A./Orange County
  http://www.cybertoday.com/cybertoday/isps/Areas.html#Southland

CyberToday ISP List—Home
  http://www.cybertoday.com/cybertoday/isps/default.html

Personal Access Providers in L.A./Orange County
  http://www.primenet.com/~lclee/laoc.html

Providers of Commercial Internet Access (POCIA) Directory
http://www2.celestin.com/pocia/index.html

Kegel ISDN Provider List
http://alumni.caltech.edu/~dank/isdn/isp.html

Government Resources (Federal)

FBI
http://www.fbi.gov

FCC
http://www.fcc.gov/

Federal Courts
http://www.uscourts.gov/

FedWorld
http://www.fedworld.gov/

Federal Web Locator
http://www.law.vill.edu/Fed-Agency/fedwebloc.html

House "Law Library"
http://www.pls.com:8001/d2/kelli/httpd/htdocs/his/17.GBM

IRS
http://www.irs.ustreas.gov/

Library of Congress
http://www.loc.gov/

National Telecommunications and Information Administration
http://iitf.doc.gov:80/

Patent Office
http://www.uspto.gov

SEC EDGAR Database
http://town.hall.org/edgar/edgar.html

Supreme Court Decisions
http://www.law.cornell.edu/supct/

United States Codes
http://www.law.cornell.edu/uscode/

United States House (Thomas)
http://thomas.loc.gov/

United States Constitution
http://www.house.gov/Constitution/Constitution.html

White House
http://www.whitehouse.gov/

Government Resources (State of California)

California Assembly
  http://www.assembly.ca.gov/

California Codes
  http://www.law.indiana.edu/codes/ca/codes.html

California Constitution
  ftp://leginfo.public.ca.gov/pub/constitution/constitution_text

California Electronic Government Information
  http://www.cpsr.org/cpsr/states/california/cegi.html#toc

California Senate
  http://www.sen.ca.gov/

California Legislative Info
  http://www.leginfo.ca.gov/

Charlotte's Web California
  http://emf.net:80/~cr/calif.html

State of California Home Page
  http://www.ca.gov/

How to Build Web Sites

Bob Allison's Tips for Web Spinners
  http://gagme.wwa.com/~boba/tips1.html

HTML FAQ
  http://www.umcc.umich.edu/~ec/www/html_faq.htmlQ

HTML Primer (A Beginner's Guide to HTML)
  http://www.ncsa.uiuc.edu/General/Internet/www/HTMLPrimer.html

Style Guide for Online Hypertext
  http://www.w3.org/hypertext/WWW/Provider/Style/Overview.html

The Web Developer's Virtual Library
  http://WWW.stars.com/

The Web Masters' Page
  http://gagme.wwa.com/~boba/masters1.html

Intellectual Property Resources

Berne Convention
  gopher://gopher.law.cornell.edu:70/00/foreign/fletcher/BH006-1971.txt

Copyright Act
  http://www.law.indiana.edu/codes/ca/codes.html

Lanham Act
  http://www.law.cornell.edu/usc/15/22/overview.html

Patent Act
  http://www.law.cornell.edu/usc/35/i_iv/overview.html

Patent Searches
http://town.hall.org:80/patent/patent.html

Patent Searches—STO
http://sunsite.unc.edu:80/patents/intropat.html

Internet Guides and Tools

Arc Toolbox
http://www.arc.org/webtools/toolbox.html

Browsers
http://gagme.wwa.com/~boba/browsers.html

EFF's Extended Guide to the Internet
http://www2.infoseek.com/

Guide to Computer Mediated Communications
http://www.rpi.edu/Internet/Guides/decemj/icmc/toc3.html

Internet Guides
http://www.brandonu.ca/~ennsnr/Resources/guides.html

Internet Tools Summary
http://www.rpi.edu/Internet/Guides/decemj/itools/toc3.htmls

Multimedia File Formats on the Internet
http://ac.dal.ca/~dong/contents.htm

Yahoo
http://www.yahoo.com/

Yanoff List
ftp://ftp.csd.uwm.edu/pub/inet.services.html

Whole Internet Catalog
http://nearnet.gnn.com/wic/

WWW FAQ
http://sunsite.unc.edu/boutell/faq/www_faq.html

Internet Searches

AltaVista
http://www.altavista.digital.com/

CUI W3 Catalog
http://cuiwww.unige.ch/w3catalog

Deja News
http://www.dejanews.com/forms/dnq.html

Excite
http://www.excite.com/

Hotbot
http://www.hotbot.com

InfoSeek
http://www2.infoseek.com/

Lexis/Nexis
  telnet://nex.lexis-nexis.com/

Lycos
  http://www.lycos.com/

One4All
  http://all4one.com/

Saavy Search
  http://www.cs.colostate.edu/~dreiling/smartform.html

Ultra
  http://ultra.infoseek.com

W3 Search Engines
  http://cuiwww.unige.ch/meta-index.html

Webcrawler
  http://webcrawler.com/

Yahoo
  http://www.yahoo.com/search.html

Law Firm Websites

Arent Fox
  http://www.arentfox.com/

Brobeck
  http://www.brobeck.com/

Buchalter
  http://www.buchalter.com/

Burke, Williams
  http://www.bwslaw.com/

Cooley Godward
  http://www.cooley.com/

Coudert
  http://www.coudert.com/

Fenwick
  http://www.fenwick.com/

Fried, Frank
  http://www.ffhsj.com/

Graham & James
  http://www.gj.com/

Gray Cary
  http://www.gcwf.com/

Hale & Dorr
  http://www.haledorr.com/

Heller Ehrman
  http://www.digital.com/gnn/bus/hewm/index.html

Jeffer Mangels
http://www.jmbm.com/jmbm/jmbm.htm

Jones Hall
http://www.jhhw.com/

Kelley Drye
http://www.kelleydrye.com/

Luce
http://www.luce.com/

Litwak, Mark
http://www.laig.com/law/entlaw/

McCutchen
http://www.mccutchen.com/

Orrick
http://www.orrick.com/

Paul Hastings
http://www.phjw.com/

Pepper Hamilton
http://www.constructlaw.com/index.html

Pepper & Corazzini
http://www.commlaw.com/pepper/

Sabo & Zahn
http://www.webcom.com/~sabozahn/

Sidley
http://www.sidley.com/

The Virtual Law Firm
http://www.tvlf.com/tvlf/

Venable
http://199.34.61.2/vbh.htm

Wilson Sonsini
http://www.wsgr.com/

Law Libraries

Boalt
gopher://law164.berkeley.edu:70/11/Boalt%20Hall%20Law%20Library

Chicago Kent
http://www.kentlaw.edu/

Cornell
http://www.law.cornell.edu/

Hastings
http://www.uchastings.edu/

UCLA
http://www.law.ucla.edu/

USC
http://www.usc.edu/dept/law-lib/index.html

U.S. House
http://law.house.gov/1.htm

Legal Directories

Lawyer Search
http://www.counsel.com/lawyersearch/

Martindale
http://www.martindale.com/

Yahoo Firms
http://www.yahoo.com/Business_and_Economy/Companies/
LawFirms/

Legal Research Guides

Finding Law Resources
http://www.well.com/user/cchick/sources.html

FindLaw
http://www.findlaw.com/

How Do I Find Law-Related Internet Resources?
http://www.well.com/user/cchick/sources.html

Irell & Manella Research List
ftp://ftp.netcom.com/pub/dj/djames/lynx/menu.html

Legal Research Starting Points
http://sparky.abanet.org/lawlink/home.html

Meta-Index for Legal Research
http://www.gsu.edu/~lawadmn/lawform.html

Newsgroups for Legal Research
http://virgo.gem.valpo.edu/~medic/news1.html

Meta-Index for Legal Research
http://gsulaw.gsu.edu/metaindex/

Starting Points
http://www.abanet.org/lawlink/home.html

Legal Research Hotlists

Kent LawLinks
http://www.kentlaw.edu/lawnet/lawlinks.html

LawMarks
http://www.iwc.com/entropy/marks/bkmrkjsm.html

Legal Info Hot Spots
http://law.wuacc.edu/scall/hotnam.html

The Legal List
http://www.lcp.com/The-Legal-List/TLL-home.html

Lexis Counsel Connect—Topical Law Materials
http://www.counsel.com/topical.htm

LOMEX
http://www.lomex.com/

Practicing Attorney's Page
http://www.legalethics.com/pa/main.html

PC Computing's Web Map—Law
http://www.zdnet.com/~pccomp/webmap/law.html

The Seamless Web: Legal Hotlist
http://www.ingress.com/tsw/road.html

The Source (San Diego Transcript) Legal Page
http://www.sddt.com/files/law.html

USC Links
http://www.usc.edu/dept/law-lib/legallst/topiclst.html

The Virtual Magistrate
http://vmag.law.vll.edu:8080/

WWW Virtual Library Law Listings
http://www.law.indiana.edu:80/law/lawindex.html

Yahoo Law
http://www.yahoo.com/Government/Law/

Legal Publishers and Commercial Sites

Bancroft Whitney
http://www.bancroft.com

CalLaw
http://www.callaw.com/

Law Journal Extra
http://www.ljextra.com/

Law Office Management
http://www.review.net/Lawyer/office_tech/index.html

Lawyers Cooperative Publishing
http://www.legal.net/

Legal dot Net
http://www.legal.net/

Lexis Counsel Connect
http://www.counsel.com/

Lexis/Nexis Communication Center
http://www.lexis-nexis.com/

Nolo Press
http://www.nolo.com/

San Diego Transcript
http://www.sddt.com/

West's Legal Directory
  http://www.westpub.com/WLDInfo/WLD.htm

West Publishing
  http://www.westpub.com/

Mailing Lists

Law Lists
  gopher://lawnext.uchicago.edu:70/00/.internetfiles/lawlists

Law Related Discussion Lists
  gopher://lawnext.uchicago.edu/hh/.web/lists.html

Law-Related Mailing Lists
  http://www.kentlaw.edu/lawlinks/listservs.html

LawNet Lists
  http://www.kentlaw.edu/lawnet/lawnet.html

Miscellaneous Reading

An Economy of Ideas by John Barlow
  http://www.wired.com/Etext/2.03/features/economy.ideas.html

American Bar Association
  http://www.abanet.org/home.html

Business Models for the Internet
  http://www.upside.com/upside/1f9508.html

Catching Money in the Web
  http://www.zdnet.com/~people/gina/950427/svalley.html

Cool Site of the Day
  http://www.infi.net/cool.html

Five Reasons for Lawyers to be on the Internet
  http://www.law.cornell.edu/papers/5reasons.html

Law Office Technology
  http://www.review.net/Lawyer/office_tech/index.html

Obscenity and the Supreme Court
  http://www.hotwired.com/Lib/Wired/2.03/departments/electro
      sphere/obscenity.html

News

Bloomberg
  http://www.bloomberg.com/

Christian Science Monitor
  http://www.csmonitor.com/

CNN
  http://www.cnn.com/

CNNfn
http://www.cnnfn.com/index.html

enews
http://www.enews.com/

Entertainment Headlines
http://pathfinder.com/News/Reuters/Latest/Entertainment/

Los Angeles Times
http://latimes.com/HOME/

MSNBC
http://www.msnbc.com/

Nando
http://nando.net/

New York Times
http://nytimes.com/yr/mo/day/front/index.html

NYT TimesFax
http://nytimesfax.com:80/cgi-bin/tmp/timesfax.pdf

Reuters
http://www.yahoo.com/headlines/news/summary.html

SF Gate
http://www.sfgate.com/

Time Daily
http://pathfinder.com/time/daily

trib.com
http://www1.trib.com/NEWS

USA Today
http://www.usatoday.com/

Other Commercial Sites

Activision
http://www.activision.com/

Apple
http://www.apple.com

Budweiser
http://budweiser.com/

Coca-Cola
http://coca-cola.com/

Federal Express
http://fedex.com/

Ford
http://www.ford.com/

IBM
http://www.ibm.com/

id Software
http://www.idsoftware.com/

Intel
http://www.intel.com/

Kodak
http://www.kodak.com/

L.L. Bean
http://www.llbean.com/parksearch/

Levi-Strauss
http://www.levi.com/

Microsoft
http://www.microsoft.com/

Olympic Games
http://olympics.nbc.com/

Penthouse
http://penthousemag.com/

Perrier
http://perrier.com/

Pop Rocket
http://poprocket.com/welcome.html

Saturn Cars
http://saturncars.com

Sega
http://www.sega.com/

SGI
http://www.sgi.com/

SGI Silicon Studio
http://www.studio.sgi.com/

Sony
http:/www.sony.com

Sun
http://www.sun.com/

Tide
http://tide.com/

Toyota
http://toyota.com/

Voyager
http://voyagerco.com/

Worlds Inc.
http://worlds.net/

Other Entertainment/Multimedia
Law Related Sites

Advertising Law
http://www.webcom.com/~lewrose/home.html

CyberLaw/CyberLex
http://www.portal.com/~cyberlaw/

EFF Multimedia Law Primer
http://www.eff.org/pub/CAF/law/ip-primer

Entertainment Law
http://www.laig.com/law/intnet/

Entertainment Law Resources
http://www.laig.com/law/entlaw/

Internet Law CyberCenter
http://www.hollywoodnetwork.com/Law/

Internet Law Hypercourse
http://www.umassp.edu/legal/HYPERCOU.HTML

Running a WWW Service—10 Legal and Ethical Issues
http://nswt.tuwien.ac.at:8000/htdocs/kelly/handbook-10.html

Privacy, Encryption, and Free Expression

ACM Internet Privacy Forum
http://www.vortex.com/privacy.htm

Bill Watch (Newsletter about Exxon, etc.)
http://anansi.panix.com:80/vtw/billwatch/

Computer Professionals for Social Responsibility
http://cpsr.org/home

Electronic Frontier Foundation
http://www.eff.org/

Electronic Privacy Information Center
http://epic.digicash.com/epic/

Pretty Good Privacy (PGP)
http://web.mit.edu/afs/net/mit/jis/www/pgp.html

Voter Telcomm Watch
http://anansi.panix.com:80/vtw/

Internet (Size and Growth)

Allison Web Survey Averages
http://gagme.wwa.com/~boba/survey.html

IBC WWW Size and Growth Statistics
http://tig.com/IBC/stats/html/index.html

The Internet Index
http://www.openmarket.com/info/internet-index/

Internet Size

http://www.netrex.com/business/basics.html

NSFNet Statistics
 ftp://nic.merit.edu/nsfnet/statistics/

WWW Growth
 http://www.netgen.com/info/growth.html

Security

Rutgers WWW Security Page
 http://www-ns.rutgers.edu/www-security/

W3C Security Page
 http://www.w3.org/hypertext/WWW/Security/Overview.html

Virtual City Halls

City of Los Angeles Home Page
 http://citynet.ci.la.ca.us/

West Hollywood Virtual City Hall
 http://www.deltanet.com:80/cityhall/

VRML

IMF VRML Page
 http://vrml.arc.org/

VRML from Hell
 http://www.well.com/user/caferace/vrml.html

Wired VRML Page
 http://vrml.wired.com/

Newsgroups for Legal Professionals

misc.legal
misc.legal.moderated
misc.legal.computing
misc.int-property
us.legal

Entertainment/Multimedia Newsgroups

rec.arts.cinema
rec.arts.movies
rec.arts.tv
rec.arts.movies.production
rec.games.misc
rec.games.video.misc
rec.video
alt.rock-n-roll
alt.showbiz.gossip

alt.tv.90210
comp.multimedia
comp.publish.cdrom.hardware
comp.publish.cdrom.multimedia
comp.publish.cdrom.software
alt.cdrom
alt.online-service
alt.online-service.america-online
alt.online-service.compuserve
rec.video.cable-tv
rec.video.production
rec.video.satellite
sci.engr.advanced-tv
alt.radio.pirate
clari.living.entertainment
clari.living.movies
clari.living.music
clari.living.tv
clari.apbl.entertainment
clari.apbl.movies
clari.apbl.music
clari.apbl.tv
clari.biz.industry.broadcasting
clari.biz.industry.print_media

NOTES

Chapter 1

[1] *Being Digital*, Nicholas Negroponte, Vintage Books, 1996, page 17.

[2] Ibid. page23

[3] Ibid. page26

[4] Alternatively, a program could be sponsored by advertisers and made freely available to viewers.

[5] Moreover, unsolicited e-mail may not be welcome by recipients. While the law is unsettled, it would appear at the present time that service providers, like AOL, have the right to stop "junk e-mail" from being sent to their subscribers.

[6] *Being Digital*, Nicholas Negroponte, Vitage Books, January 1996, page 22.

[7] A new technology, Asymmetrical Digital Subscriber Line (ADSL) permits conventional copper wires to carry enough data for one channel of precompressed movies. Technological advances are expected to increase capacity four-fold. Nevertheless, broadband coaxial cable can transmit data a thousand times faster than ordinary copper wires.

[8] One notable exception is Sony which owns a major movie studio (Columbia/Tristar) and is a significant presence in computer software, especially computer games (Sony PlayStation).

[9] "Building the Data Highway," Andy Reinhardt, *Byte*, March 1994, page 46.

[10] "Infobahn Warrior," David Kline, *Wired*, July 1994, page 130.

[11] "Malone Says TCI Push Into Phones, Internet Isn't Working for Now," Mark Robichaux, *Wall Street Journal*, January 2, 1997, page 1.

[12] "Arkansas Power & TV," *Wired*, July 1994, page 29.

[13] Indeed, a government attempt to regulate publishing would likely be considered a violation of publisher's FIrst Amendment rights.

[14] "Building the Data Highway," Andy Reinhardt, *Byte*, March 1994, page 46.

[15] "Infobahn Warrior," David Kline, *Wired*, July 1994, page 131.

[16] Although cable giant TCI apparently has plans to empower their subscribers to become originators not just consumers of content. The theory is that this will make cable subscription more value and indispensable to consumers. The cable companies are interested in providing their customers with enough upstream bandwidth to compete against the phone companies.

[17] "Focus Euronalysis," *Digital Media*, May 10, 1995, Volume 4, Number 12, page 7.

[18] *Fast Forward*, Richard Carlson & Bruce Goldman, Harper Business, page 5.

[19] Ibid. page 27.

[20] To keep these numbers in context, DBS has fewer than 5 million U.S. subscribers compared to 64 million U.S. cable subscribers. "Satellite Merger Signals a Rising Star," James Flanigan, *Los Angeles Times*, March 2, 1997, Section D, page 12.

[21] "Means for Better Surfing at Internet World Show," by David Colker, *Los Angeles Times*, March 14, 1997, Section E, page 1, 8.

[22] A write-once disc could hold 3.9GB per side. Rewritable discs hold 2.9GB per side.

[23] A DVD can hold 135 minutes of video on one side of a five inch disc.

[24] "The Digital Versatile Disc," Luke Hones, *The Independent*, June 1996, page 18.

[25] "Building the Data Highway," Andy Reinhardt, *Byte,* March 1994, page 52.

[26] The decision is on appeal.

[27] The Baby Bells have been in the cellular business for years.

Chapter 2

[1] 3 Nimmer on Copyright §10.08, page 10-71, et seq.

[2] Bartsch Metro-Goldwyn-Mayer, Inc., 391 F.2d 150 (2d Cir. 1968).

[3] Ibid.

[4] Cohen v. Paramont Pictures Corp., 845 F.2d 851 (9th Cir. 1988).

[5] Ibid.

[6] 17 U.S.C. § 102 (1994).

[7] The Copyright Act was revised in 1976 with changes effective as of 1978.

[8] Although, before March 1, 1989, failure to put a copyright notice on work if published, could result in the loss of the copyright.

[9] The Berne Convention Implementation Act of 1988 enabled the United States to establish copyright relations with twenty-five more countries. Notice requirements were dropped for works published after March 1, 1989 (although notice is still advisable and can affect the amount of damages recoverable). Recordation of an interest in a copyrighted work is no longer required as a prerequisite to bringing an infringement suit.

[10] Copyright does not extend to any idea, procedure, process, system, method of operation, principle or discovery, regardless of the form in which it is described, explained, illustrated or embodied. 17 U.S.C. § 102(b) (1994).

[11] Takeall v. Pepsico, Inc., 29 U.S.P.Q.2d 1913 (4th Cir. 1993) (unpublished per curiam decision).

[12] Ibid.

[13] Morrissey v. Procter & Gamble Co., 379 F2d 675 (1st Cir. 1967); Herbert Rosenthal Jewelry Corp. v. Kalpakian, 446 F.2d 738 (9th CIr. 1971).

[14] Beal v. Paramount Pictures Corp., 20 F.3d 454 (11th Cir. 1994); Engineering Dynamics, Inc. v. Structural Software, Inc., 26 F.3d 1335 (5th Cir. 1994).

[15] An infringement is not confined to literal and exact repetition or reproduction. Universal Pictures Co., Inc., Harold Lloyd Corp., 162 F.2d 354, 360 (9th Cir. 1947).

[16] See Sid & Marty Krofft Television Productions, Inc. v. McDonald's Corp., 562 F.2d 1157, 1162 (9th CIr. 1977).

[17] This example is taken from International Copyright Litigation in United States Courts: Lionel S. Sobel, Jurisdiction, Damages and Choice of Law, in Emerging Issues in Intellectual Property Practice, Continuing Education of the Bar 73 (1994).

[18] *The Gold Rush*, 2IIC 315 (Switzerland S. Ct 1970).

[19] Pub. L. 103-465.

[20] See section 17 U.S.C. 104A.

[21] Grants made after 1978 can be terminated under certain circumstances by serving written notice and filing a notice with the copyright office thirty-five years from date of grant or if grant covers right of publication, then thirty-five years from date of publication or forty years from date of grant, whichever is earlier. Works for hire and dispositions by will cannot be terminated. See §203 of the Copyright Act.

[22] International FIlm Exch. v. Corinth Films, 621 F. Supp. 631 (S.D.N.Y. 1985).

[23] French law provides authors with a limited right to decide when to release their works to the public (the right of divulgation), and the right to remove the works from the public arena (the right of retraction).

[24] "Multimedia: Stretching the Limits of Author's Rights in Europe," Andre R. Bertrand, *The Journal of Propriety Rights*, Vol. 7, No. 11, November 1995, page 4.

[25] Sobel, supra note 17, at 83 (citing Huston Turner Entertainment, Cuss. ass. plen. (1991).

[26] Under French law, the creators of audiovisual works and composite works retain moral rights in their contribution while employers are considered the authors of computer programs created by their employees. "Multimedia: Stretching Limits of Author's Rights in Europe," Andre R. Bertrand, *The Journal of Propriety Rights*, Vol. 7, No. 11, November 1995, pages 2-4.

[27] When the law was changed in 1976, those copyright owners with works in the second renewal period were given an additional extension of nineteen years added to the second term, for a total copyright of seventy-five years. Current copyright law grants copyright for the lifetime of the author plus fifty years.

[28] In 1994, President Clinton signed the Uruguay Round Agreements Act (URAA), Pub. L. 103-465, modifying U.S. copyright, patent and trademark law to comply with a new World Trade Organization (WTO) Agreement. See section 17 U.S.C. 104A which provides for the restoration of copyright protection in the United States for foreign works that have been in the public domain in the United States but were protected under copyright law in their source countries.

[29] Note that the NAFTA Implementation Act can revive copyright to movies first fixed or published in a NAFTA country. The Law revives only those movies that went into the public domain between 1978 and February 1989 because they lacked a copyright notice as required under prior copyright law. Since movies published without a valid copyright notice during that time were subject to a five-year cure provision upon publication, the effect of this law is to lengthen the cure provision to the present. Resurrection of the copyright requires filing with the U.S. Copyright Office. N.A.F.T.A. Implementation Act, Pub. L. No. 103-182 § 104A.

[30] Apple Computer, Inc. v. Microsoft Corp., 821 F. Supp. 616 (N.D. Cal. 1993) (citing Landsberg v. Scrabble Crossword Game Players, Inc., 736 F.2d 485 (9th Cir, 1984).

[31] Twin Peaks Prod. v. Publications Int'l, 996 F.2d 1366 (2nd Cir. 1993).

[32] See The Lanham Act, 15 U.S.C.A. § 1125 (1994).

[33] See, e.g., Lutz v. De Laurentiis, 260 Cal. Rptr 106 (1989); Metro-Goldwyn-Mayer Inc., v. Lee, 27 Cal Rptr. 833 (1963).

[34] A trademark owner's rights extend only to injurious, unauthorized commercial uses of the mark by another and does not allow the trademark owner to quash an unauthorized use of the mark by another who is communicating ideas or expressing points of view. L.L. Bean v. Drake Publishers, Inc., 811 F.2d 26 (2d Cir. 1989).

[35] Walt Disney Prods. v. Air Pirates, 581 F.2d 751 (9th Cir. 1978), cert. denied, 439 U.S. 1132 (1979).

[36] Detective Comics, Inc. v. Bruns Publication, 111 F.2d 432, 433-34 (2d Cir. 1940); DC Comics Inc. v. Filmation Assocs., 486 F. Supp. 1273, 1277 (S.D.N.Y. 1980).

[37] The Lanham Act should be construed to apply to artistic works only where the public interest in avoiding consumer confusion outweighs the public interest in free expression. Rogers v. Grimaldi, 875 F.2d 994 (2d Cir. 1989).

[38] DC Comic, 486 F. Supp. at 1277.

[39] Kimmerle v. New York Evening Journal, Inc. 262 N.Y. 99, 102 (1933).

[40] The common law is the law precedent that arises from cases decided by courts. Another type of law is statutory, or law that has been enacted by a legislative body such as Congress.

[41] New York Times Co. v. Sullivan, 376 U.S.254 (1964).

[42] Gertz v. Robert Welch, Inc., 418 U.S. 323 (1974).

[43] Philadelphia Newspapers, Inc. v. Hepps, 475 U.S. 767 (1986).

[44] McCuddin v. Dickinson, 300 N.W. 308, 309 (Sup. Ct. of Iowa 1941).

[45] An absolute privilege to defamation cannot be lost through bad faith or abuse. McCuddin v. Dickinson, 300 N.W. 308, 309 (Sup. Ct. of Iowa 1941).

[46] See Philadelphia Newspapers, 475 U.S. at 767

[47] Cohen v. Cowles Publishing Co., 273 P.2d 893, 894 (1954).

[48] See Sullivan, 376 U.S. at 279.

[49] Gertz, 418 U.S. at 344-45.

[50] Sullivan, 376 U.S. at 254.

51 *Bindrim v. Mitchell*, 155 Cal. Rptr. 29 (1979). See *Middlebrooks v. Curtis Publishing Co.*, 413 F.2d 141 (1969).

52 *Garner v. Triangle Publications, Inc.*, 97 F. Supp. 546, 548 (S.D.N.Y. 1951).

53 *Sullivan*, 376 U.S. at 279.

54 See *Cox Broadcasting Corp. v. Cohn*, 420 U.S. 469 (1975).

55 Privacy actions need not fall within one of these four categories to be actionable.

56 See, e.g. *Diaz v. Oakland Trib., Inc.*, 188 Cal. Rptr. 762 (1983).

57 *Hayes v. Alfred A. Knopf, Inc.*, 8 F.3d 1222 (7th Cir. 1993).

58 See Restatement Second of Torts § 652C; *Martinez by Martinez v. Democrat-Herald Publishing Co., Inc.*, 669 P.2d 818, 820 (OR. Ct. App. 1983).

59 See *Estate of Presley v. Russen*, 513 F. Supp. 1339, 1353 (D.N.J. 1981).

60 See e.g. *Sharrif v. American Broadcasting Company*, 613 So.2d 768 (1993); *cox*, 420 U.S. at 469.

61 Voice and signature are also protected.

62 *Carson v. Here's Johnny Portable Toilets, Inc.*, 698 F.2d 831 (6th Cir. 1983).

63 *White v. Samsung Elec. Am., Inc.*, 971 F.2d 1395 (9th Cir. 1992), rehearing en banc denied, 989 F.2d 1512 (9th CIr. 1993).

64 See *McFarland v. Miller*, 14 F.3d 912 (3rd Cir. 1994).

65 The Copyright Act of 1909, 35 Stat. 1075, 17 U.S.C. § 1 et seq. (1976 ed.).

66 Assuming the estate renewed the copyright.

67 *Stewart v. Abend*, 495 U.S. 207, 219 (1990).

68 There are some limitations on termination of derivative rights. See 17 U.S.C. § 304(c) (1994).

69 2 U.S.C. § 179 (1994).

70 Note that publication of a photograph of a person whose underwear was exposed in public was held to be an invasion of privacy. *Daily Times Democrat v. Graham*, 162 So.2d 474 (1964).

71 See, e.g. *Finger v. Omni Publications Intern*, 566 N.E.2d 141 (N.Y. 1990).

72 This is a grey area. See, for example, *Astaire v. Best Film*, U.S. Ct of Appeals (ninth circuit), no. 9556632 (June 20, 1997). The plantiff is seeking to appeal the decision.

73 *Motschenbacher v. R.J. Reynolds Tobacco Co.*, 498 F.2d 821 (9th Cir. 1974).

74 *Waits v. Frito-Lay Inc.*, 978 F.2d 1093 (9th CIr. 1992).

75 *Hicks v. Casablanca Records*, 464 F. Supp. 426 (S.D.N.Y. 1978).

76 See *Faber v. Condecor, Inc.*, 477 A.2d 1289 (1984).

77 Only original sound recordings fixed and published as of February 15, 1972, are copyrightable. Earlier recordings, however, may be protected under state law.

78 *Midler v. Ford Motor Co.*, 849 F.2d 460 (9th Cir. 1988).

79 See *Tomlin v. Walt Disney Prod.*, 96 Cal. Rptr. 118 (1971).

[80] The Digital Performance Right in Sound Recordings Act of 1995 created a limited public digital performance right in sound recordings. The act is effective as of February 1, 1996 and applies only to public performances by digital transmission. Pub. L. no. 104-39, 109, Stat. 336, certified at 17 U.S.C. §§ 106, 114, 115 (1996).

[81] The compulsory license applies only to phonorecords, not to works that have accompanying audio visual elements. Moreover, the compulsory license does not cover the right to use music in synchronization with images.

[82] "Digitized Music Adds Notes to Copyright," Heather D. Rafter, *San Francisco Daily J.*, Intellectual Property Supplement, March 30, 1994, at 15.

[83] *Acuff-Rose Music, Inc. v. Campbell*, 972 F.2d 1429 (6th Cir. 1992).

[84] Ibid.

[85] *Campbell v. Acuff-Rose Music*, 114 S. Ct. 1164 (1994).

[86] See e.g. *United States v. Taxe*, 380 F. Supp. 1010, 1014-15 (C.D. Cal. 1974).

[87] See e.g. *Grand Upright Music Ltd. v. Warner Bros. Records, Inc.*, 780 F. Supp. 182 (S.D.N.Y. 1991); *Jarvis v. A&M Records*, 827 F. Supp. 282 (D.N.J. 1993).

[88] The Harry Fox Agency, 711 3rd Avenue, 8th floor, New York, N.Y. 10017. (212) 370-5330.

[89] BZ Rights Stuff, Inc., sells an encyclopedia of public domain music for $249. BZ Rights Stuff., Inc., 125 West 72nd St., New York, N.Y. 10023. Phone (212) 580-0615, Fax (212) 769-9224.

[90] See 17 U.S.C. § 102 (Supp. V 1993).

[91] 17 U.S.C. § 120 (1994).

[92] 17 U.S.C. § 102a(5) (1982).

[93] Cal. Civil Code § 982(c) (1994). See *Playboy Enterprises, Inc. v. Dumas*, 831 Supp. 295 (S.D.N.Y. 1993).

[94] *Frank Schaffer Publications, Inc. v. The Lyons Partnership, L.P.*, Civic Action No. CV 93 3614R (C.D. Cal. 1993).

[95] It is good practice to clear rights to background artwork as well.

[96] 17 U.S.C. § 106A (Supp. V 1993).

[97] 17 U.S.C. § 101 (1994).

[98] *Atari Games Corp. v. Nintendo of Am., Inc.*, 975 F.2d 832 (Fed. Cir. 1992).

[99] See *Enter. Ltd. v. Accolade, Inc.*, 977 F.2d 1510 (9th Cir. 1992) cited in, Christopher Ottenweller, "Emerging Issues in Intellectual Property Practice," in Emerging Issues in Copyright Law pg 91, (CEB Program Handbook, April 1974).

[100] *Attari Games Corp. v. Nintendo of America Inc.*, 975 F.2d 832, 834 (Fed. Cir. 1992).

[101] *Apple Computer, Inc. v. Microsoft Corp.*, 799 F Supp. 1006 (N.D. Cal. 1992), 35 F.3d 1435 (9th Cir. 1994), cert. denied, 115 S. Ct. 1176 (1995).

[102] Ibid.

[103] *Lotus De Corp. v. Borland Int'l, Inc.*, 799 F. Supp. 203 (D. Mass 1992), 831 F. Supp. 202 (D. Mass 1993), 831 F. Supp. 223 (D. Mass. 1993).

[104] Ibid.

[105] *Mai Systems Corp. v. Peak Computer, Inc.*, 991 F.2d 511 (9th Cir. 1993).

[106] *Playboy Enterprises, Inc. v. Frena*, 839 F. Supp. 1552 (M.D. Fla. 1993).

[107] James F. Brelsford, Trademark Case Will Affect Multimedia, *San Francisco Daily J.*, Intellectual Property Supplement, March 30, 1994, at 14.

[108] 35 U.S.C. § 101 (1994).

[109] 35 U.S.C. § 154 (1994).

[110] 35 U.S.C. § 102 (g) (1994).

[111] 35 U.S.C. § 103 (1994).

[112] Cal. Commercial Code § 2314 (1993); <u>see</u> U.C.C. § 2314(c).

[113] To be effective, the disclaimer should be prominent.

[114] Publishers may want to purchase insurance to protect themselves in regard to the marketing of the product, such as liability that may arise from advertising. Publishers may also want to seek coverage to protect themselves form damages for recalls of a product, although this coverage may be difficult to obtain.

Chapter 3

[1] 17 U.S.C. 101. The types of works that may be works for hire by special order or commission are: contribution to a collective work, part of a motion picture or other audiovisual work, a translation, a supplementary work, a compilation, an instructional text, a test, answer material for a test and an atlas. Note that the work for hire provisions of the 1976 Copyright Act differ from the prior copyright law, the 1909 Act. The 1976 Act does not operate retroactively to change the ownership of work created before the 1976 Act became effective on January 1, 1978. Consequently, for works created before 1978, the 1909 Act needs to be consulted to determine ownership.

[2] See *Playboy Enterprises, Inc. v. Dumas*, 831 F. Supp. 295 (S.D. N.Y. 1993).

[3] See *Community for Creative Non-Violence v. Reid*, 490 U.S. 730, 109 S. Ct. 2166 (1989).

[4] 490 U.S. 730, 109 S. Ct. 2166 (1989).

[5] For a more detailed review of this case and other noteworthy cases, see D. Peter Harvey, Structuring Employment Relationships to Insure Ownership and Control of Intellectual Property, Practising Law Institute, February, 1995 (PLI Order No. G4-3934), 403 PLI/Pat. 35 (1995).

[6] Renewal rights exist in works created prior to January 1, 1978. The renewal can extend the term of copyright. A work in its renewal period prior to January 1, 1978, can obtain a 19-year extension. A work first eligible for renewal after January 1, 1978 can obtain a 47-year renewal term. As for termination rights, for works created prior to January 1, 1978, an author or his heirs can terminate a transfer and recover the last 19 years of the renewal term. 17 U.S.C.§ 304(c). For works created after January 1, 1978, an author or his heirs can terminate a transfer either thirty-five years from the date of publication of the work or forty years from the date of execution of the grants of rights in the work, whichever is earlier. 17 U.S.C. § 203(a)(3).

[7] 17 U.S.C. § 203 (a)(5).

[8] 17 U.S.C. § 203 (a) (3).

[9] See, *McClurg v. Kingsland*, 41 U.S. (1 How.) 202, 11 L.Ed. 102 (1843); *Gill v. United States*, 160 U.S. 426, 40 L.Ed. 480 (1896); *United States v. Dubilier Condenser Corp.*, 289 U.S. 178, 77 L.Ed. 1114 (1933).

[10] See, *McElmurry v. Arkansas Power & Light Company*, 995 F.2d 1576 (Fed. Cir. 1993).

[11] See, Restatement of Torts § 757, Comment b (1939).

[12] See, Uniform Trade Secrets Act, § 1, Commissioner's Comment, 14 Uniform Laws Annot. 439 (1990).

[13] California Business & Professions Code § 16600.

[14] See California Business and Professions Code § 16600.

[15] Pub. L. No. 99-508, 100 Stat. 1860.

[16] 18 U.S.C. §§ 2701 et. seq.

[17] See Keitt, Jr. and Kahn, "Cyberspace Snooping," Legal Times 24, 28 (May 2, 1994) as cited by Kent D. Stuckey in Internet and Online Law, § 5.03[1][b], ftnote 14, Law Journal Seminars-Press (1996).

[18] *Smyth v. Pillsbury Co.*, 1996 U.S. Dist. LEXIS 776 (E.D. Pa. Jan. 23, 1996).

[19] See Multimedia Law: Forms and Analysis, Raysman, Brown & Neuburger, Law Journal Seminars-Press (updated to 1996), § 10.09[2].

[20] See, *Hetes v. Schefman & Miller Law Office*, 393 N.W. 2d 577 (1986).

[21] "DGA' Historic Interaction," David Robb, *The Hollywood Reporter*, October 26, 1993.

Chapter 4

[1] See Chapter 7 for a sample agreement.

[2] Insurance companies generally don't want their insured companies accepting unsolicited material.

[3] Another drawback is that oral agreements are not enforceable for some kinds of transactions. State have enacted "Statute of Frauds" laws which require that certain transactions, such as the transfer of real estate, be in writing. The purpose of these laws is to encourage parties to put agreements in writing in order to reduce fraudulent claims.

[4] Since the letter has not been signed by the producer, his agreement to the terms is merely implied if he does not object. The writer would be in a stronger position if he had a letter from the producer confirming the agreement and its terms.

Chapter 5

[1] Sony, Nintendo and Sega consoles are for games only at the present time.

[2] Bundling is also used when a product is near the end of its life cycle.

[3] A publisher may be reluctant to accept a "best efforts" or "no-less- favorable" clause especially if the contract is made before the product is finished . If the product turns out poorly, the publisher will not want to be obliged to promote it in the same manner as better products. A possible compromise would be language in which the publisher agrees to promote the product in its "reasonable business judgment." The least protection is afforded a developer when the contract states that marketing is in the sole discretion of the publisher.

[4] An important issue may be the return of source code and development tools which the Developer may want to retain in order to produce future product.

[5] A publisher may desire exclusivity for all platforms even if it does not publish to all platforms. A possible compromise is for the developer to hold back exploitation of the product on other platforms for a certain period unless the Publisher exploits the program on those platforms. The developer should keep in mind that porting the program to another platform may entail a considerable expense.

[6] Granting these rights to a publisher may greatly reduce the ability of a developer to enter into an agreement with another company.

[7] Indeed, many programs are too expensive for developers to fund on their own.

[8] In book publishing, on the other hand, royalties are typically based on a percentage of retail price.

[9] It may take more than 10,000 copies shipped to recoup the advance, because the publisher may not be obliged to pay a royalty on product given for promotional purposes or to secure shelf space.

[10] Note that the U.S. publisher may receive an advance against royalties. The developer's share of any royalties may be reduced if there is an outstanding advance that the publisher is entitled to recoup.

[11] Although most revenue is typically received by the publisher during the first year of the product's release.

[12] Even with access to source code, the publisher may find it difficult to complete a program.

[13] "The Doom Boom," Wired July 1994, page 31.

[14] Publisher may want to limit Developer from creating products with a similar look and feel.

[15] Advances might be paid in smaller increments in accordance with milestone schedule.

[16] The agreement may provide that Publisher does not have to pay a royalty on copies sold at a price below the cost to produce.

[17] If agreement may provide for a royalty if the sequel uses characters or the same engine as the original product. [14] Publisher may want to limit Developer from creating products with a similar look and feel.

[15] Advances might be paid in smaller increments in accordance with milestone schedule.

[16] The agreement may provide that Publisher does not have to pay a royalty on copies sold at a price below the cost to produce.

[17] If agreement may provide for a royalty if the sequel uses characters or the same engine as the original product.

Chapter 6

[1] These figures are from *How to Make a Fortune on the Information Superhighway*, by Laurence A. Canter and Martha S. Siegel, HarperCollins, 1994, pages 41-45. Costs may vary depending on volume. Note, for example, that a full access line, T-1 or better, costs about $1,800 a month. Moreover, unsolicited advertising messages may be restricted. Note also that hundreds of web sites sell ads for anywhere from $100 per month to $20,000 or more. HotWired, for instance, charges up to $15,000 a month to post advertising banners. Netscape sells advertising banner space at $8,500 to $20,400 per month. In 1996 advertising prices ranged from 2.5 cents for a general impression, such as any search on Yahoo, to 12 cents per impression for a highly targeted ad. A present a relatively small number of companies dominate Web advertising. The number one advertiser for the first three quarters of 1996 was Microsoft at $5.8 million, followed by AT&T ($3.8 million).

[2] *How to Make a Fortune on the Informa tion Superhighway*, by Laurence A. Canter and Martha S. Siegel, HarperCollins, 1994, pages, page 204.

[3] While there may be no restriction on advertising per se, that does not mean that those who transmit ads for child pornography or defame others could not be held criminally or civilly liable.

[4] An argument can be made that cyberspace should be considered a public forum and therefore the owner of a forum cannot restrict speech activities. See, Edward J. Naughton, "Is Cyberspace a Public Forum? Computer Bulletin Boards, Free Speech, and State Action," 81 Georgetown Law Journal 409, December 1992 cited in Cyberspace and the Law, by Edward A. Cavazos and Gavino Morin (MIT Press, 1994) page 71.

[5] *Bradenburg v. Ohio*, 395 U.S. 444 (1969).

[6] *Miller v. California*, 413 U.S. 15, 93 S.Ct. 2607, 37 L.Ed.2d 419 (1973).

[7] The Communications Decency Act of 1996, 47 U.S.C. § 223 et seq, which is part of the Telecommunications Act of 1996, 47 U.S.C. § 151 et. seq (1996).

[8] United States v. Thomas, 74 F. 3d 701 (6th Circuit), reh'g, en banc, denied 1996 U.S. App. LEXIS 4529 (6th Cir. Mar. 12, 1996), cert. denied, 65 U.S.L.W. 3257 (1996).

[9] 18 U.S.C. § 1465.

[10] 47 U.S.C. § 223.

[11] *Stanley v. Georgia*, 394 U.S. 557 (1969).

12 See *United States v. 12,200 Ft. Reels of Film*, 413 U.S. 123 (1973), *United States v. Orito*, 413 U.S. 139 (1973), *United States v. Reidel*, 402 U.S. 351 (1971).

13 776 F. Supp. 135 (S.D.N.Y. 1991).

14 *Stratton Oakmont v. Prodigy*, 1995 W.L. 805178 (N.Y. Supp.), Motion for Renewal Denied, (December 1995), 24 Media L. Rep. 1126.

15 47 U.S.C. § 230(c).

16 See, "A Prodigious Decision: Stratton Oakmont and the Telecommunications Act of 1996, Ian C. Ballon, Vol. 1, No. 2 (May, 1996), Cyberspace Lawyer, page 13.

17 907 F. Supp. 1361 (N.D. Cal. 1995).

18 907 F. Supp. 1361, 1369 (N.D. Cal. 1995).

19 *Playboy Enterprises, Inc. v. Frena*, 839 F. Supp. 1552 (M.D. Fla. 1993).

20 Sega Enterprises Ltd. v. MAPHIA, 857 F. Supp. 679 (N.D. Cal. 1994).

21 *New York v. Ferber*, 458 U.S. 747 (1982).

22 18 U.S.C. § 2252.

23 18 U.S.C. § 2251.

24 *Osborne v. Ohio*, 495 U.S. 103 (1990).

25 The law was construed to apply only to depictions of minors engaged in sexual conduct.

26 18 U.S.C. § 2510-2521.

27 See, 18 U.S.C. Chapters 119, 121.

28 See, 18 U.S.C. § 2511 3(b).

29 18 U.S.C. § 2701(b).

30 A defamation action might be appropriate as well.

31 *Talley v. California*, 362 U.S. 60 (1960).

32 *Cyberspace and The Law*, Edward A. Cavazos and Gavino Morin, MIT Press, 1994, page 15.

33 See *Gibson v. Florida Legislative Investigation Committee*, 372 U.S. 539 (1963).

34 42 U.S.C. § 2000aa, et seq.

35 816 F. Supp. 432 (W.D. Tex. 1993), 36 F.3d 457 (5th Cir. 1994).

36 17 U.S.C. § 102.

37 The requirements of copyright law are discussed in greater length in Chapter 7.

38 Mai Systems Corp. v. Peak Computer, Inc., 991 F.2d 511 (9th Cir. 1993).

39 *Playboy Enterprises, Inc. v. Frena*, 839 F. Supp. 1552 (M.D. Fla. 1993).

40 17 U.S.C. 506 (a).

41 18 U.S.C. 1343.

42 *U.S. v. LaMacchia*, 871 F. Supp. 535, 541-542 (D. Mass. 1994).

43 *U.S. v. LaMacchia*, 871 F. Supp. 535 (D. Mass. 1994).

Chapter 7

[1] Atari Games Corp. v. Oman, 888 F.2d 878, 885-86 (D.C. Cir.1989).

[2] Copyright Office, Registration Decision, Docket 87-4, Fed. Reg. 21817 (June 10, 1988).

[3] 17 U.S.C. § 101.

[4] See generally, Midway Mfg. Co. v. Artic Int'l, Inc., 547 F. Supp. 999 (N.D. Ill. 1982), aff'd 704 F.2d 1009 (7th Cir. 1983), cert. denied, 464 U.S. 823 (1983).

[5] Congress is considering dropping this requirement for U.S. authors so that they are treated the same as foreign authors.

[6] See 17 U.S.C. 401 (1988).

[7] 17 U.S.C. § 401(d).

[8] Scott, Multimedia: Law & Practice § 9.27, page 9-78.

[9] Works that are contributions to a collective work, part of a motion picture or other audiovisual work, a translation, supplementary work, a compilation, an instructional text, a test, answer material for a test or an atlas. See 17 U.S.C. § 101.

[10] For works created but not copyrighted or published before 1978, copyright will not expire before December 31, 2002. If published before this expiration date, copyright protection will last until December 31, 2027.

[11] 15 U.S.C. § 1065.

[12] The MTV case was settled on undisclosed terms. The Kaplan dispute was resolved in arbitration. Princeton was ordered to transfer all rights to the name to Kaplan but Kaplan's request for damages and attorneys' fees was denied. The McDonald's dispute was settled after McDonald's unsuccessfully challenged the defendant's right to the domain name. McDonald's agreed to make a charitable contribution.

[13] Federal Trademark Dilution Act of 1995, P.L. No. 104-98, 109 Stat. 985, amending the Trademark Act of 1946, 15 U.S.C. § 1125 et seq.

[14] *Avon Products v. Carnetta Wong Associates*, E.D. N.Y. (CV 96 0451), Feb. 2, 1996.

[15] *Hasbro, Inc. v. Entertainment Group Ltd.*, 1996 WL 84858 (W.D. Wash.), No. C96- 0130.

[16] In *Diamond v. Diehr*, 450 U.S. 175, 101 S. Ct. 1048, 67 L.Ed.2d 155 (1981) the United States Supreme Court held that a software-based invention could be patented.

[17] 35 U.S.C. § 101 (1994).

[18] 35 U.S.C. § 103 (1994).

[19] 35 U.S.C. § 154 (1994).

[20] 35 U.S.C. § 102(g) (1994).

GLOSSARY

Access Provider University or company that provides access to the Internet.

Algorithm A series of instructions to solve a specific problem.

Alpha Version The first complete version of a program delivered by the developer for internal testing and evaluation.

Analog Signal A type of signal characterized by a continuous, wave-like transmission. They are measured by the wave's cycles. Compare to Digital signals, which are a series of on/off pulses, corresponding to the binary states 0 and 1.

Anonymous Server A computer in Finland that allowed computer users to transmit messages and maintain their anonymity. The Finnish server scrambled the transmitter's address and forwarded the message. Replies could only be made through the server.

Archie A software tool for locating files on FTP sites.

ARPANet Advanced Research Projects Agency Network, the precursor to the Internet.

ASDL Asymmetric Digital Subscriber Line. Technology that allows the transmission of digital data over copper telephone wires.

ATM Asynchronous Transfer Mode. High-speed switching technology used to transfer large amounts of audiovisual data.

AUP Acceptable Use Policies. Rules that govern the use of a network.

Automatic Response Robot A program that automatically replies to Internet inquiries when the sender includes in his or her message key words such as "send info."

Avatar An online, real-time graphical image of a computer user visible to other computer users in the same virtual world.

Backbone A high-speed connection that forms a major pathway in a network.

Bandwidth The range of signal frequencies that can be carried on a channel. It is the measure of data transmission capacity, usually expressed in bits per second. Conventional phones need very little; interactive digital video requires a great deal.

Baud measure of data flow across telecommunications channels.

Beta Version The developer's final version, after changes made to Alpha Version. The Beta Version is sent out for external testing.

Bit Listserv Mailing Lists Electronic mailing lists, each of which concerns an interest or organization the subscribers have in common. Every computer user on a list receives all messages posted to the list via E-mail.

BBS Bulletin Board Service. An electronic bulletin board that allows users to post messages. Many are devoted to specialized topics and are run by individuals. Sometimes there is a charge for access. Other times, the system operator (Sysop) operates it as a hobby. There are an estimated 60,000 public BBSs in the United States.

Binary A system of numbers comprised of two digits, 0 and 1. This is the system used by computers.

Bit A binary digit; either 0 or 1. The smallest measure of computer information.

Broadband Large bandwidth, which enables a greater amount of data to be transmitted. A broadband telecommunications could permit the interactive transmission of medical images, voice data, and video data. A Narrowband system, conversely, has less capacity and might only be able to transmit voice and data communication (phone calls and faxes) with limited interactivity.

BPS Bits Per Second, a measure of how fast data can move.

Bug A defect in a computer program.

Bundled A group of software and/or other product(s) sold as one unit.

Byte A string of eight bits. The amount of storage required to store one keystroke of information.

CD-I Compact Disc Interactive. An interactive CD-ROM format.

CD-R Compact Disc-Recordable. A CD-ROM format on which data can be recorded once.

CD-ROM Compact Disc-Read Only Memory: An optical disc storage medium.

CD-V Compact Disc Video. Also known as as "LaserDisc," this format combines analog video and digital stereo.

Central Processing Unit (CPU) An electronic chip that is the heart of a computer.

Chat Live or "real-time" communication or "talk" by computer. Also known as "Internet Relay Chat" (IRC).The computer user types a message, which immediately appears on the screen of all computer users logged onto the channel and allows multiple parties to converse simultaneously. Some systems allow for "private rooms" for intimate conversations between selected people.

Chip A tiny circuit board containing instructions for processing data.

Compression A two-step process (encoding and decoding) in which digital data that represents an image is reduced. The principal compression standards are Joint Photographic Expert Group (JPEG) and Motion Picture Expert Group (MPEG-1 and MPEG-2). The reverse procedure is Decompression.

CPM Cost per thousand. The cost of reaching one thousand individuals with an advertisement. When used in regard to online ads, it refers to the cost of an ad per one thousand impressions.

CPU Central Processing Unit, the principal processing unit of a computer.

Database An organized collection of information.

Digital Signal Electromagnetic signals composed of binary information. All computer data is digital. Unlike analog technology, bits can be stored, retrieved, reproduced, and manipulated an unlimited number of times without any loss in quality.

Digital Sampler A machine that can store sound in digital form.

Domain Name Electronic address of a computer server. Domain names are reserved by filing an application with a central registry in Virginia

Download The transfer of information from one computer to another, typically from a centrally located large computer via modem to a personal computer. Upload is sending the information the other way.

Encryption The process of encoding electronic communications to safeguard the data from access by unauthorized persons.

Electronic Bulletin Board Like its corkboard counterpart, a repository for posting messages for others to read. A Bulletin Board System (BBS) is a central system accessed via modem and phone lines where data is posted for dissemination.

E-mail Electronic mail.

File Server A large computer that either directly stores movies and other video programming as a digital database or interfaces with a storage device to access programming.

Flame An insulting or harassing electronic message.

FTP File Transfer Protocol. A common method for sending and/or obtaining files from another Internet site.

Freenet Provide free Internet access. Usually offered by a government entity to local residents.

Full Motion Video (FMV) Video at thirty frames per second.

Gigabyte one billion bytes.

Golden Master The final version of a program delivered by the developer after alpha and beta testing. The version that is the basis for reproducing the program commercially.

Gopher A program with menus to help users retrieve material from the Internet.

GUI Graphical user interface. The use of images and icons that the user can click on to instruct the computer.

Handle Assumed name or pseudonym.

Hardware The physical components of a computer system. Includes the Central Processing Unit (CPU) and peripheral equipment such as a monitor, keyboard, and mouse.

Hard Drive The magnetic storage disc within a computer used to store information.

Head Ends Cable programming distribution points that receive programming via satellite or feeds from local broadcasters and transmit them via coaxial cable to viewers.

High-Definition Television (HDTV) The proposed standard for the next generation television, based on all-digital, MPEG-2 standard with a 9x16:1 aspect ratio. This new technology that projects a much sharper image.

Home Page The main or opening page of a web site.

Hyperlink A way of connecting web pages on the World Wide Web. Usually consists of a highlighted word or image that takes the user to a different page when clicked upon.

Hypertext A type of non-linear writing by computer in which groups of text are linked to one another. In other words, the reader is able to jump from within one body of text to another body of text. Hyperfiction is a story based on hypertext, allowing the reader to determind his own path and storyline.

Hypertext Links A document with words or graphics that contain links to other documents, which usually may be accessed by simply clicking a highlighted word.

HTML Hypertext Markup Language. The code used to create Hypertext documents for use on the WWW.

HTTP Hypertext transfer protocol. The dominant information-carrying protocol of the World Wide Web.

Icon A picture or graphic image on a computer screen that represents a command or thing. Typically, a computer user will click on an icon with a mouse in order to direct the computer to take some action.

Impression The number of times an ad is displayed online.

Interactive Multimedia Combines the interactivity of computers with access to multiple media sources. The viewer is able to participate in the program. One type of interactive program is the video game, where the player's choices determine which part of the software is accessed.

Interactivity The ability of the user to interact with a computer that can be used to control the flow, pace, and content of a program.

Interexchange Carrier Long-distance phone carrier such as MCI, Sprint, and AT&T.

Internet A worldwide network of computer networks. Comprised of trunk lines, routers, dedicated access lines, software protocols, and data servers, linking million of users. Evolved from the ARPANet.

Internet Service Provider An entity that provides access to the Internet.

Intranet A network that functions like the Internet by allowing sharing of data, but use is restricted within an organization or company. A private network not accessible to outsiders.

Interoperability The ability to handle messages from a variety of equipment in various formats.

IRC Internet Relay Chat. Real-time chat service over the Internet.

ISDN Integrated Services Digital Network. ISDN lines are digital phone lines that can transmit data much faster than a high-speed modem communicating over traditional phone lines.

ISP Internet Service Provider, a company that provides access to the Internet.

Java A programming language that allows programs to be downloaded from the Internet and run immediately on the user's computer. Java programs can provide graphics, sound, and interactivity to users.

KBPS Kilobytes per second. Measure of the speed at which data can be transferred.

Kilobyte 1,024 bytes.

LAN Local Area Network. A computer network limited to the immediate area, such as an office suite.

Listserv A program that manages E-mail lists. Mail lists permit people to E-mail a message to one address, where it is then forwarded to all subscribers to the list.

M-Bone Multicasting Backbone Protocol, which can provide one-way signal distribution of traditional video programming and real-time, two-way conferencing between distant users over the Internet.

Megabyte 1,048,576 bytes of data.

Microprocessor A computer chip such as the Intel Pentium chip used in IBM computers or the Motorola 68040 used in Macintosh computers.

MIDI Musical Instrument Digital Interface. Standard for recording digital audio signals in multimedia applications.

MIPS Millions of Instructions Per Second.

Millisecond One one-thousandth of a second.

Modem Abbreviation for Modulator, Demodulator. A device that allows a computer to communicate with other computers over a phone line.

MPEG Motion Picture Experts Group. The standard for digital compression and decompression of video and audio signals.

Multimedia Using more than one media. For example, weaving sound, text, graphics, and moving images into a presentation. Multimedia programming is not new—after all, movies combine sound and visual media. At one time the term was associated with a multi-projector slide show accompanied by a soundtrack. Today, multimedia is associated with the storage of full-motion video, audio, and other digital data in one integrated product such as a CD-ROM title. With digital transmission, audio, video, text, data, and graphics can be transmitted in the same manner.

Multiplexing Programs are transmitted over several channels making individual programs available to viewers at several different times.

Narrowband Signal A signal that occupies little bandwidth. Transmissions of data, text, voice, electronic mail, and faxes require little bandwidth.

Near Video-on-Demand When a movie is carried on a number of channels simultaneously but the movies have staggered start times. Thus, the movie starts every fifteen minutes, for instance. This way viewers can see a movie without having to wait more than fifteen minutes.

Netiquette The unofficial code of manners for Internet users.

Netscape Navigator A popular browser developed Netscape Communications, Inc.

Newsgroup A discussion group on Usenet on a particular topic. Postings to a Newsgroup are sent to every subscriber in the group.

Node Any single computer user connected to a network.

Object Code Code that is understandable to a computer. Source Code is translated from its high-level programming language into object code's base-two form.

OEM Original Equipment Manufacturer.

Online The state of a computer when it is connected to another via modem.

Pixel Picture element. One glowing dot on a television screen or computer monitor. Screen resolution is measured in pixels.

Platform The type of machine used to access software. Optical disc platforms include CD-ROM, CD-I and the Laser Disc. Some programming is designed for use on multiple platforms. For example, many video games can be played on either the Sega Genesis or Nintendo machines.

POTS Plain Old Telephone Service.

Public Domain Material that is not protected under copyright law.

RAM Random Access Memory. Memory within a computer from which applications operate.

Read Only Memory (ROM) A device that can be read but not written onto.

Regional Bell Operating Companies (RBOCS) They are Ameritech, Bell Atlantic, BellSouth, Nynex, Pacific Telesis, Southwestern Bell, and US West. They provide local phone service.

ROM See Read Only Memory.

Scanning The process of ditigizing a printed picture or text. Frame Grabbing is digitizing from video.

Servers Computers that organize, store, and distribute content on a network.

Set-Top Converter The device that provides an interface between the signal source and a TV set.

Shareware Computer software that is distributed to others for free or for a voluntary contribution; sometimes a demo version.

Software Computer programming. There are two principal types: operating-system software like MS-DOS that organizes and controls the allocation and usage of hardware resources, and application software like WordPerfect, which allows the user to perform a certain type of work or function.

Software Developer The person or company that develops software. The developer may license the software to others, in which case he may be referred to as a licensor, supplier, or vendor.

Software Distributor A company that acquires the right to market and distribute the software of others.

Spam To flood others with irrelevant or inappropriate e-mail messages such as advertisements.

Sysop System Operator. The person responsible for the operation of a computer system or network resource.

Telcos Telecommunication companies.

Telnet A program that allows those on distant computers to access and operate another computer on the network as if they were sitting at the terminal.

Terrestrial Television signals that are broadcast from a fixed, earth-based site or antennae.

Trunk Lines Backbone or long-line telephone lines, today usually made of fiber optics. These lines carry telephone traffic from one local service area to another. Typically owned by long distance carriers such as AT&T, MCI, and Sprint.

URL Universal Resource Locator. The address of a given site on the Web, such as http://www.laig.com/law/entlaw.

Usenet A collection of 10,000 Newsgroups devoted to a wide variety of topics. These forums for public discussion allow users to post messages to one another.

Veronica Very Easy Rodent Oriented Net-Wide Index to Computerized Archives. A database of names of menu items on thousands of gopher servers.

Video-on-Demand (VOD) A means of delivery that allows subscribers to select and order individual programs to view at whatever time they like. The programming is stored on a server.

Video Dialtone Providing video programming over the telephone network.

Videodisc A 12" optical disc used for recording films and music.

Virtual Reality A computer environment that simulates reality by creating a multisensory experience.

WAIS Wide Area Information Server is a tool to search databases that have been indexed with keywords.

Web Browser A software package that allows users to view web pages.

Web Page   A specific site on the World Wide Web that incorporates one or more of the following: text, images, motion picture clips, audio files, and hyperlinks to other web pages.

World Wide Web (WWW)   A hypertext-based system for linking databases. The fastest-growing portion of the Internet.

Zines (also "E-Zines")   Electronic periodicals.

ABOUT THE AUTHOR

Mark Litwak is a veteran entertainment and multimedia attorney known for aggressively representing writers and independent filmmakers. He has won large awards for clients after distributors tried to defraud them through creative accounting. He also functions as a producer's representative, assisting filmmakers in the marketing and distribution of their films.

Litwak is the author of numerous articles and several books, which include: *Reel Power: The Struggle for Influence and Success in the New Hollywood, Contracts for the Film and Television Industry,* and the forthcoming *Litwak's Multimedia Producer's Handbook.*

Litwak has been a lawyer for nineteen years and is of counsel to the Beverly Hills law film of Berton & Donaldson. As a law professor, he has taught entertainment and copyright law at the University of West Los Angeles, U.C.L.A., and Loyola Law School. He has lectured before many filmmakers and university audiences, including presentations at the American Film Institute, Columbia University, N.Y.U., U.S.C., U.C.L.A., The New School for Social Research, the University of British Columbia, San Francisco State University, and the Royal College of Art in London.

As an authority on the movie industry, he has been interviewed on more than fifty television and radio shows including "The Larry King Show," NPR's "All Things Considered," and the Cable News Network.

For additional information, visit Litwak's web site—Entertainment Legal Resources at: http://www.laig.com/law/entlaw

CONTRACTS ON COMPUTER DISK

Obtain all of the contracts included in *Litwak's Multimedia Producer's Handbook* on computer disk:

Film-Clip License With Warranties
Model Release
Music and Sound Recording License
Photograph License Agreement
Text License Agreement
Video License Agreement
Art Work License Agreement
Results and Proceeds of Services Clause
Employment Agreement
Consultant Agreement
Work for Hire Agreement With Independent
Contractor (Programmer)
Production Agreement
Submission Letter
Submission Release
Submission Release
Software Publishing Agreement
Escrow Agreement
Virtual Shopping Mall Advertiser Agreement
Agreement for Online Distribution of Multimedia Program
Non-Disclosure Agreement

ORDER FORM

Qty	Title	Price @	Total
	Multimedia Contracts	$99.00	

Contracts are sent on 3.5 inch high-density disks formatted for IBM and IBM compatibles. Please indicate desired format:

☐ Microsoft Word

☐ Wordperfect

☐ ASCII

Sub-total _____

Sales Tax
(Los Angeles County residents add 8 1/4 %. Other California residents add 7 1/4 %) _____

Shipping & handling $ 3.00

Ship to: **TOTAL** _____

_____
(Name)

_____
(Company)

_____
(Street Address)

_____
(City/State/Zip)

Send check or money order payable to **Hampstead Enterprises, Inc.** , **P.O. Box 3226, Santa Monica, CA 90408. (310) 859-9595**

Orders are shipped via UPS (we cannot ship to P.O. boxes). Prices are subject to change without notice. All sales are final. Allow 2-4 weeks for delivery.